THE INVENTION OF LATIN AMERICAN MUSIC

Currents in Latin American & Iberian Music

ALEJANDRO L. MADRID, SERIES EDITOR
WALTER AARON CLARK, FOUNDING SERIES EDITOR

The Invention of Latin American Music

A TRANSNATIONAL HISTORY

Pablo Palomino

OXFORD
UNIVERSITY PRESS

OXFORD
UNIVERSITY PRESS

Oxford University Press is a department of the University of Oxford. It furthers
the University's objective of excellence in research, scholarship, and education
by publishing worldwide. Oxford is a registered trade mark of Oxford University
Press in the UK and certain other countries.

Published in the United States of America by Oxford University Press
198 Madison Avenue, New York, NY 10016, United States of America.

Library of Congress Cataloging-in-Publication Data
Names: Palomino, Pablo, author.
Title: The invention of Latin American music : a transnational
history / Pablo Palomino.
Description: New York : Oxford University Press, 2020. |
Series: Currents in Latin American and Iberian music |
Includes bibliographical references and index.
Identifiers: LCCN 2019047291 (print) | LCCN 2019047292 (ebook) |
ISBN 9780190687410 (paperback) | ISBN 9780190687403 (hardback) |
ISBN 9780190687434 (epub) | ISBN 9780197510483 (online)
Subjects: LCSH: Music—Social aspects—Latin America—History—20th century. |
Music—Political aspects—Latin America—History—20th century. |
Regionalism—Latin America.
Classification: LCC ML3917.L27 P35 2020 (print) |
LCC ML3917.L27 (ebook) | DDC 780.98—dc23
LC record available at https://lccn.loc.gov/2019047291
LC ebook record available at https://lccn.loc.gov/2019047292

9 8 7 6 5 4 3 2

Paperback printed by Marquis, Canada
Hardback printed by Bridgeport National Bindery, Inc., United States of America

Contents

Acknowledgments

This book began as a doctoral project at the University of California, Berkeley, where Mark Healey and Margaret Chowning welcomed me and guided it with their wisdom, warmth, and generosity. I thank as well the teachings and insights of Richard Cándida-Smith, Tyler Stovall, Jocelyne Guilbault, Irv Scheiner, David Henkin, and Yuri Slezkine, and of my dear friends and colleagues Sarah Selvidge, Greg Leventis, Sarah Hines, Celso Castilho, Jessica Long, Germán Vergara, David Tamayo, Michiko Yokomizo, Greta Marchesi, Kathleen Grady, Gabe Milner, Filippo Marsili, Julie Caine, Jason Blalock, Noah Miller, T. K. Revane, Aggie Lumbang, Gustavo and Amalia Faerman, Sapna Thottathil, David Gardner, and the late Charles "Todd" Friend. Paula Mandel made me realize, among many other things, the very structure of this research.

The project grew thanks to the splendid colleagues around the Center for Latin American Studies and the History department at the University of Chicago. Mauricio Tenorio helped me to reconceptualize it: *gracias, profesor.* Brodie Fischer, Natalie Arsenault, Jamie Gentry, Claudia Giribaldi, Robert Kendrick, Dain Borges, Emilio Kourí, Ramón Gutiérrez, Julio Postigo, Ricky Davila, Chris Dunlap, Emilio de Antuñano, Joseph Maurer, Rohan Chatterjee, and Eleonor Gilburd enriched it with their dialogue. I also thank the participants at the workshops on Latin American History, Latin American Studies, and Music History/Theory, and the colloquium "The Worlds of Latin American Music."

Fortuna then led me to two Oxfords. Alejandro Madrid, Suzanne Ryan, and three anonymous reviewers at Oxford University Press gave excellent suggestions to the book proposal and to the manuscript. I finished it in the company of wonderful colleagues at Oxford College and the wider community of Emory University: I especially thank Bridgette Gunnels, Josh Mousie, Erin Tarver, Monika Kirloskar-Steinbach, Doug Hicks, Jeff Lesser, Yanna Yannakakis, Tom Rogers, Teresa Davis, and Sergio Delgado Moya for their dialogue and for making Atlanta so welcoming. The manuscript was greatly improved by Kelly Besecke, with support from Oxford College and from Emory's Center for Faculty Development and Excellence. My students' curiosity and feedback were and are of the essence.

Many colleagues and friends contributed to this project along the way. I thank Adriana Brodsky, for her guidance when the project was taking shape; Lena Suk, for her reading and support to finish it; Matthew Karush, for his dialogue and for illuminating some of its key arguments; and Anaïs Fléchet, for animating so many conversations about history, globalization, and music. Chris Batterman, Esteban Buch, Aníbal Cetrangolo, Eduardo Contreras Soto, Lorena Díaz Nuñez, André Guerra Cotta, Beatriz Hernández Gutiérrez, Julio Moreno, Jorge Myers, Carlos Palombini, Edwin Seroussi, Inés de Torre, Hernán Vázquez, and Vera Wolkowicz shared with me their insights on crucial aspects of this project. I also benefited from conversations with Lance Ingwersen, Paul Kramer, and Celia Applegate at the Vanderbilt History Seminar; with the Atlantic Geographies Institute at the University of Miami; the departments of Spanish and Portuguese and of History at Emory; the Georgia, Atlantic, Latin American, and Caribbean Studies Initiative (GALACSI); and with William Acree, Leandro Benmergui, Ted Cohen, Alejandro Dujovne, Brenda Elsey, Paula Park, Raanan Rein, Jessica Stites-Mor, Cecilia Tossounian, Mary Kay Vaughan, Corinna Zeltsman, and Eric Zolov at several AHA, LASA, and LAJSA conferences.

The research was supported by fellowships from the Council on Library and Information Resources and the Social Science Research Council. I thank the inspiring Amy Lucko and the CLIR team, and the hospitality and friendship during my research travels of my uncle Hugo Lovisolo and the late Tania, Dimitris Mavridis, Alejandro Costábile, Jeannine Manjarrez, Priscila Fujiwara, Poliany Figueiredo, Maria Sales, and Rebecca Zabel.

Thanks also to the librarians and staff at the Acervo Francisco Curt Lange, Universidade Federal de Minas Gerais, in Belo Horizonte; Museu da Imagem e do Som, and Museu Villa-Lobos, in Rio de Janeiro; Centro Nacional de Investigación, Documentación e Información Musical "Carlos Chávez" (CENIDIM), Archivo Gerónimo Baqueiro Foster, and Archivo de la Secretaría de Educación Pública, in Mexico City; Ibero-Amerikanisches Institut, in Berlin; IWO Jewish Research Institute, Museo Antropológico Nacional, and Sociedad Argentina de Autores y Compositores de Música (SADAIC), in Buenos Aires; Organization of American States, Columbus Library, in Washington, DC; Bancroft Library, in Berkeley; Woodruff Library, in Atlanta, especially Phil McLeod; and Oxford College's Library. A previous version of chapter 5 was published in the journal Nuevo Mundo—Mundos Nuevos in 2015 as part of the dossier "Musique et politique en Amérique Latine, XXe-XXIe siècles."

Profound thanks to my maestras and maestros, also model historians and friends: Dora Barrancos, Alberto Ferrari Etcheberry, and Danny James. I became a historian learning from Fernando Devoto and the Theory and History of Historiography group, Patricia Funes, Fernando Rocchi, my classmates and professors at the History Department of the University of Buenos Aires, Los Verdaderos Niveladores, and Vera Carnovale, Federico Lorenz, Gonzalo Conte, and the Memoria Abierta team. Special thanks to Silvia Rebecchi, who taught me about this curious endeavor—"cultural history"—when I was fourteen years old.

Insights on this project, and on everything else, I owe to my young old friends Ezequiel Adamovsky, Valeria Arza, Claudio Benzecry, the remembered Gastón Beltrán, Martín Bergel, Tania Carol Lugones, Leandro Castagnari, Verónica Chapperon, Natalia Cosacov, Gabriel Di Meglio, Ximena Espeche, Laura Goldberg, José González Ríos, Nicolás Kwiatkowski, Hernán Lucas, Eli Monteagudo, Pablo Ortemberg, Mónica Ranero, Mariano Salzman, Daniel Sazbón, Pablo Spiller, and Alejandra Zina.

My biggest thanks are to my beloved sisters Mariana and Laura Palomino, my brother Kuri Cousandier, and my parents Mirta Libchaber and Héctor Palomino, for their teachings, love, and fun. Also to Pupi and the Fluk family, and to the memory of Rita Libchaber, Marcos Fluk, and Pedro Arriague. The book is dedicated to my remembered grandparents, whose lives and times inspired it: Ofelia Andón, Francisco "Pancho" Palomino, Juanita "Memé" Silberberg, and Jacobo "Jack" Libchaber. Pancho gave me a guitar when I was a kid and reappeared in my dreams as I finished the manuscript.

Oskar purred at every thought in these pages. And in Oakland, Buenos Aires, la gran Tenochtitlán, Chicago, Atlanta, and everywhere else, Xochitl enchanted everything with her magic—this book and my life.

Abbreviations

AFCL   Acervo Francisco Curt Lange, Universidade Federal de Minas Gerais, Belo Horizonte

AHVL   Arquivo do Museu Villa-Lobos, Arquivo Nacional, Rio de Janeiro

AGBF   Archivo Gerónimo Baqueiro Foster, Centro Nacional de las Artes, Mexico City

BLAM   Boletín Latino-Americano de Música

IWO   Jewish Research Institute, Buenos Aires

SEP   Archivo de la Secretaría de Educación Pública, Mexico City

INTRODUCTION

Music Is Latin American History

THE HETEROGENEITY OF this region—linguistic, ethnic, geographic—is also musical: how could a classificatory label encompass sonic and poetic streams as disparate
as the ones coexisting in these Americas of multiple Native, Afro-Atlantic, European,
Circum-Caribbean, Andean, urban, rural, commercial, religious, and national musical traditions?

And yet the aesthetic category of "Latin American music" is everywhere, naturalized by listeners throughout the world, as in the name of this Oxford University Press
series. Like the songs collected in Europe by folklorists since the eighteenth century,
it is more than just "music": it stands as symbol of an entire region. Its history is
in fact enmeshed with the history of other categories, like "pan-American," "Ibero-
American," "national," and more recently "world" music, with which it converged and
competed for about a century. And it is also intertwined with the conceptualization
of the region in other domains, such as international relations, scientific organizations, and the entertainment industry. Tracing the category of Latin American music
means dealing with the wider history of the conceptualizations of Latin America as a
cultural space, and with its overlapping with those of individual nations, the Western
hemisphere, and the world.

The history of this category suggests that Latin America, as a region, is in fact
the result of the *sedimentation of projects*—diplomatic, aesthetic, political—that
"invented" it. This book deals with the crucial role of one among those projects: that
of promoting a distinct musical discourse, recognizable within the world's polyphony,

The Invention of Latin American Music. Pablo Palomino, Oxford University Press (2020). © Oxford University Press.
DOI: 10.1093/oso/9780190687403.001.0001

Latin American music. It traces the multiple actors that, between the 1920s and the 1960s, and through aesthetic, political, commercial, and institutional programs, "invented" Latin American music. The book illuminates thus, from the perspective of the formation of a regional musical space, the history of the representation of the world as made of discrete geocultural regions—upon which we still organize our universities and music catalogues, and whose interactions we call globalization.

Through practices that crisscrossed the region's internal and external boundaries, such as cultural essays, state musical education, music commerce, musicology, and cultural diplomacy, Latin American music was accepted and naturalized by audiences, artists, and cultural brokers both regionally and globally.

The research for this book was conducted in archives located in five specific countries—Mexico, Brazil, Argentina, and the United States, the demographically and economically largest countries of the hemisphere during the twentieth century, and also in Germany—but the focus is on the role of music in the imagining of the entire region. The idea of Latin America as a region originated in the early nineteenth century, when the former Iberian colonies began to coalesce around national projects, and continues in our own turbulent time. But this idea was decisively strengthened in the first half of the twentieth century by practices, programs, and a whole rhetoric around *music*. We know very well how music served nationalism; this book shows how it also produced Latin America as a *cultural region*, and why it remains at the core of the ever-evolving Latin American identity.

Music is labor—Caetano Veloso described it as the job of connecting sentiments, reason, rhyme, and sounds[1]—by a variety of musical actors: composers, performers, producers, pedagogues, musicologists, diplomats, and audiences. As a cultural historian, I searched the archives looking less for music itself than for traces of those intellectual, economic, political, expert, and social forces shaping musical labor in Latin America. I began the research with the innocent and ambitious goal of understanding, beyond the individual national histories, the larger structures or connections that historically formed what we call Latin American music. Over the years, I learned from several generations of ethnomusicologists and musically minded sociologists and historians that the formal qualities of the region's music are inseparable from broader aesthetic, aural, and social meanings and practices, and it became clear to me that Latin American music is in fact just the name of a vast, almost endless, heterogeneous web of specific histories of musical transmission and creation. Among them, there was an identifiable series of key actors and practices that, with more or less success, and through operations of exclusion and inclusion, organized those

---

[1] *Acima do coração, que sofre com razão / A razão que vota no coração / E acima da razão, a rima / e acima da rima, a nota da canção / bemol, natural, sustenida no ar / Viva aquele que se presta a esta ocupação / Salve o compositor popular* (Above the heart, which suffers with reason / The reason that votes in the heart / /And above reason, rhyme / And above rhyme, the song's note: / flat, natural, sharp in the air / Long live who devotes to this profession / Hail to the popular composer), Festa Inmodesta (Immodest celebration), in Buarque de Hollanda, Chico. *Sinal Fechado.* LP. Vol. 6349 122 (Brazil: Phillips, 1974).

disperse musical threads. From the myriad intellectual, business, artistic, and diplomatic stories that popped up from the archives, one came rapidly to the center of my research: the discipline of musicology itself. By valorizing old and new, erudite and popular, native and diasporic music, some of the characters in this book created in the 1930s the transnational field of Latin American musicology. This in-appearance merely scientific field provided, through the mediation of artists, markets, and state policies, the vocabulary and legitimacy through which heterogeneous populations in multiple countries began to see themselves as part of a common cultural tradition. The resulting image was that of Latin America as a *transnational musical region*, defined by exchanges among its different cultural nationalist projects, transnational musical networks, and last but not least, imperial geopolitics.

Latin American music is both a geographic frame of reference and an aesthetic category. It shapes how we listen to and how we talk about music within and beyond academia. Far from primordial, self-evident, or organically elaborated since the European conquest of the New World, the category is in fact a relatively recent invention. Let us locate its emergence, within the longer history of the projects that created the region as such.

MUSIC AND LATIN AMERICA

The idea that Latin America is a region was shaped over two centuries by imperial and anticolonial wars, political reformism, and racial ideologies.

Since the seventeenth century priests and Spanish imperial officers referred in occasions to an encompassing unit, "our America" (*nuestra América*), when describing the people and things of their colonies.[2] A concept of Latin America a bit closer to ours is in Simón Bolívar's *Carta de Jamaica* in 1815, when the Independence leader addressed the Spanish American classes (people of Spanish origins born in America) in its hemispheric war against the Spanish monarchy: "*We*, neither Indians nor Europeans, but a species in between the legitimate owners of the land and the Spanish usurpers."[3] That "we," initially referring to "*Americanos*," as opposed to Spaniards and Europeans, was the basis for his attempt to create a federation of republics.

---

[2] Such as the "ability of the naturals of our America ... who hunt tigers with the confidence with which we play with bulls in our Spain," as a Jesuit friar wrote in "Vida del Padre Roberto Nobilis" in 1656 ("la habilidad que tienen en nuestra América los naturales, en quienes la destreza suple las fuerzas, y cazan tigres, con la seguridad que en nuestra España se juega con los toros"). Joseph Cassani, *Glorias del segundo siglo de la compañia de Jesus, dibuxadas en las vidas y elogios de algunos de sus varones ilustres en virtud, letras y zelo de los almas que han florecido desde el año de 1640, primero del segundo siglo desde la aprobacion de la Religion* (Madrid: Manuel Fernandez, Impresor, 1734), 535.

[3] "*Nosotros*, que [...] no somos indios ni europeos, sino una especie media entre los legítimos propietarios del país y los usurpadores españoles" (34). Tulio Halperin Donghi, "Dos siglos de reflexiones sudamericanas sobre la brecha entre América Latina y Estados Unidos," in *La Brecha entre América Latina y Estados Unidos*, comp. Francis Fukuyama (Buenos Aires: Fondo de Cultura Económica, 2006), 31–78.

Contemporaneous notions of *Americanos* were more inclusive, such as among the Rio de la Plata revolutionaries who proposed the enthroning of an "Inca-king," who "after four centuries" would recover its legitimate rights emanating from "the general will of the peoples"—both the indigenous "descendants of the dispossessed" and their "brothers," the descendants of the Spaniards, "blancos" who also had "indigenous blood" (*sangre Indiana*).[4] It was thus a combination of blood and citizenship what defined this region against Europe.

Once coined in 1836 by a French observer of the United States,[5] "Latin America" evolved as a *geopolitical* term, in the work of diplomats and intellectuals from the emerging republics reacting against the United States' military expansion into Mexico and Central America.[6] Some of its first advocates explicitly favored racial integration.[7] But the idea that Latin America was a region composed of "pueblos," as in "los pueblos de América Latina,"[8] did not have a cultural nor aesthetic dimension: it was a strictly political and institutional construct. The *Revista Latino-Americana*, founded and printed in Paris in 1874 to promote "the patriotic duty of promoting in France, England, and Spain the interests of Columbus' people . . . will be liberal and republican in politics, and eclectic in scientific and literary matters."[9]

As the national projects in the region began to turn their heterogeneous populations into "Mexicans" or "Uruguayans," ethnic hierarchies (and slavery de jure or de facto) persisted. People of Indigenous and African origin became "problems," subjected to programs of assimilation, erasure, forced labor, and mythification, having to fight to resist or even to be also agents of those national projects. The *Latin* in Latin America meant to criollo elites and larger population a cultural affiliation to Spain, France, and Europe.[10]

[4] Salvador Rivera, *Latin American Unification: A History of Political and Economic Integration Efforts* (Jefferson, NC: McFarland & Co., 2014). José Victorino Lastarria et al., *La patria común: pensamiento americanista en el siglo XIX*, 2013. Gabriel Di Meglio, *1816: La trama de la independencia* (Buenos Aires: Planeta, 2016), 205–206.

[5] Michel Chevalier, "Letters on North America," trans. Steven Rowan, University of Missouri-St. Louis Institutional Repository Library, n.d., 434. (original edition Paris: Gosselin, 1836).

[6] The Chilean writer Luis Bilbao popularized the term in dialogue with central and eastern European exiles in Paris in the aftermath of the 1848 revolutions, a moment of anti-imperial national projects that led to a political reconsideration of concepts such as democracy, socialism, sovereignty, capitalism, and history. See Rafael Mondragón, "Anticolonialismo y socialismo de las periferias: Francisco Bilbao y la fundación de *La tribune des peuples*," *Latinoamérica. Revista de Estudios Latinoamericanos*, no. 56 (June 2013): 105–39.

[7] Mónica Quijada, "Sobre el origen y difusión del nombre 'América Latina' (o una variación heterodoxa en torno al tema de la construcción social de la verdad)," *Revista de Indias* 58, no. 214 (1998): 602.

[8] *El Comercio*, Lima, Peru, September 26, 1858, p. 1.

[9] "La patriótica tarea de sostener en Francia, Inglaterra y España los intereses del pueblo de Colón . . . será liberal y republicana en política, ecléctica en materias científicas y literarias." *Revista Latino-Americana*, Primer Año, Tomo 1, París, Librería Española de E. Denné Schmitz, 1874, pp. 4–5.

[10] Michel Gobat, "The Invention of Latin America: A Transnational History of Anti-Imperialism, Democracy, and Race," *American Historical Review* 118, no. 5 (December 1, 2013): 1345–75. Rebecca Earle, *The Return of the Native: Indians and Myth-Making in Spanish America, 1810–1930* (Durham, NC: Duke University Press, 2007).

The success of the term Latin America among those elites expressed, above all, geopolitical pressure and necessity. Their most lucid members realized that it was the neocolonial nature of their relationship with the north Atlantic powers what threatened the viability and autonomy of these young national projects.[11] They saw the need to build some kind of regional voice and system.

The unifying idea of Latin America had many sources. It benefited from two older georacial imperial projects: *iberismo* (in Spain) and *latinité* (in France), present on both sides of the Atlantic.[12] The idea of an America *criolla*, Catholic, and distinct both from the indigenous population and from the protestant Anglo America sustained in 1857 the idea of "the two Americas" by Colombian José María Torres Caicedo.[13] French imperial propagandists promoted the idea of Latin America when they invaded Mexico in the 1860s. Hence, "Latin" and "our" América coexisted for several decades among both imperial and anti-imperial projects. Argentine historian and jurist Carlos Calvo published in 1863 his influential work (he proudly wrote that it was read by Napoleon III[14]), which provided an erudite view of the region as having its own legal history, and hence reclaimed for the civilizing criollo elites the figure of "our America" (*nuestra América*) from its colonial and imperial origins. In 1887 the Colombian minister of foreign relations and the French ambassador to Venezuela cofounded an "asociación latino-americana universal" in Paris to foster relations among "peoples of Latin origins in both hemispheres."[15] Diplomats and statesmen, particularly from Argentina, promoted conferences and treaties to strengthen the links among the Latin American states, and in the opening speech to a congress of the "South-American governments" in 1888 the Uruguayan foreign affairs minister celebrated the progress of *Nuestra América*.[16] Hence, both a racial and an internationalist juridical discourse defined Latin America in the turn of the century.

---

[11] Carlos Marichal and Alexandra Pita, "Algunas reflexiones sobre la historia de los intelectuales/ diplomáticos latinoamericanos en los siglos XIX y XX," *Revista de Historia de América* 156 (January 2019): 97–123.

[12] Mauricio Tenorio Trillo, *Latin America: The Allure and Power of an Idea* (Chicago: University of Chicago Press, 2017).

[13] Arturo Ardao, "Panamericanismo y Latinoamericanismo," in *América latina en sus ideas*, ed. Leopoldo Zea (Mexico, D.F.: Unesco-Siglo XXI, 1986), 160–64.

[14] Carlos Calvo, *Anales históricos de la revolución de la América Latina, acompañados de los documentos en su apoyo: Desde el año 1808 hasta el reconocimiento de la independencia de ese extenso continente* (A. Durand, 1865), vi.

[15] "Los pueblos de origen latino de ambos hemisferios," *La Época*, Madrid, September 7, 1887.

[16] Ernesto Restelli, ed., *Actas y tratados del congreso sud-americano de derecho internacional privado (Montevideo 1888–1889)* (Buenos Aires: Imprenta y encuadernación de la Cámara de Diputados, 1928), 52. This congress aimed at regulating also intellectual property, including musical publications ("las obras dramáticas, operas, zarzuelas, cánticos en sus dos formas, la de impresión y representación escénica," 760). See Juan Pablo Scarfi, "La emergencia de un imaginario latinoamericanista y antiestadounidense del orden hemisférico: de la Unión Panamericana a la Unión Latinoamericana (1880–1913)," *Revista Complutense de Historia de América* 39 (July 5, 2013): 81–104. Greg Grandin, "The Liberal Traditions in the Americas: Rights, Sovereignty, and the Origins of Liberal Multilateralism," *American Historical Review* 117, no. 1 (2012): 68–91.

Fighting the continent's last anti-colonial war against Spain, the Cuban revolutionary leader José Martí gave a multiracial and democratic sense to the figure of "Nuestra América," now critical of both Iberianism and Latinity, but also of the "Yankee specs" of the elites, and closer instead to "the peculiar elements of the American peoples."[17] The US takeover of Cuba and Puerto Rico through the 1898 war with Spain reinforced this popular, republican, and radical Americanist tradition in Cuba and beyond. It became synonymous with Latin America as an anti-imperialist project.[18]

A spiritual rhetoric emerged in 1900. The Argentine scholar Ernesto Quesada opposed "we, the Latin-Americans" to the "Yankees" in terms of language and general philosophical attitude toward the world.[19] In 1906 the Nicaraguan poet Rubén Darío announced a magazine in Paris called *El Latinoamericano* dedicated to "la política y la sociedad latinoamericana en la capital francesa."[20] A "Latin American race" was invoked in 1912 in Mexico City by university students attending conferences by the Argentine writer Manuel Ugarte. The goal of the expression, according to Rafael de Torres Beleña, a Mexico-based Spanish correspondent of *El Heraldo de Madrid*, was to

> arouse in the peoples of America of Iberian language a feeling of solidarity and strengthen a current of opinion of spiritual communion in the soul of these countries, resulting in the creation of a solid and robust Latin American block capable of counterbalancing the influence of the grand Anglo-Saxon republic to the north, whose impulse of absorption and imperialism nobody doubts.[21]

Ugarte's rhetoric was echoed in 1918 by a Federation of Latin American Students in the United States. According to their speakers, these "Latin American youth" had abandoned the comfort of their wealthy families because they felt a "spiritual necessity" to pursue rigorous and austere studies in the United States.[22]

---

[17] José Martí and Pedro Henríquez Ureña, *Nuestra América* (Santo Domingo: Cielonaranja, 2016).

[18] Oscar Terán, "El primer antiimperialismo latinoamericano," in *En busca de la ideología argentina* (Buenos Aires: Catálogos Editora, 1986), 85–97.

[19] *El problema del idioma nacional* (Buenos Aires: Revista Nacional Casa Editora, 1900), p. 10. The epigraph to the book on the cover page refers to the contrary to "Hispano-América."

[20] *La Nación*, Buenos Aires, August 30, 1906, p. 9.

[21] "Despertar en los pueblos de América—de habla íbera—el sentimiento de solidaridad y fortificar una corriente de opinión de mancomunidad espiritual en el alma de estos países, qué por resultado la formación del bloque latinoamericano tan robusto y fuerte como es necesario para contrarrestar la influencia de la gran República anglosajona del Norte, cuyas ansias de absorción e imperialismo ya nadie pone en duda." "Desde Méjico—Por la raza latinoamericana," *El Heraldo de Madrid*, February 18, 1912, p. 4.

[22] Federación de Estudiantes Latino-Americanos, *El estudiante latino-americano* 1, no. 1 (1918): 2, "Un nuevo lazo entre las dos Américas." A similar organization functioned in Paris from 1924 to 1928, the Asociación General de Estudiantes Latinoamericanos (AGELA). See Michael Goebel, "Una sucursal francesa de la Reforma Universitaria: jóvenes latinoamericanos y antiimperialismo en la París de entreguerras," in *Los Viajes Latinoamericanos de La Reforma Universitaria*, ed. Martín Bergel (Rosario, Argentina: HyA Universidad Nacional de Rosario, 2018), 177–79.

At the Centennial commemorations of the Independence between 1910 and 1925 across the region, rituals and speeches reinforced the idea of a regional fraternity to ease territorial conflicts and geopolitical rivalries. In contrast to the massacres of the European Great War, diplomats, statesmen, and intellectuals portrayed the region as civilized and peaceful. Even the traditionally isolated Brazil fostered links with its neighbors since the 1890s, and embraced regionalism with Argentina, against which it held a war in 1825–1828.[23] In 1922, the scholars at the Brazilian Institute of Geography and History invited the leader of their Argentine peers, Ricardo Levene, to participate in the First International Congress for the History of America, part of the events for the Centennial of Brazil's Independence.[24]

Intellectuals and political activists after the Great War adopted this regionalism in their anti-imperialist critique of the United States, and promoted a new Latin Americanist imaginary.[25] The university reform movement spanning from Córdoba (Argentina) to Havana, the associations of Latin American students in Paris and in the United States, the Peruvian Latin-Americanist political movement (APRA), and even the pan-American policies from Washington, DC that aimed to hegemonize the hemispheric relations, they all consolidated Latin America as a geopolitical entity. Latin America expanded also into the convergence of liberal professions and public services: in 1928 a First Latin American Conference on Legal Medicine in Buenos Aires gathered medical doctors interested in promoting modern standards of legal medicine within the state and juridical systems of Latin America.[26]

Until the 1930s, however, none of the categories used to define Latin America was a *cultural* one. None of the actors that had until then shaped it, either from within or from without, claimed that the region shared a distinct *culture*. On a few occasions,

---

[23] In the words of the notable Brazilian diplomat Ruy Barbosa, what linked both countries was "the emotion of the true brotherhood, with which my *pátria* embraces its glorious sister" ("a emoção da verdadeira fraternidade, com que minha Pátria abraça a sua gloriosa irmã, a quem o adiantamento na cultura das instituições liberais e a magnificência da sua civilização asseguram um dos primeiros lugares na família dos Estados republicanos"). In Pablo Ortemberg, "Ruy Barbosa en el Centenario de 1916: apogeo de la confraternidad entre Brasil y Argentina," *Revista de Historia de América* Enero-Junio, no. 154 (2018): 118. See also by Ortemberg "Geopolítica de los monumentos: los próceres en los centenarios de Argentina, Chile y Perú (1910–1924)," *Anuario de Estudios Americanos* 72, no. 1 (June 30, 2015): 321–50, and Ori Preuss, *Transnational South America: Experiences, Ideas, and Identities, 1860s–1900s* (New York, NY and Abingdon, UK: Routledge, 2016).

[24] The Second Congress expected for 1923 in Buenos Aires would finally take place in 1937. See Martha Rodriguez, "De historiadores y de los posibles usos de su saber: la contribución de los Congresos Internacionales de Historia de América en la conformación de una identidad americana (décadas de 1930 a 1960)," *História da Historiografia: International Journal of Theory and History of Historiography*, no. 27 (2018): 91–117.

[25] Martín Bergel, "América latina, pero desde abajo: prácticas y representaciones intelectuales de un ciclo histórico latinoamericanista, 1898–1936," *Cuadernos de Historia (Santiago)*, no. 36 (June 2012): 7–36. Alexandra Pita González, *La Unión Latino Americana y el Boletín Renovación: redes intelectuales y revistas culturales en la década de 1920* (México, D.F.; Colima: Colegio de México; Universidad de Colima, 2009).

[26] "Primera Conferencia Latinoamericana de Medicina Legal," *Caras y caretas* n. 1537, Buenos Aires, November 24, 1928, p. 25.

in the 1920s, Latin Americanist intellectuals reached into the realm of culture, but to signal its absence. When the Chilean nationalist writer Joaquín Edwards Bello spoke in 1925 (from Madrid) of a unified "Latin American nation," he lamented that America had so far just applied "tracing paper upon Europe" (*el papel de calco a Europa*).[27] The same year—also in Madrid—José Vasconcelos published his influential definition of the Latin American *mestizaje* as a process that produced the first "race-synthesis . . . that inhabits the Ibero-American continent," "the truly universal, truly cosmic *culture*." Despite appearing profusely in this text, the word "culture" stands not as a reality but as the *future* result of the mixing of the old races—Hellenic, Saxon, Iberian, Western, Indostanic, and from the mythical Atlantis—into the Iberian American or "cosmic" one.[28]

Neither foreign institutions addressed the region as a cultural one. The Washington, DC-based Pan American Union, founded in 1890, promoted hemispheric intellectual cooperation as a tool for commerce, and considered Latin America as a collection of "American republics" to be integrated under the legal and economic direction of the United States. A *US-based* "Pan-American Culture" would result from scientific, technical, and patent-related collaboration between the two Americas.[29] In part to counterbalance this hegemonic project, in 1926 many Latin American countries joined a competing, French-sponsored intellectual cooperation organization through the League of Nations, while continuously participating in pan-American conferences. But these organizations never fully took off and failed to actually produce or disseminate a Latin American regional culture, other than a few commercially remarkable artists.[30]

---

[27] Joaquín Edwards Bello, *El nacionalismo continental. Crónicas chilenas* (Madrid: Impr. G. Hernández y Galo Sáez, 1925), 17. See also Fabio Moraga Valle, "¿Una nación íbero, latino o indoamericana? Joaquín Edwards Bello y el nacionalismo continental," in *Pensar el antiimperialismo: ensayos de historia intelectual latinoamericana, 1900–1930*, ed. Alejandra Pita González and Carlos Marichal Salinas (Mexico, D.F. y Colima: El Colegio de México y Universidad de Colima, 2012), 247–79 and Olivier Compagnon, *L'adieu à l'Europe: l'Amérique latine et la Grande Guerre (Argentine et Brésil, 1914–1939)* (Paris: Fayard, 2013).

[28] "La primera cultura verdaderamente universal, verdaderamente cósmica." José Vasconcelos, *Misión de la raza iberoamericana. Notas de viajes a la América del Sur* (Madrid: Agencia Mundial de Librería, 1925), prólogo. In the prologue to the 1948 edition, he mentions the "spiritual" influence of Africans in the Unites States through music.

[29] See for instance International Bureau of American Republics, *Bulletin of the International Bureau of the American Republics* (Washington, DC: US Government Printing Office, 1910).

[30] Despite setting in 1929 the "cultural development of the Continent" as a goal, the Pan American Institute of Intellectual Cooperation never took off, due to the Latin American diplomats' mistrust of the United States and alignment with the European-based League of Nations. Juliette Dumont, "Latin America at the Crossroads. The Inter-American Institute of Intellectual Cooperation, the League of Nations, and the Pan American Union," in *Beyond Geopolitics: New Histories of Latin America at the League of Nations* ed. Alan McPherson and Yannick Wehrli (Albuquerque: University of New Mexico Press, 2015), 155–67. For the cultural aspects of the PAU policies vis-à-vis Latin America, and the wider process of cultural and literary translation of Latin American productions into the United States' art world and the public sphere, see Richard Cándida Smith, *Improvised Continent: Pan-Americanism and Cultural Exchange* (Philadelphia: University of Pennsylvania Press, 2017).

A few initiatives insinuated the view of Latin America as a cultural region, but inconsequentially. A short-lived music bulletin was published in Paris in 1918, the *Revue Mensuelle Franco-Latino-Américaine—Bulletin Musical*, but in fact it took Latin America as a regional market for French music, not as a musical culture in itself.[31] In Barcelona, a failed attempt to write a musical encyclopedia (no musician responded to the author's call!) led Lucas Cortijo Alahija to write in 1919 the first history of Latin American music. Cortijo had been born in Mendoza, Argentina, the son of a Spanish composer and immigrant who had run a zarzuela company and migrated to Argentina in 1889.[32] His solitary and improvised book (to which we will return) included work on the music creators, performers, and traditions of Latin America as a space, but was not influential at all. More visible, but also more abstractly "American" than explicitly "Latin American," was a text published in 1920 at the *Revista de América* in Buenos Aires by the champion of nationalist education, Ricardo Rojas, who reflected on possible *future* links between "our musicians" and a continental "American art."[33]

"Latin American literature" was a phrase in some encyclopedias written in the United States at the turn of the century, to refer to either one undistinguishable body of texts written south of the Rio Grande, or the sum of separate national developments, but always as a minor prolongation of its Spanish, Portuguese, or French origins.[34] When the Great War displaced from Paris to Madrid the book production for Latin America, a curiously Euro-centric overlap of geographic categories occurred: the *Revista Hispano-americana Cervantes* was published by the publishing house *Mundo Latino*.[35]

An important event was the coinage of the category "Latin American art" in 1923–1924 in Paris by a network of artists, students, curators, philanthropists, and cultural bureaucrats from France and many Latin American countries. Art historian Michelle

[31] This happened as part of a larger "war" between French, German, and English music publishers during the Great War. I thank Rachel Moore for this reference. See Rachel Moore, *Performing Propaganda: Musical Life and Culture in Paris in the First World War* (Woodbridge, UK: Boydell Press, 2018).

[32] Lucas Cortijo Alahija, *Musicología latino-americana. La música popular y los músicos célebres de la América latina* (Barcelona: Maucci, 1919). See also María Antonieta Sacchi de Ceriotto, *La profesión musical en el baúl: músicos españoles inmigrantes radicados en Mendoza a comienzos del siglo XX* (Mendoza, Argentina: Editorial de la Universidad Nacional de Cuyo, 2007).

[33] Ricardo Rojas, "El arte americano," *Revista de América* 1, no. 1 (Marzo 1920): 1–2.

[34] The author of a 1896 literary study of Latin America argued in fact that *Celtiberian*—the "great Celtic race" and its Iberian progeny—would be a more appropriate name than Latin America, confirming the racial connotations of these regionalist views. M. M. Ramsey, "Latin-American Literature," in *Library of the World's Best Literature: Ancient and Modern*, vol. XXII, 46 vols., ed. Charles Dudley Warner (New York: R. S. Peale and J. A. Hill, 1896), 8903. See also Frederick Converse Beach and George Edwin Rines, eds., *The Encyclopedia Americana: A Universal Reference Library.* (New York: Scientific American Compiling Department, 1904) and *The Encyclopedia Americana: A Library of Universal Knowledge : In Thirty Volumes*, vol. 17 (New York: The Encyclopedia Americana Corporation, 1919).

[35] Cecilio Alonso, "Semblanza de Editorial Mundo Latino (1915–1931)," Biblioteca Virtual Miguel de Cervantes—Portal Editores y Editoriales Iberoamericanos (siglos XIX-XXI), 2017.

Greet showed that the exhibit of *Art Américain-Latin*, from pre-Columbian to modern, at the Galliera museum, between March and April of 1924, was the first survey that took the region as a whole (preceded by a smaller exhibit the year before and the creation of a short-lived Latin Americanist journal in that city).[36] Intended to support Latin American artists in Paris and to promote French art in Latin America, the exhibit reflected the exoticism that the Parisian academies and galleries assigned to the "primitive" art from the rest of the world. Interestingly, it opened with a concert in which painters, diplomats, and public enjoyed the Brazilian Heitor Villa-Lobos and other artists (both French and Latin American) performing a repertoire of works by then young composers who would later become both Latin American and nationalist titans: Villa-Lobos himself, the Argentine Alberto Williams, the Uruguayan Alfonso Broqua, the Guatemalan Alfredo Wyld, and the Chilean Pedro Allende Saron. The Galliera exhibit lasted just one month, but prompted Parisian galleries to work with those artists in the following years. In 1930 the Uruguayan Joaquín Torres García organized an exhibit of purely avant-garde works by a "Groupe Latino-Américain." (The regional Latin American format reappeared in New York at the World Fair of 1939 and at the MoMA in 1943, and consolidated since then.)[37] This Latin American art, which later became a staple in the postwar art museums and markets, was initially a section of the "imperial" charting of the art world in Paris: the prestige it gave to the artists back home remained circumscribed to their small and *national*—not regional—art fields.

Visual arts were still a disjointed space, in which artists from Latin America sought to create distinct national scenes in direct connection to foreign centers of legitimacy: the Spanish painters of 1898, the successive French schools, and the Venice Biennale, among others. These are the origins of the "illustrated" modern magazines that mushroomed during the second half of the nineteenth century, shaping the taste of literate urban classes, both creators and targets of nationalist programs.[38] The artistic innovations of the 1920s and 1930s, despite valorizing popular vernacular cultures, maintained the relationship between Europe and each individual nation as the primary aesthetic relationship. The increased circulation of artists, magazines, and techniques between Havana, Mexico City, Lima, and Buenos Aires created a regional modernism. But its actors conceptualized their practice as modernist, national or universal, not as Latin American.[39] By the 1930s there was no such a thing

[36] Michele Greet, *Transatlantic Encounters: Latin American Artists in Paris between the Wars* (New Haven, CT: Yale University Press, 2018), esp. introduction and chapter 3. See also Goebel, "Una sucursal francesa de la Reforma Universitaria," 177–99.

[37] Michele Greet, "Occupying Paris: The First Survey Exhibition of Latin American Art," *Journal of Curatorial Studies* 3, no. 2–3 (2014): 218 and 233–34.

[38] María Isabel Baldasarre, "América Latina y la idea de una 'modernidad global', 1895–1915," *DezenoveVinte. Arte no Brasil do Século XIX e Início do XX*, December 2015 (http://www.dezenovevinte.net/).

[39] Harper Montgomery, *The Mobility of Modernism: Art and Criticism in 1920s Latin America* (Austin: University of Texas Press, 2017).

as *a* Latin American art; instead, diverse but structurally similar aesthetic nationalist and modernist programs developed in different centers throughout the region.

A crucial institution was founded in 1930 to foster Germany's interests in the region, explicitly intended to preserve and promote Latin American culture: the Iberian-American Institute (Ibero-Amerikanisches Institut, or IAI), in Berlin. Like the pan-American and the Parisian artistic categories, this was an external, imperial formulation of the region; but the IAI represented the first stable institutional and comprehensive effort to distinguish, collect, and valorize Latin American culture, as part of a wider Iberian tradition. It was built upon a collection of documents donated by an Argentine erudite intellectual.[40]

The *cultural* sense of Latin America appeared, finally, as the historian Jorge Myers has shown, in the disparate works of a generation of anthropologists, historians, and writers who began to valorize the "transcultural" roots of Latin America—with an emphasis in African and mestizo cultural traditions—against the positivist, biologicist, and also Marxist Europeanist traditions of the intellectual national fields of the region.[41] Some of these intellectuals proposed regional syntheses, like the Peruvian philosopher Antenor Orrego who in 1939, in the style of the cultural-philosophical synthetic essays of the time, reflected on Latin America as a "Pueblo-Continente."[42] By the late 1930s a Latin Americanist approach to literary studies flourished in the United States, whose programs had been dominated by pan-Americanist and Hispanist currents.[43] But it would be much later, in 1944, that the "Tierra Firme" series by the Fondo de Cultura Económica publishing house in Mexico City established the idea of a distinct Latin American cultural and literary tradition.

This cultural dimension of Latin America invented in the 1930s became so entrenched and influential that as historian Mauricio Tenorio Trillo put it, "Latin America" does not name a historically or culturally homogeneous entity, but "is the title of a cultural history" (*es el título de una historia cultural*). Latin America became

---

[40] The initial collections were largely based on a donation by Ernesto Quesada, praised by Haya de la Torre with these words: "Siendo el Doctor Quesada admirador de [anti-imperialist Argentine intellectual José] Ingenieros, no es panamericanista. Y éste sí que es mérito apreciable en hombre de su prestigio, porque en época en que la ofensiva cultural del imperialismo convierte a tantos hombres de la vieja generación en devotos incondicionales de la 'American-kultur,' vale mucho que nos queden algunos que no caigan en la tupida y ancha red que desde Washington tienden—trampa dorada—los cazadores de adhesiones incondicionales de los intelectuales latinoamericanos." "La biblioteca latinoamericana en Berlín," Víctor Raúl Haya de la Torre, *Obras completas*, vol. 2 (Lima: J. Mejía Baca, 1977), 287. The theory of "cultural arenas" (*kulturkreise*) was "fashionable around the turn of the century in Germany and Austria." Jürgen Osterhammel, *The Transformation of the World: A Global History of the Nineteenth Century* (Princeton, NJ: Princeton University Press, 2014), 86.

[41] Jorge Myers, "An 'Atlantic History' Avant La Lettre: Atlantic and Caribbean Transculturations in Fernando Ortiz," *Sociologia & Antropologia* 5, no. 3 (December 2015): 745–70, and "Gênese 'Ateneísta' da história cultural Latino-Americana," *Tempo Social, Revista de Sociología da USP* 17, no. 1 (2004): 9–54.

[42] Antenor Orrego, *El pueblo continente: ensayos para una interpretación de la América latina* (Santiago de Chile: Ercilla, 1939).

[43] Fernando Degiovanni, *Vernacular Latin Americanisms: War, the Market, and the Making of a Discipline* (Pittsburgh: University of Pittsburgh Press, 2018).

"a specific field of knowledge" without being a definite concept, an "essentially cultural category" that mobilizes "a flexible, dynamic, and almost indefinable amalgam of ideas and beliefs, a mix that changes its form according to the circumstances." Ultimately, "Latin America" is the cultural conversation about Latin America.[44]

In this book I explain how *music* became essential to the consolidation of Latin America as a region. Music was particularly effective to express the power of culture better than other aesthetic practices, because of its ubiquity, its cross-class nature, and its ability to link, through aesthetic, policy, and economic means, the local, the regional, the national, and the global. Far from an objective musical tradition, Latin American music is the history of a musical conversation about Latin America.

The invention of Latin American music in the 1930s enabled an array of institutional, pedagogic, commercial, and even diplomatic and intellectual musical programs to introduce Latin America into a wider conversation about cultural globalization. It was as a *musical* category—through musical policies, technologies, and sound—that Latin America acquired, for the first time, a cultural sense that involved multiple actors and spheres beyond strictly intellectual circles.

Whereas the history of musical nationalisms in the region is well known, the origins of the notion of Latin American music are fragmentary. The two earliest references mentioned before—the French music publishers in 1918 and Cortijo's book in 1919—were inconsequential. The first serious discussion of this category was by Pedro Henríquez Ureña in 1929. The Dominican scholar, who many years later founded the field of the "cultural history of Latin America," gave in La Plata, Argentina, a conference presentation, *Música popular de América*, about the music of "nuestra América latina."[45] But he started this beautiful text with a series of caveats to justify his having limited his treatment to the Antilles and Mexico: surveying the music of the rest of the region remained an unaccomplished project. Almost at the same time, other Latin American intellectuals began to listen to Latin America from abroad. The exiled leader of the Peruvian and Latin-Americanist political movement APRA, Víctor Raúl Haya de la Torre, wrote in 1930 an article on "the musical Latin-Americanization of Europe." Haya described the popularity of the "música latinoamericana" in Berlin, by distinguishing specific Latin American national styles that he considered to be at the same level as US styles: "The Argentine *gaucho* and the Mexican *charro* are today as popular as the American Black or Jew who, dressed with a tuxedo, sings, cries, and dances or does gymnastics within his jazz band." Haya considered *música latinoamericana* as a key indicator of the emergence and popularity of a distinct and proud "Latin

---

[44] "Una amalgama maniobrable, movible, dinámica y casi indefinible de ideas y creencias; una mezcla que adquiere formas según la circunstancia." Mauricio Tenorio Trillo, *Argucias de la historia: siglo XIX, cultura y "América Latina"* (México: Paidós, 1999), 171–72.

[45] Pedro Henríquez Ureña, "Música Popular de América," *Boletín de Antropología Americana*, Pan American Institute of Geography and History, no. 9 (July 1984): 137–57. This work was presented in 1929 and published originally in 1930 in *Conferencias, Primer Ciclo*, 1929, Vol. 1, Biblioteca del Colegio Nacional de Las Plata, 1930, pp. 177–236.

American culture" that was no longer a copy of the culture of the United States or Europe. The *"canciones típicas"* of *"nuestros países,"* he argued, now stood equal to the popular music of the United States and could be performed next to "serious music" (*música seria*) from Europe.[46]

The Cuban writer and musicologist Alejo Carpentier described the success of Don Aspiazú's Cuban orchestra at the Empire Theater in Paris in 1932 as the "vanguardia de la música latinoamericana." He highlighted it as a triumph of Cuban music over jazz and tango and argued that there was a thing called "Latin American music," which was for him a vessel for distinct national music styles. He voiced his sense of national distinctiveness by praising the theater's stage decorators for avoiding false stereotypes such as "a Mexican volcano or a California hacienda in a landscape intended to be Caribbean."[47] (In 1935 the Argentine writer Jorge Luis Borges acknowledged one of Aspiazú's biggest hits, "the deplorable rumba *El manisero*" [The Peanut Vendor], as well as "Handy's blues," "the Habanera—mother of tango" and the Uruguayan "candombe" as part of the hemispheric legacy of African slavery.[48])

The commercial success of orchestras and music of Latin American origin in the 1930s was the visible face of a deeper process of valorization of the region's music. Between 1928 and 1934, for instance, after the failure of the Paris-based International Composers Guild, the Mexican composer Carlos Chávez, joined by US and Latin American modernist colleagues at the Pan American Association of Composers, promoted the idea of an *Americanist*, New World musical maturity to rival Europe's established art music system.[49] He put it bluntly in his call to the Symphonic Festivals of Pan-American Music in 1930, organized by the Mexican Symphonic Orchestra and the Revista "Música." Since European music dominates—because it is "excellent" and because Europeans conduce virtually all the symphonic orchestras, "including both the South and North American ones"—the task now is to stimulate and reunite the disperse "repertoires of both Latino- and North-American" symphonic music.[50] But in the United States the label "Latin American," even within the pan-American view, was applied to classical repertoires by Latin American composers, except when

46 "El gaucho argentino y el charro mexicano son hoy tan conocidos en Europa y tan populares como el negro o el judío norteamericano que trajeado de smoking canta, grita y danza o hace gimnasia dentro de su jazz-band." "Latinoamericanización musical de Europa—Triunfo de la música típica de México," August 21, 1930, *La Industria*, Trujillo, Peru. I thank Martín Bergel for this reference. The text appears in his *Complete Works* as written in Berlin in 1929. See Víctor Raúl Haya de la Torre, *Obras completas*, vol. 2 (Lima: J. Mejía Baca, 1977): 294–97.

47 "Un volcán mexicano o una hacienda en California en medio de un paisaje que aspira a ser antillano." "Don Aspiazu in Paris," in *Crónicas*, Vol. 2, Instituto Cubano del Libro—Editorial Arte y Literatura, 1975 (orig. published in *Revista Carteles*, November 20, 1932, pp. 109–14).

48 Jorge Luis Borges, "El atroz redentor Lazarus Morell," in *Historia universal de la infamia [1935]* (Buenos Aires: Emecé, 1953).

49 Stephanie Stallings, "Collective Difference: The Pan-American Association of Composers and Pan-American Ideology in Music, 1925–1945" (PhD diss., Florida State University, 2009).

50 "Inclusive las americanas del Sur y del Norte." Carlos Chávez, "Festivales Sinfónicos de Música Panamericana—Convocatoria," *Música—Revista Mexicana* 1, no. 4 (July 15, 1930): 3–4.

touring US artists used it to refer to a purely geographical zone. Not even musical ethnographers studying indigenous music used the term; they preferred the also purely geographic "South America."[51]

The single most crucial and consequential Latin Americanist musical project was *Americanismo Musical*. It began in 1934 as a solitary text by a then unknown German émigré in Montevideo named Francisco Curt Lange, who called the project a "movement," and in 1935 turned it into a transnational platform for Latin American music, the *Boletín Latino-Americano de Música*. In part by making use of the *Boletín*, nationalist activists throughout the region began to create music education policies that articulated a Latin Americanist discourse. The importance of Lange's bulletin was immense, proportionally inverse to his gradual forsake by the following generations of scholars. Lange and his bulletin addressed Latin American music as both a discourse and a program. The bulletin made the music world fully embrace Latin America as a regional category earlier and in wider circles than other cultural fields, such the visual arts (where it really took off by the end of the Second World War) and literature (which only in the 1960s overcame the Hispanism and pan-Americanism the foreign policy of Spain and the United States imposed on the field).[52]

The idea of Latin American music, despite the ethnocentric views of some of its promoters, incorporated and valorized virtually every ethnic root in the region—the main source of distinction being "true" music versus "false" (commercial) music. The fundamental contribution of Francisco Curt Lange and his bulletin was an understanding of the history of musical practices in Latin America that valorized actors and materials from a plurality of social, geographic, and linguistic groups, through the flexible adoption of disparate aesthetic categories—such as folkloric, modernist, regionalist, religious—beyond the cultural elites, across national boundaries, and encompassing the entire region.

---

[51] Louis Moreau Gottschalk, *Notes of a Pianist, during His Professional Tours in the United States, Canada, the Antilles, and South America* (Philadelphia: J. B. Lippincott, 1881). Karl Gustav Izikowitz, *Musical and Other Sound Instruments of the South American Indians, a Comparative Ethnographical Study*, Göteborgs Kungl. Vetenskaps- Och Vitterhets-Samhälles Handlingar, 5. Földjen, Ser. A, bd. 5, n:o 1 (Göteborg: Elanders boktr, 1935).

[52] For the pan-American and Hispanic origins of the Latin Americanist field of studies and the larger academic interest in Latin America in the US, see Degiovanni, *Vernacular Latin Americanisms* and Ricardo Salvatore, *Disciplinary Conquest: U.S. Scholars in South America, 1900–1945* (Durham, NC: Duke University Press, 2016). The explicitly programmatic conversation about Latin American literature began later, with Alejo Carpentier's 1949 prologue to *El reino de este mundo*, in which he defined it as "lo real maravilloso," or magical realism, and continued in the 1960s with the "boom" of Latin American writers published by Carmen Balcells in Barcelona, and theorized in 1969 by Carlos Fuentes in *La nueva novela latinoamericana*. I thank Inés de Torres for these insights.

LATIN AMERICAN MUSIC AS RHETORIC OF THE POPULAR

The Latin Americanist rhetoric appeared in the midst of structural changes in the practice of music. The transformation of capitalism between 1870 and the Second World War reorganized musical practices across the globe. Commercial cultures expanded through the nodes and networks of the global economy, which Theodor Adorno called at the time a "cultural industry," while state, religious, bourgeois, and working-class organizations created their own musical institutions, repurposing "traditional" musical forms worldwide. In Latin America, modernizing state bureaucracies used musical education to shape populations in a context of industrialization, secularization, migrations, miscegenation, literacy, urbanization, and consumerism. Here too, traditional musical legitimacies, practices and repertoires were transformed. But in this region institutions were weak and markets unstable. The heterogeneous music worlds of Latin America only imperfectly coalesced around national systems of musical production and taste much later, in the second half of the twentieth century, like much of the rest of the world.[53] It is important to note that there was no unifying regional institution tying these emerging systems together —no Latin American Ministry of Culture or Latin American Conservatory; no shared Latin American Tin Pan Alley nor Latin American Hollywood, to dictate legitimacies, build audiences, and generate a stable labor market for musicians, producers, and critics. Hence, the archive reflects at once great expectations and grim realities: beyond reduced social circles,[54] everyone complained about lack of resources—the struggling musicologist, the performer at the radio station, the traditional folklorist, and the working-class student at the nocturnal music school. In such context, a financially precarious and ideologically amorphous project, Latin Americanist musicology, provided a legitimate rhetoric and practical tools to national bureaucracies and individual artists in their efforts to build musical organizations and audiences, and proposed a regional program for Latin American music to be developed regionally.

The ideological cornerstone of this rhetoric was the idea of music as the quintessential expression of *the people*. If by the eighteenth century music was defined in Europe by its *function*—religious or military, for example—and the repertoires, instruments, and lyrics attached to those functions had hence been policed by the competent authorities (such as the Inquisition, for instance), by the mid-nineteenth

---

[53] Frédéric Martel, *Mainstream: enquête sur cette culture qui plaît à tout le monde* (Paris: Flammarion, 2010). Martel shows that music markets are nowadays mainly national: the globalization of formats coexists with the nationalization of contents. EMI expanded the recording industry globally, the same way MTV globalized the video-clip, but even within those globalized formats, Brazilians tend to listen Brazilian music, and the same applies to Iranian, Mexican or French consumers. The intense expansion of global communications in the late twentieth century and in the first fifteen years of the twenty-first did not challenge this. (The national system is based on a mix of cultural factors, such as language, and policy factors, such as the national quotas in radio.)

[54] Omar Corrado, "Victoria Ocampo y la música: una experiencia social y estética de la modernidad," *Revista Musical Chilena* 61, no. 208 (December 2007): 37–65.

century, music's *origins* became paramount, and a distinction was drawn between "Art music" produced by individual geniuses, and the anonymously created "folklore." Both Art music and folklore served to build national music canons. And with the global transformation of capitalism and the dissemination of new commercial music, a third form emerged: "popular" music.[55] In Latin America, to the contrary, the three categories—nationalist art music, folklore research, and urban commercial music—developed almost synchronically and consolidated in the 1930s. Marginal urban commercial genres became, through multiple interactions with art and folklore music, national symbols. Hence, popular legitimacy turned this music into national music—*música del pueblo, do povo, popular*—exactly when the very idea of Latin American music was taking shape. The "people" was identified with each specific nation and at the same time evoked as a wider regional cultural source—a wider regional, transnational *Volk* not yet politically organized.[56]

The first generation of musicologists based their own legitimacy on the ability to separate legitimate from illegitimate music. Pedro Henríquez Ureña, in his 1929 conference, used "popular" to refer to the spontaneous, *true* art of the people, in contrast to both "cultivated" art music and "vulgar" or fake music—the market presented according to him a distorted image of the reality of the "people." Carlos Chávez explained in 1930 that popular art is essentially "innocent" and not reflexive. Popular art "does not know whether itself is popular or not"; "the popular chants of the indigenous people, so to speak, have never pursued an artistic goal," and the "'spirituals' of Black people have a purely religious intention." The popular artist is conscious of the expressiveness of the materials he uses, but the result—the work of art—is experienced by him and the audience as "a surprising mystery." Chávez wrote this with admiration: like the "indios de Guadalajara," the ancient Greeks also created art in this innocent, true, popular fashion, one that alien to market convenience or vanity was in fact the way for the "art for art's sake."[57] The candid condescendence of this definition of popular art pertains to the Europeanist idea of the composer as a genius, but it also permeated the scientific pretensions of musicologists. The founding father of Argentine musicology, Carlos Vega, called in 1950 "*mesomúsica*" ("middle music" or "everyone's music") the urban musical culture that was distinct from both art music and rural folklore but shared elements of both of them.[58] The

---

[55] Javier Marin Lopez, "A Conflicting Relationship: Music, Power and the Inquisition in Vice-Regal Mexico City," in *Music and Colonial Society in Colonial Latin America*, ed. Geoffrey Baker and Tess Knighton (Cambridge: Cambridge University Press, 2011), 43–63. Matthew Gelbart, *The Invention of "Folk Music" and "Art Music": Emerging Categories from Ossian to Wagner* (Cambridge: Cambridge University Press, 2007).

[56] Johann Gottfried Herder, *Song Loves the Masses: Herder on Music and Nationalism*, ed. Philip Bohlman (Berkeley: University of California Press, 2017), 24.

[57] Carlos Chávez, "Nacionalismo Musical—II—El Arte Popular y El No Popular," *Música—Revista Mexicana* 1, no. 4 (July 15, 1930): 18–22.

[58] Vega created the notion of mesomúsica in the 1950s, which was first used in 1959 by his disciple, the Uruguayan Lauro Ayestarán, before Vega fully elaborated it in 1965. Coriún Aharonián, "Carlos Vega y la teoría de la música popular: un enfoque latinoamericano en un ensayo pionero," *Revista*

idea of popular art defined in relation to a "true" music remained at the basis of the musicologists' epistemology. It took a long time for commercially and industrially mediatized music to be fully accepted by musicologists as legitimate and as proudly Latin American. The Latin American branch of the International Association for the Study of Popular Music was created in 1997, the effort of musicologists and musicians trained between the 1960s and 1980s, who elaborated a critique of the musical hierarchies of the previous generation.[59] But the popular legitimacy of music had already been there since the 1930s, when expert discourses located the value of musical work in its connection to the people.

The struggle to musically define "the people" happened in all the cultural metropolises of the industrialized and industrializing world. It was visible in policies by Soviet cultural officers, British unions, US New Dealers, German nationalists, Italian communists, and French popular front-era cultural brokers.[60] In China, the commercial musical forms that shaped Shanghai's popular culture became tools for both Nationalist and Communist musical policies successively.[61] In Latin America, the main forces in the definition of the popular were the emerging state cultural bureaucracy, the founding generation of musicologists, the US entertainment industry, and a constellation of impresarios, artists, and journalists. In this book, the cases of Mexico, Brazil, and Argentina illuminate the larger region's musical policies during the populist era.

The musical field was certainly postcolonial in that, for instance, governments sponsored young talents to be trained at European conservatories, to come back and, in their view, elevate and civilize the musical taste of the people. The European epistemology of the local intelligentsia, and the *neocolonial* expansion of US recording

---

Musical Chilena 51, no. 188 (1997): 61–74. Carlos Vega, *Danzas y canciones argentinas: Teorías e investigaciones : Un ensayo sobre el tango.* (Buenos Aires: G. Ricordi y C., 1936). Carlos Vega, "Mesomúsica: Un Ensayo Sobre La Música de Todos," *Revista Musical Chilena* 51, no. 188 (1997): 75–96. This concept resembled, perhaps unknowingly, the one of "mass music" utilized by T. Adorno, the Frankfurt School, and US sociology in the 1930s.

[59] Musicologist Juan Pablo González, protagonist and analyst of that process of legitimation of the popular, reflects on the Latin Americanist musicological and epistemological stakes of the past half century in *Pensar la música desde América Latina: problemas e interrogantes* (Buenos Aires: Gourmet Musical, 2013).

[60] See Pauline Fairclough, *Classics for the Masses: Shaping Soviet Musical Identity under Lenin and Stalin* (New Haven, CT: Yale University Press, 2016); Gareth Stedman Jones, "Working-Class Culture and Working-Class Politics in London, 1870–1900; Notes on the Remaking of a Working Class," *Journal of Social History* 7, no. 4 (1974): 460–508; Francis V O'Connor and Federal Art Project, *Art for the Millions; Essays from the 1930s by Artists and Administrators of the WPA Federal Art Project* (Greenwich, CT: New York Graphic Society, 1973); George L. Mosse, *The Nationalization of the Masses: Political Symbolism and Mass Movements in Germany from the Napoleonic Wars through the Third Reich* (New York: Howard Fertig, 1975); Antonio Gramsci, *Gli intellettuali e l'organizzazione della cultura* (Torino: Einaudi, 1950); Jeffrey H Jackson, *Making Jazz French: Music and Modern Life in Interwar Paris* (Durham, NC: Duke University Press, 2003); and Danièle Pistone, *Musiques et musiciens à Paris dans les années trente* (Paris: H. Champion, 2000).

[61] Szu-Wei Chen, "The Rise and Generic Features of Shanghai Popular Songs in the 1930s and 1940s," *Popular Music* 24, no. 1 (2005): 107–25.

and radio industry over the region, also considered popular taste something mold-able by experts—even if, as historian Matthew Karush showed, local entrepreneurs in the music industry adapted those neocolonial market relations to local and pop-ular aesthetic forms. Nostalgically postcolonial was also the ideology that valued Iberian music as the matrix of Latin America's folk music against modern pollutants. But these views were not the only ones. The *popular* legitimacy of music was pro-duced by other political framings of music and culture.[62] Musicians from the Afro-Brazilian diasporas, for instance, claimed to be popular, and like criollo and mestizo musicians, foreign and local entertainment industry agents, conservative and radi-cal indigenists, and cosmopolitan modernists, they too proposed forms of musically representing the "popular," some times reinforcing, other times subverting, and fre-quently displacing the "colonial" conflict into more inclusive configurations. When tango musicians—Afro-Argentine, immigrant, and criollo—dressed-up as gauchos to play or record, at home or abroad, "creole," "typical," or "Argentine" songs, they literally brandished and owned their work as legitimate because popular, therefore resignifying, in a populist sense, any colonial meaning.[63]

The cultural rhetoric of the popular and the idea of Latin American music emerged hence more or less simultaneously, and both marked the region's heterogeneous musical worlds.

MUSIC AS MODERNIZING TOOL

Most actors in this book had a *programmatic* stance toward music. They projected on it a conscious activism, with expectations of growth and expansion—be it musical education, markets, aesthetic quality, or truthfulness. The manager of a broadcast-ing system, the street performer, the orchestra director, the musicologist, and the music pedagogue engaged—as it happens today as well—in forms of labor based on creativity, opportunities, and networks, informed by musical ideologies.[64] On some

---

[62] For the politics of the popular in music see Jocelyne Guilbault, *Governing Sound: The Cultural Politics of Trinidad's Carnival Musics* (Chicago: University of Chicago Press, 2007). Julio Mendívil suggests that ethnomusicology does not need to adopt a *postcolonial* perspective to de-essentialize the concept of "music" and address the always contextual and situated nature of musical and cultural practice. See Julio Mendívil, *En contra de la música: herramientas para pensar, comprender y vivir las músicas* (Buenos Aires: Gourmet Musical, 2016), especially 149 and 197. Silvia Rivera Cusicansqui pointed out that the postcolonial perspective in Andean, and more broadly Latin American studies, risks to reify the essentializing otherness of the subaltern condition it seeks to criticize. See Silvia Rivera Cusicanqui, "Ch'ixinakax Utxiwa: A Reflection on the Practices and Discourses of Decolonization," *South Atlantic Quarterly* 111, no. 1 (Winter 2012): 95–109.

[63] Julia Chindemi Vila and P. Vila, "La música popular argentina entre el campo y la ciudad: música campera, criolla, nativa, folklórica, canción federal y tango," *ArtCultura (Universidade Federal de Uberlândia)* 19, no. 34 (2017): 9–26. Marina Cañardo, *Fábricas de músicas. Comienzos de la industria discográfica en la Argentina (1919–1930)* (Buenos Aires: Gourmet Musical, 2017), chapter 5.

[64] Kaley Mason, "Musicians and the Politics of Dignity in South India," in *The Cambridge History of World Music*, ed. Philip Bohlman (Cambridge: Cambridge University Press, 2013), 441–72; Howard

occasions, for instance, Latin American musicians organized in unions and societ- ies of composers, responding to a context of commercial opportunity and state pro- motion of unionization and labor protections. Composing, broadcasting, enforcing pedagogy programs, and building regional organizations were conscious programs aimed at transforming existing musical practices by expanding their reach, their ideological appeal, their economic benefits, or their political impact. This program- matic and transformative understanding of musical practices is what makes them *modern.* These actors and institutions purposely promoted and regulated the inter- action between institutionalized elite and marginal subaltern music, state and ple- beian practices, and vernacular and foreign sounds. What we consider today Latin American music results from that modernizing labor.[65]

Textbooks were modernizing tools par excellence, and Latin America was for their authors a space to conquer. The Chilean Pedro Allende published in 1937 a music ini- tiation method "for lyceums and elementary schools of Latin América."[66] The first *Historia de la música latinoamericana* was written for the Argentine national middle- school system and published in Buenos Aires in 1938, with the assistance of Lange and other Uruguayan musicologists. It presented a history of the music of several Latin American nations as examples of the same cultural arena. Latin American music appears here as an array of regional and national "mestizajes" or *mixings* of each nation's indigenous and Iberian roots—"la conjunción maravillosa de dos razas poderosas"—and, in the cases of Cuba and Brazil, their African roots as well.[67]

The Latin Americanist discourse, with its positive view of a diverse popular cul- ture and its pedagogical and musicological activism, was well received by key United States cultural diplomats during World War II. The United States and Latin America had exchanged popular music commercially beginning in the nineteenth century and throughout the first decades of the twentieth.[68] But between 1939 and 1947 the Pan American Union expanded its traditional concerts in Washington, DC, and the

Becker and Robert R. Faulkner, *Do You Know . . . ?: The Jazz Repertoire in Action* (Chicago: University of Chicago Press, 2009); Marc Perrenoud, *Les musicos: enquête sur des musiciens ordinaires* (Paris: La Découverte, 2007).

[65] Modernist and avant-garde artists in those years also wanted to bridge those oppositions. The circulation across cultural divides became later on the subject of historians of the cultural, ideo- logical, and musical worlds of past societies. See for instance Carlo Ginzburg, *The Cheese and the Worms: The Cosmos of a Sixteenth-Century Miller* (Baltimore: Johns Hopkins University Press, 1980); Beatriz Sarlo, *Una modernidad periférica: Buenos Aires, 1920 y 1930* (Buenos Aires: Ediciones Nueva Visión, 1988); Andreas Huyssen, *After the Great Divide: Modernism, Mass Culture, Postmodernism* (Bloomington: Indiana University Press, 1986); Hermano Vianna, *O mistério do samba* (Rio de Janeiro: Jorge Zahar & Editora UFRJ, 1995).

[66] Pedro Humberto Allende, *Método original de iniciación musical para Liceos y Escuelas Primarias de la América Latina* (Santiago de Chile: Imp. y Lit. Casa Amarilla, 1937).

[67] Rolando García, Luciano Croatto, and Alfredo Martín, *Historia de la música latinoamericana* (Buenos Aires: Librería Perlado, 1938).

[68] Eugenio Pereira Salas, *Notas para la historia del intercambio musical entre las Américas antes del año 1940* (Washington, DC: Pan American Union, Music Division, 1941); Robert Stevenson, "Visión musical norteamericana de las otras Américas hacia 1900," *Revista Musical Chilena* 31, no. 137 (1977): 5–35.

strictly avant-garde sphere of the Pan American Association of Composers began to include musical folklore and music mass pedagogy explicitly based on Latin American musical programs and expertise.[69] Lange's musicological network was thus tapped and almost absorbed by US wartime cultural programs.

The legitimacy gained by the modernizing rhetoric of Latin American music as popular during World War II was crucial for the further expansion, in the postwar years, of the definition of Latin America as a region to nonmusical realms. From the visual arts to economics and social sciences, by the 1960s it had become an established geocultural notion, and music was at its core. Latin American *music* is since then indivisible from both the popular and the modernizing uses of the regional category "Latin America."

TOWARD A TRANSNATIONAL LATIN AMERICAN CULTURAL HISTORY

This book is not about specific genres, nor about music in the sense of "the way it intensifies experience."[70] It does not address either the specifically sonic and aural dimension of music. For historians and social scientists, sound is a wide and promising frontier, and we can rely on the work of two pioneer generations that located sound at the intersections of musicology, anthropology, sociology, and history.[71] Their insights appear here and there in the text.

This book is instead about how people came to categorize some music as Latin American. The question orienting it is how an array of musical cultures organized sound and formed a regional category and identity around it. As will become clear, Latin American music does not exist. It is impossible to demarcate anything Latin

---

[69] For instance, a 1940 program for farm women and girls' clubs in the state of Iowa offered music lessons using "traditional" songs from Peru and Martinique, an "Argentine cowboy song," and "Spain-Mexico" and "Italian-Brazil" ones. The introduction highlighted Latin America's "magical" and multiracial history and culture. Fannie Buchanan, *Musical Moments from Latin America* (Ames: Iowa State College of Agricultural and Mechanic Arts, 1940).

[70] Celia Applegate, "Introduction: Music Among the Historians," *German History* 30, no. 3 (2012): 330.

[71] Steven Feld, "Acoustemology," in *Keywords in Sound*, ed. David Novak and Matt Sakakeeny (Durham, NC: Duke University Press, 2015), 12–21; Veit Erlmann, *Reason and Resonance: A History of Modern Aurality* (New York: Zone Books, 2014). Xochitl Marsilli-Vargas, "Listening Genres: The Emergence of Relevance Structures through the Reception of Sound," *Journal of Pragmatics* 69 (August 2014): 42–51; Ana María Ochoa Gautier, *Aurality: listening and knowledge in nineteenth-century Colombia* (Durham, NC: Duke University Press, 2014); Alejandra Bronfman and Andrew Grant Wood, *Media, Sound, & Culture in Latin America and the Caribbean* (Pittsburgh: University of Pittsburgh Press, 2012); Claudio Benzecry, *The Opera Fanatic: Ethnography of an Obsession* (Chicago: University of Chicago Press, 2011); Suzanne G. Cusick, "'You Are in a Place That Is out of the World . . .': Music in the Detention Camps of the 'Global War on Terror,'" *Journal of the Society for American Music* 2, no. 1 (February 2008): 1–26; Jonathan Sterne, *The Audible Past: Cultural Origins of Sound Reproduction* (Durham, NC: Duke University Press, 2003); Peter Szendy, *Écoute, une histoire de nos oreilles* (Paris: Minuit, 2001); Richard A. Peterson and Roger M. Kern, "Changing Highbrow Taste: From Snob to Omnivore," *American Sociological Review* 61, no. 5 (October 1996): 900–907; and James Johnson, *Listening in Paris: A Cultural History* (Berkeley: University of California Press, 1996).

American in Latin American music, given the heterogeneity intrinsic to the category itself. And yet the archive provides evidence of the utility, prestige, popularization, and acceptance of this category among ordinary listeners, art programmers, educators, activists, and cultural brokers, making Latin American music a relevant category for understanding both Latin America and the globalization of music.

It has been a long time since anthropologists and, later, cultural historians and sociologists challenged the idea that *culture* matches *space*, thinking instead of culture as a practice of conflict, translation, or accommodation between places, people, and things. The global turn in the humanities and social sciences helps us see musical practices as produced by networks and social relations that cross boundaries of space and origin.[72] In Latin America, the transnational circulation of capital and ideas fed, over two centuries, national systems of taste and culture. But they also produced a *regional* space. The musical practices studied in this book, like all cultural practices, are tools that humans use to unsettle their social and cultural boundaries and build new ones, places they can call "home," thereby "keeping even spatially rooted cultures in motion."[73] The commercial category *world music* of the 1980s, with its relabeling and reorganizing of supposedly rooted folkloric forms, anticipated our global, internet-mediated soundscape. Today, through algorithms, both users' personal taste and corporations' strategies constantly recategorize music spatially and generically to create intimate and social worlds.[74] Many decades ago, in the 1930s, and with other tools, people produced another kind of "home," a regional one, for musical programs unleashed by that other wave of cultural globalization.

Like the roots of a redwood tree, the arguments in this book extend horizontally. No individual case study could suffice to show the width of the regional and transnational articulations that created Latin American music. Because musical practices cross-pollinated through the entire region, the research had to be necessarily multisited: the archives are located Buenos Aires, Belo Horizonte, Rio de Janeiro, Mexico City, Washington, DC, Berlin, and Berkeley. The list of cities, countries, and archives could of course have been longer, but that would have turned this project into an endless encyclopedia. I present here a key set of actors, repertoires, and ideas that traveled across the region, constructing it musically.

The regional ambition of this book is purposeful. Regional blocks are formed in general to engage with globalization and are not opposed to national identities. This book shows precisely how cultural nationalism and cultural Latin Americanism grew

[72] Peter Burke, *Cultural Hybridity* (Cambridge: Polity, 2014).

[73] Daniel T. Rodgers, Bhavani Raman, and Helmut Reimitz, *Cultures in Motion* (Princeton, NJ: Princeton University Press, 2014), 3.

[74] Jocelyne Guilbault, "Interpreting World Music: A Challenge in Theory and Practice," *Popular Music* 16, no. 1 (1997): 31–44; Bob W. White, *Music and Globalization: Critical Encounters* (Bloomington: Indiana University Press, 2014); Gabriel Vaz de Melo, Ana Flávia Machado, and Lucas de Carvalho, "Música digital no Brasil: uma análise do consumo e reproduções no Spotify" (Cedeplar, Universidade Federal de Minas Gerais, November 2018); Ignacio Siles González et al., "Genres as Social Affect: Cultivating Moods and Emotions through Playlists on Spotify," *Social Media + Society* 5, no. 2 (May 25, 2019): 1–11.

together. In 1940 Carmen Monroy Niecke, Secretary of the Mexican Institute of Musicology and Folklore, expressed a typical argument when linking, in support of a musical union among Spanish American peoples, "the love for the fatherland, and its culmination in the love for the race, that in our case creates an endless chain of nations."[75] Regional formations—with their racial imagination—are with globalization the very grammar of national formation. This is why this book focuses precisely on the climactic period of nationalist populism: to show how transnational dynamics between nations were crucial to them. Transnationalism is thus not just a postcolonial, periphery-center relationship (such as, for instance, Puerto Rico and New York, Rio de Janeiro and Paris, or Santiago de Chile and London). Transnationality *within* and *between* Latin American spaces was fundamental. A powerful example is that of the "dialogues" of danzón, which crossed national, social, and racial borders at once.[76] Another is the incredible dissemination of cumbia throughout the hemisphere.[77]

My reading, many years ago, before starting my doctoral studies, of a handful of texts by anthropologists, musicians, historians, cultural critics, and philosophers, animated me to interrogate music in order to illuminate relevant zones of the past.[78] As I conducted my research, I engaged with three wide questions in Latin American and cultural history: the interdependence of cultural pluralism and cultural populism; of nationalism and globalization; and of nationalism and Latin Americanism.

Many cultural innovations in recent decades—the blossoming of rock in Spanish made in Buenos Aires, Mexico City, Bogotá, and Los Angeles; state policies at the *pontos de cultura* of the Worker's Party administration under Gilberto Gil; the grassroots musical markets and parties of the Brazilian interior; the global replications of the Venezuelan *Sistema* of youth orchestras; the musical encounters along the US–Mexico border; and the array of techno-cumbias across the region—represent music as a continuous mediation, a dialogue between art and popular, urban and rural, and local, national, regional, and global forms. Many of these materials consolidated, originally, at the time of nationalism.[79] It was under the supposedly inward-looking

---

[75] "El amor patrio, y la culminación de éste con el amor a la raza que en la nuestra forma una cadena interminable de naciones, todas ellas en condiciones parecidas." "La música como lazo de unión en Hispano América," *Diario Nuevo*, San Salvador, El Salvador, April 8, 1940, Archivo Gerónimo Baqueiro Foster.

[76] Alejandro L. Madrid and Robin D. Moore, *Danzón: Circum-Carribean Dialogues in Music and Dance* (New York: Oxford University Press, 2013).

[77] Héctor Fernández L'Hoeste, "All the Cumbias, the Cumbia," in *Imagining Our Americas: Toward a Transnational Frame*, ed. Sandhya Shukla and Heidi Tinsman (Durham, NC: Duke University Press, 2007), 338–64.

[78] Fundamental for my perspective were Hermano Vianna, *O mistério do samba* (Rio de Janeiro: Jorge Zahar & Editora UFRJ, 1995); Caetano Veloso, *Verdade tropical* (São Paulo: Companhia das Letras, 1997); Esteban Buch, *La Neuvième de Beethoven: Une histoire politique* (Paris: Gallimard, 1999); Carlos Monsiváis, *Aires de familia: cultura y sociedad en América Latina* (Barcelona: Anagrama, 2000); and Ricardo Ibarlucía, "La perspectiva del zorzal: Paul Celan y el 'Tango de la muerte,'" *Revista Latinoamericana de Filosofía* 30, no. 2 (2004): 287–312.

[79] Matthew Karush, *Musicians in Transit: Argentina and the Globalization of Popular Music* (Durham, NC: Duke University Press, 2017); Deborah Pacini Hernandez, Héctor Fernández L'Hoeste, and

populist nationalisms of the second third of the twentieth century that musical markets, platforms, pedagogies, and mythologies enabled the emergence of a Latin American culture that continues thriving.

Anthropologist Néstor García Canclini argued that the region's modernity was built around national cultures until the crisis of the 1970s and 1980s, which affected the national state's ability to foster an autonomous and inclusive modernization, and surrendered the region to the current neoliberal, corporate-led globalization, which in turn disrupted the old national borders, hierarchies, frameworks, and legitimation—producing our "hybrid cultures." But some years later, the essayist and critic Carlos Monsiváis noticed that the region's old national cultures of the early and mid-twentieth century had been in fact quite *trans*national already, shaped by pan-Latin American relations as well as by the United States cultural industry, an insight later confirmed by cultural historians.[80] This book continues this conversation and suggests that our current, twenty-first-century Latin American culture is not being built over the ruins of the national projects, but in fact it continues their work of bringing together disparate cultural threads and fostering regional integration.

In chapter 1, I map the continental patchwork of music circuits since the late nineteenth-century that provided the context to the emergence of the category of Latin American music, and identify the agents, institutions, and discourses throughout the hemisphere and in Europe that contributed to its emergence. Chapter 2 provides a map of four disparate and concrete circuits of musical practice to illuminate how Latin America was created as a modern musical space: (1) a very brief study of the entertainment scene's repertoire of Manila, Philippines, in the early 1920s; (2) the place of the Latin American repertoire in the career of Isa Kremer, a Russian Jewish singer who migrated to Argentina in the 1930s; (3) the copyright strategy of the Sociedad Argentina de Autores y Compositores de Música (SADAIC), the Argentine society for composers of tango and other popular styles, in the late 1920s;

Eric Zolov, *Rockin' Las Américas: The Global Politics of Rock in Latin/o America* (Pittsburgh: University of Pittsburgh Press, 2004); Maria Majno, "From the Model of El Sistema in Venezuela to Current Applications: Learning and Integration through Collective Music Education," *Annals of the New York Academy of Sciences* 1252, no. 1 (April 2012): 56–64; Hermano Vianna, "Technobrega, Forró, Lambadão: The Parallel Music of Brazil," in *Brazilian Popular Music and Citizenship*, ed. Idelber Avelar and Christopher Dunn (Durham, NC: Duke University Press, 2011), 240–49; Alejandro Madrid, *Nor-Tec Rifa!: Electronic Dance Music from Tijuana to the World* (Oxford: Oxford University Press, 2008); Ketty Wong, *Whose National Music?: Identity, Mestizaje, and Migration in Ecuador* (Philadelphia: Temple University Press, 2012).

[80] In 2000, Canclini even argued that the history of globalization "had hardly begun," as if the culture of the region had been until recently mostly "national." Néstor García Canclini, "Contradictory Modernities and Globalisation in Latin America," in *Through the Kaleidoscope: The Experience of Modernity in Latin America*, ed. Vivian Schelling (London: Verso, 2000), 37–52. The classic thesis is in Néstor García Canclini, *Culturas híbridas : estrategias para entrar y salir de la modernidad* (México, D.F.: Grijalbo : Consejo Nacional para la Cultura y las Artes, 1990). Monsiváis, *Aires de Familia*. A study of the history of music styles of Latin America that focuses on their "hybrid" character since colonial times is Carmen Bernand, "'Musiques métisses', musiques criollas. Sons, gestes et paroles en Amérique hispanique," *L'Homme. Revue Française d'Anthropologie*, no. 207–208 (2013): 193–214.

and (4) the Mexican broadcasting system XEW, and its commercial attempt to build a Latin Americanist regional musical platform. Chapter 3 shows the emergence of a regional Latin Americanism as part of the musical pedagogy of the nationalist states, particularly in Brazil, Mexico, and Argentina, from the 1910s through the 1950s, through a comparative history of Latin American musical populisms. In chapter 4 I tell the history of Francisco Curt Lange and the Latin-American Music Bulletin, a musicological project founded in Montevideo and intended as a forum for musicians and music-related people interested in creating a regional field. There I examine policies and rhetorics about disc collection, score printing and distribution, musical ethnographies, musical analysis, conferences, concerts, and regional institutions, and trace relevant aspects of Lange's professional journey between Germany, Uruguay, Argentina, Brazil, and the United States, among other places. Chapter 5 is about the pan-American absorption of Latin Americanism and the formation of a world music discourse. It focuses on the work of Charles Seeger as director of the Pan American Union's Music Section during World War II, and its influence over the consolidation of Latin American music as a field of study. In chapter 6, I trace the consolidation of Latin America as a musical region since the 1950s, through the commercial, political, diplomatic, and musicological practices and discourses that shaped our current musical understanding of the region. In the brief epilogue, I reflect on how music can shed light on the place of Latin American regionalism in global history.

1

A CONTINENTAL PATCHWORK

UNTIL THE 1930S, the music composed, performed, listened to, and danced to in
Latin America was not Latin American. Whether local, regional, translocal, national,
diasporic, old, or new, no musical practice in the region was considered Latin
American. Songs were instead, for instance, "mexicanas, españolas y habaneras," as
a Mexico City newspaper advertised in 1870.[1] Music circulated in many circuits, but
not in a Latin American one. To understand how actual Latin American circuits and
explicit Latin Americanist discourses slowly emerged in the 1930s, we first need to
understand the hemispheric musical panorama at the turn of the twentieth century,
paying attention to both its striking heterogeneity and the connections among its
regions and actors.

CIRCUITS

The hemisphere has always been a site of vastly diverse musical practices and traditions. Around the turn of the twentieth century, a patchwork of circuits of music—
disparate elements coexisting without apparent order—in what today we call Latin
America contrasted to the increasingly cohesive musical market in the United
States, which created a unified space of musical production and consumption. This is

---

[1] *El Ferrocarril*, Mexico City, September 29, 1870.

The Invention of Latin American Music. Pablo Palomino, Oxford University Press (2020). © Oxford University Press.
DOI: 10.1093/oso/9780190687403.001.0001

perhaps the single most important structural factor in the comparison between the musical histories of the United States and Latin America. The US nationally extended network of commercial entertainment circuits was produced by several forms of syndication, which allowed the commodification and expansion of technological innovations and consumption of music, from phonographs to cinemas and, later on, radio, across that national space—and by the 1920s, beyond its borders. This national system emerged *before* the modern technological wonders that expanded it—in fact, it stimulated their creation and diffusion: already in the 1880s, vaudeville shows toured thousands of miles, from the East to the West Coast and from the Midwest to the South, performing a standardized repertoire and collecting revenue in a single currency. Like film and sound recording later on, vaudeville became a national business under a quasi-monopolistic system. It based its popularity by incorporating virtually everything, from folk traditions of minstrelsy to "ethnic" novelties from immigrants, as well as the Shakespearian tradition. This nationally integrated entertainment market turned a diverse popular culture, made of multiple geographic and cultural origins, into a positive category, *American music*. When Aaron Copland and other composers in the 1930s proposed erudite nationalist musical discourses, they could count on musical materials already processed by that vast system, as well as with state cultural policies such as the Library of Congress' official musical archive of folk music recordings by John and Alan Lomax.[2]

The US network of musical circulation that connected countless small and midsize urban areas across the nation was organized around key large cities. By 1890, New York, then the largest city in the Americas, hosted the headquarters of the oligopolistic companies that controlled the national entertainment market of music publishing, vaudeville, and an evolving variety of mechanical devices for music enjoyment that preceded the emergence of the recording industry. By 1900, Chicago was the second largest city in the Americas and in the United States; its booming bourgeoisie sustained a splendid concert music scene, and its expanding neighborhoods were a hotbed of immigrant musical traditions. In the 1920s it would give

---

[2] Lawrence W. Levine, *Highbrow/Lowbrow: The Emergence of Cultural Hierarchy in America* (Cambridge, MA: Harvard University Press, 1988); Richard Butsch, *The Making of American Audiences: From Stage to Television, 1750–1990* (Cambridge: Cambridge University Press, 2000); Gunther Paul Barth, *City People: The Rise of Modern City Culture in Nineteenth-Century America* (New York: Oxford University Press, 1980); William Robert Taylor, ed., *Inventing Times Square: Commerce and Culture at the Crossroads of the World* (New York: Russell Sage Foundation, 1991). On blackface and minstrelsy, see Eric Lott, *Love and Theft: Blackface Minstrelsy and the American Working Class* (New York: Oxford University Press, 1993); Karl Hagstrom Miller, *Segregating Sound: Inventing Folk and Pop Music in the Age of Jim Crow* (Durham, NC: Duke University Press, 2010); Annemarie Bean, James Vernon Hatch, and Brooks McNamara, *Inside the Minstrel Mask: Readings in Nineteenth-Century blackface Minstrelsy* (Hanover, NH: Wesleyan University Press, 1996); and Robert C. Toll, *Blacking Up: The Minstrel Show in Nineteenth Century America* (New York: Oxford University Press, 1974). On the commodification of sounds, see David Suisman, *Selling Sounds: The Commercial Revolution in American Music* (Cambridge, MA: Harvard University Press, 2009). On John and Alan Lomax, see John Szwed, *Alan Lomax : The Man Who Recorded the World* (New York: Viking Penguin, 2010).

birth to its own stream of jazz, by migrants from the Southern states. Jazz, a modern American genre, kept developing with the migration of Southern laborers to industrial cities across the country, and later on at a global scale with the expansion of the New York-based—and later on, the Los Angeles-based—entertainment business, through the recording and movie industries.[3] Philadelphia, Boston, and other large cities were also nodes in this national entertainment system. The old port city of New Orleans—one of the largest US cities before the Civil War—was also a hub for the circum-Caribbean area, where European and African music traditions fed the work of many art and popular composers.[4]

In contrast to this expansive and integrated system, Latin America was a patchwork of disparate and smaller systems. The circuits of music—commercial and noncommercial alike—did not coincide with national borders, but rather with cultural and demographic areas within and across nations. Many of these areas had urban hubs in them, but the cities weren't as interconnected as analogous hubs in the United States and Europe—with some exceptions, like Buenos Aires and Montevideo, which shared intense entertainment traffic since colonial times.[5] In these hubs, cultural productions of European cities and mobile peoples converged with the traditions of nearby rural areas through sheet-music trade, long-distance tours, and local entrepreneurship. For instance, to audiences in the bustling export-oriented cities along the Uruguay River, Italian opera was as lively as local folklore.[6] But these hubs were not articulated in larger national systems.

Diverse sociological realities produced in each city a distinctive "cosmopolitan formation."[7] The end of slavery and a series of export-related economic booms in

---

[3] E. Taylor Atkins, *Blue Nippon: Authenticating Jazz in Japan* (Durham, NC: Duke University Press, 2001); Andrew Jones, *Yellow Music: Media Culture and Colonial Modernity in the Chinese Jazz Age* (Durham, NC: Duke University Press, 2001) and "Black Internationale: Notes on the Chinese Jazz Age," in *Jazz Planet*, ed. E. Taylor Atkins (Jackson: University Press of Mississippi, 2003), 225–43; Jeffrey H Jackson, *Making Jazz French: Music and Modern Life in Interwar Paris* (Durham, NC: Duke University Press, 2003).

[4] Charles Hersch, *Subversive Sounds: Race and the Birth of Jazz in New Orleans* (Chicago: University Of Chicago Press, 2007); Floyd, Samuel A. "Black Music in the Circum-Caribbean." *American Music* 17, no. 1 (1999): 1–38.

[5] Alex Borucki, "From Colonial Performers to Actors of 'American Liberty': Black Artists in Bourbon and Revolutionary Río de La Plata," *The Americas* 75, no. 2 (April 2018): 261–89; Daniel Richter, "Mirrored Imaginaries: Urban Chroniclers in Buenos Aires and Montevideo, 1910–1936," *Journal of Urban History* (December 29, 2018): 1–20; Kristen McCleary, "Ethnic Identity and Elite Idyll: A Comparison of Carnival in Buenos Aires, Argentina and Montevideo, Uruguay, 1900–1920," *Social Identities* 16, no. 4 (July 1, 2010): 497–517.

[6] John Rosselli, "Latin America and Italian Opera: A Process of Interaction, 1810–1930," *Revista de Musicología* 16, no. 1 (1993): 139–45; John Rosselli, "The Opera Business and the Italian Immigrant Community in Latin America 1820–1930: The Example of Buenos Aires," *Past & Present* no. 127 (May 1, 1990): 155–82; Aníbal Enrique Cetrangolo, "Del arpa de Viggiano al organito porteño, músicos ambulantes y ópera," *Etno-Folk: Revista Galega de Etnomusicoloxía* 14 (2009): 596–621, *Il teatro di due mondi. Rapporti Italo-Iberoamericani: Il 'teatro musicale,' s/f,* and *Ópera, barcos y banderas: el melodrama y la migración en Argentina (1880–1920)* (Madrid: Biblioteca Nueva, 2015).

[7] Thomas Turino, "Are We Global Yet? Globalist Discourse, Cultural Formations and the Study of Zimbabwean Popular Music," *British Journal of Ethnomusicology* 12, no. 2 (2003): 51–79.

different parts of the region all fostered the movement of multiple populations in multiple directions, both internally and from Europe and Asia to Latin America. From Andalusia to Cuba, from Sicily to the Pampas, from Bahia to São Paulo, and from Sonora to Yucatán, migrations broke apart and at the same time multiplied new musical worlds. Uprooted and relocated in new lands, especially in cities, new artists and audiences further diversified the musical patchwork of Latin America. The region's neocolonial order was based not on a pan-regional integration but on its opposite: separate national alliances of economic power, each one around a dominant production—the coffee lands, the cattle areas, the mines—that attracted population in free or compulsory ways in response to North Atlantic consuming and industrial demand.[8]

Cities with a dense colonial history and modern export booms, such as Rio de Janeiro, produced a bourgeois *belle époque* at the turn of the century that combined traditions of imperial sociability (such as the *saraus*) and an emerging class of composers and entertainers—some highbrow, some lowbrow, and all in interaction—who articulated local and regional styles with North Atlantic repertoires.[9] The limits for the circulation of music were not musical but socio-racio-political: the criminalization of popular practices by the authorities, which contrasted with the more fluid cultural and musical exchanges.[10] On the other hand, cities that lacked colonial cachet but that were economically prosperous, such as Buenos Aires, produced a more plebeian but no less cosmopolitan musical scene. In the "old guard" tango orchestras, for example, local *criollo* musicians joined first- or second-generation Italian, Spanish, or Eastern European Jewish immigrants to develop a local style of varied social uses, from the brothels and outskirt fairs of the 1900s to the modern theaters, cafés, cinemas, dance halls, and carnivals of the 1920s.[11]

Mexico City had been the main center of a large network of regions and cities since colonial times, and continued to be afterward a hub in which multiple forms of musical patronage converged. For instance, the federal authorities in Mexico City granted fellowships to enable promising young performers from the interior regions to train

---

[8] Tulio Halperín Donghi, *Historia contemporánea de América latina* (Madrid: Alianza Editorial, 1969).

[9] Cristina Magaldi, "Cosmopolitanism and World Music in Rio de Janeiro at the Turn of the Twentieth Century," *The Musical Quarterly* 92, no. 3–4 (September 21, 2009): 329–64. The larger picture was captured in Jeffrey Needell, *A Tropical Belle Epoque: Elite Culture and Society in Turn-of-the-Century Rio de Janeiro* (New York: Cambridge University Press, 1987).

[10] Marc A. Hertzman, "Making Music and Masculinity in Vagrancy's Shadow: Race, Wealth, and Malandragem in Post-Abolition Rio de Janeiro," *Hispanic American Historical Review* 90, no. 4 (November 1, 2010): 591–625; Leonardo Affonso de Miranda Pereira, "Os Anjos da Meia-Noite: trabalhadores, lazer e direitos no Rio de Janeiro da Primeira República," *Tempo* 19, no. 35 (2013): 97–116.

[11] Luis Adolfo Sierra, *Historia de la orquesta típica: evolución instrumental del tango* (Buenos Aires: A. Peña Lillo, 1976); Pablo Kohan, *Estudios sobre los estilos compositivos del tango (1920–1935)* (Buenos Aires: Gourmet Musical, 2010), 20 and "Europa y el tango argentino: intercambios culturales en el origen del tango," in *Los caminos de la música: Europa y Argentina*, eds. Pablo Bardin et al. (Jujuy: Universidad Nacional de Jujuy, 2008), 153–75.

in Berlin,[12] while "Comisiones de señoras" organized "patriotic events" at the main theaters, such as a 1849 concert of German songs to benefit orphans.[13] Mexico City's centrality accelerated with the civil and foreign wars of the nineteenth century, and then with the Porfiriato (1876–1910), when it continued to be the main destination for musicians from all corners of Mexico, whose village bands and military bands had already concocted styles and instruments. The revolution and the ensuing industrialization kept attracting musicians from the neighboring regions and countries and from Europe. Migrants found a place where music was constantly being transmitted and created—in circuses, military and police bands, and popular *carpas*, with their shows under provisory tents. With almost half a million inhabitants in 1885, and over a million by 1930, Mexico City was the point of encounter and sounding board of the circum-Caribbean and Atlantic circuits and the Center, South, and Northern regions.[14]

Regional identities had their musical expression as well, such as in the wandering popular bards who connected cities and towns in the immense Brazilian Northeast, turning it into a cultural unity, the *nordeste*.[15] Other regions did not even exist as autonomous musical spaces until well into the twentieth century. At the turn of the century, for instance, the sparsely populated southern Brazilian state of Mato Grosso do Sul, which Brazil had incorporated after the Paraguayan War of 1865–1870, hosted soldiers from Rio de Janeiro and São Paulo who brought Carnival sambas with them, and thereafter Paraguayan and Argentine litoraleño music, such as *chamamé*, entered the mixture. The region itself was a patchwork.[16]

---

[12] For instance, in July 1922 the young Felipe Cortés Teixeira asked the legislature of the state of Guanajuato for a grant to study music and orchestra conduction in Berlin, while the Escuela Nacional de Música y Arte Teatral asked Manuel Toussaint, head of the Departamento de Bellas Artes, to complement the Guanajuato grant with more resources so he could travel to Berlin, where he was admitted to the Stern'sches Konservatorium der Musik Gustav Hollaender, an institution directed by Alexander von Fielitz. Departamento de Bellas Artes, Caja 46, SEP.

[13] Newspaper *El siglo diez y nueve*, Ciudad de Mexico, April 20, 1849.

[14] Guy Thomson, "The Ceremonial and Political Role of Village Bands, 1846–1974," in *Rituals of Rule, Rituals of Resistance : Public Celebrations and Popular Culture in Mexico*, ed. William Beezley, Cheryl Martin, and William French (Wilmington, DE: SR Books, 1994), 564–625; Ricardo Pérez Montfort, "Circo, teatro y variedades: diversiones en la Ciudad de Mexico a fines del Porfiriato," *Alteridades* 13, no. 26 (2003): 57–66. Local and foreign opera and zarzuela companies would tour a network of cities roughly between Guadalajara and Veracruz, with Mexico City at its center. Lance Ingwersen, "Mexico City in the Age of Theater, 1830–1901" (PhD diss., Vanderbilt University, 2017).

[15] Linda Lewin, "A Tale of Two Texts: Orality, Oral History, and Poetic Insult in the Desafio of Romano and Inacio in Patos (1874)," *Studies in Latin American Popular Culture* 26 (2007): 1–25; Diósnio Machado Neto, "Administrando a Festa: Música e Iluminismo No Brasil Colonial." (PhD diss., Escola de Comunicação e Artes–USP, São Paulo, 2008); Courtney Campbell, "The Brazilian Northeast, Inside Out: Region, Nation, and Globalization (1926–1968)" (PhD diss., Vanderbilt University, 2014); Durval Muniz de Albuquerque Jr., *A invenção do Nordeste e outras artes* (São Paulo: Editora Massangana, 1999).

[16] Álvaro Neder, *"Enquanto este novo trem atravessa o Litoral Central": música popular urbana, latino-americanismo e conflitos sobre modernização em Mato Grosso do Sul* (Rio de Janeiro: Mauad, 2014); Felipe Batistella Alvares, "Milonga, chamamé, chimarrita e vaneira: origens, inserção no Rio Grande do Sul e os princípios de execução ao contrabaixo" (Licenciatura en Música, Universidade Federal de Santa María, 2007).

Other cities and regions maintained their musical autonomy from colonial times. These spaces created their own internal forms of musical circulation, which led their music to evolve in tension with the larger national rhetoric of which they were part. In São João del Rei, Minas Gerais, for example, from the nineteenth to the twentieth century, popular classes and elites diverged and converged around shared local musical forms such as the *cateretês*. Through contacts and circulation across socioeconomic and urban divides, they eventually consumed "the same culture," a culture that was unique among the regions of Brazil.[17]

Many of these regional musical practices were also transnational: like the Italian opera companies in the cities and rivers along the Atlantic shore, other theatrical troupes traveled seasonally. The tours of Sarah Bernhardt and other European stars produced a *rioplatense* theatrical region, which included cities and towns around the Rio de La Plata basin linking Argentina, Uruguay, and Brazil.[18] Cuban classical pianists, singers, and flautists traveled to the cities of the US northeast, where they trained, founded music institutions, directed orchestras, became famous, or simply earned a living.[19] The Zarzuela companies that toured the Americas—from Havana to Yucatan to Buenos Aires[20]—would be deemed today "Pan Hispanic," and the repertoire of "stars" like Louis Moreau Gottschalk, who linked the circum-Caribbean region with US and South American port cities, was not identifiable with any national tradition or style.[21] In 1914 the Mexican actress, singer, and businesswoman Virginia Fábregas was praised for her South American tour—Peru, Ecuador, Bolivia and Chile, Argentina and Uruguay—as an "eminent Latin American artist" (*eximia artista latinoamericana*) by a Barcelona newspaper.[22]

Genres themselves were transnational. The *zamacueca* intersected with multiple social groups in Chile, Peru, Bolivia, and Argentina.[23] Montevideos' *murga* developed

[17] Marcelo Crisafuli Nascimento Almeida, "Música Popular em Minas Gerais no século XIX: São João del Rei, um estudo de caso," *Temporalidades* 2, no. 2 (2010): 43–49.

[18] William Acree, "Hemispheric Travelers on the Rioplatense Stage," *Latin American Theatre Review* 47, no. 2 (2014): 5–24; Erminia Silva, *Circo-Teatro: Benjamim de Oliveira e a Teatralidade Circense No Brasil* (São Paulo: Editora Altana, 2007).

[19] Louis A Pérez, *On Becoming Cuban: Identity, Nationality, and Culture* (Chapel Hill: University of North Carolina Press, 1999), 43.

[20] Mario Roger Quijano Axle, "Zarzuela y ópera en Yucatán (1863–1930). Actividad del teatro lírico y creación local" (PhD diss., Universidad Complutense de Madrid, 2016)

[21] Kristen McCleary, "Popular, Elite and Mass Culture? The Spanish Zarzuela in Buenos Aires, 1890–1900," *Studies in Latin American Popular Culture* 21 (2002): 1–27. Janet Lynn Sturman, *Zarzuela: Spanish Operetta, American Stage* (Urbana: University of Illinois Press, 2000). Louis Moreau Gottschalk, *Les Voyages Extraordinaires de L. Moreau Gottschalk, Pianiste et Aventurier*, Collection "Voies et Chemins" (Lausanne: P.-M. Favre, 1985). Francisco Curt Lange, *Vida y muerte de Louis Moreau Gottschalk en Rio de Janeiro, 1869; el ambiente musical en la mitad del segundo imperio* (Mendoza: Universidad Nacional de Cuyo, 1951). Frederick Starr, *Bamboula!: The Life and Times of Louis Moreau Gottschalk* (New York: Oxford University Press, 1995).

[22] *Mercurio*, Barcelona, June 11, 1914, p. 9.

[23] Christian Spencer Espinosa, "Imaginario nacional y cambio cultural: circulación, recepción y pervivencia de la zamacueca en Chile durante el siglo XIX," *Cuadernos de Música Hispanoamericana* 14 (2007): 143–76.

in the nineteenth century in subtle dialogue with musical forms of Cadiz and Madrid.[24] The central musical scene of Cuba and the Caribbean, Havana, exported in the 1870s and 1880s, through exiled orchestras in the context of the independence wars, the dance and music genre *danzón* to a large network of cities, including Mexico City but also New Orleans, Mérida, and many others in Puerto Rico, Central America, and the northern fringe of South America.[25] Son and rumba, also originating in Cuba and also a mix of African and Iberian colonial roots, expanded all over the region, and later on into the nightlife of the entire world, through its success in Hollywood and the US dance craze of the 1920s to the 1950s.[26] The *son montuno* songs of Arsenio Rodríguez, for example, represented for his listeners different things—and different nostalgias—depending on whether they were Cubans in Havana, former Curaçaoan migrant workers in Cuba, or Caribbeans in New York, Chicago, or Los Angeles.[27]

These circuits were thus neither Latin American nor national, but rather *nordestino*, *rioplatense*, Andean, intra- or circum-Caribbean. The reason is obvious: no national markets or demographic relations sustained anything like a national space, let alone a Latin American one.

In every city, a cluster of musical institutions intended to promote at once a national music and a civilized Europeanist canon.[28] The nation-states' cultural civilizing projects attempted to impose some order in this patchwork, despite the modest means of the emerging bureaucracies. In the words of Francisco Manuel da Silva, the composer of Brazil's national anthem and founder of the Brazilian imperial conservatory in 1848, "human institutions must be based on morality, and fine arts are essentially moral, since they turn the individuals who cultivate them into happier and better citizens."[29] The intentions of Brazil's imperial court drew on a spiritual civilizing rhetoric: to form morally apt citizens through music, but also to provide professional training. Da Silva lauded the conservatory for its many social advantages,

---

[24] Dorothée Chouitem, "Cádiz, cuna de la murga uruguaya: ¿mitificación de los orígenes?," *Memorias: revista digital de historia y arqueología desde El Caribe* 32 (2017): 39–61.

[25] Alejandro Madrid, and Robin D. Moore, *Danzón: Circum-Carribean Dialogues in Music and Dance* (New York: Oxford University Press, 2013), chapter 3.

[26] The association between these Cuban genres and the modernist ethos of the 1930s is still alive. In 1999 the German film *Aimée and Jaguar* used Ernesto Lecuona's 1935 *Rumba Azul* by the Lecuona Cuban Boys orchestra to provide the aural and dance context of a lesbian love scene in Berlin at the beginning of World War II.

[27] David F. García, *Arsenio Rodríguez and the Transnational Flows of Latin Popular Music* (Philadelphia: Temple University Press, 2006).

[28] Claudio E. Benzecry, "An Opera House for the 'Paris of South America': Pathways to the Institutionalization of High Culture," *Theory and Society* 43, no. 2 (March 1, 2014): 169–96; John Rosselli, "The Opera Business and the Italian Immigrant Community in Latin America 1820–1930: The Example of Buenos Aires," *Past & Present*, no. 127 (May 1990): 155–82.

[29] "As instituições humanas devem ter por base a moralidade, e que as Belas-Artes são essencialmente morais, porque tornam o indivíduo que as cultiva mais feliz e melhor cidadão," quoted in Antonio Augusto, "A civilização como missão: o Conservatório de Música no Império do Brasil," *Revista Brasileira de Música* 23, no. 1 (2010): 67–91, 70.

making affordable to all social classes the regular and systematic learning of an art whose pure and pleasant enjoyment strengthens the worker in his tiring duties, lessens the deprivations of the poor by giving him a useful and lucrative tool, liberates the well-off from their boredom, and beautifies human existence.[30]

Rio's conservatory included both men and women—in 1871 its director celebrated that it "had given an honest means of living to a great number of poor young women who now can subsist by practicing music."[31] With ten professors and 150 to 200 students, its practice was limited to official choirs and celebrations. It became the National Music Institute under the republic in 1889 and the National School of Music since 1937.

But state efforts were just a drop in an ocean of musical practices. Together, Northeastern migrants, Portuguese and Italian immigrants, and the local population expanded Rio's entertainment sector. The cosmopolitan scene they produced was made of musical theater organized by companies that connected the city with Lisbon[32] and of another New World modern hybrid: samba. In 1917, at the time when the first modern jazz recording was produced ("Livery Stable Blues"), the first successful modern samba ("Pelo telefone") was legally registered in Rio de Janeiro.[33] Like Mexico City, Rio was the sounding board of all sorts of musical migrations and ideological debates—about nativism, exoticism, Europeanism, nationalism, and modernism.

The music scene of São Paulo, which would later become the largest city in Brazil, was in its infancy, its most dynamic section being the music of the Italian community.[34] The first modern tango ("Mi noche triste") was also performed in 1917, in Buenos Aires, another very Italian city and one that was larger than any other south of Chicago and New York. Buenos Aires was the main musical scene within a sub- and transnational area that included Montevideo (Uruguay), Rosario, and a host of smaller cities along the Paraná and Uruguay rivers and across the agricultural

---

[30] "Facilitando a todas as classes da sociedade o ensino regular e metódico de uma arte, cujas fruições puras e agradáveis dão vigor ao operário em suas fadigosas tarefas, minoram as provações do pobre, dando-lhe uma profissão útil e lucrativa, expelem o tédio do abastado, e embelezam a existência do gênero humano." Official textbook *Compêndio de Princípios Elementares de Música*, quoted in Antonio Augusto, "A civilização como missão: o Conservatório de Música no Império do Brasil," *Revista Brasileira de Música* 23, no. 1 (2010): 67–91, 76.

[31] Antonio Augusto, "A civilização como missão," 36: "Tem dado um meio de vida honesto a grande número de donzelas pobres, que tiram os meios de sua subsistência do exercício da música."

[32] Joao Luis Meireles Santos Leitao Silva, "Music, Theatre and the Nation: The Entertainment Market in Lisbon (1865–1908)" (PhD diss., Newscastle University, 2012), 29.

[33] There were sambas recorded earlier than that, in 1913 and 1914, but the tradition of musicians, journalists, and writers canonized "Pelo Telefone" as the "original" modern samba. Luiza Mara Braga Martins, *Os Oito Batutas: história e música brasileira nos anos 1920* (Rio de Janeiro: Editora Universidade Federal de Rio de Janeiro, 2014), 139.

[34] Aiala Levy, "Stages of a State: From São Paulo's Teatro São José to the Teatro Municipal, 1854–1911," *Planning Perspectives* 28, no. 3 (July 1, 2013): 461–75.

hinterland of the Pampas, and tango expanded throughout this network. Bogotá, Lima, and Santiago de Chile also experienced a wave of cosmopolitan modernism in dance manners and musical habits, and they too concocted modern "local" styles out of regional and global influences.[35]

By the first decades of the twentieth century, all these cities housed social groups with enough disposable income to sustain entertainment markets. In all of them, a class of impresarios developed and adapted commercial and technological novelties for musical consumption. This fostered the dissemination of modern hybrid music genres within and beyond the urban borders and offered opportunities of professionalization in incipient musical markets, ranging from the culturally prestigious to the culturally marginal. Mexico's military bands were perhaps the most stable positions for music-making in the region in the nineteenth and early twentieth centuries.[36] In Rio de Janeiro, Marc Hertzman's study of judiciary records shows how hard popular classes had to fight to make music-making a legitimate and regulated profession.[37] In Argentina, chauffeurs, barbers, and other urban workers made music as a side activity, together with the semirural *payadores*, those wandering guitar players, popular poets, and improvisers that entertained small towns, camps, and rural outskirts of the cities.[38] These musicians had no national market to work in. The main nationalizing forces were the war against the foreign intervention in Mexico (in the 1860s) and the presence of the imperial court in Brazil (until 1889), both of which brought together composers and artists from different regions. But most of the musical life happened either locally or through subregional circuits, such as those between city and rural surroundings in the Rio de La Plata.

In the 1930s larger musical cultures emerged, due to economic and demographic growth, increasing pervasiveness of phonographs, radio, the commercial music world, and the expansion of public and private musical academies. Modern state apparatuses expanded and began to construct a collective "we" as a symbolic and political unit.[39] Nationalists tried to turn specific fragments of this musical heterogeneity

---

[35] Peter Wade, *Music, Race, & Nation: Música Tropical in Colombia* (Chicago: University of Chicago Press, 2000); Juan Pablo González Rodríguez and Claudio Rolle, *Historia social de la música popular en Chile, 1890–1950* (Santiago, Chile: Ediciones Universidad Católica de Chile, 2005); Gérard Borras, *Chansonniers de Lima: le vals et la chanson criolla, 1900–1936* (Rennes: Presses Universitaires de Rennes, 2009).

[36] Guy Thomson, "The Ceremonial and Political Role of Village Bands, 1846–1974," in *Rituals of Rule, Rituals of Resistance : Public Celebrations and Popular Culture in Mexico*, ed. William Beezley, Cheryl Martin, and William French (Wilmington, DE: SR Books, 1994), 564–625.

[37] Marc Hertzman, *Making Samba: a New History of Race and Music in Brazil* (Durham, NC: Duke University Press, 2013).

[38] Brian Bockelman, "Between the Gaucho and the Tango: Popular Songs and the Shifting Landscape of Modern Argentine Identity, 1895–1915," *American Historical Review* 116, no. 3 (June 1, 2011): 577–601.

[39] Robin Moore, *Nationalizing Blackness: Afrocubanismo and Artistic Revolution in Havana, 1920–1940* (Pittsburgh: University of Pittsburgh Press, 1997); Bryan McCann, *Hello, Hello Brazil: Popular Music in the Making of Modern Brazil* (Durham, NC: Duke University Press, 2004); Marco Velázquez and Mary K. Vaughan, "Mestizaje and Musical Nationalism in Mexico," in *The Eagle and the Virgin: Nation and Cultural Revolution in Mexico, 1920–1940*, eds. Mary Kay Vaughan and Stephen E. Lewis (Durham, NC: Duke University Press, 2006), 95–118; Oscar Chamosa, *The Argentine Folklore Movement : Sugar*

into national symbols. But the emerging modern national musical cultures were heterogeneous and combined genres of multiple origins. The Colombian city of Medellín, for instance, developed its modern musical taste and habits of listening through the combination of tango, bolero, and bambuco. These genres originated variously in Buenos Aires, the Mexico City–Yucatan–Havana axis, and the Colombian Andes, and each provided Medellín with a distinct geocultural imaginary: tango signifying the city, bolero representing cosmopolitanism, and bambuco symbolizing the belonging to the Colombian nation.[40] (Far away, in Dutch-colonized Indonesia, several Latin American and US styles made it to local *kroncong* versions in the 1930s: "kroncong-foxtrot, kroncong-swing, kroncong-tango, kroncong-rumba, kroncong-carioca, kroncong-paso doble."[41])

None of the Latin American nations achieved a high degree of market integration, neither at the continental geographic and demographic scale of the United States, nor at the smaller scale of countries like France or England. Europe provided social status and key music urban professions: private teachers imparted the European musical tradition, whether they were German Jews, Italians, Portuguese, or immigrants from other places who worked in Latin America as music teachers, sheet music entrepreneurs, or crafters and repairers of musical instruments. These musicians were often proud of their role as representatives of Italian or German music, and their dissemination throughout the Americas from Rio Grande do Sul to Massachusetts contributed to strengthen a widely shared transnational Europeanist musical ideology within the urban classes—the ideal of music as universal language. John Philip Sousa's US Army Band, famous and active worldwide between 1880 and 1930, performed a repertoire that included and was inspired in modern European music: Verdi, Tchaikovsky, or Dvorjak.

There was no common market in Latin America enabling a Latin Americanist musical identity. Musicians, performers, producers, and audiences organized their practice with other labels, either modeled after Europeanist civilizational ideals, or more closely connected to their actual space of activity and to their audiences. Demographics and economic networks in the region's largest urban hubs connected local musical cultures with larger spaces and with other cities within regions, as I already shown, but the contours of these networks did not coincide with those of Latin America.

Countering that Europeanism at that dispersion, *national* music was a project of small circles of composers like Manuel Ponce, who called for a folk-based musical

---

Elites, Criollo Workers, and the Politics of Cultural Nationalism, 1900–1955 (Tucson: University of Arizona Press, 2010); Matthew B Karush, *Culture of Class : Radio and Cinema in the Making of a Divided Argentina, 1920–1946* (Durham, NC: Duke University Press, 2012).

[40] Carolina Santamaría Delgado, *Vitrolas, rocolas y radioteatros: hábitos de escucha de la música popular en Medellín, 1930–1950* (Bogotá, DC: Editorial Pontificia Universidad Javeriana, 2014).

[41] Philip Bradford Yampolsky, "Music and Media in the Dutch East Indies: Gramophone Records and Radio in the Late Colonial Era, 1903–1942" (MA thesis, University of Washington, 2013), 330.

identity in Mexico in 1913.[42] Brazilian musicians and intellectuals had invented musical nationalism in the context of the empire and continued it through folklore research during the republic. They documented Brazilian musical roots to sustain a Brazilian cultural identity that would recognize the African and, to a lesser extent, the Indigenous history of Brazil. Nationalist music compositions and folkloric research were based on the idea of a cultural uniqueness and were produced by applying Western aesthetic and scientific frameworks to vernacular traditions.[43] But for these early nationalist musicians and folklorists, Latin America was simply not a useful category. It did not help them construct a Brazilian identity. Neither sponsors nor producers nor artists nor audiences before the 1930s had Latin America in mind—neither as a territory nor as an aesthetic discourse.

Latin Americanism, a diplomatic and political discourse, had not yet reached the field of music. None of the first three "Latin American scientific congresses" (Buenos Aires 1898 and Montevideo 1901, and Rio de Janeiro 1905), nor the fourth (Santiago de Chile 1908), which was also the first pan-American one because it included US representatives, included music whatsoever.[44] During World War I, England and France published a propaganda magazine in Spanish, *América-Latina*, that targeted Spain, Portugal, Latin America, and the Philippines. And at the same time, the Second Pan American Scientific Congress reunited scientists from the entire hemisphere. But music played no role in either of these activities.[45] Music was absent at the American International Conferences—only culture and folklore would appear, later on, at the 1936 Inter-American Conference for the Consolidation of Peace in Buenos Aires, in a mere recommendation to the Pan American Union "to study a plan to organize a closer collaboration between Academies and Museums of Arts, Sciences, History, Archeology and Folklore throughout the Americas."[46]

---

[42] Alejandro L. Madrid, "Renovation, Rupture, and Restoration. The Modernist Musical Experience in Latin America," in *The Modernist World*, ed. Allana Lindgren and Stephen Ross (London: Routledge, 2015), 409–16.

[43] Martha Abreu and Carolina Vianna Dantas, "Música popular, folclore e nação no Brasil, 1890–1920," *Nação e cidadania no Império: novos horizontes* (Rio de Janeiro: Civilização Brasileira, 2007), 123–51, and Martha Abreu, "Histórias musicais da Primeira República," *ArtCultura* 13, no. 22 (2011): 71–83; Antonio Augusto, "A civilização como missão: o Conservatório de Música no Império do Brasil," *RBM* 23, no. 1 (2010): 67–91.

[44] "Conferencias y Congresos Técnicos Panamericanos—Derecho Internacional Público," accessed March 11, 2017, http://www.dipublico.org/category/tratados-y-documentos-internacionales/conferencias-y-congresos-tecnicos-panamericanos/.

[45] María Inés Tato, "Propaganda de guerra para el Nuevo Mundo. El caso de la revista América-Latina (1915–1918)," *Historia y Comunicación Social (Madrid)* 18 (2013): 63–74; Roberta Marx Delson, "Some Brief Reflections on the Centennial of the Second Pan American Scientific Congress of 1915–1916," *Revista de Historia Iberoamericana* 9, no. 1 (2016): 90–102.

[46] "Cooperación artística y cultural (Conferencia Interamericana de Consolidación de la Paz—Buenos Aires, 1936)," Derecho Internacional Público, https://www.dipublico.org/15095/cooperacion-artistica-y-cultural-conferencia-interamericana-de-consolidacion-de-la-paz-buenos-aires-1936/, January 3, 2013.

It would be in 1938, at the eighth Inter American Conference in Lima, when, responding to a current of Latin Americanism that is at the core of this history and is treated in chapters 4 and 5, diplomats specifically addressed "musical exchange in the Americas" and recommended the creation of an Institute of Music that would encompass the Americas.

How had the idea of Latin American music emerged, to be able to be adopted by these diplomats?

EMERGENCE OF A MUSICAL DEFINITION OF LATIN AMERICA

The idea of Latin American music appeared for the first time in the historical record not in a cosmopolitan hub, but in a regional musical scene far away from the Atlantic space: the Andean province of Mendoza, Argentina.

In the early 1900s Mendoza was for many Italian and Spanish theater companies mainly a stop before crossing to Chile, and the first cohorts of local musicians played temporary roles in those productions. By the 1910s professional composers were already feeding piano music to bourgeois salons and military, religious, and dance bands. They competed with publishers of sheet music in Italy, Spain, and Buenos Aires. Beginning in the 1890s composer Mariano Cortijo Vidal, an immigrant himself, composed music in all those registers, from religious to theatrical, including political tunes, and later became a recognized *criollista* by composing "tangos americanos" in the style of the Spanish *zarzuelas*. An active cultural broker, he funded Mendoza's first children's theater and the Conservatorio Musical Mendocino. At the 1910 centennial celebrations, children choirs sang *La mendocina* and other songs Vidal had penned and national educational authorities awarded a prize to his textbook *School Songs*, which had been adopted by schools and conservatories "of the Argentine and Hispano-American Republics."[47]

Cortijo Vidal's son, Lucas Cortijo Alahija, was a pianist himself. In 1909, Cortijo Alahija attempted to produce a volume containing the musical profiles of each

---

[47] "Cantos escolares y de la enseñanza mutual de la música. Método graduado y adaptado a los programas vigentes del Consejo Nacional de Educación para uso de la escuelas y conservatorios de la República Argentina y las Repúblicas Hispano-Americanas." Mariano Cortijo Vidal had come to Argentina as the director of a zarzuela troupe. Trained first at the children choir of the Cathedral of Valladolid, Spain, and later at the Royal Conservatory (at his time, already the Escuela Nacional de Música y Declamación in Madrid), in Buenos Aires (and also in Montevideo) he worked as church organist, director of orchestras and Spanish immigrant music choirs (*orfeones*), composer of popular and "serious" musical works, music critic, and even a *luthier* and inventor of music instruments. In Mendoza, where he eventually moved due to health issues, Vidal became a *criollista*, composing and publishing vidalitas, "tangos Americanos," and *cuyanas*—songs from Cuyo, the traditional name of that region of Argentina (Mariano Cortijo Vidal, *Cuyanas, aires criollos. Letra y musica de M. Cortijo Vidal*, Buenos Aires: Breyer Hermanos, 1911). See María Antonieta Sacchi de Ceriotto, *La profesión musical en el baúl: músicos españoles inmigrantes radicados en Mendoza a comienzos del siglo XX* (Mendoza, Argentina: Editorial de la Universidad Nacional de Cuyo, 2007).

"república américo-latina," by sending requests to "the press from all Hispanic American nations . . . and to the directors of conservatories and museums and professors" asking about the musical situation of the region. He did not get many responses. In 1919, in Barcelona, he published an incomplete compendium of what he called "musicología latino-Americana," by which he meant the music composers and educators of the region.[48]

Cortijo Alahija's book was not influential—it did not spark similar works in the 1920s, and was barely referenced in the literature on the subject published in the 1930s.[49] But it revealed interesting ideological features that were symptomatic of the Europeanism that dominated Latin America's musical patchwork, on the one hand, and of the indigenista-folkloric discourse that marks musical Latin Americanism until today. In a book in which Europe (and especially Spain) appears as the central aesthetic source, an apparently brief rhetorical afterthought provides the key to the argumentative architecture of the work: the "indigenous race" had given the region its "original poetry" and art, and it was the duty of its musicians to capture it in order to recover a glorious and unfairly dismissed history. The "soul" of this race can be found in the "sparkles" of its art, which "reveals to us the people's sentimental background" (*el fondo sentimental predominante en el pueblo*), which far from an archeological, unanimated remain, is the basis of an aesthetic project for the future.

I set myself to demonstrate that before the absolute immobility to which the indigenous race has arrived, there was an era when the arts flourished spontaneously and the original poetry lived . . . the final sparks of which we must use, before they are forever lost, in order to penetrate the glorious past of an unjustly slandered people. Through the mist, we perceive the supreme soul of that race . . . shedding its reflections over its defeated land, calling the slaves for the good redemption. Art fulfills thus an immediate function: it reveals the people's sentimental background, and we know that a race that feels is not lost for the future.[50]

A Spaniard-Argentine invoking the "indigenous race" as guarantee of a future musical art in Latin America was not surprising. The racialization of art as an aesthetic representation of a biologically defined "people" was a Romantic approach to art history that shaped

---

[48] Lucas Cortijo Alahija, *Musicología latino-americana. La música popular y los músicos célebres de la América latina* (Barcelona: Maucci, 1919).

[49] For example, Daniel Castañeda, "La música y la revolución mexicana," *Boletín Latino Americano de Música* 5 (1941): 440.

[50] Lucas Cortijo Alahija, *Musicología latino-americana*, 100: "Nos propusimos demostrar que antes de la inmutabilidad absoluta a que ha llegado la raza indígena, floreció el arte espontáneamente y vivió la poesía original . . . (cuyos) últimos destellos de luz [. . .] debemos aprovechar, antes que se pierdan, para penetrar en la historia y esclarecer el pasado glorioso de un pueblo injustamente calumniado. A través de las nieblas se percibe el alma soberbia de la raza [. . .] que esparce sus reflejos sobre la tierra de los vencidos, llamando a los esclavos a la buena redención. Así el arte [. . .] cumple una función de utilidad inmediata; nos revela el fondo sentimental predominante en el pueblo, y sabemos que la raza que sabe sentir no está perdida para el porvenir."

the academic organization of aesthetic production well into the twentieth century.[51] Race was a central argument in the intra-European conflicts that shaped the making of a musicological discourse on Latin America as well. Spain's musical elites explicitly antagonized both pan-Americanism (sponsored by the United States) and "Latin Americanism" (promoted by France and other European powers, which wanted to "dissolve," as a Madrid newspaper put it in 1929, "the Hispanic spirit in a sentiment of Latinity [*disolviendo el espíritu hispánico en un sentimiento de latinidad*]), perceiving both as competitors, "spiritually and commercially, closer to the nineteenth countries we gave birth (*a quienes dimos el ser*)."[52] Cortijo Alahija was not the only one attempting to musically capture this region. As he was conducting his research, the musical bulletin *Franco-Latino-Américaine* published in Paris at the end of the Great War saw Latin America as a market for French music, and released its material in both French and Spanish. Its goal was to promote, against its German and English rivals, the French industries of publishing and music instruments, among composers and musicians "of Latin American nationality" widely understood, "from Mexico to Tierra del Fuego, from the Atlantic to the Pacific."[53] (In Spain, the region was officially called *Hispanoamérica*, as in the "becas hispanoamericanas" that the state awarded to journalists and students "of those countries."[54])

Latin American intellectuals adopted the racial rhetoric to define a regional music project. Immediately after Alahija's book, the magazine *Revista de América* published in Buenos Aires opened its first issue in 1920 with a text in which the Argentine nationalist champion Ricardo Rojas links the emergence of a national music with a larger "American" music composed and performed by musicians who formed a "fraternity of spirits initiated in the mystery of America":[55]

For a long time in salons and newspapers there is talk about an American music, and even of an Argentine musical school . . . If our musicians had found before enough inspiration in the rhapsody of the European maestros, today they feel an emancipating fervor that is already a creative principle.

"Our musicians" are here both Argentines and Latin Americans. The purpose of the magazine was to address the national, regional, and programmatic nature of the new music from several angles:

One is the basic folklore data on the traditional music of the American peoples; another is the technical value of musical folklore as it appears in the work of

[51] We will reencounter this approach in later chapters. Éric Michaud, *Les invasions barbares: une généalogie de l'histoire de l'art* (Paris: Gallimard, 2015), esp. chapter 3.
[52] "¿Confederación latinoamericana?," *La Correspondencia Militar*, Madrid, October 1, 1929, p. 1.
[53] Paul Lansoge, "Nôtre But," *Bulletin Musical—Revue Franco-Latino-Americaine* 1, no. 1 (October 1918): 2.
[54] "Instrucción pública," *El Heraldo de Madrid*, March 3, 1933, p. 10.
[55] "Hermandad de espíritus iniciados en el misterio de América." Ricardo Rojas, "El arte americano," *Revista de América* 1, no. 1 (Marzo 1920): 1–9.

contemporary artists; the third one is about the Argentine musician regarding the past indigenous tradition and the current cosmopolitan culture. All this concurs to posit one single aesthetic problem: *the possibility of creating an American music* [emphasis orig.], recognizable in spirit and form. Crìtical and historic treatises refer to "Greek music," to "Italian music" . . . Will they refer one day to an "American music"? Such is the problem this magazine wants to pose, and this issue in itself is enough to signal its importance in Argentina's culture.[56]

Rojas quoted his own *Restauración Nacionalista* (1908, p. 371) to make it clear that he had been claiming the existence of an American art and arguing for an American aesthetic education in the fine arts curriculum for many years. He mentioned that in 1914, at the University of Tucumán, he had created a "school of American industrial arts" where "the vernacular art of the textile mills and vases is coming out of the abstract speculations and entering commerce and the public taste." It was in the same vein, Rojas continued, that composer Pascual de Rogatis presented his "Indian" music (*música "india"*) at the Colón theater. In a programmatic connection of past, present, and future, Rojas proclaimed that "The 'music of America,' even if inspired in the past, is an art of the future; only the inspired ones will create it, and only the emancipated ones will understand it."[57]

Rojas referred to a *"tradición folklórica americana"* in terms that resemble José Vasconcelos's later reference to "the cosmic race":

The American folkloric tradition offers four formations: the autochthonous, the colonial or Hispanic-American, the *gauchesca*, and finally the current creole one or cosmopolitan . . . But it is in the first and second ones where we find continental transcendence and pre-historic mystery, i.e., human universality,

---

[56] Ibid., 1: "Tiempo hace que en tertulias y periódicos se viene hablando de una música Americana, y hasta de una escuela de música argentina [. . .] Si nuestros músicos hallaron antes suficiente expresión en la rapsodia de maestros europeos, hoy sienten esa inquietud emancipadora que es ya principio de creación [. . .] Una es de mera información folklórica sobre la música tradicional en los pueblos americanos; otra es la del valor técnico del folklore musical en sus relaciones con la obra personal de artistas contemporáneos; la tercera consiste en la posición del músico argentino con respecto a la pretérita tradición indígena y a la presente cultura cosmopolita. Todo esto concurre a plantear un solo problema estético: *la posibilidad de crear una música de América*, individualizable por su espíritu y por su forma. Tratados de crítica y de historia hablan de una 'música griega,' de una 'música italiana,' [. . .] ¿Hablarán algún día, asimismo, de una 'música americana'? Tal es el problema que esta revista viene a plantear, y ello solo basta para señalar su carácter y definir la importancia de esta empresa en la cultura argentina."

[57] Ibid., 2: "Escuela de artes industriales americanas . . . el arte autóctono de los telares y los vasos va saliendo de la mera especulación teórica para entrar en la actividad mercantil y en el gusto público . . . la 'música de América,' aunque reciba su soplo inspirador del pasado, es arte del porvenir; solo podrán crearlo los inspirados, pero solo podrán comprenderlo los emancipados."

together with primitive melodies, scales, cadences, rhythms, and original timbres. The colonial folklore is linked to the Spanish one, which is a synthesis of the European tradition; and the indigenous folklore is linked to the Oriental one, which is the synthesis of the Asian tradition. As we can see, we have in the old America doors through which, by penetrating its own genius, we penetrate into the genius of the most ancient humanity.[58]

The sections of *Revista de América* indicate the musical imagination of this generation of modernists: "Our aboriginal music" (referring to indigenous, colonial, and gauchesca dance and music), "Lyrical Theaters" (new operatic works and singers), "Concerts" (concert criticism), and "Conservatories" (education and pedagogy dedicated to the student and young concertist).

Music began to appear in other Latin Americanist discourses as well. In 1927 in Cuba, Alejo Carpentier linked the national folklore with a consciousness of a sphere of musical qualities that was larger than the nation. He wrote that specific melodic attributes of "our" Cuban music were in fact part of a larger Latin American tradition, and that it was the Afro-Cuban rhythmic tradition that separated Cuba's music from the rest:

> However interesting are the purely melodic aspects of our folklore, the rhythmical ones are superior in providing material for further stylization. Our voluptuous, languid melodies have many equivalents in the popular music of Latin America; but what is impossible to compare with other folkloric elements, due to their very character, are the inexhaustible rhythmic riches of the forms commonly known as "Afrocuban."[59]

In the same vein, Pedro Henríquez Ureña presented two years later the first comprehensive attempt at a general image of the "popular music of America," based on his consideration of Caribbean traditions. His analysis dismissed the academic

---

[58] Ibid., 7: "La tradición folklórica Americana ofrece cuatro formaciones: la precolombiana o autóctona; la colonial o hispanoamericana; la gauchesca; y finalmente la criolla actual o cosmopolita [. . .] Pero en las dos primeras es donde encontramos trascendencia continental y misterio prehistórico, es decir, universalidad humana, a la vez que melodías primeras, escalas, cadencias, ritmos y timbres originales. El folklore colonial lígase con el español, que es resumen de la tradición europea, y el folklore indígena lígase con el folklore oriental, que es resumen de la tradición asiática. Como se ve, tenemos en la vieja América puertas por donde, al penetrar en su propio genio, se penetra en el genio de la más vieja humanidad."

[59] "Si bien los elementos puramente melódicos de nuestro folklore son interesantes, los rítmicos los superan de tal modo, que no cabe duda posible en la elección de elementos estilizables . . . Nuestra melodía voluptuosa, lánguida, tiene equivalencias innumerables en la música popular de América Latina; lo que nos sería casi imposible comparar con otros elementos folklóricos, por su carácter, son los ritmos riquísimos, inagotables, de las formas que suelen considerarse a la ligera como 'afrocubanas'." "Amadeo Roldán y la música vernácula, *Carteles*, 13 de febrero de 1927, quoted in Bernat Garí Barceló, "La ensayística musicológica de Alejo Carpentier: eufónica vía a una poética de la novela" (PhD diss., Universidad de Barcelona, 2015), 162.

composers that had been the center of Cortijo Alahija's book, and instead focused on popular practices. His is the first attempt at a cultural history of music in Latin America.[60]

The first conscious transnational association of musicians in the region, the Pan American Association of Composers (PAAC), organized in New York in 1928. These composers wanted to promote the exchange of "new music" composed in "America" so that South and Central American work could become known in North America and vice versa. They explicitly articulated the goal of instigating "the composers of these countries to create a music that is distinctive of this hemisphere."[61] The association's "unofficial conductor" was the Russian émigré, conductor, composer, and critic Nicolas Slonimsky, who promoted the modernist work (the "new music") of the PAAC composers in Europe. Members included the Americanized Frenchman Edgar Varese; Americans Henry Cowell, Ruth Crawford, and Charles Ives; Mexicans Carlos Chávez and Silvestre Revueltas; Chilean Acario Cotapos; Argentine José André; and Cuban Amadeo Roldán. "Latin American" here meant one half of a pan-American musical front. The PAAC did not last long as an active institution, but it did promote the idea of the New World as an engine of modern music against the until then hegemonic Europeanist view in the realm of art music.

In 1930 the Mexican composer José Rolón celebrated the fact that "the contemporary musical production in the Latin America" was marked by "a radical and complete revolution in the mentality of the musicians of this continent," but at the same time noticed that capturing this change required observing it from afar—from "the old and erudite Europe, site and haven of the artists and intellectuals of the entire world. The energy for this renovation came from the rejection of Italian opera by a new generation of composers and the search of a new language."[62] Rolón noticed that this was a continental phenomenon.

US cultural officers also perceived Latin American music as a cultural unity, but through an imperial perspective. In 1930 a cheerful cultural counselor named Franklin Adams wrote a report to the Pan American Union (PAU) in Washington, DC about the "indigenous music of Latin America." He defined this music as the ancient music of the Maya and Inca transmitted over "thousands of years" through the "musical memory" of this "race" (the Latin American) to contemporary Latin American

[60] Pedro Henríquez Ureña, "Música Popular de América," *Boletín de Antropología Americana* no. 9 (July 1984): 137–57. This work was presented in 1929 and published originally in 1930 in *Conferencias, Primer Ciclo*, 1929, Vol. 1, Biblioteca del Colegio Nacional de Las Plata, 1930, pp. 177–236.

[61] "A los compositores de estos países en la creación de una música distintiva de este hemiferio." Deane L. Root, "The Pan American Association of Composers (1928–1934)," *Anuario Interamericano de Investigación Musical* 8 (1972): 49–70, and especially Carol A. Hess, *Representing the Good Neighbor: Music, Difference, and the Pan American Dream* (New York: Oxford University Press, 2013), chapter 2.

[62] "La vieja y culta Europa, asiento y refugio de los artistas e intelectuales del mundo." José Rolón, "El porvenir de la música Latino Americana," *Música: Revista Mexicana* 1, no. 2 (May 1930): 31.

composers, whose compositions represented its "modern development."[63] Adams considered the ancient, colonial, and modern musical traditions of Latin America as a single, organic, continued tradition, which United States institutions had to preserve. His report lumped together the multiple native populations of Latin America in a single group. Adams explained that the United States Army Band was preparing a selection of "New World music" to be performed at the Ibero-American Exposition in Seville in 1929 and at the International Exposition organized in Barcelona simultaneously and that at its debut in Madrid, the band's repertoire had consisted of only music "existing in Mexico, Central, and South America, at the time of the Conquest." It was, according to the PAU counselor, "the first time" that "Mother Spain" had listened to "music by her children and grandchildren."[64]

In this imperial fantasy—the United States army bringing together the Iberian mother and her New World children—Latin American music expressed millennia of cultural continuity. This imperial essentialism was one of the main sources of the idea of Latin America as a region at a time when most of the region's national elites were focusing more on their individual links to London, Paris, or Washington than on their links to one another.

The term also began to appear in the entertainment sections of newspapers, from Texas to Argentina, referring to a US musical craze. Whereas in San Antonio a journalist proclaimed that "Latin American music is a craze among New Yorkers,"[65] two years later an article titled "Latin American music" in an Argentine magazine explained that

the enthusiasm that from the beginning has been provoked in the United States by the music here [in the United States] known as Latin American . . . continues to grow. Before, the "rumbas" and "sones" were played and danced only in "dancing halls" and cabarets; today, that music has reached to the highest social spheres of the United States.[66]

---

[63] These composers included even the most innovative and most alien to folklore, such as Julián Carrillo, with his avant-garde, microtonal *Sonido 13* project. Alejandro L. Madrid, *In Search of Julián Carrillo and Sonido 13* (New York: Oxford University Press, 2015).

[64] The counselor added that "military bands of Spain have secured through the leader of the United States Army Band, Captain William J. Stannard, arrangements of sixty of the most prominent Latin American selections, in the repertoire of the Army Band" (3). Franklin Adams, "Indigenous Music of Latin America and Its Modern Development," Report to the Pan American Union, Washington, DC, 1930. University of Rochester, Eastman School of Music—Sibley Music Library.

[65] "La música latino americana enloquece a los neoyorquinos," *La Prensa* (San Antonio, Texas), April 25, 1931, p. 10.

[66] "El entusiasmo que desde el primer momento ha causado en todos los Estados Unidos la música aquí conocida por latinoamericana . . . aumenta cada día. Antes, las 'rumbas' y 'sones' eran sólo tocadas y bailadas en 'dancing-halls' y cabarets; hoy en día, esa música ha penetrado hasta la más exquisita sociedad de Norte América." Música Latinoamericana," *Caras y Caretas* N. 1.805, June 5, 1933, p. 63.

The article describes the orchestra director Emil Coleman as one of the first to introduce Latin American music instruments into the American bands that performed at the most distinguished families' *"parties."*[67] Meanwhile, in early 1935, Radio Belgrano in Buenos Aires began to broadcast "música folklórica latinoamericana" performed by a new orchestra under the direction of the Neapolitan, tango composer, and former director of the city's municipal orchestra Carlos Percuoco. According to the journalist, this programming decision was a response to public demand for folklore on a radio station otherwise focused on jazz. On the exact same page, another director explains how classical orchestras can sound right on the radio and a reader's letter argues that tango is a more cherished genre than jazz. Here, clearly, Latin American music meant something different from classical music, jazz, and tango.[68]

The patchwork of the turn of the century was slowly being addressed by encompassing regionalist views. In parallel to the popularization of the term Latin American music in the realm of journalism and entertainment, well-established writers and intellectuals adopted transnational notions of Latin America as a cultural framework. In 1932, a multinational group of writer-diplomats writing in favor of Argentine writer Manuel Ugarte grounded their case in "the professional solidarity and in the appreciation and common interest of Latin American culture," and argued that Ugarte's "spiritual influence encompasses the entire Latin America, whose race has received from him vital doctrine and advise."[69] In December of that year the president of the American Historical Association, Herbert Bolton, gave a famous speech calling on his colleagues to expand their intellectual horizon to "the epic of the greater America"—or the "history of the Western hemisphere" as a unit—by incorporating in their view of the United States the historical experience of "the Latins."[70]

In 1931 the University of Buenos Aires founded the Institute of Latin American Culture as a department of its Facultad de Filosofía y Letras, presented in the very first article of the resolution that created it as an "organ for intellectual relations

---

[67] "Triples, timbales, maracas y claves . . . instrumentos generalmente tocados por músicos latinoamericanos, especialmente antillanos, colombianos, venezolanos y centroamericanos," In the same page, the advertisement of a Phillips radio receptor entices consumers to "escuchar todas las broadcastings de la República Argentina y también las del mundo entero, Argentina, Europa, Estados Unidos, Canadá, Australia, Africa, Japón, etc."

[68] "Orquesta folklórica en Radio Belgrano," *Caras y Caretas*, November 1934.

[69] "La solidaridad profesional y en el aprecio y el interés común de la cultura latinoamericana . . . [Ugarte's] influencia espiritual se extiende a la América latina entera, y la raza ha recibido de él doctrina y consejo en asuntos vitales." Letter signed by Mexican, Chilean, Spanish, and "hispanistas franceses" urging the Argentine minster of public instruction to award Manuel Ugarte the National Literary Prize. (Chilean Gabriela Mistral, Mexican José Vasconcelos, Peruvian Francisco García Calderón, Spaniard-Mexican Enrique Diez Canedo, Venezuelan Rufino Blanco Fombona, Colombian Max Grillo, and many others.) See "El gran premio de literatura para Manuel Ugarte," newspaper *Luz*, Madrid, September 13, 1932, p. 4.

[70] Herbert E. Bolton, "The Epic of Greater America," *American Historical Review* 38, no. 3 (April 1933): 448–74.

among the Iberian-American countries" around their "cultural problems."[71] *Iberia* served as a deeper foundation for a still undefined Latin American cultural area. The institute slowly established a regional network by designating an affiliated scholar in Colombia. Its first initiatives, in 1934, aimed to overcome the lack of communication among the Iberian American countries through a speech at the Uruguayan state broadcasting system, S.O.D.R.E., a supporting gesture by the Uruguayan government. The Dominican scholar Pedro Henriquez Ureña and three assistants began organizing a "Hispanic-American bibliography," starting with an important donation of books by the Argentine National Library. At the official inauguration of the institute on July 5, 1934, the main speech, by Professor Arturo Gimenez Pastor, was titled "The Spirit of America." In May 1935 the institute cosponsored talks on romanticism in Brazil with the Instituto Argentino-Brasileño and sponsored conferences with Peruvian writers and intellectuals, such as Luis Alberto Sánchez, whose conference had the programmatic title "Toward the Cultural Autonomy of America."[72] In 1937 Sánchez was invited to a new series of conferences as part of the "direct intellectual communication among the peoples of the "la América *hispana*." This series included courses with colleagues from the "closest countries—Chile, *Brazil*, Uruguay, Bolivia—and will be extended to the totality of the peoples that form the *continental* society." All these activities stemmed from the mission of the Instituto de Cultura Latino-Americana.[73] In this paragraph the erudite director of the institute mixed four geocultural traditions with which Argentina would develop its cultural relations: continental, Hispanic, Iberian, Latin, and Brazilian cultural traditions.

The institute amassed an impressive bibliography of cultural, literary, archeological, folkloric, and historical literature produced in and on Latin America, brought invited speakers, and promoted courses in many South American universities. In 1939 it joined the new Paris-based International Institute of Iberian-American Studies, which was directed by the towering jurist and historian Rafael Altamira, exiled from his native Spain in 1936 and who had begun to promote a project of "liberal Americanism" from the University of Oviedo.[74] In 1940 the institute promoted a talk by Colombian historian and sociologist, then ambassador in Argentina Germán Arciniegas, called "The History of America Seen from the Bottom Up," a sort of populist view of the Iberian Conquest from the perspective of the natives and of the "new human type" that colonial society had created.[75] The Boletín's countless bibliographic

---

[71] "Órgano de relaciones intelectuales entre los países ibero-americanos."*Boletín del Instituto de Cultura Latino-Americana*, Universidad de Buenos Aires—Instituto de Cultura Latino-Americana, 1:1, 1937, p. 1.

[72] Ibid., 3–4.

[73] "Voces de América en la cátedra argentina," *Boletín del Instituto de Cultura Latino-Americana*, 1:4, June 1937, pp. 29–30.

[74] Gustavo Prado, *Rafael Altamira en América, 1909–1910: historia e historiografía del proyecto americanista de la Universidad de Oviedo* (Madrid: Consejo Superior de Investigaciones Científicas, 2008).

[75] "La historia de América vista desde abajo hacia arriba," *Boletín del Instituto de Cultura Latino-Americana*, May-June 1940, Año IV no. 21, 217.

notes, until the end of the publication in 1947, reflect a musicological research boom catalogued as a subtopic of folklore that appears as a national, or subnational (regional) category.

The idea of Latin America reached the realm of musical pedagogy in Argentina by 1938, when historian Manuel Salas published the textbook *Historia de la música (América Latina)* for use in Argentina's middle schools. Salas proposed a panorama of "popular music in Latin America" to provide students with a "vision of the development of the musical sentiments of these American peoples" (*una visión del desarrollo del sentimiento musical de estos pueblos Americanos*). Latin America appears here as a specific geographic space and population, as a "young" world region that is "open to the world," as a promise for those who seek an honorable working life (*promesa segura para el trabajo digno*), and as a crucible of races and ideas (*crisol de razas e ideas*). In the textbook, a very simple map divides Latin America into "civilizations" (Aztec, Mayan, Inca), indigenous groups (Chibcha, Araucan, Tupí), and wide empty spaces: Northern Mexico and Argentina. In the prologue, Salas acknowledges a regional set of collaborators, from individual pedagogues to artists such as Gabriela Mistral to diplomatic representatives of Brazil, Venezuela, Bolivia, Uruguay, Cuba, Chile, and Mexico. Salas thanks this pan-Latin American set of contributors for expressing "an honorable spirit of American solidarity."[76] The first of the mentions goes to Francisco Curt Lange, who had founded, a few years earlier, as I will show in chapter 4, the musical idea of Latin America.

I showed in this chapter how a series of journalists, intellectuals, and critics began to disseminate in the 1920s, in isolation from one another, an idea of Latin American music, when actual musical practices and traditions were not in fact actually "Latin American," and not even national, but a disparate array of local and subnational and transregional circuits. This fragmentary and imaginary *idea* of Latin American music converged in the 1930s with a similarly vague view of Latin America as a cultural region, also marked by multiple definitions—was this "continent" culturally Iberian, Latin, Hispanic, or a crucible? In the next chapter I will move away from the intellectual realm to analyze four quite diverse transnational commercial circuits, with the goal of identifying when, where, how, and why specifically *musical* actors proposed a regional Latin Americanist discourse and practice.

---

[76] Samuel J. A. Salas, Pedro I. Pauletto, and Pedro J. S. Salas, *Historia de la música (América latina) adaptada a los nuevos programas de tercer año de la enseñanza secundaria* (Buenos, Aires: Editorial Araujo, 1938), 5–8.

2

TRANSNATIONAL NETWORKS

MULTIPLE COMMERCIAL CIRCUITS, carrying sounds and musical categories, criss-crossed the region in the first half of the twentieth century, dramatically transforming its soundscape.[1] It is in fact striking that in the 1930s a commercial repertoire and circuit specifically deemed Latin American could emerge at all, out of the dense juxta-position of local, regional, diasporic, and global circuits of music and entertainment.

In this chapter I reconstruct four transnational histories of commercial music. They illuminate both the limits and the possibilities for a regional space and dis-course of Latin American music. First, a very brief reconstruction of the Philippines musical entertainment in the 1920s will allow us to appreciate the global reach of the forces that shaped commercial music in Latin America. Second, the journey of a nomadic Jewish singer, Isa Kremer, which ended in Córdoba, Argentina, will illu-minate the ideologies of musical authenticity and musical "populism" that became intrinsic to the category of Latin American music in the 1930s. Third, the copyright

---

[1] Like the landscape, the *soundscape* is both a physical reality and a cultural construction. I am referring here to the multiple styles, poetics, and aesthetic evocations generated by music and to the different cultural worlds the new musical technologies brought to Latin Americans at that time. See R. Murray Schafer, *The Soundscape: Our Sonic Environment and the Tuning of the World* (Rochester, VT: Destiny, 1977). Ana María Ochoa Gautier and Alejandra Bronfman explored not the music repertoires but the specifically aural experience of the past in Colombia and the Caribbean: Ana María Ochoa Gautier, *Aurality: Listening and Knowledge in Nineteenth-Century Colombia* (Durham, NC: Duke University Press, 2014) and Alejandra Bronfman, *Isles of Noise: Sonic Media in the Caribbean* (Chapel Hill: University of North Carolina Press, 2016).

The Invention of Latin American Music. Pablo Palomino, Oxford University Press (2020). © Oxford University Press.
DOI: 10.1093/oso/9780190687403.001.0001

strategy of the Buenos Aires-based union of composers, the Sociedad Argentina de Autores, Intérpretes y Compositores de Música (SADAIC, previously called Asociación Argentina de Autores y Compositores de Música), will show the transnational interests of local popular composers. Finally, the broadcasting system XEW reveals the convergence of Mexican and US entertainment interests around the formation of a Latin American space of musical circulation.

GLOBAL ENTERTAINMENT AND LOCAL STYLES: MANILA

The Spanish empire fostered multiple colonial musical cultures in counterpoint to metropolitan forms and institutions; the Philippines and especially Manila became in the sixteenth century a colonial economic and musical hub in the modern world system.[2] By the early twentieth century, folk music developed in the Philippines in counterpoint to yet another imperialism: the US and its commercial music genres. Thus the *Philippines Herald*, Manila's first English-language newspaper, advertised in the 1920s, next to each other, records of Italian opera, American jazz, and the local folk genre, *Kundiman*. Manila's nightlife offered classic opera at the Manila Opera House as well as a kind of pan-Asian series of acts—in 1922 one would have enjoyed Singapore acrobats and an intelligent dog dancing the Charleston, Hawaiian music and "Hawaiian blues," boxing, dance, several jazz bands, Chinese artists, shimmy, and a "Sox-o-Phone."[3] Borromeo Lou was the Philippines' most important entertainment organizer of the 1920s and a widely celebrated composer and director. He continued a late nineteenth-century tradition of Filipino *vodavil* that developed Spanish zarzuela as local form of vaudeville. In 1921 one of his shows included a song called "'My bamboo Girls,' presented as 'tango-foxtrot'."[4] On any given night, his "Borromeo jazzers . . . tickled the audience with a touch of jazz" and "jazzy selections . . . played by a syncopating orchestra," a troupe of "Chinese, Moro, and Filipino players" that used to present "a masterful review of the evolution of the classic jazz."[5] Performances as varied as "Tagalog operette," "Filipino comedian," Japanese "Maruki-Hioki" artists, "Jazz," and "Spanish dances" were announced for the same night.[6]

Many Filipino folksongs had been modeled in the nineteenth century on polkas, and among them the romantic *Kundiman* became popular during the revolution of 1896–1898 against Spain. Filipino classical composers combined it with European

---

[2] David Irving, *Colonial Counterpoint: Music in Early Modern Manila* (New York: Oxford University Press, 2010).

[3] *Philippines Herald*, October 20, 1926, and March 2, 1922.

[4] Peter Keppy, "Southeast Asia in the Age of Jazz: Locating Popular Culture in the Colonial Philippines and Indonesia," *Journal of Southeast Asian Studies* 44, no. 3 (October 2013): 444–64, 451–52.

[5] *Philippines Herald*, September 15, 1921.

[6] *Philippines Herald*, January 4, 1922.

forms to build up a Filipino classical tradition.[7] Once under US occupation, industrial recordings of Kundiman songs were objects of double legitimacy, local and imperial. Sung in Tagalog by baritone soloist Professor Jose Mossesgeld Santiago—"at the present giving concerts at the Metropolitan Opera House in New York City"—Kundiman songs were recorded on the Columbia label and advertised with both Spanish and Tagalog names. Advertisers enhanced thus the local tradition through its association with US business and "art" music; emphasized the artistic value of the singer by mentioning that he was performing at the New York Opera; targeted a nation-wide marketplace for music machines and records; and finally highlighted the mixed inheritance—Spanish and Tagalog—of Kundiman music. On their part, the Victor record label had the Philippines in the same business area as the Americas, China, and Japan, after it had "agreed to divide the globe" with Gramophone (which in fact it partially owned) in 1907. In the 1920s the company's factories in Japan, China, and South America produced recordings that it also sold to migrants from those countries in the United States. The Philippines were also one of the many marketplaces where German companies became serious competitors of the British and US ones: in 1929 German companies exported 3.4 million discs, mainly to China, the Dutch East Indies, Egypt, British Malaya, and Turkey, but also to India, Thailand, Japan, Ceylon, Palestine, Persia, the Philippines, Tunisia, and Morocco. That same year, the Philippines imported 486,000 discs (China imported 1.1 million): in the 1920s, the recording industry was already reproducing all kinds of music in and for the Philippines—local and foreign, opera and dance—in Tagalog, Spanish, and English.[8]

Hence, when the first radio broadcasting schedules appeared in 1925 on the pages of the *Philippines Herald*, their content featured that musical diversity: Hawaiian waltzes, Kundiman songs, Spanish dances, foxtrots, and classical music by Filipino Orchestras. Music from Spain, the United States, and the Philippines dominated the airwaves. It is not surprising that from such musical crossroads, by 1936 Filipino musicians became a "musical proletariat," regularly hired on the pan-Asian steamship line and hotel circuit because of their excellence at "'faking' (playing from charts) and their willingness to work at low wages."[9]

The absence of any Latin American reference in the quite heterogeneous musical worlds of the Philippines, which did include Spanish-language music—not only from Spain but from Mexico[10]—and were targeted by the same US media companies as

---

[7] Antonio C. Hila, *Music in History, History in Music* (Manila: University of Santo Tomás, 2004), 7; Ramón P. Santos, *Musika: An Essay on the American Colonial and Contemporary Traditions in Philippine Music* (Manila: Cultural Center of the Philippines, 1994), 6.

[8] Pekka Gronow, "The Record Industry Comes to the Orient," *Ethnomusicology* 2 (1981): 251–84.

[9] Joaquín González III, *Philippine Labour Migration: Critical Dimensions of Public Policy* (Singapore: Institute of Southeast Asian Studies, 1998), quoted in Stephanie Ng, "Filipino Bands Performing in Hotels, Clubs and Restaurants in Asia: Purveyors of Transnational Culture in a Global Arena," PhD diss. (University of Michigan, 2006), 46.

[10] See Rafael Bernal, *México en Filipinas: estudio de una transculturación* (México: Universidad Nacional Autónoma de México, 1965), 124. I thank Paula Park for this reference. See also Paula Park,

Latin America, indicates that until the 1930s the region was neither a unified circuit nor a recognizable musical discourse.

Considering the globalization of music from a very different geographic angle— the diasporic career of a Russian-Jewish singer—will allow us to understand the *ideological* frameworks of the musical globalization in which Latin American music emerged.

HIGHBROW, LOWBROW, AND FOLK: THE DIASPORIC POPULISM OF ISA KREMER

In a 1924 advertisement brochure, a range of "most eminent musicians" praised the products of New York piano makers Knabe and Co., and next to Pyotr Tchaikovsky, Camille Saint-Saëns, and Giacomo Puccini, we see a young singer, today forgotten, named Isa Kremer.[11] At the time she was a musical icon but also an ethnic one. In 1926, Zionist ideologue Vladimir Jabotinsky wrote in *The Jewish Tribune* that he was "not quite sure whether it is quite lawful for a Zionist to be so madly patriotic about a city somewhere in the Diaspora—but that is how we [Odessans] feel about Odessa." He entitled this loving tribute, "Odessa, Isa Kremer's City."[12] In fact, Kremer's life was not attached to any city—hers was a truly nomadic life. Born on October 21, 1887, in the tiny village of Beltz, Bessarabia (today's Ukraine, very close to the Polish border), Kremer moved with her parents in 1899 to Odessa, where she grew up but eventually left and never returned. She arrived in Argentina at age fifty-one, in 1938, and died eighteen years later in Córdoba on July 7, 1956. Her prestige and artistic life spanned four decades, but then fell into oblivion just until recently.[13]

According to the notes Isa Kremer left among her papers at the IWO archive in Buenos Aires,[14] her father, a not very successful merchant, sent her to study music in Italy, where in 1904 she began giving concerts to pay for her studies. In 1914 she returned to Odessa to work with a local opera company. The war started, and in 1916, not seeing any future in the opera, she moved to Moscow as a popular singer, and

---

"Transcolonial Listening: Dissonances in Cuban and Philippine Literature" (MA thesis, University of Texas, Austin, 2014), 33, n51.

[11] The company's website proudly states that Francis Scott Key, composer of "The Star-Spangled Banner," commissioned a Knabe piano for his house in 1838, and Tchaikovsky used one at the inauguration of Carnegie Hall in 1891. https://www.knabepianos.com/history.php (accessed February 18, 2012).

[12] Michael Katz, "'Go Argue with Today's Children': The Jewish Family in Sholem Aleichem and Vladimir Jabotinsky," *European Judaism* 43, no. 1 (May 30, 2010): 63–77, 69 and n14.

[13] Ted Schillinger, *Isa Kremer: the People's Diva* (New York: Women Make Movies, 2000); Sandra McGee Deutsch, *Crossing Borders, Claiming a Nation: a History of Argentine Jewish Women, 1880–1955* (Durham, NC: Duke University Press, 2010), 187–88.

[14] The autobiographical notes were dictated to a certain "M. Iardeni," probably Mordecai Yardeini, author of several books on Yiddish music and musicians; Yardeini was affiliated with the pro-Soviet New York Yiddish newspaper *Morgn-frayhayt*. I thank Zachary Baker for this reference.

there, according to her memoir, she did succeed. When the Russian Revolution began, she moved to Turkey.

Among the earliest documents of her artistic life is a series of press clips from 1920 in Constantinople (today's Istanbul). A *"Grande Soirée en l'honneur de Mme Isa Kremer"* included in its repertoire "the most cherished Russian, Neapolitan, Jewish, and Gypsy songs" (*les plus aimées chansons russes, napolitaines, juives et tziganes*). That same year at another concert she performed Franz Liszt and David Popper's *Hungarian Rhapsody*, Pablo de Sarasate's *Zigeunerweisen* ("Gypsy airs"), *Chansons Juives et Napolitaines* (composer not indicated), Henryk Wienawski's *Souvenir de Moscou*, Leo Zeitlin's *Eli Sion*, Popper's *Fileuse*, and finally *Hatikvah* ("The Hope," a Zionist anthem since the 1897 First Zionist Congress, then Israel's unofficial anthem since 1948 and official anthem since 2004). This list includes thus Romantic pieces, a nationalist anthem, and not only Jewish but also Neapolitan *chansons* presented as anonymous repertoire.

A chronicler of these concerts revealed the main aesthetic and ideological categories of the global music of the time:

The Russian *diseuse* Isa Kremer. Possibly the word *diseuse* is not accurately descriptive but what she gave us was an endless series of the most *charming light songs in Russian, Neapolitan, and Hebrew* [my emphasis]. She possesses quite the finest talent in this genre we have ever seen possessed by a woman artiste. Her voice is almost contralto and you can see that she adores what she sings. The programme had, in fulsome adulation, compared her to Occidental artistes of the same kind, but she is undoubtedly far superior to any such artistes in the west. The fact is that *in the west this genre is either confined to the cafe-chantant and vulgarised thereby, or to the drawing room*, where a certain number of little misses with semi-educated voices do occasionally give us some of the old folk songs . . . It is true that we could not understand the Russian words, nor even— so fast did Isa Kremer sing—the Neapolitan. As for the Hebrew, having never studied the Bible in the original, we again have to confess ourselves defeated. But this did not make any difference to our understanding of the art. It was perfectly clear they were full of that *touching folk element which has been preserved integrally in the East*, and that they phrased with charm light emotions and momentary sorrows. In her Neapolitan songs Isa Kremer put into her voice *the warmth and passion of the South* and the hoyden gaiety of Naples street girls. Elsewhere in her songs, you felt her voice laughing in rounds of glee and in others again in felt to an extraordinary sadness. The Russian present gave her a great reception and it was very well deserved. She could teach a great deal to the stage of the West.[15]

---

[15] *The Orient News* (Constantinople), February 13, 1920.

Seven crucial definitions of music are revealed in this paragraph.

First, the multiple criteria to define national origins in music: Kremer sang a Zionist anthem accompanied by two musicians who were also Jewish, but having been trained in Moscow made her a *Russian* artist. Second, a musical hierarchy: art, folk, and commercial music. Kremer offers an educated, uplifted version of folk, and both training and folk save music from the vulgar "drawing room." Third, *style* hierarchies: she was a *diseuse*—a talker, teller, monologist, or dramatic performer—of *light songs*, not opera arias or more sophisticated works. Fourth, the Orientalist "folk," opposite to the corny, semi-improvised old folk repertoire of ordinary café-chanteuses of "the West," artistically superior because it had "the touching folk element which has been preserved integrally in the East." "Oriental," in this context, means *truer*—preserved from the vulgarization of the West. Fifth, the myth of "the South," the *Australist* version of Orientalism;[16] the "warmth and passion of the South" define her as an *authentic* singer. "East" and "South" share, under this light, a common distance from the "West." Sixth, the ethnocentric convergence of all folk traditions: in other words, that folk music ultimately expresses a transcultural, global tradition. The power of this ideology is noteworthy: Kremer's Russian, Neapolitan, and Hebrew songs reveal the authentic folk art in such an evident way that the musical critic can perceive it, *even without knowing Russian, Neapolitan, or Hebrew*. Seventh, and finally, both *talent* and *authenticity* as key to popular genius. Isa is not only more authentic, but "possesses quite the finest talent" and is "undoubtedly superior" to any comparable "woman artiste."

Kremer's repertoire expressed thus a widespread ideology of popular music as being an authentic and talented take on multiple, potentially global, musical origins. Her career illuminates the possible connections across geographic areas and musical categories. Let us reconstruct it.

From Istanbul she jumped to the most prestigious stages. At a concert at Berlin's Philharmonic Great Hall in 1922, the program began with Chopin's nocturne and waltz and followed with Russian, French, Italian, and Yiddish songs.[17] In October of that year she made her debut at Carnegie Hall in New York City. By 1923 her name was widespread in both the United States and Europe. A Russian-language sheet music published by the trading firm Milan Auman & Co. in Krsko, Slovenia, presents a drawing of her in a Flamenco style and the title *"chansons d'*Isa Kremer."

In 1927 she was back in the United States, but this time, surprisingly, in a different kind of stage and presenting a different artistic persona. Kremer offered at the Palace Orpheum in Milwaukee her "first venture in vaudeville" with a "program of those

---

[16] José Moya proposes and discusses Australism in "Latin America: The Limitations and Meaning of a Historical Category," *The Oxford Handbook of Latin American History* (New York: Oxford University Press, 2011), 1–24.

[17] The April 7, 1922, program quoted praise of Isa Kremer's numerous previous concerts, including praise for a concert in Moscow written by the *Russkija Wedomosti* critic Joel Engel, composer and leader of the revalorization of Jewish musical folklore in Eastern Europe.

exquisitely interpreted folksongs of different nations, for which she is celebrated," sharing a bill with acrobats, dancers, and movies—a diversity of performances similar to the one we saw in Manila. She carried prestige with her: "The concert stage has lost one of its most talented singers and the broad boards of vaudeville are the richer for it . . . Strangely, she proved to be a knockout. [. . .] she has IT written large all over her. Monday night she sang in four languages and was applauded to the rafters in each one."

In an interview she inverted the musical hierarchy, valorizing the "real music lovers" and "folks" in the vaudeville audience over the "high-brows" as the ultimate musical judge:

According to her own telling, she is better known by the "high-brows" than by real music lovers . . . On the vaudeville stage she comes out to sing ballads and folk songs of many countries, in many languages. She says this is her first experience in singing folk songs to "folks," that is to people who don't go to the music places because it's fashionable or the thing to do. "I must win over a vaudeville audience," she said. "Many of them never heard of me. They don't clap when I come on, they wait to hear what I can do."[18]

In another interview ("Artists Who Sings in 12 Tongues Makes Debut in Vaudeville Here") she explained her artistic career as a populist choice: "I wanted to try vaudeville. For there you play to the people who want to be amused. I love Milwaukee, its people, and vaudeville . . . I was in Russia throughout the war. When the Bolsheviks won I was given a government contract. They spared me because they said I was of the people. I am proud that I am of the people." Another chronicler explained how her multilingual repertoire was an appropriate container for interpreting each audience's language: "It's the *coquetery* [sic] of her eyes and voice aided by just a touch of foreign accent, that give these English and American songs a color all their own, gives them that something different that strikes the listeners' fancy and willingly makes him forgive some of the other songs that he did not understand."[19] The article explains Isa's "stage" style as a result of her earliest training in opera: "Her early experiences go back to the time when she sang Mimi to Tito Schipa's Rudolfo in *La bohème*." This success in vaudeville led her, later that year, to Broadway.

Isa Kremer toured Europe in 1929 and 1930 and was celebrated by critics from all over the ideological spectrum, including the Italian newspaper *Il Lavoro Fascista* [the Fascist labor] (April 3, 1930), whose review Kremer incorporated into her concert programs: "a woman with a soul so great that all the other peoples can be mirrored into it." In London in 1930, she published a songbook called *Album of Jewish Folk-Songs*, all of them in Yiddish. In 1934 a tour brought her for the first time to distant Buenos Aires, where she performed at the Odeón Theater. The program included the praise of

[18] *The Milwaukee Sentinel*, August, 23, 1927.
[19] *Milwaukee Leader*, August 24, 1927.

a famous admirer, Albert Einstein: "Isa Kremer is the most marvelous interpreter of folk music of all peoples and I greet her as a sign of deep admiration and gratitude."

Kremer moved to Buenos Aires in 1938. There she became fully internationalist. Performing in November 1938 at the Young Men's Hebrew Association concert, her program began with a Yemenite, a Greek, and a Tartar song, then followed with a section of three "cradle songs" ("French, Negro, Jewish"), and by another described as "Jewish children songs." The pianist, the Russian Ivan Basilevsky, performed two solo pieces: a "Polonaise" by Chopin and the 1927 "Malagueña" by Cuban composer Ernesto Lecuona. This piece (a Cuban love song to an archetypical Andalusian woman) and "Mucho te quiero," a *bailecito* (an Argentine traditional folk song), were probably the first pieces in her repertoire we would call Latin American.[20]

In August 1939 the main Argentine radio magazine, *Radiolandia*, interviewed "the famous Russian balladist" before a series of shows on Radio Belgrano in Buenos Aires, where she would sing "*all the folklores of the world.*" The published interview, titled "Isa Kremer: The Voice that Sings the Emotion of the People," presented her as an interpreter of the "soul of the people" acclaimed in France, England, and the United States as "one of the most authentic voices of the regional accent." She was authentic enough to make a commentator on her previous shows in 1934 write that Kremer "gave the impression of having born Argentine, from Argentine parents, and having an extraordinary voice for interpreting our folklore." Kremer described Argentine folklore as

> very sad and very beautiful. Maybe the most beautiful of the world . . . it doesn't seem like any other else. Maybe a little bit like Spain's, but the *cante jondo* [flamenco singing] isn't sad, but tragic. Yours is sweet, peaceful, sentimental . . . The sweetness of a *Vidalita* [a folk style from Argentina's Northwestern provinces] is unique among all the singings of the earth. And the *Triste* [another folk style] has the entrancing suggestiveness of religious music.

Kremer praised local folk styles, compared them to Spain's, and then, asked about tango, showed a subtle understanding of it, and of how authenticity works in global entertainment. She had a great collection of tango records,

> and in my travels and stays in Europe I heard it being sung. Tango is in the spirit of Argentines . . . An Argentine is an Argentine in any country, in any city in the world. He's been known for his way of looking at women . . . In the eyes of a *porteño* [inhabitant of Buenos Aires] citizen there is a special gaze; mix of tenderness, gallantry, and superiority. When I feel observed like this on the street, I would never respond to such a gaze for anything in the world . . . The women who don't live in Buenos Aires feel somewhat intimidated . . . Which is attractive! Alas, the Argentine men look this way at every woman that comes

---

[20] "Isa Kremer" Box, Jewish Research Institute (IWO), Buenos Aires.

in their way . . . Going back to the tango: please tell the audience that in my show at Radio Belgrano I will sing Argentine tangos. Not at all English-language American tangos, nor German or Italian ones . . . your tangos . . . I swear that if I manage to correctly sing a *porteño* tango in Buenos Aires, I'll have the right to sing it anywhere else.[21]

The pictures show her at the Radio Belgrano studio, accompanied at the piano by *maestro* Rodolfo Sachs, another European exile.[22] In June of that same year, she performed in a show titled "The Soul of the Song of All Peoples" (*El alma de la canción de todos los pueblos*). Kremer's first years in Buenos Aires were marked by benefit concerts related to World War II, including the *Junta de la Victoria*, an anti-fascist organization that drew upon previous socialist, communist, and suffragist movements and included women from all ethnic and social origins.[23] As her repertoire grew, it incorporated songs from the Americas and from Soviet Russia.

How did Kremer organize such a diverse repertoire? In 1941 at the National School of Music in Rio de Janeiro, Brazil, and in a July 1942 program in Buenos Aires, Kremer divided the twenty-two songs thematically into eight categories: Labor, Lullabies, Love, Women, Children, Soldiers, Blacks, and Chassidim, poetic themes presented as universal. She performed on October 6, 1942, in Montevideo, at the concert hall of the national public broadcasting system (S.O.D.R.E., the official and largest broadcasting station in the country, whose music library and record collection was directed by the German musicologist Curt Lange, who will play a decisive role in our history.) That night Kremer, accompanied by Dr. Pablo Manelsky at the piano, sang twenty-four multinational songs, and the program includes her explanation of each of them.

The first part presented eight songs: "Wide River" (very likely, "The River is Wide"), an American spiritual, the type of song "by which black people arrive at religious ecstasy." Then "Piccaniny," an American lullaby, a "product of the infinite tenderness of black mothers toward their children"; "Volga," a song which conveys "sailing images of the famous river that has dragged so much pain . . . We have loved your old songs, Volga; wouldn't you like to listen to our new Soviet songs now?"; "Moscowa," a love song to the bright future of the capital; "Chittarata," an ironic and melancholic Italian song about the witty smile of a peasant woman; "La Marcha de los Pioneros" ("March of the Pioneers"), a Soviet children's song dedicated to the fatherland; and "¡No Señor!" ("No Sir!"), the Spanish version of a sentimental English song.

[21] "Isa Kremer: la voz que canta la emoción del pueblo," *Radiolandia*, Agosto 1939.

[22] "Sachs . . . went to Argentina in 1933 as Austrian and became citizen of Argentina in 1941; there he developed a career as musician, composer of popular songs and film music, pianist, accompanist, music director; in autumn 1944 cofounded in Buenos Aires the night cabaret 'Mosquito;' later on worked in trading business as importer; in 1953 opened a restaurant with a friend in Barcelona; died in September 1956 in Barcelona; buried in Buenos Aires." Klaus Völker, *Ich verreise auf einige Zeit*, c1999, p. 54, quoted at the Library of Congress Name Authority catalogue, http://id.loc.gov/authorities/names/n00034010.html (accessed February 25, 2012).

[23] McGee Deutsch, *Crossing Borders*, 185–89.

The second part was about love and began with three "Oriental songs": "Yafim haleiloth," a Yemenite love song set in the desert; "Bibikey Kiz," a Tartar song sung by a man while his fiancée dances, "because Tartar men never dance and Tartar women never sing"; and "Egia Mola," a patriotic Greek song. The following four were "Dance Songs": the English "The second minuet," about grandparents who meet each other dancing a minuet; the Bavarian "Philys," in which a young woman refuses to obey her mother's order to enter a convent; the French "En dansant," a love song set in a picnic; and the Russian "Molodka," about the conflict between an old peasant and his young wife.

The third part was about war and still included popular love songs: "Si mañana viene la guerra" ("If the War Comes Tomorrow"), a Soviet song about the necessity of being ready today to fight tomorrow; "Madelon," a popular French military song; the American "Inky Dinky," in which an American attempts to talk with a French woman but just knows two words: *"parlez vous?"*; "Morena salada," a "song of the Spanish soldier, full of emotion and poetic feeling"; the Jewish song "Der Prisiv," in which a Jewish man "defends his Soviet fatherland where there are no more pogroms or persecutions"; two Soviet songs: "Pájaros libres" ("Free Birds"), which praises the invincible Soviet youth ready to die for its fatherland, and "Marineros rojos," the hymn of the Red Navy; the American "Little Sparrow," in which an unmarried seamstress sings about her distrust of men; and finally the French revolutionary anthem "La marsellaise," which "doesn't belong only to France anymore. It is the universal song of freedom, of anybody who loves the life and wishes the resurrection of all the enslaved peoples." Soviet, African American, Spanish, Jacobin, Jewish, Yemenite— the ambition of singing "the Song of All the People" was almost literal.[24]

In Argentina Kremer married doctor Gregorio Bermann, the communist and active anti-fascist organizer who a few years before had created the Argentine medical brigade that served the Republican armies in Spain during the Civil War. This could explain the incorporation into her programs of Spanish translations by Rafael Alberti, the famous Spanish poet, Republican, and Communist, who arrived in Argentine exile the same year as Kremer. His are the Spanish versions of "Little Sparrow," "Wide River," "Le petit navire," "A vieglied," "Bibikey Kitz," and many other Greek, Tartar, American, Yiddish, and Russian songs.

Toward the end of the war the war she toured New York and London with recitals of folk song, which included a piece by Manuel de Falla (the "Ritual Fire Dance" from his 1915 ballet *Love the Magician*), another Spanish Republican exiled in Argentina in 1939, who had moved from Buenos Aires to Córdoba soon after his arrival and died

---

[24] Kremer's own archive included a collection of folk songbooks: *French-Canadian Folk-Songs* (London and New York, 1927); *Smokey Mountain Ballads*, by The Carter Family (New York, 1934); *New Songs the Soviets Sing*; a publication by the Ukranian National Chorus; and scores of Russian, Gipsy, Caucasian, Soviet, and French songs, among others, printed by publishing houses in New York, London, Warsaw, Moscow, Buenos Aires, and Paris. "Isa Kremer—Partituras Música Folklórica," IWO.

there in late 1946. Kremer kept performing her folk repertoire until at least 1951, when she toured Tel Aviv and Paris. She died in Córdoba, Argentina, in 1956.

Kremer's musical practice challenges our national and hierarchical preconceptions in music history. It clearly defies the binary approaches to Latin American culture, such as art/popular, highbrow/lowbrow, European/native, hegemonic/subaltern, and cosmopolitan/folkloric. In the United States, critics celebrated her populist step from the art scene to vaudeville, while in Argentina her repertoire was praised as a global folklorist project, comparable to Carl Sandburg's *American Songbag*, or to Andés Chazarreta's performance of Santiagueño culture for Buenos Aires audiences.[25] Kremer's journey indicates the emergence in the 1920s and 1930s of shifting musical cartographies and hierarchies.

Her journey also suggests that gernes defined with tags such as Cuban, folk, Argentine, tangos, vidalitas and others reveal a Latin American circulation that not required an encompassing "Latin American" category. Finally, her claim of performing *the music of the people* across linguistic and geographic borders suggests that musicians in the 1930s were embracing a *transnational populist* rhetoric that would be essential to musical Latin Americanism as well.

BETWEEN LOCAL AND TRANSNATIONAL MARKETS: BUENOS AIRES TANGO COMPOSERS

To consider tango Argentine and Latin American is to a significant extent a retrospective effect. The examples mentioned in the previous chapter of Indonesian and Filipino uses of the genre in the 1920s, and the distinction made in Buenos Aires between tango and "Latin American folklore" suggest that in its origins and development it was mainly considered a cosmopolitan genre and also, as Argentine traditional historiography emphasized, as the genre by excellence of Buenos Aires and the Rio de la Plata. In recent decades scholars have explored tango as a global cultural artifact. Now we know that transnational circulation turned tango into a global genre *before* and *during* its association with Buenos Aires, the Rio de la Plata, and Argentina.[26]

[25] Ricardo Jonatas Kaliman, "Dos actitudes ilustradas hacia la música popular: para una historia social de la industria del folklore musical argentino," *Revista Argentina de Musicología* 17 (December 2016): 37–56.

[26] Carlos Vega, *Danzas y canciones argentinas: teorías e investigaciones* (Buenos Aires: G. Ricordi y C., 1936) and *Estudios para los orígenes del tango argentino* (Buenos Aires: Editorial de la Universidad Católica Argentina, 2007); José Sebastián Tallon, *El tango en sus etapas de música prohibida.* (Buenos Aires: Instituto Amigos del Libro Argentino, 1959); Instituto Nacional de Musicología "Carlos Vega," *Antología del tango rioplatense* (Buenos Aires: Instituto Nacional de Musicología "Carlos Vega," 1980); Horacio Salas, *El tango* (Buenos Aires: Planeta, 1986); Enrique Cámara de Landa, "Tango 'de Ida y de Vuelta,'" *Revista de Musicología* 16, no. 4 (January 1, 1993): 2147–69; Marta Savigliano, *Tango and the Political Economy of Passion* (Boulder, CO: Westview Press, 1995); Julio Nudler, *Tango judío: del ghetto a la milonga* (Buenos Aires: Editorial Sudamericana, 1998); José Judkovski, *El tango y los judíos de Europa*

Tango music and dance were present since the 1880s in the ports, fairs, and broth-els of Buenos Aires and Montevideo (and Brazil, although the expression *tango brasileiro* suggests that Brazilians were designing with that name a national version of a foreign style).[27] Before that it was part of the musical repertoire of porteños of African origins.[28] But even before that, as early as 1856, a dance handbook published in the United States described tango as a "South American dance."[29] Tango was one of the names of the musical dialogues around the contradance between La Habana, Sevilla, Madrid, and Paris, cities where tangos, tonadillas, and habaneras borrowed and adapted from each other transnationally.[30] Even earlier, the records of the Mexican archives of the Inquisition mention, among other musical styles related in

---

oriental (Buenos Aires: Academia Porteña de Lunfardo, Fundación IWO, 2010) and *El tango: una histo-ria con judíos* (Buenos Aires: IWO, 1998); Eduardo Archetti, *Masculinities: Football, Polo, and the Tango in Argentina* (Oxford: Berg, 1999); Pablo Palomino, "Tango, samba y amor," *Apuntes de Investigación del CECYP* 12 (October 7, 2007): 71–101; Florencia Garramuño, *Primitive Modernities: Tango, Samba, and Nation* (Stanford, CA: Stanford University Press, 2011); Esteban Buch, ed., *Tangos cultos: Kagel, J.J. Castro, Mastropiero y otros cruces musicales* (Buenos Aires: Gourmet Musical, 2012); Esteban Buch, "La censura del tango por la iglesia francesa en vísperas de la Gran Guerra (con una post-data de Erik Satie)," *Revista Argentina de Musicología* 15–16 (2014–2015): 79–102; Morgan James Luker, *The Tango Machine: Musical Culture in the Age of Expediency* (Chicago: University of Chicago Press, 2016); Kacey Link and Kristin Wendland, *Tracing Tangueros: Argentine Tango Instrumental Music* (New York: Oxford University Press, 2016); Matthew B. Karush, *Musicians in Transit: Argentina and the Globalization of Popular Music* (Durham, NC: Duke University Press, 2017); Marina Cañardo, *Fábricas de músicas. Comienzos de la industria discográfica en la Argentina (1919–1930)* (Buenos Aires: Gourmet Musical, 2017).

[27] "Hence, we see that lundu, polca-lundu, cateretê, fado, chula, tango, habanera, maxixe and all the combinations of these names, even if on other contexts could have had their particular determina-tions, when printed on the covers of Brazilian music sheets of the nineteenth century they informed basically that it was 'syncopated,' 'typically Brazilian' music appropriated to mixed-raced swing [*requebrados mestiços*]." Carlos Sandroni, *Feitiço Decente: Transformações Do Samba No Rio de Janeiro, 1917–1933* (Rio de Janeiro: Jorge Zahar Editor : Editora UFRJ, 2001), 31.

[28] Leonardo Affonso de Miranda Pereira, "Do Congo ao tango: associativismo, lazer e identidades entre os afro-portenhos na segunda metade do século XIX," *Mundos do Trabalho* 3, no. 6 (2011): 30–51.

[29] "The Tango was originally a South American dance, composed in two-fourth time. Arranged for the ballroom, by M. Markowski." The section dedicated to "Tango" in this 1856 dance textbook describes a dance different from current tango dance and provides a drawing of a dancing couple of Spanish air ("Le Tango Valse—A Fancy Ball Room Sketch"). Charles Durang, *The Fashionable Dancer's Casket, Or, The Ball-room Instructor: A New and Splendid Work on Dancing, Etiquette, Deportment, and the Toilet* (Philadelphia: Fisher & Brother, 1856), 151–53. Jo Baim analyzes this text and develops a fascinating hypothesis about possible connections in the 1850s and 1860s among a variety of characters that could have been behind the articulation of habanera and waltz dance music under the name of tango. Baim mentions the top Parisian dance arranger Markowski, his disciple the American dancer Charles Durang (the one who published the 1856 description), Parisian dancer Celeste Mogador, Spanish composer Sebastian Yradier (author of "María Dolores," which was a "Tango Americano compuesto sobre un ayre habanero" published in Madrid in 1860, and which fits Markowski's indications for tango), and Georges Bizet (who arranged an Yradier work, "El areglito," for his habanera piece in the opera *Carmen*). Jo Baim, *Tango: Creation of a Cultural Icon* (Bloomington: Indiana University Press, 2007), 133–39.

[30] Hervé Lacombe and Christine Rodriguez, *La Habanera de Carmen: Naissance d'un tube* (Paris: Fayard, 2014), 100; the wider history of contradance was pan-Caribbean, as studied in Peter Manuel, ed., *Creolizing Contradance in the Caribbean* (Philadelphia: Temple University Press, 2009).

one way or another with its prosecutions, a tango in 1802.[31] In the twentieth century, some of the earliest tango recordings took place in Paris and featured the Argentine composers Villoldo and Gobbi in 1907, and on the eve of World War I, many Argentine musicians and wealthy patrons established Argentine tango as a fashionable dance and music in Paris.[32] Tango was the name of an amusement ride at Coney Island's Luna Park, where the "convenient cars in which one comfortably reclines go through the motions of the dance . . . they also wind through the wilds of South America, where the Tango originated."[33] Tango began to spread to other big European cities— in 1914 the *futurista* writer Marinetti mocked those dancers as "hallucinated dentists who stare at each other's teeth"[34]—and spread even more intensely during the inter- war years. At that point its Argentine credentials were relative at best: several dance texts published between 1913 and 1915 mention Argentina most frequently when discussing tango's origins but also attribute it to Spain and Cuba, and also mention Mexico as the birthplace of an evolved version of a form that was originally Cuban or Spanish.[35] The proliferation of references suggests that tango was at once a dis- tinct musical genre and dance form, and a cultural label. Ethnomusicologist Ramón Pelinski defined tango as a nomadic style particuarly well suited to globalization.[36] By the 1930s, tango's prestige as a category was mainly cosmopolitan: a dance club in Shanghai was called "Tango Palace,"[37] and the 1934 tango habanera "Youkali" composed by the German composer Kurt Weill the year after he fled from Berlin to New York, is an example of its ubiquity. Many "tangos" were composed and recorded in Indonesia in the 1930s.[38] In Germany, Poland, the Soviet Union, and the shifting

---

[31] Javier Marin Lopez, "A Conflicting Relationship. Music, Power and the Inquisition in Vice-Regal Mexico City" (Cambridge: Cambridge University Press, 2011), 54.

[32] Juan Corradi, "'How Many Did It Take to Tango? Voyages of Urban Culture in the Early 1900s," in *Outsider Art: Contesting Boundaries in Contemporary Culture*, 1997, 194–214.

[33] Rem Koolhaas, *Delirious New York: A Retroactive Manifesto for Manhattan* (New York: Monacelli Press, 1994), 42–43.

[34] Filippo Tommaso Marinetti, "Abasso il Tango e Parsifal!," *Milano*, January 1914.

[35] Baim, *Tango*, 75.

[36] Ramón Pelinski, "Tango nómade: una metáfora de la globalización," *Escritos sobre tango en el Río de la Plata y en la diáspora*, eds. Teresita Lencina, Omar García Brunelli and Ricardo Salton (2008): 65–128. "It can be said that there is a de-territorialized tango in the Rio de la Plata, capable of detaching from its territorial links and de-territorialize in transnational circulation to reterritorialize on other cul- tures and places, assuming (some of) their traits, transforming them and giving origin to new types of tango" (3–4). Pelinski notes that tango was introduced as far away as Melanesia, in the summer nights of 1914, by one of the founders of modern anthropology. See Bronislaw Malinowski, *A Diary in the Strict Sense of the Term* (Stanford, CA: Stanford University Press, 1989), 21 and 259.

[37] A tale by New Sensationist and film critic Liu Na'ou, translated from Chinese by Andrew Jones, describes Shanghai's Tango Palace in 1930 as a place of "jazz": "Everything here in this Tango Palace is in melodic motion—male and female limbs, colored lights and glowing drinks, red and green liq- uids enfolded by slender fingers, lips the color of persimmon, smoldering eyes [. . .] Suddenly the air shudders with a wave of music, and a startling cry begins to sound. A musician in the middle of the bandstand holds that demon of jazz, the saxophone, and begins to blow crazily toward the crowd." Andrew Jones, "Black Internationale: Notes on the Chinese Jazz Age," in *Jazz Planet*, ed. E. Taylor Atkins (Jackson: University Press of Mississippi, 2003).

[38] Yampolsky, "Music and Media in the Dutch East Indies," 241.

boundaries of Eastern Europe, tango became nationalized and at the same time a nightlife lingua franca.[39] Around the same years in New York, middle- and upper-class female patrons at *Thé Dansants* paid male "ethnic" dancers (usually Italians and Jews) called "tango pirates."[40] After World War II, it became popular in Japan and a national symbol, although in a quite different form, in Finland.[41] Especially since the 1970s, tango has dialogued with other styles, from jazz to classical and contemporary music, and electronic tango eventually gave it a new life globally. Beginning in the early 2000s, it regained a central place in Buenos Aires through a new generation of musicians, dancers, and composers, as well as both public and civil grassroots promotion.[42] Tango became thus "Argentine" as it was being disseminated throughout Europe and beyond. Therefore, rather than an Argentine form that was disseminated globally, tango was a global form that became nationalized—as marketed Argentine authenticity by the French recording industry,[43] but also as Soviet, Polish, Finnish, or simply as a marker of bohemian, nocturnal, and global modernity.

Broadcasting and cinema expanded tango throughout Latin America in the 1930s. Like the similarly-named *rumba, mambo, cumbia,* and *samba,* it was synonym for Latin American music, although in this regional context it gained a distinctively Argentine identity. People born in the region between the 1920s and the 1950s became adults by singing tangos—together with boleros, sones, valses, and rancheras, often disseminated by Mexican movies that promoted not only Argentine but also Venezuelan, Colombian, and Cuban artists, styles, and scripts.[44] This process overlapped with the records, movies, and tours that carried the songs of one Buenos Aires singer in particular, Carlos Gardel, across the region. Gardel's life illustrates this transnational era

---

[39] Eleonor Gilburd, "Weary Sun. Tango in Soviet Russia," Colloquium: The Worlds of Latin American Music in the 20th Century, University of Chicago, Center for Latin American Studies, April 18, 2017; Didier Francfort, "Le tango, passion allemande et européenne, 1920–1960," in *Littératures et musiques dans la mondialisation: XXe-XXIe siècles,* ed. Anaïs Fléchet and Marie-Françoise Lévy (Paris: Publications de la Sorbonne, 2015), 95–114.

[40] Lewis Erenberg, *Steppin' Out: New York Nightlife and the Transformation of American Culture, 1890–1930* (Westport, CT: Greenwood Press, 1981), 83–86.

[41] Baim, *Tango;* Enrique Cadícamo, *La historia del tango en París* (Buenos Aires: Ediciones Corregidor, 1975); Marta Savigliano, "Tango in Japan and the World Economy of Passion," in *Re-Made in Japan: Everyday Life and Consumer Taste in a Changing Society,* ed. Joseph Jay Tobin (New Haven, CT: Yale University Press, 1992), 235–51; Corradi, "'How Many Did It Take to Tango?"; Ramón Adolfo Pelinski, *El tango nómade: ensayos sobre la diáspora del tango* (Buenos Aires: Corregidor, 2000).

[42] For instance, the Orquesta Típica Fernández Fierro and the Club of the same name; Orquesta-Escuela de Tango Emilio Balcarce; Tangovía's Digital Tango Archive; Festival & Mundial de Tango Buenos Aires; countless milongas; electronic tango bands like Gotán Project and Bajofondo; and an emerging "queer tango."

[43] Cañardo, *Fábricas de Músicas.*

[44] Maricruz Castro and Robert McKee Irwin, *El cine mexicano "se impone": mercados internacionales y penetración cultural en la época dorada* (México: Universidad nacional Autónoma de México, Coordinación de Difusión Cultural, Dirección de Literatura, 2011); sometimes impresarios worked transnationally, like Max Glücksmann; see Jessica Stites Mor and Daniel Alex Richter, "Immigrant Cosmopolitanism: The Political Culture of Argentine Early Sound Cinema of the 1930s," *Latin American and Caribbean Ethnic Studies* 9, no. 1 (January 2, 2014): 65–88.

of popular music: born in Toulouse and raised in Buenos Aires, he combined folk and tango in his initial repertoire, then moved to Paris, filmed in New York and Buenos Aires, and died in a plane crash in Medellín in 1935 while touring Colombia.[45]

My modest contribution to the vast literature on tango is a reconstruction of the collective copyright startegy by a key group of tango composers. It suggests that for tango composers of the golden age, tango was *at the same time* their own local style, a language of cultural nationalism, and a global business, whose transnational deployment engaged them with audiences beyond the Río de la Plata. Here it is where Latin America appears only fragmentarily, as part of an even larger map.

A Union of Popular Music Composers

A society that protected the rights of a few theater authors in Buenos Aires had existed since 1895, and a larger number of artists were protected in 1910 by Law 7092, which established artistic, literary, and scientific works as intellectual property. In 1918, music composers organized independently from theater authors by forming the Sociedad Nacional de Autores, Compositores y Editores de Música. The founders were eleven tango composers, mostly native citizens of Italian descent, and a music publishing house, Breyer Brothers, which since 1885 had been an agent of Ricordi publishers in Milan, Italy (and would later be aqcuired by Ricordi in 1924). The goal of this society was to set a minimal monthly fee that commercial establishments— "cabarets, teatros, biógrafos, cafés, sociedades"—would pay for the use of members' songs. In April 1921 the Society expelled the publishers and became the Asociación Argentina de Autores y Compositores de Música (AAACM).[46] The association first adopted foreign standards: the person in charge of collecting the rights was the representative of the French association of authors and composers in Argentina, Oscar Ossotevsky (he was suceeded later on by his right-hand man, Mario Bénard.) In 1928 the association initiated a campaign for more effective copyright enforcement by pushing Congress to reform the old Law 7092.

In 1930 some of the most famous and successful tango composers broke away and created a new entity: Juan de Dios Filiberto, Carlos Gardel, Roberto Firpo, Francisco Canaro, Cátulo Castillo, and Enrique Santos Discépolo together founded the Círculo Argentino de Autores y Compositores de Música. Whereas some key composers remained in the Asociación—the Fresedo brothers, Alfredo Gobbi, Juan Carlos Cobián, and Vicente Greco—the new Círculo authors composed the large majority of the popular tango songs of the 1920s and 1930s. Between 1931 and 1936, agents from the two associations competed to collect copyright fees from theater owners who did not know which song belonged to whom. Because the Circle composed about 80% of

---

[45] Simon Collier, *The Life, Music, and Times of Carlos Gardel* (Pittsburgh: University of Pittsburgh Press, 1986).

[46] Jesús Martínez Moirón, *El mundo de los autores. Incluye la historia de S.A.D.A.I.C.* (Buenos Aires: Sampedro Ediciones, 1971), 44–48.

the most popular tangos and therefore had rights over about 80% of the repertoire of the *orquestas típicas*, the association chose instead to focus on the repertoire of jazz bands.

The Circle had a contract to represent United States American Society of Composers, Authors and Publishers (ASCAP) rights in Argentina and worked with representatives of equivalent societies in Spain, Italy, France, and Germany.[47] Regarding the expanding business of radio in the 1930s, it approached it as follows: Circle officers received lists of broadcast songs from the Argentine radio stations; they passed these lists along to each foreign representative, who would mark with a specific color the songs his society owned; and finally the Circle officers would mark off the songs the Circle owned. Under this unreliable system, representatives sometimes assigned a song's rights to the Italian society simply because its author had an Italian last name, when in fact its author was a New Yorker. Many rights were assigned based on guesses, on the Circle's inspectors' ability to recall the authorship of a musical piece—"our minds were the real archives of the repertoires," remembered a former inspector—and on economic interest, because the representatives received the payments first and distributed them to the associates in Argentina and abroad without any oversight.[48]

September 1933 was a watershed: the Congress passed the awaited Law 11.723, which gave both the Circle and the Association the effective means to collect copyright. Article 56, directly inspired by the Italian intellectual property legislation of November 1925 (under Fascism), extended the rights to performers as well, and protected any artist of any origin who recorded a music composition in the country.[49] The Circle soon promoted (unsuccessfuly) a similar law to be passed in neighboring Uruguay—it would take more than a decade for the Uruguayan Congress to pass it, in 1937.[50] The Argentine law was celebrated with a tango gala at the Teatro Colón that included a super-orchestra ("the largest *Orquesta Típica*[51] ever registered in the history of tango," according to composer and promoter of the law Francisco Canaro) composed of musicians from the best orchestras of the city and featuring a performance by the popular singer, composer, and actress Azucena Maizani. By making copyright enforcement more profitable for all composers and performing artists, the 1933 law led the Circle and the Association to combine in 1936 as the Sociedad Argentina de Autores, Intérpretes y Compositores de Música (SADAIC), which today still collects and distributes musical copyrights in Argentina.[52]

---

[47] Respectively: SGAE, SIAE, SACEM, and GEMA.

[48] Moirón, *El mundo de los autores*, 84–86.

[49] Vanessa Roghi, "Il dibattito sul diritto d'autore e la proprietà intellettuale nell'Italia Fascista," *Studi Storici* 48, no. 1 (January 1, 2007): 217–18.

[50] Francisco Canaro, *Mis bodas de oro con el tango y mis memorias*, 1906–1956 (Buenos Aires: CESA, 1957), 322.

[51] A name designing popular dance music band, with varying instruments in different countries throughout Latin America.

[52] Moirón, *El mundo de los autores*, 103 and Canaro, *Mis bodas de oro*, 322–23.

These were years of increased regulation of labor relations also in the realm of recorded music. Although the 1933 law was intended to protect the performers' rights, it in fact benefited the recording companies, who purchased the copyrights individually, in exchange for a one-time, up-front payment. In 1936 the new and strong SADAIC signed an agreement with the record makers (themselves unified under COMAR, Argentine Musical Corporation), to share equally in the performers' rights.[53] The *individual* legal right, which industrial companies had abused by making automatic purchases, now became a collectively negotiated right by which interpeters *as a group* benefited to the same degree as companies.

Composers and performers had always held a weak position in relation to publishers, as well. Authors traditionally received a few cents in exchange for the rights to the music sheets, transcribed by publishers at cafés and dancehalls, of musical pieces composed and performed without notation. It was not even good business for the publishers: since anyway performers illegally copied any song they liked, the publishers' consumer market was reduced to the families of girls who played piano at home. The 1933 law made it easier to police "records, radio, theaters, cabarets, boites, [and] cinemas," and both publishers and recording companies finally began to make money. Musicians gained as well, but to a much smaller degree. Canaro lamented that whereas in the United States and Europe the publisher paid the artist and then did the advertising and distributing of the work of art, in Argentina the artists sold their work first and then were still responsible for promoting it. Whereas in the US market a song was recorded and performed multiple times, in Argentina and other smaller markets, an artist's only choice was to pursue the prestige of being a work's first performer or recorder. There were no incentives to buy the rights to a song that had already been performed.[54]

What lay beyond this local market (the city of Buenos Aires) to these tango composers? In the 1930s and 1940s Argentina's national music market was in fact merely incipient. SADAIC's mission—protecting the rights of its members as music composers and performers—was defined, given the circumstances, locally and transnationally rather than nationally.

A Metropolitan and Transnational Strategy

In 1929, in the only surviving yearbook of the old AAACM I could find, its leaders listed their "tributary locals," from which the association collected its associates' copyrights. The list is a telling portrait of the commercial musical life of Argentina. That year the organization collected fees from 292 musical venues. 60% of them (174) were located in the city of Buenos Aires; 24% (70) in the province of Buenos Aires; 13% (37) in other provinces and national territories; and 3% (11) were in neighboring countries: Uruguay (7, of which 6 in Montevideo and one in Salto) and Chile (4)

---

[53] Canaro, *Mis bodas de oro*, 377.
[54] Ibid., 380–81.

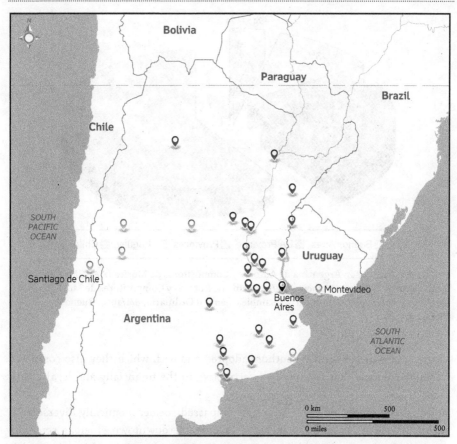

FIGURE 2.1 Asociación Argentina de Autores y Compositores de Música (AAACM) tributary locals, 1929 on Google Maps. The black pin (Buenos Aires metropolitan area) represents 75% of the total. The grey pins are cities generating a mid-size revenue. The light ones represent individual locals in smaller cities (not all of them are signaled). Source: Asociación Argentina de Autores y Compositores de Música. Memoria y Balance Presentado a la Asamblea General Ordinaria, 8/1/1929, Buenos Aires, 1929.

(see Figures 2.1 and 2.2). The metropolitan area—the City of Buenos Aires plus its contiguous sections in the province of Buenos Aires, such as Avellaneda—amounted to three-quarters of the tributary sites.

Within the city, 58% (102) of the locales were cinemas, located not just downtown but in virtually every neighborhood (this changed dramatically a few years later, with the transition from silent to sound film). The rest were cafés, bars, hotels, cabarets, restaurants, *confiterías*, and department stores (such as Harrods' and Gath & Chaves). The association thus collected at least 35% of its total revenue from cinemas—and probably more, since many of the tributary sites outside Buenos Aires were cinemas as well.[55] Some tributary locals were big and famous and also worked with foreign

---

[55] Asociación Argentina de Autores y Compositores de Música, *Memoria y Balance Presentado a la*

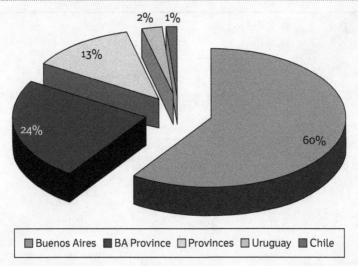

Buenos Aires ■ BA Province □ Provinces □ Uruguay ■ Chile

FIGURE 2.2 Asociación Argentina de Autores y Compositores de Música (AAACM) tributary locals per region. Source: Asociación Argentina de Autores y Compositores de Música. Memoria y Balance Presentado a la Asamblea General Ordinaria, 8/1/1929, Buenos Aires, 1929.

repertoires, which Argentine authors adopted and with which they also competed. Others were small but commercially attractive to the financially and legally weak association.

This mainly metropolitan market encompassed socioeconomically diverse audiences. Buenos Aires cinemas included fashionable downtown cinemas screening primarily foreign movies and charging more for tickets than the working-class neighborhood theaters, which screened primarily local films for an affordable ticket.[56] But the association's list of tributary locals did not distinguish between downtown and neighborhood cinemas, and did not specify the amount collected at each local. Some of these locals were outside the fancy downtown area, in the neighborhoods of Almagro, Flores, Boca, Saavedra, and Once, suggesting that any financial or aesthetic differences between *barrio* and *centro* did not influence the composers' strategy. Like working-class moviegoers, music listeners were likely to attend both downtown and neighborhood cinemas, depending on the occasion, their budget, and their changing status on the social ladder. In a heterogeneous and mobile city, it is hard to neatly distinguish a working-class or popular audience from a middle-class one. Buenos

---

Asamblea General Ordinaria, 1 de Agosto de 1929 (Buenos Aires: Asociación Argentina de Autores y Compositores de Música, 1929).

[56] Matthew Karush, *Culture of Class: Radio and Cinema in the Making of a Divided Argentina, 1920–1946* (Durham, NC: Duke University Press, 2012).

Aires workers were politically combative and autonomous as well as culturally open to mass entertainment.[57]

The culture of Buenos Aires and the *pampa húmeda*—the broader region of the agricultural export economy, demographic growth, and immigration—had undergone by 1930 several decades of three simultaneous processes of nationalization, creolization, and class formation. Nationalization began as a top-down, elite program of state policies, but rapidly became an extended reality through market and popular culture.[58] Creolization was a dialogue with a variety of cultural "others," both internal and foreign, out of which resulted a new culture identified as Argentine but infused by those multiple strands.[59] Working-class organizations and identity emerged stronger than anywhere else in Latin America and much of the world.[60] The three processes articulated in fascinating and changing ways. The culture of nationalism was deemed *criollo*, meaning "native," as opposed to both European and Indigenous, and was an avenue for foreigners to become Argentine. At the same time, labor organizations also *creolized* workers from multiple origins. Social mobility in this frontier of global capitalism was of course unevenly distributed, ethnically and chronologically speaking—some grandchildren of Basque or Italian farmers arrived in the 1860s accessed land and joined the old patrician class by the 1920s, whereas rural mestizos either remained in the lowest social strata or became at best urban administrative or professional class during the same period of time. But social mobility, consumerism, and educational levels were high enough to create a shared culture that celebrated a European (and increasingly US)-based modernity and capitalist advancement,[61] and at the samet time was infused by working-class cultural strands—the international culture of socialists and anarchists, and the rural culture of old criollos. The working-class critique of capitalism and social inequality made it to the big screen and to recordings in the 1920s and 1930s, through the rhetoric of melodrama.[62] And folklore and traditional rural symbols played an important role in the cultural history, often as countercultural weapons.[63] But at the same time, as in the rest of Latin America,

---

[57] Beatriz Sarlo, *El imperio de los sentimientos: narraciones de circulación periódica en la Argentina, 1917–1927* (Buenos Aires: Catálogos Editora, 1985).

[58] William G. Acree, *Everyday Reading: Print Culture and Collective Identity in the Río de La Plata, 1780–1910* (Nashville: Vanderbilt University Press, 2011).

[59] Sergio Pujol, *Las canciones del inmigrante: Buenos Aires, espectáculo musical y proceso inmigratorio : de 1914 a nuestros días* (Buenos Aires: Editorial Almagesto, 1989) and Eduardo Archetti, "Nationalisme, football et polo: tradition et créolisation dans la construction de l'Argentine moderne," *Terrain : carnets du patrimoine ethnologique* 25 (1995): 73–90.

[60] Julio Godio, *Historia del movimiento obrero latinoamericano* (San José, Costa Rica: Editorial Nueva Sociedad, 1987) and *Historia del movimiento obrero argentino: 1870–2000* (Buenos Aires: Corregidor, 2000).

[61] Ezequiel Adamovsky, *Historia de la clase media argentina: apogeo y decadencia de una ilusión, 1919–2003* (Buenos Aires: Planeta, 2015).

[62] Karush, *Culture of Class.*

[63] Ezequiel Adamovsky, "La cuarta función del criollismo y las luchas por la definición del origen y el color del ethnos argentino (desde las primeras novelas gauchescas hasta c. 1940)," *Boletín del Instituto de Historia Argentina y Americana Dr. Emilio Ravignani*, no. 41 (December 2014): 50–92.

melodrama and mass entertainment encompassed both the critique of modern urban capitalism and its rosy celebration—hence its appeal.[64] The ability to contradictorily showcase separation and unity in changing societes turned modern cultural production, like literature and cinema, into truly mythical devices.[65]

But for the Association composers, in the top ranks of the popular music scene, professional organization and aesthetic quality always prevailed over any class or nationalist concern. They adopted nationalist and folkloric rhetorics only reticently, and late, under the legal and economic coercion of government officials in the conservative 1930s. Tango composers followed a strictly corporatist strategy: they organized themselves to collect revenue from all sorts of outlets and to track the spread of their repertoire. Any ideological messages conveyed by their music, was subordinated to the basic claim of being representative of what they called *the popular taste*.

Something similar happened among the top popular composers in Brazil, even if their market was less developed. Legal protection had been established only for a tiny elite of Brazilian authors in the early years of the Republic (1898), and Brazilian popular musicians did not unionize until the 1930s.[66] As late as 1937, "more than 90% of almost 2,800 registered artists and workers in Rio's theaters were white," leaving a larger number of ethnically diverse artists working at poorer venues unprotected by the law.[67] Elite composers worked with African musical "sources" (as if these were freely available and anonymous), while black composers had to fight legally for the rights to their music. But despite these constraints, many Afro-Brazilian popular musicians attained fame and success.[68] In 1922, after a tour in France, the popular samba star Pixinguinha declared to the press that his band Oito Batutas was "simply a group of modest but profoundly sincere artists, making heard the easy, unpretentious music of our popular songs."[69] Pixinguinha's words expressed both the expanding role of Black Brazilians in the music business and an awareness of being a medium of popular culture. His discovery of new music in France, and the opportunity to play "sincere" popular songs, were for Pixinguinha material aspects of music making more important than ethnic or political considerations. Upon that 1922 Parisian tour,

---

[64] Maricruz Castro and Robert McKee Irwin, *El cine mexicano "se impone": mercados internacionales y penetración cultural en la época dorada* (México: Universidad Nacional Autónoma de México, 2011).

[65] Claude Levi-Strauss, "The Structural Study of Myth," *Journal of American Folklore* 68, no. 270 (1955): 428–44.

[66] But there were city-based unions, such as the Sindicato Musical de Porto Alegre, founded in 1934. Immigration to the city was noticeable in their ranks: Italian, German, and Argentine musicians, among other nationalities, joined the majority of Brazilian ones. See Julia da Rosa Simões, "Na pauta da lei : trabalho, organização sindical e luta por direitos entre músicos porto-alegrenses (1934–1963)" (PhD diss., Universidade Federal do Rio Grande do Sul, 2016), 41.

[67] Marc Hertzman, "A Brazilian Counterweight: Music, Intellectual Property and the African Diaspora in Rio de Janeiro (1910s–1930s)," *Journal of Latin American Studies* 41, no. 4 (2009):709–12.

[68] José Ramos Tinhorão, *História social da música popular brasileira* (Lisboa: Editorial Caminho, 1990); Vianna, *The Mystery of Samba*; McCann, *Hello Hello Brazil*; Sandroni, *Feitiço Decente*; Hertzman, *Making Samba*.

[69] Hertzman, "A Brazilian Counterwight," 715.

Pixinguinha measured his success in terms of how much money the Oito Batutas collected, the number of orchestras that performed their songs throughout France upon their tour, the creative partnership with a French composer, and the fact the the French bourgeoisie and "aristocracy" learned and admired his Brazilian music. Interestingly, his "Brazilian" music was a series of "polcas, tangos, choros, *nordestina* music, and also samba," that is, a combination of regional and international music styles, played in the Oito Batutas way, intended and perceived as "Brazilian." The fluidity of the music genres of the time was striking: even the members of the same band had heterogeneous views and valued the music genres they played differently. So whereas Donga valorized the Afro-Bahia roots of samba, Pixinguinha dismissed them as "primitive" and simple; whereas the first celebrated samba, the other missed the old-fashioned choro that since 1914 had declined in favor of samba. The members of Oito Batutas also held conscious and diverse visions of themselves ethnically: they identified with diverse forms of black, mixed-race, and white racial selves, each in turn celebrating the African origins of the music they played but displaying different attitudes and strategies toward the different levels of racism they encountered in different professional milieux.[70] All musicians performed with an eye on their audiences' cultural and ethnic expectations—hence tango players dressed as gauchos, and Josephine Baker played in her 1929 Latin American tour at once the exotic, the Parisian, and the US modernity[71]—to foster their commercial interest. But the identity rhetoric of these Argentine and Brazilian popular artists was subordinated to their professional strategy.

In Buenos Aires, the association membership by 1929 included about 750 authors, nearly 400 of which participated regularly. They identified themselves as popular authors, not performers (grouped separately in the Argentine Association of Musicians), nor art musicians (who had formed the Argentine Society of Composers). Its leaders—Emilio Fresedo, José Razzano, Francisco Lomuto, Francisco Canaro, Julio de Caro, and Agustín Magaldi—were mostly native Argentines (and Uruguayans) of Italian heritage, and many had studied music at home as children. The overwhelming majority were men.

The association registered repertoire by 1929 reached 7,287 songs, which they classified into 91 styles. More than half were registered as tangos (4,107, or 56%). Jazz-related danceable music (fox-trots, shimmies, one-step, two-step, etc.) amounted to around 13%.

Around 18% could be categorized as "traditional," I lumped the *pasodobles, cuplés, zambas, canciones*, and *estilos* (between 150 and 350 songs each of them), and other styles of criollo or Spanish origins (18%). The rest are hard to group: almost 10%, for

---

[70] Luiza Mara Braga Martins, *Os Oito Batutas: história e música brasileira nos anos 1920* (Rio de Janeiro: Editora UFRJ, 2014), 144–51.

[71] Jason Borge, "The Portable Jazz Age: Josephine Baker's Tour of South American Cities (1929)," in *Urban Latin America: Images, Words, Flows and the Built Environment* (New York: Routledge, 2018), 127–41.

TABLE 2.1

Compositions By Members of the Argentine Association of Music Authors and
Composers by 1929 (Founded 1921), By Genre

Total	7287	
Tango	4107	56%
Traditional*	1343	18%
Jazz*	933	13%
Vals	663	9%
Others*	241	3%

*My encompassing categories (P.P.).

Source: Asociación Argentina de Autores y Compositores de Música, Memoria y Balance, p. 35.

instance, are works catalogued as *vals* (waltz), some of which may be tangos with a ¾ rhythm, whereas other may designate something different. Around 3% of the total represented an impressive variety: there were maxixes, *schotis, fados, cuecas, tarantelas*, can-can, *milongas*, polkas, *habaneras*, Basque songs, nocturnes, and a symphony (see Table 2.1).

The same musicians composed and performed in those different styles: tango pianist Francisco Lomuto, one of the association leaders, advertised his *Lomuto* orchestra services as "Jazz-Band y Típica," next to Pedro Maffia's advertisement of tango bandoneon lessons and direction of "grandes orquestas típicas y americanas."[72]

The association managed to create a small but hardworking body of inspectors to audit the accounts of theaters and venues where this music was performed. The revenue generated by theaters and cinema-theaters was much bigger than the one from strictly music concerts.[73] Downtown cinema-theater impresarios would pay up to four times more for the rights of foreign works, a "privilege of the foreign repertoire"[74] that had a minimal impact in more popular venues such as cabarets, and none at all at the Carnival celebrations.

The composers lamented this situation, particularly the strength of foreign competitors in Buenos Aires, but were thrilled by the success of their own repertoire abroad. As one member of the board put it:

The spread of our repertoire, slow and steady at the beginning, entered an era of notorious prosperity and absolute supremacy. In Spain, France, Germany, Brazil, Mexico, United States, etc., our music is executed at theaters, cinemas,

---

[72] *La Canción Moderna*, April 2, 1928.

[73] María Florencia Caudarella, *La necesidad del espectáculo: aspectos sociales del teatro porteño, 1918–1930* (Rosario, Argentina: Prohistoria, 2016), 30.

[74] Asociación Argentina de Autores y Compositores de Música, *Memoria y Balance*, 12.

bar cabarets, in a way that, besides being flattering to our authors, puts before us increased chances of collecting revenue.[75]

The system was clearly metropolitan. A comparison with the United States illuminates this fact: already in 1891 the Copyright Act gave organizations of composers and performers concentrated in New York a mechanism to collect income from a system that spanned a vast US national market, that was more important than foreign markets for US firms.[76] But the sheer size and density of Buenos Aires attracted most of the association's efforts, and from this metropolitan center they expanded into foreign and wealthy consumer markets *before* creating a national one.

The expansion abroad relied nonetheless on loosely controlled individuals and unpredictable local aesthetic tastes. Opportunities were usually individual and based on pesonal networking. For instance, in Paris in 1931 tango star Carlos Gardel met the man who would become his inseparable composing partner, Alfredo Le Pera, a former journalist then working as a translator, creating Spanish subtitles for French movies intended to be screened in Spanish-speaking markets (he also translated for United Artists, the US film company). He had been hired by Oscar Ossovetsky, the association manager, who in Buenos Aires collected royalties for French composers and in Paris collected royalties for Argentine compositions. Le Pera was recommended to Ossovetsky by his Buenos Aires successor, Mariano Hermoso. Both Ossovetsy, until his death in the mid 1920s, and Hermoso were reponsible for expanding the association's international grasp.[77]

AAACM built its strategy upon those personal networks. The association began to establish agreements with agents in foreign markets, granting them a percentage in exchange for collecting royalties for Argentine works. Its main handicap was that until the 1933 law it had no legal standing (*personería jurídica*) to collect the money and so was forced to repeatedly ask every affiliate individually, even those living far away, to give the association's lawyers legal permission to represent the affiliate's rights. But even under such constraints, by 1929 the association had managed to close a deal with a local agent in Brazil, was in the process of sealing another in Spain, and planned to further extend to what it considered the other four important markets: France, Mexico, Germany, and North America.

In 1928 the association made an agreement with a Brazilian agent who, as the exclusive legal representative of the authors, would receive 25% of the rights collected from the execution of AAACM affiliates' works anywhere in Brazil.[78] At the

---

[75] Ibid., 15–16.

[76] Suisman, *Selling Sounds*.

[77] On Ossovetsky, see Cadícamo, *La historia del tango*, 139 and Canaro, *Mis bodas de oro*, 312–313.

[78] Shortly afterward, the AAACM board realized that many Argentine publishers were also interested in collecting revenue in Brazil and had assigned their own representatives there. This created a legal dilemma in Buenos Aires: which representative was authorized to collect the rights—the publisher's or the association's?

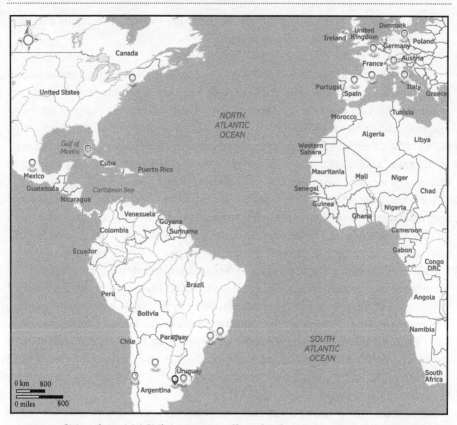

FIGURE 2.3 Cities where AAACM's inspectors collected rights. Source: Asociación Argentina de Autores y Compositores de Música. Memoria y Balance Presentado a la Asamblea General Ordinaria, 8/1/1929, Buenos Aires, 1929.

Pan American Peace Conference celebrated in Buenos Aires in 1936, the directors of the now unified SADAIC approached the Mexican representative to request that his government establish reciprocal copyright legislation to protect composers' and performers' artistic rights in both countries.[79] By 1950, SADAIC had regular interactions with equivalent societies in Brazil, Chile, Uruguay, and most European countries. In their exchanges with Mexico and Cuba, the amount received and sent was so asymmetrical that it raised suspicions in Argentina about how zealous their colleagues really were about collecting the rights of Argentine works. In the rest of Latin America there were no equivalent associations, nor legal frameworks to operate within, and the United States was not a member of the International Confederation and had a different way of organizing the field. This lack of an established system meant that

---

[79] Víctor Reyes, "Gestión formal de autores y compositores de América para asegurar su propiedad," *Excelsior*, February 12, 1937. Press Clips, AGBF.

the Argentines were still studying the issue to find the best way to proceed.[80] In sum, AAACM–SADAIC composers operated in a perpetually shifting and heterogeneous legal geography.

Within that geography, the AAACM's raison d'être, its "basic, fundamental function [. . .] the determining factor of its own existence, the main cause of its movement, the synthesis of its gremial goals, the reason for all its fights," was to collect the *pequeño derecho*, or performance right. Its interests thus followed the geography not of Argentina but of the songs: a cabaret in Rio de Janeiro and a club in Paris were more important commercially than most provincial theaters, even a few miles away from downtown Buenos Aires (see Figure 2.3). As a result, organized composers developed an economic strategy abroad without first promoting a national musical system domestically.

A Transnational Definition of Argentine Music

As tango composers developed strategies to profit from the nightlife and dance culture in Buenos Aires and many other cities abroad, a series of conservative groups took over the state after the coup of 1930, and government cultural officials became increasingly concerned about the cultural connotations of tango, especially its lyrics. Several official decrees and regulations limited musical expression on the airwaves of the Río de la Plata *lunfardo* urban poetry, so present in many tangos—a language that offered a meditation on, if not a praise of, vanity, criminality, and prostitution, which contrasted with the rural poetics of the folkloric repertoire that was on the rise in the 1930s. Especially between 1938 and the mid-1950s, nationalist administrations forced SADAIC to revise the aesthetic and moral grounds of song lyrics, their regulation, the internationalization of the musical scene, and the nationalization of music.

In August 1938, the conservative government of Roberto Ortiz established a censorship on the airwaves and threatened to close any stations that did not comply. SADAIC and several associations that had formed to protect radio artistic workers—including playwrights, writers, actors, and music performers—produced a public statement that offered three quite telling arguments. First, they argued that the aesthetic level of Argentine broadcasting was among the highest in the world because of the talented artists, "*both national and foreign*," enjoyed by the audiences. Second, they pointed out that censorship menaced the jobs of authors, composers, playwrights, musicians, and technicians, generating a "*social* problem." And third, quoting Herder, they argued that because "popular songs are *the living voice of the people and of humanity itself*," a legitimate government should not censor them.[81]

---

[80] *Crítica*, January 19, 1950, "SADAIC estudia un replanteo de sus relaciones internacionales," in Moirón, *El mundo de los autores*, 284–87.

[81] "En defensa del cancionero popular argentino," Revista Social de SADAIC (August 1938), in Moirón, *El mundo de los autores*, 429.

Three principles sustained thus both national and foreign music: the audiences' taste, professional interests, and popular legitimacy. Music was hence less a matter of national identity, than an aesthetic, labor, and political issue. Herder was astutely invoked in support of a universalist—"and of humanity itself"— defense of the Argentine artists against the censorship of popular lyrics. Like Jorge Luis Borges's *criollista* view of Argentine literature of the 1920s, SADAIC considered that music lyrics were made of "expressions,"

born certainly in the city streets, but then accepted at home because they did not bring any improper or mean resonance, but added instead a colorful note to ordinary conversation, or often put the necessary grain of salt on certain phrase, with irreplaceable expressivity.

Censors applied absurd regulations "through metaphysical reactions [. . .] by crossing-out with red ink the guilty and proscribed terms: 'God,' 'kisses,' 'love,' 'money . . .' 'Money,' yes!"[82] The "true Buenos Aires and Argentine popular songbook" (*cancionero*), with its references to money, God, and love, did not need any reform.

From an international perspective, SADAIC considered its repertoire "not inferior to any similar one in the world" and in some ways "superior to all the rest, because in a country so cosmopolitan, so eclectic in the way it looks and feels, it was natural for the people to bring to the songs most of their troubles." SADAIC took pride not in national identity, but in the attachement of Argentines to a repertoire that expressed their cosmopolitan views and concerns.

Against this cosmopolitan view, the traditionalist movement behind state censorship of music promoted a different *cancionero* intended to rescue the national Hispanist heritage and to "discover" an indigenous component in provincial and rural popular music.[83] By the late 1930s, this movement included projects of musicological archeology carried out by provincial intellectuals, along with a growing audience of radio listeners both in the provinces and among provincial migrants to Buenos Aires.[84] It also had several fervent Catholic promoters within the conservative cadres of the state office in charge of censoring the SADAIC repertoire.

SADAIC argued that the proven quality of the *porteño*-Argentine repertoire put its members—the best and truest composers—and not any state agent, in the position of deciding about the value of their music.

At the same time, SADAIC had to adopt chauvinistic and ethnocentric arguments to defend its music. For instance, it argued that censorship missed its target by letting

---

[82] Ibid.

[83] Andrea Alejandra Bocco, "Tensiones entre proyectos intelectuales, políticas estatales y emergencia de las masas en los cancioneros populares," *Anclajes* 13, no. 1 (June 2009): 27–40.

[84] Chamosa, *The Argentine Folklore Movement.*

foreign songs (those *"rumbas y marchiñas,"* i.e., Cuban and Brazilian music[85]) freely populate broadcasting, which ended up benefiting the "snobbism that admires the argot of the Apache and the twisted slang (*zurda jerigonza*) of the mulattos [. . .] born under the sketchy bridges of the Seine or in smelly and slimy attics" (*bajo tenebrosos puentes del Sena o en zaquizamíes malolientes y pringados*).[86] In other words, street music is good only when it is a Buenos Aires street and not a Parisian or Rio de Janeiro one. These remarks coexisted with SADAIC's usual praise of international standards as measures of local production. They were a reaction against what SADAIC perceived as an unfair attack on local production that left untouched trendy foreign tunes, be they African American, Parisian, Afro-Cuban, or Afro-Brazilian. Again, politics and economics foisted a national strategy on musicians who were actually thoroughly transnational in their musical practice.

Interestignly, the airwaves showed, to the contrary, a *convergence* of local and foreign musical streams. For example, the programming of Radio LS11 in 1938 categorized music segments by *type* rather than origin, in contrast with older practices in the record business of the 1920s (for instance, both Victor and Odeon segmented their offerings into Argentine and foreign categories), and with radio ads of the 1930s that used code words to distinguish Argentine origin (*orquesta típica*, for example) from foreign music.[87] Radio LS11 devoted many hours to "música ligera" and "música popular" and, in a second tier, "música selecta" and "música folklórica," and finally "bailables," "ópera," and selections of "singers" and "operetas."[88] And this was an official station promoted by a leading figure of popular conservatism, the governor of the Buenos Aires Province, Manuel Fresco.[89]

Radio LS11 was targeting the booming population of Greater Buenos Aires, a convergence of immigrant and criollo traditions as a result of a growing migration from poorer provinces and regions. Cosmopolitan and tradional repertoires converged as well in 1938 when the first national broadcasting system, Radio Belgrano, was launched with its headquarters in Buenos Aires. Radio *El Mundo* and Radio *Splendid* followed in 1940, although it took them several years to incorporate affiliate stations outside Buenos Aires.[90] A golden age of tango coincided with the conversion of

---

[85] Or perhaps Chilean: several rumbas were composed in Chile in the 1930s. See Juan Pablo González, "El trópico baja al sur: llegada y asimilación de música cubana en Chile, 1930–1960," *Boletín de Música Casa de Las Américas*, no. 11–12 (2003): 3–18, 10.

[86] Moirón, *El mundo de los autores*, 430.

[87] Luis Adolfo Sierra, *Historia de la Orquesta Típica: evolución instrumental del tango* (Buenos Aires: Corregidor, 1985) [1976]; Cañardo, *Fábricas de música*; and Karush, *Culture of class.*

[88] Noelia Fernández, "'Hablando con el pueblo'. La creación de LS 11 bajo la gestión de Manuel Fresco en la provincia de Buenos Aires, 1936–1940," *Question* 1, no. 38 (June 28, 2013): 67–80, esp. Cuadro 1.

[89] In those years music occupied about half the broadcasting time. More precisely, it fell from 60% to 40% between the late 1930s and the mid-1940s. See Andrea Matallana, *Locos por la radio: una historia social de la radiofonía en la Argentina, 1923–1947* (Buenos Aires: Prometeo, 2006), 101.

[90] Matallana, *Locos por la radio.* Another sign of the centralization of the entertainment world was that SADAIC began to establish provincial branches only in 1944 (Rosario, Santa Fé, Córdoba, La Plata, Mar del Plata, and Bahía Blanca; in 1945 added Mercedes, in 1950 a Cuyo office in charge of

folklore into a legitimate field not only on the radio but at universities, conservatories, and research institutes.

SADAIC had to adapt to tighter regulations on language brought by the June 1943 military coup d'état and its authoritarian traditionalism. Inspired by an understanding of folklore as a rural and traditional symbol of the nation, the new regulations treated urban music as a threat to the national spirit because of its foreign and immoral origins. SADAIC leadership astutely responded by defining urban popular music as folklore.

Popular urban music was, SADAIC leaders argued, a continuation of longstanding folkloric traditions of Spanish and *criollo* theater, poetry, and music, ranging from (Spanish modernist writer) "García Lorca's Gypsy motifs" to "the gauchesco, regional and folkloric." According to them, authorities in fact had gone too far: if they applied their own standards strictly, they would have rejected even *Martín Fierro*, the gaucho epic and national symbol, since, as nationalist intellectual Ricardo Rojas had noted, it was certainly not "academically correct." SADAIC offered to do the censorship themselves under government guidelines. This, they argued, would avoid the risk of turning the task over to "people alien to literature." Concretely, they wanted to control the advisory commission in charge of overseeing radio broadcasting—a shift that would also have allowed SADAIC leadership to regulate access to the airwaves.[91]

The case of SADAIC suggests two important insights to understand the history of modern music in Argentina and in Latin America. First, musicians were concerned above all with giving their audiences good music, improving their own labor and economic interests, and promoting their prestige locally and abroad; fostering a national or ethnic identity was secondary, if it was even a goal at all. Second, cultural nationalism, far from emerging from audiences and from the music establishment, was rather both a matter of bureaucratic and culture wars initiated by conservative policymakers, and also a structural response to the transnational music business.[92]

When Peronism came on the scene, SADAIC readapted once again its aesthetic, labor, and economic concerns to the new official rhetoric, but it did not need to modify its populist ideology—that music belongs to, expresses, and serves *the people*.

Peronism and the Problem of the National Culture

Restrictions on certain uses of language in broadcasting, based on moral standards defined by state personnel, remained in effect under the democratic government of

---

Mendoza, San Juan and San Luis, and one in Corrientes as late as 1963). Moirón, *El Mundo de los autores*, 499–509.

[91] Moirón, *El mundo de los autores*, 434–35.

[92] These culture wars included, for instance, the military regime's creation of a "Commision on Folklore and Nativism" that allowed the regime to influence public education. Ataliva Herrera and Consejo Nacional de Educación, *Folklore y nativismo en la enseñanza primaria: resolución del Consejo Nacional de Educación creando la Comisión de Folklore y Nativismo* (República Argentina: Consejo Nacional de Educación, 1945).

General Juan Perón since 1946. SADAIC adopted the official rhetoric of an "Argentine soul" and the idea of music and poetry as "folkloric tradition" and "heritage." But this meant defending tango as "traditional music," as if it were folklore: the argument was that it had emotionally touched several generations of Argentines.[93] And in arguing for freedom from excessive regulation, SADAIC kept promoting the acceptance of popular parlance, and invoked Perón's statement that if everyday language had been suppressed, "we would all still speak Latin."

SADAIC also began to police itself to avoid confronting the Sub-Secretary of Information and Press (SSIP). The military government had created this office in 1943, acquired the radio stations Belgrano, Splendid, and El Mundo, and submitted all programming to the SSIP inspectors. In 1949 Perón suspended official censorship after a meeting with the SADAIC directors, which in exchange began to practice an informal self-policing, blocking lyrics that could compromise its public image of moral correctness, gaining in exchange a relative degree of autonomy.

But this was a culture war and on the very last day of 1949 Perón issued Decree 33.711 on "the Safeguarding of National Music." One of the clauses transferred censorship authority from SADAIC back to state functionaries, but SADAIC managed to force a personal intervention by Perón to reverse this part of the decree. Another part of the decree was left untouched: the government policy on "national music," which ruled that 50% of *any* public musical supply had to be national and threatened to close any public establishment that did not comply—"broadcasters, booster stations, loud-speaker trucks or automobiles, restaurants, *confiterías*, cafés, 'boites,' 'cabarets,' stores, salons, or dancing clubs" with live music, varieties, orchestras, phonographs, or singing, with our without instruments. "National" was widely defined as "everything classified as autochthonous, traditional, or criollo, including tangos, waltzes, rancheras, milongas and other popular music of national authors."[94] SADAIC authors had been composing in these genres since the 1920s and applauded the spirit of the measure.

The decree also specified that national music was "any composition *of Argentine or foreign resident authors, that interprets the musical feelings of the Argentine people or Argentine traditions, excluding those works whose genre or rhythm is foreign*."[95] The menaces, thus, were not foreign *compositions*, but *musical genres and rhythms*. This rule fostered the popularity of folklore in the airwaves, and also opened the door to traditionalists who had been promoting folklore from universities, conservatories, and the ministry of culture. The National Institute of Musicology had been created in 1944 by the country's first "scientific" folklorist, Carlos Vega (his 1944 *Panorama de la música argentina* included an "Essay on the Science of Folklore"), and in 1949 a new radio station, increasingly associated with Perón, promoted folklore as a national symbol.

---

[93] "Para que los tangos guarden el debido equilibrio, ni restricciones ni licencia reclama la canción popular," *Noticias Gráficas*, March 26, 1949, in Moirón, *El mundo de los autores*, 442.

[94] Boletín Oficial de la República Argentina, January 12, 1950.

[95] In Moiron, *El mundo de los autores*, 283.

Buenaventura Luna and many other folklore singers and composers became popular in Buenos Aires broadcasting and entertainment by promoting mestizo (criollo) and indigenous traditions from the provinces through "folkloric" (though composed by them) songs, in an aesthetic and identitarian discourse opposed to Europe and modernity. This folkloric nationalism was rooted in Argentina's Northwest, but on some occasions, artists presented it as indigenous to the Andes and even to the larger "Nuestra América." Interestingly, some of these artists were descendents of Irish and Italian immigrants and came from well-off families, but their ideological and aesthetic connection to the "Andean roots" and with "the people" or the oppressed classes led them to a social and political critique of inequality that led them to converge with Perón's government.[96]

The decree thus forced SADAIC to control the *musical origins* of its repertoire. Argentine musicians used to compose "foreign" boogies or boleros precisely because they resonated with the "feelings of the Argentine people"—like foreign artists who made money by composing tangos to markets abroad for the exact same reason, or like folklorists on Buenos Aires' commercial airwaves, who appealed to urbanites with the invocation of the spectral archetype of a downtrodden and defeated mestizo rural population. The metropolis was hence animated by all sorts of popular forms of "otherness" and aesthetic inclinations.

In a professional sense, however, the effects of Peronism were beneficial for composers and SADAIC's corporatist strategy. In 1943 it inaugurated its own mausoleum at the city's main cemetery, and in 1946 its leaders participated in the XIV International Congress of Authors at the Library of Congress in Washington, DC, where they lobbied to organize the next meeting in Buenos Aires, having obtained full financial and political support from Perón. During that trip SADAIC leadership strengthened agreements with its partner associations in the United States, Mexico, and Cuba.[97]

Francisco Canaro recalled meetings in Buenos Aires, Havana, Los Angeles, New York, Washington, DC, and Mexico City that included legal and economic conversations as well as artistic fraternity among colleagues. Canaro describes encounters with Argentine artists who were touring those cities, such as Paulina Singerman, who was working in Cuba, and with foreign stars, such as Irving Berlin, Marlene Dietrich, and Agustín Lara; as well as shows by Paul Whiteman. These were events of comradeship and opportunities to consolidate personal bonds and international partnerships. At a private lunch in New York, SADAIC representatives met the czar of the Mexican broadcasting business, Emilio Azcárraga ("sort of our Yankelevich,"

[96] Tânia da Costa Garcia, "Mundo Radial e o cancioneiro folclórico nos tempos de Perón," *Nuevo Mundo Mundos Nuevos—Nouveaux mondes mondes nouveaux—Novo Mundo Mundos Novos—New World New Worlds*, dossier "Musique et politique en Amérique Latine, XXe-XXIe siècles," June 11, 2015; Ezequiel Adamovsky, "Criollismo, política y etnicidad en las ideas y el folklore de Eusebio Dojorti (Buenaventura Luna)," *Studies in Latin American Popular Culture* 34, no. 1 (2016): esp. 258–59.

[97] Canaro, *Mis bodas de oro*, 329–45.

Canaro says, referring to the Argentine radio mogul). These connections served to consolidate the association's foreign income and institutional power. The case of Cuba offered to him a telling counterpoint: divided into three independent and weak associations, Cuban composers and performers were subordinated to a handful of foreign music publishers who sold the artists' work in Cuba and abroad without redistributing the profit.[98]

In 1948 SADAIC, together with ARGENTORES (Argentine Association of Writers), hosted the XV Congress of the International Confederation of Authors in Buenos Aires. In his inaugural speech Canaro stated the association's "vows for the worldwide unification of Intellectual Property, turning creativity into one common fatherland."[99] President Perón expressed his support of "the universal recognition of the rights of the intellectual worker" at another meeting, while the association was trying to make Argentina sign the Berne Convention for the Protection of Literary and Artistic Works and at the same time promoting the Pan American Council. Canaro wrote a letter to Brazilian composer and state music organizer Heitor Villa-Lobos, inviting him to come to Buenos Aires; he wrote,

> It will be the first time that, on Iberian-American soil, representatives from the Confederation and from all the authorial societies of the world will meet to consider the serious issues that, regarding authorial rights, concern all of us in order to improve the social and economic condition of the intellectual creators.[100]

Peronism's understanding of musicians as nationally and internationally organized workers was a natural consequence of its labor corporatism—an ideology that was also expressed in its global labor diplomacy.[101] It also produced its own understanding of Latin Americanism, in the cultural magazine *Sexto Continente*.[102]

Self-policing worsened in March 1952, when SADAIC's Commission of Artistic Affairs published a list of banned songs, calling their composers "a minority of seekers of easy success, responding to the suspicious demand of a certain part of the audience" still drawn to the vulgar slang of a bygone Buenos Aires.[103] The everyday language of the Argentines that SADAIC had praised a few years before was now rejected in the name of an abstract and conservative Argentine soul. And yet in 1953

---

[98] Canaro, *Mis bodas de oro*, 340 and 344.

[99] "También hago votos para que se unifique en el mundo el Código de Derecho de Autor, haciendo de la creación una sola patria." Canaro, *Mis bodas de oro*, 353.

[100] Letter from Francisco Canaro to Heitor Villa Lobos, June 4, 1948, AHVL.

[101] Ernesto Semán, *Ambassadors of the Working Class: Argentina's International Labor Activists and Cold War Democracy in the Americas* (Durham, NC: Duke University Press, 2017).

[102] Daniel Sazbón, "Sexto Continente: una apuesta por una Tercera Posición latinoamericanista en la cultura peronista," in *Polémicas intelectuales, debates políticos. Las revistas culturales en el siglo XX*, dir. Leticia Prislei (Buenos Aires: Facultad de Filosofía y Letras, Colección Cátedra, 2015), 149–91.

[103] SADAIC, "Informe de la Comisión de Asuntos Artísticos," March 4, 1952, in Moirón, *El mundo de los autores*, 443–44.

José Gobello published his *Lunfardía*, an erudite vindication in folkloric terms of the Rio de la Plata slang featured in many tangos. In fact, the issue of the "national language" SADAIC had to navigate had been debated for decades at this point—is it in Argentina's Iberian roots, its traditional folklore, or its immigrant-inflected Spanish? Nationalism was debated in those terms—respectively Hispanist, traditionalist, and modernist. But none included an explicit relationship with Latin America.[104]

The world of tango in Argentina slowly became inward-looking and nationalist. When a Latin Americanist perspective re-emerged in Argentine music in the 1960s, it centered on folklore, not tango. The 1963 Argentine "New Songbook," by an explictely Latin American-oriented, avant-garde group of popular musicians, recovered neither lunfardo nor tango, but a rural-based folkloric poetry.[105]

But tango had in fact been incorporated to a regional Latin Americanist repertoire. Not in Argentina, but in the US-backed Mexican broadcasting enterprise XEW, which had significant resources and an ambitious scope: to become "the Voice of Latin America."

US–MEXICAN BROADCASTING AND THE BIRTH OF COMMERCIAL MUSICAL LATIN AMERICANISM

Our fourth and final transnational case developed in Mexico, where the Revolutionary State made room for Latin America in its cultural initiatives: in 1920 the National University (UNAM) adopted its current seal, in which, as instructed by Rector José Vasconelos, an Andean condor and a Mexican eagle, standing on volcanos and "Aztec nopales," protect a region referred to as both "gran patria Hispano-Americana" and "América Latina."[106] When commercial radio took off in Mexico ten years later, it also had an explicitly Latin American musical repertoire at its center. As I will show, this was a result of the aesthetic openess of musicians and audiences and of a business strategy built upon them.

[104] Mara Glozman and Daniela Lauría, eds, *Voces y ecos: una antología de los debates sobre la lengua nacional (Argentina, 1900–2000)* (Buenos Aires: Cabiria, 2012); Mara Glozman, "Corporativismo, política cultural y regulación lingüística: la creación de la Academia Argentina de Letras," *Revista Lenguaje* 41, no. 2 (May 12, 2013): 455–78; "Combatir y conservar: posiciones y saberes sobre el lenguaje popular en los Boletines de la Academia Argentina de Letras (1933–1943)," *Gragoatá* 17, no. 32 (June 30, 2012): 227–45; and "Lenguas, variedades y filología en los discursos estatales (1946–1947): entre la comunidad hispánica y la identidad nacional," *Actas de las Primeras Jornadas Interdisciplinarias: Lenguas, Identidad e Ideologías, Facultad de Filosofía y Letras, Universidad de Tucumán* (2006): 52–61.

[105] Karush, *Musicians in transit*, chapter 5.

[106] Adalberto Santana, "Bicentenario de la independencia, centenario de la Revolución Mexicana y de la UNAM," *Archipiélago. Revista cultural de nuestra América* 18, no. 68 (2010): 15.

Weak Unions

The main drivers of Mexico's musical life were the impresarios, not the musicians. "Working associations and unions, not organized and strong enough to balance their members' interests with the law of supply and demand, instead of broadening up the economic opportunities for its members, remain passive," wrote Estanislao Mejía, director of the University's Facultad de Música, in August 1933. Labor legislation only benefited a tiny elite of musicians. Unions failed to gain state help to "guarantee the rights of a noble and useful profession, so necessary to the education of the masses." For Mejía, "the problems of the Mexican musician got worse with the introduction of the radio," which encouraged unpaid work and other abuses, and whose corny songs attacked "the musical soul of the Mexican race" (*el alma musical de la raza*).[107] In Germany, he argued, taxes supported radio stations that broadcast orchestras and choirs "that elevate the spirit of the people, dismissing the cheesy and hollow songs," and performers were paid and copyright was enforced every time a composition was performed. German radio was also a meritocracy: it favored talented composers and performers with decent incomes and excluded mediocre artists. The Mexican state should follow the German example, he argued, and force every musical organization to expand musical education, help organize musicians, and favor "good music"— "good" in a universal sense, and good for Mexican listeners. Unions, Mejía argued, should request a law from Congress to protect musicians' rights to organize and to a decent income.

Mexico City musicians worked at orchestras, military bands, "orquestas típicas" and "orquestas de jazz," as well as at a variety of small "hybrid orchestras" of the entertaining world, and others pejoratively called "amateurs" and also "músicos de arrabal"—with the disdainful connotation of "coming from the city borders"—which were hired by radios and downtown cabarets, and sometimes made more money than conservatory-trained musicians. As a whole, musicians had been unable to set up a collective system that would benefit both employed and unemployed musicians, as a few years later musicologist Gerónimo Baqueiro Foster explained in a series of newspaper articles.[108]

The old Sindicato de Músicos (SM) had been up until the 1920s one of the strongest unions within Mexico's national unified union CROM, representing musicians from symphonic orchestras, churches, restaurants, cabarets, and especially cinema theaters, which used to hire up to three orchestras each. But in the 1930s, as sound films replaced silent ones, cinema theaters began firing their orchestras. Each time a theater owner offered to keep an orchestra for a lower salary, the SM refused to

---

[107] Estanislao Mejía, Director de la Facultad de Música, "La crisis del gremio musical," *El Universal*, August 11, 1933, Mexico City, Press Clips, AGBF.

[108] "La música y los músicos entre bastidores: Sindicato de Músicos, Unión Filarmónica, Sindicato de Filarmónicos, Sindicatos Blancos y Unión de Músicos Libres," I, II & III. April 16 and 23, and May 14, 1936, Mexico City. Manuscripts, AGBF. These are Gerónimo Baqueiro Foster's original articles to be published in *El Universal Ilustrado*; the date and content could have been modified by the newspaper.

negotiate, and musicians ended up accepting a lower salary under the table to keep their jobs.[109] Another union split from the SM, the Unión de Filarmónicos (UF), led by directors of theater orchestras who worked in zarzuelas, operettas, "bataclán," variety shows, and later, radio. The UF organized cooperative groups in association with theater impresarios and music directors of other commercial entertainment, such as radio stations, cabarets, restaurants, and carpas, as well as churches. Income was barely decent for regular members, but quite high for the leadership, on a level with the state bureaucrats and members of the political establishment. The SM remained composed by the members of the National Symphonic Orchestra and sustained by the state budget, intended precisely to save its members from the allure of the "caimans," impresarios and orchestra managers from radio stations, cabarets, and some restaurants, who hired these highly skilled artists to perform in lowbrow settings.

According to Baqueiro Foster, the leadership of both unions also blocked attempts to create zarzuela and opera companies of unemployed musicians. In sum, intransigency, corruption, and strife between SM and UF weakened musicians' labor rights and benefited opportunistic "formadores de orquestas" and caimans. Musicians shifted between both organizations and even worked as "free musicians," pushing salaries down. With low salaries, bad musicians earned the same income as good ones, and the overall consequence was that impresarios got the lion's share of the music business.

Radios thrived in this context. The UF worked in association with company-controlled union sections "whose offices are in the radio stations, very close to the offices of the administrators and directives." Radio managers were thus able to keep their own artistic payrolls virtually free from union interference.[110] The UF became a bureaucratic caste ruling a series of cooperatives of impoverished musicians who performed under business control. The expansion of commercial entertainment benefited only an elite of composers, directors, and arrangers with personal ties with the impresarios. Both amateur and classically trained musicians ready to work for low salaries at radio stations fostered cross-pollination of musical styles and origins, but endured a poor income.

Inequality was the norm. Musicians in orchestras "like Riestra, Curiel, Girón, Carter, Rosales and many others," in some cases were "paid in dollars and make in one week what the concertmaster or any member of the Symphonic Orchestra" made in a month, on top of having weekly rest days and professional training. Others managed some income, such as the "80 professors with minimum salary at the Symphonic

---

[109] Mexican newspapers published worrisome articles in these years about the decline in jobs for musicians at cinemas in Spain due to sound movies. For instance in Málaga, theater owners refused to increase ticket values by a few cents to sustain an orchestra that would play during intermissions, instead offering the hall to any musician willing to perform for tips. El Nacional, January 16, 1935, Press Clips, AGBF.

[110] According to Baqueiro Foster, by 1936 the Frente Unico de Músicos de Orquesta (FUMO) was the only real alternative for the musicians' interests.

Orchestra" that were the core of the SM, and the "the 35 or 40 individuals behind the music stands of the reduced and poorly paid theater orchestras" represented by the UF. Some musicians chose to form new, smaller unions. But the large majority of musicians was unprotected and poorly paid by prosperous caimans and impresarios.

Of all the actors in the internationalization of Mexico City's music scene, it was not the musicians, but the radio impresarios, the ones who produced an explicit Latin Americanist discourse.

Mexican Broadcasting in the Thirties

An American scholar of the National Broadcasting Company pointed out in 1940 that Mexican radio, unlike France, England, and the United States, "knew no child-hood": its early years were marked by strong state regulation because the 1917 Constitution gave the federal government control of radio-telegraphic services.[111] Later, several laws and decrees, especially the 1931 Radio Law, prohibited granting licenses to foreign individuals and firms and using radio for announcing political or religious activities. Inter-American conferences in this period also advocated for state regulation, a position rejected only in the United States, where amateur and experimental broadcasting were followed by massive commercial radio stations managed by private firms.[112]

The roles of state and private firms in broadcasting were debated throughout the world. In 1940, Barbour identified at least four model systems for managing broadcasting: the American, in which broadcasting companies were owned and operated privately; the Italian, which featured just one company licensed by the government; the Japanese, in which the government managed different stations; and the Mexican, which included both state and (licensed) private stations, all strongly regulated by the government.[113] In the case of Mexico, regulation was intended to control the expansion of American private interests in broadcasting, which were seen since the 1920s as a threat to the Mexican state. To further counter that threat, presidents Carranza and Obregón set up a Mexican-Central American network of radio stations, expanding infrastructure first to El Salvador and then to Costa Rica, Guatemala, Honduras, and Nicaragua, using German technology developed by the pioneer broadcasting company Telefunken. Throughout the 1920s, Central Americans listened to Mexican programming of music, advertisements, and health campaigns, instead of just the radio stations owned by the US company United Fruit.[114] This combination of private

---

[111] Philip Barbour, "Commercial and Cultural Broadcasting in Mexico," *Annals of the American Academy of Political and Social Science* 208 (March 1, 1940): 94–95.

[112] Arthur Scharfeld, "The Mexican Broadcasting Situation," *Journal of Radio Law* 1, no. 2 (July 1931): 193; James Schwoch, *The American Radio Industry and Its Latin American Activities, 1900–1939* (Urbana: University of Illinois Press, 1990), chapter 3.

[113] Barbour, "Commercial and Cultural Broadcasting," 95.

[114] J. Justin Castro, *Radio in Revolution: Wireless Technology and State Power in Mexico, 1897–1938* (Lincoln: University of Nebraska Press, 2016), 123–27.

and state stations was at odds with the entirely commercial model of the United States, which was rejected at the 1924 Inter American Committee on Electronic Communications held in Mexico City by all the other countries in favor of state regulations of the airwaves. But no hemispheric regulatory framework emerged from this conference, evidencing both the inability of US commercial interests to hegemonoize the region, and the impossibility of building an inter-American system contrary to them.

Hence Mexico developed a hybrid radio system in which US interests were mediated by a local businessman, creating a consequential and "tumultuous relationship between the state and the Azcárraga family that has survived into the twenty-first century," under the constant pressure of US companies.[115]

The main state network in the 1920s was the Secretary of Public Education (SEP) educational radio, which included indigenous music as well as jazz bands and the Yucatan bolero star Guty Cárdenas. "When educators brought the receivers to villages, the community usually put on a large celebration. In Acatlán, Puebla, one such party included orchestral performances, poem recitations, a tango, inauguration speeches by community leaders, an address by SEP zone inspector . . ., and lastly, listening to the radio."[116]

But in the 1930s the dominant station was XEW, through which US radio companies expanded their exports of radio receivers, precisely when the National Broadcasting Corporation (NBC) and the Columbia Broadcasting System (CBS) started broadcasting commercially in Spanish and Portuguese for Latin America.[117]

In Mexico, as in Argentina, cultural concerns shaped regulatory frameworks. In 1937 a regulation went into effect limiting radio stations to a maximum of two minutes of continuous advertisement without the transmission of a musical piece and requiring that "every program must contain at least 25% of *typically Mexican music*"— not just music of "Mexican authorship," because according to the Department of Communications, "not all our authors create *typically Mexican* music."[118]

That same year, the *Departamento Autónomo de Prensa y Publicidad* (DAPP) began broadcasting its cultural and educational transmissions through an official station. As Barbour shows in his analysis of DAPP archives for the period 1937–1939, the president's suggestion of a "National Hour" program was established for all broadcasters for Sunday evenings, and many radio programs on national issues were transmitted throughout the country, some of them including music. Some of these programs were produced through collaboration between the Mexican government and American

---

[115] Ibid., 106.

[116] Ibid., 168–69.

[117] Fernando Mejía Barquera, *La industria de la radio y la televisión y la política del estado mexicano* (México, D.F.: Fundación Manuel Buendía, 1989), 51–53; Roderick Deihl, "South of the Border: The NBC and CBS Radio Networks and the Latin American Venture, 1930–1942," *Communication Quarterly* Communication Quarterly 25, no. 4 (1977): 2–12.

[118] Barbour, "Commercial and Cultural Broadcasting," 96–97.

foundations and universities. Hence, Mexican regulators applied similar rules to the ones their Argentine colleagues would apply soon after, although the interests of American firms and relatively weaker local production probably explain why the national music requirement was set at 25% and not 50%. The National Hour was contemporaneous to an identical Brazilian program enforced by radio regulators under the *Estado Novo*. But unlike Brazilians and Argentines, Mexican regulators accepted the collaboration of US cultural initiatives as a means of "elevating" broadcasting's aesthetic level.

Compared with Brazil and Argentina, Mexican broadcasting was much more strongly regulated by the state almost from its beginning. State educational radio stations in the 1920s and 1930s is proof of this, as is the 1937 national content policy requiring private broadcasters to promote the national identity. Nationalism was above all due to "the unique role that radio broadcasting played in a country of historically isolated localities and regions" and therefore to the fact that "the government [investment] in radio as a powerful new medium for building national identity and allegiance."[119]

State policies' definition of "Mexican" music originated among composers and intellectuals-cum-bureaucrats.[120] As Minister of Education in the early 1920s, José Vasconcelos had raised the issue of the importance of state-sponsored musical education by compiling and diffusing folk music under the idea of musical *criollismo*. This project was partially inspired by the musical proposals of the *Ateneo de la Juventud* in 1913, during the violent phase of the revolution. In 1925, composer Carlos Chávez—who in 1934 would become the head of the Department of Fine Arts in the Ministry of Public Education—proclaimed the Indo-Spanish identity of Latin American music. (This was just one year after the Argentine nationalist writer Ricardo Rojas advanced the idea of the American arts as a convergence of indigenous and European forms in *Eurindia*.)[121] In September 1926, the newspaper *El Universal* sponsored the First National Congress of Music in Mexico City. Various generations of Mexican composers and arrangers debated the modernization and definition of "national music." The debate was limited to art music, with folk music considered valuable mainly as source for erudite translation into the musical language of Europe. But the interrogation of popular musical traditions became a truly "public discussion."[122] This recognition of a specific Mexican folk music tradition was fundamental to the establishment of the

---

[119] Joy Elizabeth Hayes, "National Imaginings on the Air: Radio in Mexico, 1920–1950," in *The Eagle and the Virgin*, ed. Mary K. Vaughan and Stephen E. Lewis (Durham, NC: Duke University Press, 2006), 243–58; Gilbert M. Joseph and Daniel Nugent, "Popular Culture and State Formation in Revolutionary Mexico," in *Everyday Forms of State Formation: Revolution and the Negotiation of Rule in Modern Mexico*, eds. Gilbert M. Joseph and Daniel Nugent (Durham, NC: Duke University Press, 1994), 244.

[120] Alejandro Madrid, "The Sounds of the Nation: Visions of Modernity and Tradition in Mexico's First National Congress of Music," *Hispanic American Historical Review* 86, no. 4 (2006): 681–706.

[121] Ricardo Rojas, *Eurindia* (Buenos Aires: Librería "La Facultad" Juan Roldán, 1924).

[122] Madrid, "The Sounds of the Nation," 701.

National Conservatory curriculum in the following years and to the cultural atmosphere in which the commercial radio started to broadcast "typical Mexican music."

What constitutes "typical Mexican music" is a longstanding question. In a short book published by a National Commission in charge of the celebration of the 75th anniversary of the revolution,[123] we read about three main musical trends: Mexican romantic song, classical Mexican music, and the *corrido*. The first emerged in the 1880s and mixed Spanish *tonadilla* and local *son*—itself derived from the miscegenation of other styles: its melodies and rhymes were transcribed by German folklorists, supported officially by Diaz's government for the International Fairs and Centennial celebration, and musically adapted by Miguel Lerdo de Tejada. It survived the revolution in silent movies, mixed with classical music, and merged with the political satires of urban *Teatro de Revista* (the Hispanic-American version of French *variété* and US *variety*, in which popular songs shared the spectacle with many other performance genres through a series of short acts). By the 1920s, this type of song was at the center of the bohemian *Salón México*, mixed with danzón and foreign popular music such as tango, jazz, pasodoble, polka, and waltz. The second trend emerged when a new generation of composers—led by Manuel M. Ponce, "the *maestro* of the young nationalists composers,"[124] along with Carlos Chávez and Silvestre Revueltas— incorporated popular and traditional tunes in an erudite and nationalist music project to create authentically Mexican classical music. Finally, the corrido was the rural "people's news service."[125] This official narrative does not hide the complexities of the formation of Mexican music and recognizes it as a music defined by multiple factors and actors.

Mexico's regional, aesthetic, and social diversity also appears in many musical biographies. The career of Estanislao Mejía, whose description of musical unionism we just followed, began at a local band in Hueyotlipan (a small town in Tlaxcala). He later became a bugler in Puebla's State Music Band and then, in the capital, joined the Artillery Band. He was a student, professor, and composer at the conservatory during and after the revolution and became president of the organizing committee of the First National Congress of Music in 1926. He became the director of the *Facultad de Música* of the National University in 1929 and directed the National Music Conservatory between 1934 and 1938.[126] Candelario Huizar, founder of the Mexican Symphonic Orchestra in 1928, started his career as a member of a small-town band in Zacatecas. And Gerónimo Baqueiro Foster, whose lamentation of the unions' weakness we heard about earlier, started his career in a small-town band in Campeche

[123] María Elvira Mora and Clara Inés Ramírez, *La música en la revolución* (Mexico City: Comisión Nacional para las Celebraciones del 175 Aniversario de la Independencia Nacional y 75 Aniversario de la Revolución Mexicana, 1985).

[124] Mora and Ramírez, *La música en la revolución*, 18.

[125] Ibid., 27.

[126] José Valero Silva, *Polvos de olvido: cultura y revolución* (Mexico City: Universidad Autónoma Metropolitana, Unidad Azcapotzalco, División de Ciencias Sociales y Humanidades : Instituto Nacional de las Bellas Artes, 1993), 351–52.

before ultimately becoming one of the most important researchers of Mexican folk-lore.[127] The repertoires of these village bands had been growing in complexity since Mexico became independent, when they began to include a wide diversity of styles—from Spanish-Moorish colonial songs to polkas, marches, waltzes and quick-steps—executed by musicians who often lacked formal education.[128]

The transit from the periphery to the center—from village bands to the main cultural institutions of the revolutionary state—and the overlap of classical and popular, rural and urban music, were the grounds on which commercial radio developed its influence, by attracting artists of many different origins in order to reach a broad audience.

XEW Musical Broadcasting, 1933–1934

By the 1930s, radio programmers had at their disposal many and varied musicians to play what today would be called an "omnivorous" repertoire. They were in control of an apparently minor but profoundly influential practice that emerged in the record catalogues of the 1920s and became widespread through radio in the 1930s: the commercial *labeling* of songs.

Labeling is the action by which the broadcaster *codes* a particular piece of music to offer the listener a key to understanding it. The label can be geographic, stylistic, temporal, or social. Should the famous song "Allá en el Rancho Grande" (1936) be labeled as a *ranchera, regional, Mexican, popular,* or *traditional* song? Is it *rural music* or *film music*? Labels matter contextually, signaling a classificatory decision of genre or origin understood by broadcasters, newspaper readers, and radio listeners. Labeling choices were (and still are) a powerful way of shaping modern popular culture.[129] In Mexico, commercial radio labeling escaped direct government regulation. Radio operators chose names for programs and assigned genres to music by following their managers' broad indications, the information that manufacturers provided about

---

[127] Ibid., 353–57.

[128] Guy Thomson, "The Ceremonial and Political Role of Village Bands, 1846–1974," in *Rituals of Rule, Rituals of Resistance: Public Celebrations and Popular Culture in Mexico*, ed. William Beezley, Cheryl English Martin, and William French (Wilmington, DE: SR Books, 1994), 564–625.

[129] Labeling is inherently political, as Jocelyne Guilbault argues in "The Politics of Labeling Popular Music in English Caribbean," *Revista Transcultural de Música* 3 (1997). A cultural history of music must take into account the diverse procedures by which musical meaning is constructed, organized, and disseminated into classificatory systems beyond the sound itself. It would not be until the 1980s, however, that a "new" musicology would start to study the interplay of musical language and the social signification of music. Philip Tagg, "Analysing Popular Music: Theory, Method and Practice," *Popular Music* 2 (1982): 37–67; Nicholas Cook, "Theorizing Musical Meaning," *Music Theory Spectrum* 23, no. 2 (October 1, 2001): 170–95. More recently, sociologists reconstructed contexts and processes of music categorization, with an emphasis on the interplay of music actors, listening communities, and market dynamics. Jennifer C. Lena, *Banding Together: How Communities Create Genres in Popular Music* (Princeton, NJ: Princeton University Press, 2012) and William G. Roy and Timothy Dowd, "'Race Records' and 'Hillbilly Music': Institutional Origins of Racial Categories in the American Commercial Recording Industry," *Poetics* 32, no. 3 (June 1, 2004): 265–79.

recordings, their own musical categories, and what they imagined their audience's categories would be.

In 1923 the Mexico City newspaper El Universal—the one who organized the 1926 congress on music—had launched the country's first commercial station of the country, CYL, in partnership with Luis and Raúl Azcárraga, Monterey businessmen who imported American radio parts and receivers. Emilio Azcárraga, their younger brother, moved from being the local Ford dealer in Monterrey and the distributor of RCA radio devices to building what would become the major commercial broadcaster of Mexican history: XEW, founded in 1930 as an affiliate of the National Broadcasting Company, NBC, from the United States. Other lasting stations were created that year, all independent from one another, in Veracruz and Ciudad Juárez. In 1938 Emilio Azcárraga launched another station, XEQ, associated with the Columbia Broadcasting System, CBS, as a step toward the creation of a seventeen-station network outside the capital. By the end of 1941, he was leading the institutionalization of all these stations by creating and presiding over the National Chamber of the Broadcasting Industry. This strategy led him to build a huge Latin American network that had thirty-eight affiliated stations by the end of the Second World War.[130] What was the musical ideology behind this radio empire?

In March 1933 the Mexico City newspaper *Excelsior* began to publish the XEW program schedule daily. In the first year of announcements of its daily programming, from March 1933 through May 1934, XEW station was the first to systematically attempt to organize a diverse musical world and make it intelligible to the audience by converting it into an articulated *repertoire*. During the previous three years, programming schedules had been vague and abbreviated and lacked the musical descriptions we associate with labeling. For instance, in the pages of *Excelsior*, XEX advertised "Fifteen minutes of Zapaterías Gloria," or "Fifteen minutes of beauty crème Florantón": the sponsors were more important than the music, which remained undefined. At best, for example on July 3, 1932, the station's advertising signaled that between 13 and 13:15 it would broadcast fifteen minutes of "Popular Music," without any further specification.

Musical criteria appear to have been included in scheduling for the first time in 1933. The transmissions are lost. We know they combined live and recorded music, and we can speculate about their contents by interpreting broadcasting schedules with the help of information from *Excelsior* and secondary sources.[131] The schedules

---

[130] Joy Elizabeth Hayes, *Radio Nation: Communication, Popular Culture, and Nationalism in Mexico, 1920–1950* (Tucson: University of Arizona Press, 2000), 30; Alex Saragoza, *The Monterrey Elite and the Mexican State, 1880–1940* (Austin: University of Texas Press, 1988), 140; Elizabeth Fox, *Latin American Broadcasting: From Tango to Telenovela* (Luton: University of Luton Press, 1997), 38; Fátima Fernández Christlieb, *La radio mexicana: centro y regiones* (México: J. Pablos Editor, 1991), 34–41; Mejia Barquera, *La industria de la radio*, chapter 3.

[131] Pável Granados and Mónica Barrón Echauri, *XEW, 70 años en el aire* (Mexico City: Editorial Clío, 2000); Yolanda Moreno Rivas, *Historia de la música popular mexicana* (México, D.F.: Alianza Editorial Mexicana : Consejo Nacional para la Cultura y las Artes, 1989); Jesús Flores y Escalante, *Salón México: historia documental y gráfica del danzón en México* (México, D.F.: Asociación Mexicana

suggest that broadcasters and listeners were starting to share a common musical world made of specific categories.

Between March 1, 1933, and May 20, 1934, the newspaper published on a daily basis a list of around 30 segments or programs that could be heard each day. The segments ran from five to thirty minutes each, covering the broadcast from 10 a.m. to almost midnight. They were overwhelmingly musical and were labeled in curious ways. Some sections were titled by style ("Jazz Jugglers"); others by type ("Selections by the Symphonic Orchestra"); instrument and executor ("Accordion Solo by Mr. Domínguez"); composer or performer, either already famous or promoted ("Tenor Pedro Vargas and his Tropical Orchestra"); geographical provenance ("Michoacán Trio," "Argentine Trio," "Exclusive Novelties of American Music"); instrument ("Marimba and Organ Concert"); time markers ("Old Time Melodies," "Recorded Novelties of Cuban Music"); the nature of the performance ("Recordings" or "Live Concert"); and institution ("Police Cultural Department—Police Band").

Some combined various types: "Recorded Novelties of Cuban Music" (*Novedades grabadas de música cubana*) offered music that was "recorded," "new," and "Cuban." Others appealed to images and sentiments rather than musical information: "Juan Gutiérrez, el rey del organillo" suggests the popular street player of an instrument diffused throughout the world, the hurdy-gurdy; the "Cancionero sentimental" undoubtedly refers to some kind of "romantic song"; others are more vague, such as "The Rhythm Squad" or "The Squad of Harmony."

A few nonmusical segments were oriented to children ("Tío Polito, el amigo de los niños"), mothers ("Breve plática a las madres de familia"), and broader audiences (the lottery, detective investigations such as the "Investigador policíaco del aire," etc.). And many segments included musical and nonmusical segments: on Friday, March 3, 1934, immediately after the initial "Salutaciones," the morning started with a segment apparently oriented to housewives, "The Broom and Duster Club" ("El Club de la Escoba y el Plumero"), which included recorded songs of a "Dance-Hall Orchestra" ("Orquesta de Salón").

Each label prompts questions. What was this "Dance-Hall Orchestra"? During the recording industry's first decades, discs were produced in the countries that had developed the technical manufacturing skills and patents: the United States, England, France, and Germany. The discs broadcasted on XEW were made in the United States by RCA Victor, which either mastered recordings made in Mexico or directly recorded Mexican bands in the United States. But was this "dance-hall orchestra" in the early 1930s American or Mexican? If Mexican, it could have performed a variety of tunes, including American ones. Did the broadcasters announce that they were offering recordings by American bands? Or was their intention, rather, simply to fill

de Estudios Fonográficos, 1993); Juan Garrido, *Historia de la música popular en México, 1896–1973* (México: Editorial Extemporaneos, 1974); Claes af Geijerstam, *Popular Music in Mexico* (Albuquerque: University of New Mexico Press, 1976).

a segment with American records without announcing them as such because of a possible negative reaction from the audience?

After one segment, probably live, of violin and accordion, the schedule announced the "mezzo-soprano Josefina Aguilar"—did she sing *zarzuelas* or opera arias? Recorded orchestras, the Police Band, and "Novedades musicales exclusivas de XEW" followed. It is impossible to know the actual contents of the latter section, but the word "Novedades" indicates an embryonic musical fashion system, perhaps a signal that the American model of fast replacement of songs was on the horizon. XEW scheduling was probably somewhere in between the improvisation of early American radio and the well-oiled hit-making machine of the forties. The commercial idea of "novelty" was accompanied by the strategy of building a traditional repertoire composed of the "novelties" of one, two, or five years earlier. The programming created a sort of popular "canon" of music through segments like "Musical Mosaic: Melodies of Recent Years That We Still Like" (October 19, 1933).

However, several signs suggest the lack of a standardized criterion by which to define the recordings to be transmitted. On the morning of March 4, 1933, almost all the segments included partially or completely recorded music in an overlapping way: "10 a.m.: Salutaciones. Información de Excelsior. Orquesta Típica (Discos)," then "10:30 a.m.: Club de la Escoba y el Plumero and Orquesta Típica (Discos)," followed by "11:00 a.m.: Concierto XEW: Banda internacional (Discos)," and finally "11:30 a.m.: Novedades musicales exclusivas de XEW (Discos)." The sections may have been labeled so imprecisely because listeners were already familiar with the content of such segments or, perhaps more likely, because the discs that were broadcast were chosen from an unpredictable wave of imports from the United States.[132] However, labels such as "Orquesta Típica" and "Banda Internacional" suggest a repertoire that goes beyond specific musical styles and origins. It is in this heterogeneous realm that "Mexican music" has to be considered.

The main features of this programming were hence its musical diversity and its symbiosis, not replacement, of rural and urban, and traditional and modern genres, suggesting the density of social and territorial codes involved in the population growth of Mexico City.[133] Programming was not characterized by an "urban

---

[132] How similar to the American broadcasting system was XEW at that time? A few years later, in 1941, research organized by Columbia University and Columbia Broadcasting System (CBS) pointed out that the "production" of musical hits in the United States had become a predictable, constantly updated, and profitable business. "Twenty years ago songs were 'plugged' by the song pluggers themselves, vaudeville entertainers, singers and traveling bands for a period of several months before they became hits. Now a song is introduced, exploited and 'played to death' all within a corresponding period of a few months [. . .] Publishers then could count on a popularity of a song lasting for one to two years; now a publisher knows that his song will last only three to five months," Duncan MacDougald, Jr., "The Popular Music Industry," in *Radio Research 1941*, eds. Paul Lazarsfeld and Frank Stanton (New York: Duell, Sloan and Pearce, 1941), 71–72.

[133] Pablo Piccato, *City of Suspects. Crime in Mexico City, 1900–1931* (Durham, NC: Duke University Press, 2001).

modernity" replacing old sounds;[134] instead, it was a diverse soundscape for an audience familiar with variety.

The identification of certain music as "Mexican" involved both significant musical "others" and internal categories within the "Mexican" category. The "others" were basically the United States and Spain and, in a second tier, Cuba and Argentina. Segments such as "Música española" and "Arreglos modernos de melodías norteamericanas" were frequent, but so were segments such as "Los trópicos y las pampas," which included music from the Caribbean and Argentina. Reference to other nations and cultures was an indispensable part of affirming and defining a cultural identity.[135] These international references crossed the whole Mexican entertainment system. On a single page readers found advertisements for American movies with both American and Argentine stars and the big Mexican singing star of those times, Agustín Lara, joined by other artists sponsored by XEW such as Toña la Negra. Those countries appear as the framework in which Mexican artists acquire relevance.

The definition of Mexican at this time was imprecise. On a single day, September 26, 1933, for instance, XEW transmitted four Mexican segments: "Mexican Regional Music," "José Landeros, violin: Mexican melodies," "Beautiful Program of Mexican Regional Music," and "Typical Mexican Music." The differences between a Mexican song, a Mexican melody, a typically Mexican, and a regional song are not clear in the labeling. Were they clear to the audience? Or did they indicate the instability of the process by which "Mexican-ness" emerged through the mass media? The absence of regional descriptors (e.g., "norteño" or "Jalisco" music), suggests that, like in Argentina, nationalization partly reflected commercial structures and imperatives.

Media historian Joy Hayes compared XEW programming to the official XFX, run by the Secretary of Public Education (SEP), in 1932–1933.[136] XFX was based on a pedagogical aim. It was a tool for the transmission of practical knowledge, modern behavior codes, hygiene habits, language, history, and geography. It was also a tool for transmitting, through music, both the "civilized" habit of listening to a Hispanic-inflected European classical repertoire and a sentimental attachment to the nation. XFX accomplished these aims by broadcasting popular songs from the country's many regions, interpreted by either conservatory-trained or popular musicians. Presented together, the different regional music styles tended to reinforce, rather

---

[134] Mark Pedelty, "The Bolero: The Birth, Life, and Decline of Mexican Modernity," *Revista de Música Latino Americana* 20, no. 1 (1999): 34.

[135] Brazilian and Argentine self-definitions in the realm of popular culture were analyzed through the lens of soccer and cooking. In both cases, the presence of one or a few national "others" was essential to the establishment of national characteristics. See Eduardo Archetti, "Hibridación, diversidad y generalización en el mundo ideológico del fútbol y el polo," *Prismas. Revista de Historia Intelectual* no. 1 (1997): 53–76 and "In Search of National Identity: Argentinian Football and Europe," *International Journal of the History of Sport* 12, no. 2 (1995): 201–19; Ronaldo Helal, Antônio Jorge G. Soares, and Hugo Rodolfo Lovisolo, *A invenção do país do futebol: mídia, raça e idolatria* (Rio de Janeiro: Mauad, 2001).

[136] Hayes, "National Imaginings," 248–53, and *Radio Nation*, chapter 5.

than dissolve, listeners' sentimental attachment to the nation. But listeners, Hayes suggests, preferred commercial broadcasting to official stations.[137]

The mobilization of US investments in broadcasting for the development of a nationalist canon of popular music should not be considered contradictory. Throughout Latin America, state regulations and nationalism in the 1920s and 1930s did not reject foreign capital, but aimed to attract it as a tool for economic development. The idea of Mexican-ness was a profitable business.

Already in 1937–1939 the *Excelsior* schedules showed a Mexican musical star system in the making. Famous orchestras and singers canonized the Mexican-ness of the Golden Age of the 1940s and 1950s in the form of an array of different styles, and the Mexican-ness of each of them has appeared, since then, obvious and natural.[138] But its origins were not evidently or exclusively Mexican at all: its initial impulse lay in private commercial strategies of transnational origins and materials.

Carlos Monsiváis showed that the thirties were the moment of the popularization of a new type of language: Agustín Lara's boleros were the heirs of the poems of Amado Nervo— "cursi" (corny) modernist poetry—because they translated the images of love produced in the realm of bohemian life into commercial music. Lara and commercial radio acted as mediators of urban life to new urbanites that had come to Mexico City from the provinces—and through his tours, as historian Andrew Wood showed, to Latin Americans as well—speaking to the "joyful hopelessness of nocturnal souls, love-struck adolescents, and housewives"[139] In 1930, musicologist Luis Sandi explained—and lamented—Lara's popularity through what we could call the geopolitics of Mexican music:

Mexico has suffered three musical invasions in the recent years: those of Colombian and Cuban music, the North-American one, and that of the Argentine tango. Tango and jazz entered straghtly as foreign music, without hiding their origins; Cuban and Colombian music were more diplomatic: theirs was a conquest, rather than an invasion. Arrived to our Oriental coast— Veracruz, Yucatán—they easily conquered the somewhat cosmopolitan, some-what nation-less population of the ports.

When Mexicans began to form jazz bands, and "corny" and "absurd" tango invaded, Mexicans became strangers to themselves. They found refuge in the coastal Yucateco

---

[137] Argentine teachers experimented with a similar reaction in the 1921 National Educational Survey's questions about folk culture in the Argentine provinces: when country people were asked about "their" music, they said how much they liked the tango stars they had discovered through records and performers from Buenos Aires. Chamosa, *The Argentine Folklore Movement*, Bocco, "Tensiones entre proyectos intelectuales."

[138] Jacqueline A. Avila, "Los Sonidos Del Cine: Cinematic Music in Mexican Film, 1930–1950" (PhD diss., University of California, Riverside, 2011).

[139] Carlos Monsiváis, "Feliz desesperanza de noctámbulos, enamorados adolescentes y amas de casa," *Escenas de pudor y liviandad* (México: Grijalbo, 1988), 173–74; Andrew Grant Wood, *Agustín Lara: A Cultural Biography* (New York: Oxford University Press, 2014).

and Veracruzano music influenced by Colombia and Cuba. This is exactly when Lara appeared, doing Cuban-Colombian music with tango lyrics, becoming the singer of "the low life" and its "passions." He is at once—argues Sandi with a complicated conservative logic—popular but not representative of the actual people.[140]

It was difficult for nationalists to navigate these aesthetic changes. The early era of mass radio was crisscrossed with discourses that had originated in specific social spheres: advertising, technology, new journalism, cinema, music, the United States, and bohemian life.[141]

Commercial labeling in the early 1930s was more about *organizing* music styles than about projecting a certain *identity* or *ideology* originating in the state or any other locus. Broadcasters were more interested in seducing the ears than penetrating the mind ideologically with identity aims. The "Mexican" label was as legitimate and useful as labels such as "Mosaico Musical" or references to the tropics, the Pampas, and American jazz.

A similar picture emerges from a study of the "Golden Age" of Mexican cinema between 1936 and 1955, when it exerted on many Spanish-speaking markets a "cultural imperialism" comparable to the one traditionally identified with US cinema.[142] From 1931 to 1935, the most successful Spanish-speaking hits had featured Carlos Gardel and been produced by Paramount in New York. *Allá en el Rancho Grande* marked the beginning of Mexican dominance in 1936 and elevated rancheras to one of the main Latin American music styles alongside tangos. New urban audiences across the world were fed with the exotic images and sounds of Cubans in US movies, rural Mexicans in Mexican movies, tango culture in Argentine and US movies, and other stereotypes. Combined, they recreated Latin America as a cultural zone in which movies circulated *conventions* of authenticity—shared representations of national styles. By the late 1930s, Spain, Mexico, and Argentina had shown themselves to be better than Hollywood and New York at finding the right actors, the right accent, and the right tone to reach the large Iberian American audience. By then, the Latin American market represented just 10% of Hollywood's business, which targeted mainly the United States. In 1939 and 1940 Spain and Argentina matched and surpassed Mexico's production. But in the early 1940s, Mexican cinema surpassed its rivals as an international producer, and Mexico City became the major Spanish-speaking node. The United States helped by blocking celluloid exports to Argentina, lobbying against Argentine movies in the region, and subsidizing Mexican films. By the mid-1940s the Mexican industry dominated this market. It had assimilated

[140] "La plaga del tango con sus melodías ramplonas, con sus 'letras', monumentos de cursilería y con su absurda técnica de canto . . . Es imposible considerar a Agustín Lara como un representativo de nuestra música y de nuestra poesía populares." Luis Sandi, "Agustín Lara y la canción mexicana," *Música—Revista Mexicana* 1, no. 9–10 (Diciembre 1930): 46–49.
[141] Angel Miquel, *Disolvencias: literatura, cine y radio en México (1900–1950)* (México, D.F.: Fondo de Cultura Económica, 2005).
[142] Castro and Irwin, *El cine mexicano "se impone,"* 9.

music styles and foreign artists such as Spaniard Luis Buñuel, Argentine Libertad Lamarque, and Cubans Rita Montaner and Bola de Nieve, and it exported Mexican music and accents to Cuba, Venezuela, Colombia, and virtually all Spanish-language markets.

Likewise, by the 1940s Mexican airwaves continued to host mixed origins and styles. In the March 9, 1943, programming of "Radio Mil," listeners could enjoy "Pepe Camarillo and the Bajío Messengers" (popular Mexican minstrels); "La Marimba Méndez" (popular melodies); "Paris Lights: musical parade with the great French vedettes"; Vienna romantic waltzes; "In Hawaii's Paradise," beautiful typical Polynesian songs; "Che Falgas, the first performer of Buenos Aires music, accompanied by Pepe de la Vega's Argentine Orchestra"; recorded versions of fashionable dancing hits by the greatest orchestras of the time; Los Romanceros, two beautiful romantic and popular voices; "Sliding over the stave: Light music"; Violin Concertos; "In the City of Skyscrapers: US Melodies and Rhythms"; modern sentimental songs by Carmen del Real and pianist Carlos Robledo; Mariachi concerts; Rumbos de España, Spanish popular songs; "The Taxqueños; the most Mexican and popular trio"; "The great Gran Kiko Mendive, the soul of Black Antillan song, with Arturo Nuñez's Afro-Cuban orchestra"; "Los Calaveras, the first trio of America, the best concert of Mexican popular songs"; "Hernán Molina and his Dance Orchestra"; "Miguel García Mora, piano virtuoso"; "Selection of Zarzuelas"; "Sentimental melodies by Guillermina Ríos and Pepe de la Vega's band"; "Music from Yesterday, Today, and Ever: selection of cherished operettas"; "Works by the Immortal Authors"; "Fashionable dances"; "Alejandro Rojas sings accompanied by a solovox"; "El Jarocho, la Alegría de Veracruz"; "Learning the Song: Live teaching of the modern songbook by maestros Rosa Elvira (whispering voice), Los Cadetes (trio of the moment), and Carlos Robledo"; "Mexico Lindo: Selection of Popular Music by the Great Typical Orchestra"; "Music in the Tropics: Hot rhythms"; "Brothers and Sisters Huesca, popular troubadours"; "Musical contest"; "From the Fine Arts Palace, Symphonic Orchestra of Mexico conducted by Carlos Chávez"; and "Fashionable dances by fashionable orchestras."[143]

Music was evidently not simply a nationalist expression, but a field where multiple origins and aesthetics converged to educate and please audiences in Mexico and abroad. Benefiting from US investments, the economic protectionism of the revolutionary state, and the proliferation of artists in Mexico City, XEW managers fostered musical globalization. What was the place of Latin American in this story?

The Voice of Latin America from Mexico

The first promotional advertisement of XEW makes it very clear (see Figure 2.4).

This quintessentially Mexican platform, the origins of what in the 1950s would become Mexico's main audiovisual platform and as such the stage of the entire

---

[143] *Excelsior*, September 3, 1943, AGBF.

FIGURE 2.4 "XEW. La Voz de la América Latina desde México," Excelsior, September 18, 1930, inauguration of the radio station. Hemeroteca Nacional de México.

national system of cultural symbols and power that marked Mexican life until very recently, was created as "the voice of Latin America."

The advertisement addresses the entire continent, synthesizing the station's commercial ambitions and simultaneous self-definition as Mexican and Latin American. The radio is a woman standing on Mexico and announcing something in direction to the South of the continent, with tall radio towers emerging behind her, from

FIGURE 2.5 "Books! In All Branches of Knowledge," by Alexander Rodchenko, 1924. Courtesy of Frye Art Museum, Seattle, WA. Photo: Mark Woods.

the United States. The rays—a technological motive at the same time classical[144]—divinely empower her, emiting the broadcasting waves of "the most powerful [station] of the whole of Latin America," making Mexico and XEW the nexus between North American technology and Latin American listeners. The idea that Mexico was a gateway to Latin America was very commonly promoted by United States corporations in the 1930s. But here it also appears as a cultural hybrid. The woman is a flapper—her haircut and body shape suggest it—but the ruffles on her dress are reminiscent of both nineteenth-century Spanish and colonial Mexican symbols of womanhood. While the bold letters of the radio station are typically modernist, the round photographs of the artists bring us back to the nineteenth-century press.

Finally, the flapper-Poblana's facial expression and hand position replicate the Russian constructivist painter Alexander Rodchenko's 1924 advertising poster for the literacy campaing by the Moscow publishing house *Gosizdat*, which shows a woman announcing the arrival of the new times—a likeness that invites us to search for connections between early Soviet and Mexican commercial design, mediated by painters related to the Communist Party (see Figure 2.5).

---

[144] An example among countless others is the frontispiece of Giambattista Vico's *Scienza Nuova*. Donald Phillip Verene, "Vico's Frontispiece and the Tablet of Cebes," in *Man, God, and Nature in the Enlightenment*, eds. Donald Mell, Theodore Braun and Lucia Palmer (East Lansing: Michigan State University Press, 1988), 3–11.

Among the artists showcased, singer and actor Tito Guizar became very famous—in Mexico and in Latin America[145]—as a painter of Mexico's different regions, particularly Jalisco, which became in his songs synonymous with Mexicanness. Opera singer Alfonso Ortiz Tirado, a medicine doctor from Sonora, also became famous singing boleros and rancheras. Juan Arvizu was a celebrated singer of operas and boleros. The fame of singers Josefina Aguilar and Maruca Perez, bandleader Velino Preza, and hot-jazz saxophone player and bandleader Troy Floyd from San Antonio, Texas, may or may not have been less enduring. As I argued elsewhere, there is a "hidden half" in the history of musical globalization.[146]

The comic-book aesthetic of the whole advertisement refers to a US-originated but internationally popular trend of representation. These hybrid connotations express the intertwining of nationalism and transnational circulation of cultural references in the making of the modern soundscape in Latin America.[147]

LATIN AMERICA AS A SPACE AND AS A REPERTOIRE

Copyright collection by the Buenos Aires' SADAIC and radio programming by Mexico's XEW were metropolitan initiatives explicitly understood as transnational. Argentine composers protected the intellectual property of their songs, and Mexican broadcasters promoted a Latin American repertoire, and in doing so, both contributed to the globalization of the region's music. These musical mediations served nationalizing forces in Argentina and Mexico, but their artistic and commercial practices were primarily oriented to participating in the simultaneous processes of economic globalization and cultural democratization. Let's reconstruct this specific form of transnationalism.

The patchwork of commercial music circuits in Latin America expanded dramatically in Latin America since the first half of the twentieth century, based on metropolitan, rather than actuallly national markets. Nationalist folk discourses became popular and legitimate but commercial opportunities opened up for all kinds of musicians in these large urban markets and in the circuits that linked those cities with one another and with the United States and Europe. Demographic growth and higher disposable income produced a socially broadening nightlife; events organized by civil, ethnic, and neighborly associations; printed music; a recording industry;

---

[145] Ricardo Chica Geliz and Miguel Camacho Manjarrez, *El cine mexicano y la cartelera cinematográfica de Cartagena, 1939–1945* (Cartagena: Editorial Universitaria de la Universidad de Cartagena, 2017), 93.

[146] Pablo Palomino, "Nina Sibirtzeva, or the Hidden Half of Musical Globalization," *Journal of Social History* 52, no. 2 (2018): 260–82.

[147] These tensions were expressed in the Mexican commercial advertising culture of that time, which "presented conflicting images and values that blurred the conventional boundaries between traditional or national and modern or global trends." Julio Moreno, *Yankee Don't Go Home!: Mexican Nationalism, American Business Culture, and the Shaping of Modern Mexico, 1920–1950* (Chapel Hill: University of North Carolina Press, 2003), 112.

professional orchestras; official and private conservatories; film studios; and cinemas that hired live musicians. Latin American cities became thus musical laboratories. But truly *national* music markets developed only later, imperfectly, and not everywhere.

In the late 1930s, through broadcasting, copyright law, and urban musical markets, Latin American artists participated in economic and symbolic circulations whose direction was globalizing, not just nationalizing. Class struggles in the realm of national culture, theorized then by Antonio Gramsci for that other case of nation building, Italy, happened in a context marked by the globalization of capitalist relations, not just their nationalization.[148]

The two institutional cases analyzed here became the basis of twentieth-century Mexico's largest entertaining monopoly, Televisa, and the first solid professional association representing the economic interests of a key sector of the Argentina's musicians. To both XEW and SADAIC, aesthetic, labor, and political concerns were more relevant than national or ethnic identity per se. They engaged with markets by elaborating a transnationalist and populist musical ideology, shared by artists and audiences worldwide.

The comparison of XEW and SADAIC also suggests that the emergence of national musical rhetorics did not oppose the transnationalization of the soundscape. Instead, they took advantage of it and contributed to its development by recreating foreign influences domestically and feeding foreign markets with indigenous production. Some of the very same forces that promoted musical globalization (the multinational record companies, for example) also promoted the nationalization of local musical practices.[149] But here we see how "peripheral" agents like SADAIC acted at the "center," and how the transnationalism of XEW was not imposed from abroad but resulted from the convergence of foreign capitals and local musical heterogeneity.

Like in the musical scene of Manila in the 1920s, and the career of Isa Kremer until the 1950s, a sort of cosmopolitan populism defined Latin America's music in the 1930s. Jewish artists in mid-twentieth century in Buenos Aires, like *criollo* musicians in Lima, Afro-Cuban orchestras in Havana, and blues singers in the US South, made a living in emerging urban musical markets by singing songs addressed to the people around them and participating in the increasingly global musical scene.[150] Jewish musicians adopted all sorts of attitudes toward the Buenos Aires musical scene: some integrated into it, erasing their ethnic markers, and others integrated into it while keeping them; some maintained strong linguistic and cultural links with Eastern

---

[148] Antonio Gramsci, *Gli intellettuali e l'organizzazione della cultura* (Torino: Einaudi, 1950).

[149] Karush, *Culture of Class*; Cañardo, *Fábricas de música*.

[150] Gérard Borras, *Chansonniers de Lima: le vals et la chanson criolla, 1900–1936* (Rennes: Presses Universitaires de Rennes, 2009); Robin D. Moore, *Nationalizing Blackness: Afrocubanismo and Artistic Revolution in Havana, 1920–1940* (Pittsburgh: University of Pittsburgh Press, 1997); Michelle Scott, *Blues Empress in Black Chattanooga: Bessie Smith and the Emerging Urban South* (Urbana: University of Illinois Press, 2008).

European networks of migrants, while others moved in and out multiple social and geographic worlds.[151] In some cases, both grassroots and highbrow global repertoires made it into the shows of mobile singers such as Nina Sibirtzeva and Isa Kremer. Sibirtzeva developed a career in the shadows, performing US spirituals, Argentine folksongs, Russian soviet ballads, and traditional Yiddish tunes, each piece of her repertoire considered a "people's song."[152] Kremer, to the contrary, was a celebrity and began her career performing socially elitist repertoires at "highbrow" venues before becoming an explicitly global-folk populist singer. Both of them, like the Filipino entertainers briefly analyzed in this chapter, praised folk music's connection to "the people" as their main source of aesthetic legitimacy.

By the 1930s, more powerful actors were claiming that legitimacy as well. With nationalist goals, they also produced, in some occasions, a Latin Americanist framework. These were the cultural and musical bureaucracies of the expanding Latin American states, the subject of the next chapter.

---

[151] Pablo Palomino, "The Musical Worlds of Jewish Buenos Aires, 1910–1940," in *Mazel Tov, Amigos! Jews and Popular Music in the Americas* (Leiden: Brill, 2015), 25–53. See also Julio Nudler, *Tango judío: del ghetto a la milonga* (Buenos Aires: Sudamericana, 1998); Silvia Glocer, "Músicos judíos exiliados en Argentina durante el Tercer Reich (1933–1945): los primeros tiempos en los nuevos escenarios.," *Revista Argentina de Musicología* 11 (2010): 99–116.

[152] Pablo Palomino, "Nina Sibirtzeva, or the Hidden Half of Musical Globalization," *Journal of Social History* 52, no. 2 (Winter 2018): 260–82.

3

STATE MUSICAL POPULISMS

SINCE THE BEGINNING of the twentieth century, cultural nationalists in the field of music worked with tools and ideas that circulated transnationally, proposed new understandings of the nation based on their internal regions, and some of them implicitly operated with an idea of Latin America as a transnational regional framework. On Independence Day, 1908, Uruguay's main primary school supervisor praised the collective singing of the national anthem by six thousand children and defended the inclusion of an excerpt, in Italian, from Giuseppe Verdi's opera *Nabucco* in "the solemn choir of the children, because I long for them the cultivation on the arts . . . which are the life of the spirit, which gives direction to existence, assuages the pain, and civilize the nations."[1] Incorporating songs from other nations was legitimate "as long as they are beautiful, artistic, and speak to the popular feeling."[2] For this education bureaucrat, European civilization spoke to popular feelings. But he also knew that in between Uruguay and Europe there was a *regional* identity. Uruguay was not an island, he added: "Among us (as *mutatis mutandis* must be the case of the other nations of *our race*, whose territories span *from the Gulf of Mexico to*

---

[1] "El coro solemne cantado por los niños, porque ansío para ellos el culto del arte . . . porque el arte es la vida del espíritu, el que da rumbos a la existencia, consuela los dolores y civiliza las naciones." Abel J. Pérez, "Los aniversarios patrios y los cantos escolares en la Plaza Independencia," in *República Oriental del Uruguay—Anales de instrucción primaria*, vol. 5 (Montevideo: Imprenta El Siglo Ilustrado, 1908), 643.
[2] Ibid., 641: "Siempre que sean bellas, que sean artísticas, que hablen al sentimiento popular."

The Invention of Latin American Music. Pablo Palomino, Oxford University Press (2020). © Oxford University Press.
DOI: 10.1093/oso/9780190687403.001.0001

Cape Horn) the number of active primary teachers should be multiplied by four, in order to accomplish the supreme mandate of offering primary schooling to all school-age children."[3]

Transnational regionalism was a matter of multiple scales. Foreign modernists were indispensable for revealing to nationalists from the Gulf of Mexico to Cape Horn their own exoticism, the "inner other" from peripheral areas that local intelligentsia turned into national or even supra-national symbols.[4] For instance, the "traditional" province of Santiago del Estero represented "the inner nation" of Argentina in the work of an intelligentsia that included French archeologists, sons of immigrants, and writers living many miles away in cosmopolitan Buenos Aires. Scholars and intellectuals postulated that the national culture was also an expression of a larger tradition—for example, Andean, Iberian American, or Western. As musicologist Vera Wolcowicz has shown, Ecuadorian nationalist composers, in order to draw a line with their neighboring rival Peru and to stake a nationalist "claim . . . in the global creation of Western art music," produced an Incan musical discourse, referencing their indigenous-infused work to a grandiose pre-Hispanic past shared with many other composers in South America.[5] Other "inner nations," such as Brazil's Northeast and the "Gaúcho" South, were crafted as well by regionalist cultural brokers in dialogue with foreign actors and ideas.[6]

By 1932, when Egypt's cultural minister at the Congress on Arab Music in Cairo famously advised musicologists from a variety of countries to work on "inventing and concocting foundations and principles appropriate for constructing the future of Arab music,"[7] his Latin American counterparts were also defining their national musical identities through a common regional tradition. They turned vernacular musical forms into national folklore under "universal" European norms and within a vaguely defined region. Educators, bureaucrats, musicologists, impresarios, and

---

[3] My emphasis. "Entre nosotros (y *mutatis mutandis* debe ocurrir lo mismo en las demás naciones de nuestra raza cuyos territorios se extienden desde el Golfo de Méjico hasta el Cabo de Hornos) habría que cuadriplicar el número de maestros actualmente en ejercicio para poder realizar el supremo desiderátum de proporcionar enseñanza primaria a todos los niños en edad de escuela." Joaquín R. Sánchez, "Observaciones Sueltas," in *República Oriental del Uruguay—Anales de instrucción primaria*, vol. 5 (Montevideo: Imprenta El Siglo Ilustrado, 1908), 606–31).

[4] Vianna, *O mistério do samba*; Florencia Garramuño, *Modernidades primitivas : tango, samba y nación* (Buenos Aires: Fondo de Cultura Económica, 2007).

[5] Vera Wolkowicz, "Incan or Not? Building Ecuador's Musical Past in the Quest for a Nationalist Art Music, 1900–1950," *Journal of Musicology* 36, no. 2 (April 1, 2019): 228–60, 258.

[6] Beatriz Ocampo, *La nación interior: Canal Feijóo, Di Lullo y los hermanos Wagner: el discurso culturalista de estos intelectuales en la provincia de Santiago del Estero* (Buenos Aires: Antropofagia, 2004). Courtney Jeanette Campbell, "The Brazilian Northeast, Inside Out: Region, Nation, and Globalization (1926–1968)" (PhD diss., Vanderbilt University, 2014). Ruben George Oliven, "'The Largest Popular Culture Movement in the Western World': Intellectuals and Gaúcho Traditionalism in Brazil," *American Ethnologist* 27, no. 1 (2000): 128–46.

[7] Ali Jihad Racy, "Historical Worldviews of Early Ethnomusicologists: an East-West Encounter in Cairo, 1932," in *Ethnomusicology and Modern Music History*, ed. Stephen Blum, Philip V. Bohlman, and Daniel M. Neuman (Urbana, University of Illinois Press, 1991), 70.

composers defined the music of the people (or "the masses," to use the sociological-journalistic term of the time, which in fact designated a *way of seeing* heterogeneous populations[8]) through ethno-historical sources and aesthetic frameworks that criss-crossed both the internal and the external borders of the nation.

From the perspective of the cultural elites, the three levels—subnational, national, and supra-national musical roots—provided material for the same modernizing ped-agogical challenge. State policies contributed hence to produce Latin America as a musical region. But they did it in subtle rather than in systematic or planned ways, and for this reason this dimension of musical history escaped scholarly attention until very recently.

STATE MUSICAL POLICIES

Music mattered above all as a tool for wider social reform. For example, in Mexico in the 1920s, the revolutionary state sought to make education more "progressive," in part by simultaneously teaching Spanish to the indigenous population and striv-ing to preserve the indigenous languages, and the arts were key to this agenda. The Mexican secretary of education, José Vasconcelos, sought with it to reach the "peas-ant masses" (*masas campesinas*).[9] "If you are artists," he wrote in 1922, "how could you find inspiration under the roof of your house or office, or in the stupidity of the salons? Join the ranks of the missionary teachers!"[10] State music boomed. Educational concerts now combined classical music (Franck, Haydn, R. Strauss, Dvorak) with regional or popular music. Composer Manuel Castro Padilla, charged with putting together an official regional orchestra, played *jaranas yucatecas, sonecitos chiapane-cos, huapangos veracruzanos*, and *aires del bajío* at the National Museum in 1922. The National School of Music recruited 1,500 students that year and required its alumni to give weekly conferences to *obreros*.[11] Three thousand male and female workers and their *orquestas típicas* from the Federal District *orfeones obreros* performed works by Manuel Ponce.[12] This double movement—a *narodnik* search for peasant culture and a missionary, civilizing crusade—converged with a hygienist rhetoric: at "schools,

---

[8] Renato Ortiz, *Otro territorio: ensayos sobre el mundo contemporáneo* (Buenos Aires: Universidad Nacional de Quilmes, 2005).

[9] "El segundo aniversario de 'El Maestro Rural,'" *El Maestro Rural. Órgano de la Secretaría de Educación Pública* 4, no. 5 (March 1, 1934): 1.

[10] "Si sois artistas," José Vasconcelos had written in 1922, "¿cómo esperáis hallar inspiración bajo el techo de la oficina o del hogar, o en medio de la estupidez de los salones? . . . Alistáos en las filas de los maestros misioneros." *El Heraldo de México*, December 20, 1922.

[11] "Fomento de la educación artística del pueblo," *Boletín de la Secretaría de Educación Pública* 1, no. 2 (1922): 193–97. In 1921 Castro Padilla had organized a massive *jarabe* with 300 dancing couples at the presidential palace. Ricardo Pérez Montfort, *Expresiones populares y estereotipos culturales en México, siglos XIX y XX: diez ensayos*, 1a. ed. (México, D.F.: Centro de Investigaciones y Estudios Superiores en Antropología Social, 2007), 138.

[12] *El Demócrata*, July 10, 1922.

popular masses, and military groups," music was supposed to form "healthy souls" in an aesthetic, disciplinary, recreational, and even physiological sense. Intertwined with literacy, history lessons, and labor training, music education was a language and a technique for instilling in students aesthetic, biological, and emotional discourses of both the universal and the national.

The national aspect of music as a tool for social reform emerged in part from the music pedagogues reaction against what they considered "vulgar" music disseminated by commercial brokers. This rhetoric was particularly strong in the border with the United States—the cradle of the false and invasive jazz music, symbol of the expansion of United States commerce and culture into the region. In a 1925 letter to educational authorities in Mexico City, the federation of workers unions of Tijuana (Federación de Uniones Obreras de Tijuana, then a small border town in Baja California) explained that jazz was taking over Tijuana's musical life. The workers described jazz as an "infernal noise" (*ruido infernal*) from an "excentric" neighboring society with which the city had to engage, since it was their main source of economic activity. They argued that even though the Tijuana workers weren't necessarily artists, their "tough souls" (*rudas almas*) had a predilection for "our" Mexican music. Each nation—Italy, Germany, and so on—had its own music, they argued, and every one was valuable in one way or another. Mexicans, like Hawaiians, were a subjugated race, but unlike those islanders, Mexicans did rebel against the United States, so would the Secretary of Public Education (SEP) help them counteract the influence of jazz, "that din without melody nor, even less, harmony?"[13] This was very likely a strategic expression of the Tijuana union's nationalism toward the nationalist officers in Mexico City. The musicologists at SEP took note but could do no more than just encourage the music teachers of Tijuana to "combat" jazz in ways they didn't specify.

State musical nationalism was, in fact, weak. In Mexico and everywhere else, the state had traditionally limited its funding to maintaining a small official conservatory, granting a handful of fellowships to talented students to train at European conservatories, and having military bands perform a minimal patriotic repertoire at public rituals.[14] Now, state musical policies aimed to shape a "national culture" infused with prestigious European romantic and postromantic styles, but had to counterbalance powerful forces: the emerging musical technologies (sheet music, recordings, radio), organizations (popular music societies, commercial establishments), and repertoires (vernacular and cosmopolitan popular styles).

---

[13] *"Ese estruendo sin melodía, y mucho menos sin armonía.* "Se combatirá el jazz con audiciones de música vernácula," *Boletín de la Secretaría de Educación Pública* 4, no. 2 (1925): 55–58.

[14] That was all the Latin American states could afford in the musical realm, as their bureaucratic apparatuses were oriented to public services catering the demands of the export-oriented economy. National conservatories were founded at a quite varied pace: for example, Brazil 1848, Chile 1850, Mexico 1877 (based upon a previous Society), Cuba 1885, Ecuador 1900, Bolivia 1907, Peru 1908, Uruguay 1910, Venezuela 1916, Argentina 1924 (based upon the Colón Theater's School of Dramatic and Scenic Art), and Paraguay 1997.

Grandiose aspirations ("a national music"), limited resources, and transnational forces shaped the state pedagogy. Schools were expected to discipline children's minds and bodies through practices of music, hygiene, order, gender roles, historical narratives, and ethno-patriotic symbols. For that reason, they became spaces of struggle with culturally heterogeneous populations, local balances of power, and even competing agendas within government and elite circles. The Latin American intellectuals, bureaucrats, and teachers of the early decades of the century (Antonio Gramsci's "intellectual class") crafted public policies of music education that did not stop market and foreign influences, but had a lasting influence on these nations' musical memory.[15] Like their colonial predecessors, they shared a sense of belonging to a larger whole, a supra-national area: a "Latin" civilization,[16] that shared Latin-Iberian origins, a recognition of the colonial experience, a condescending valorization of indigenous life and myths, cultural bonds with Spain, France, and Italy, the perception of a common threat (the United States), and the goal of finding cultural autonomy in a world of shifting empires. Ultimately, they saw themselves as carriers of a tradition that one scholar summarized in 1987 with the phrase "extreme Occident," the ultimate fruit of European modernity.[17]

A good example of both the strengths and limitations of these "civilizing" state policies is the history of collective singing as a political tool.

Rooted in monarchical and religious liturgy in Europe, chanting together infused all kinds of political rituals, as historian Esteban Buch and others have shown: from the Festivals of the Supreme Being under the rule of Robespierre in revolutionary France, to Schiller's poem *Ode to Joy* at the end of Beethoven's Ninth Symphony, created as a musical celebration of the European "concert of nations" in 1824 and later on adopted by Socialists, Nazis, Apartheid South Africa, and finally as the hymn of the European Union. In Germany, collective singing was key to nationalists and to the union and youth organizations of the social democratic movement between 1870 and 1939, providing sociability and symbolism to working and middle-class

---

[15] Antonio Gramsci, *Gli intellettuali e l'organizzazione della cultura* (Torino: Einaudi, 1950), 7–9. Mary K. Vaughan and Oscar Chamosa studied the everyday construction of hegemony in Mexico and Argentina during the first half of the twentieth century; see Mary K. Vaughan, *Cultural Politics in Revolution: Teachers, Peasants, and Schools in Mexico, 1930–1940* (Tucson: University of Arizona Press, 1997) and Oscar Chamosa, *The Argentine Folklore Movement: Sugar Elites, Criollo Workers, and the Politics of Cultural Nationalism, 1900–1955* (Tucson: University of Arizona Press, 2010).

[16] The Mexican intellectual Alfonso Reyes famously put it in this way: "Si validos de nuestro leve peso histórico y *hasta de haber sido convocados al banquete de la civilización cuando la mesa estaba servida -lo cual nos permite llegar a la fiesta como de mejor humor y más descansados-* queremos aportar a la obra ese calor, esa posibilidad física que haga al fin de ella un patrimonio universal, ¿qué sentido tiene hablar de latín, de latinidad y de latinismo?" Alfonso Reyes, *El discurso por Virgilio* (Buenos Aires: Coni, 1937). The first pages were published in 1932 in his own literary magazine, *Monterrey. Correo literario*, and the full text in Buenos Aires in 1937. Reyes's "civilization" was obviously European, of Latin origins, but also a resource for progressive intellectuals in Latin America. Being "late" was not a disadvantage: to the contrary, it allowed them to make a positive contribution. I thank Jorge Myers for these insights.

[17] Alain Rouquié, *Amérique Latine: Introduction à la l'Extrême-Occident* (Paris: Seuil, 1987).

Germans.[18] In France, choral societies under the Second Empire and the Third Republic channeled both amateur culture and state policies that collected and standardized repertoires, teaching techniques, and performing methods. Choral associations in cities and neighborhoods, unions, and fraternities brought together tens of thousands of singers and executants from different professional groups in contests and festivals, and were seen as an impulse to industry, commerce, tourism, press, and the strength of civil society in general. Some of them even developed pensions and health insurance for their members. The notion of *"musique populaire"* acquired in this context a legitimate connotation: choral and musical societies were a harmonic and well-ordered expression of the people.[19] In the 1920s French choirs faced the concurrence of leisure activities such as sports, theater, and cinema, and of jazz, which the musical societies' conservatism rejected. Still, choirs counted with hundreds of thousands of members. Popular Front's support of unemployed musicians during the economic crisis destined 25% of the fine arts budget to music.[20] The founding in 1935 of a Federation of Popular Music by members of the choir of the Association of Revolutionary Writers and Artists, close to the French Communist Party, exemplifies the political appeal of choral music. Collective singing was present in other modernizing contexts as well: the United States' Works Progress Administration and Federal Arts Project, Soviet, Fascist, Nazi, and Chinese Nationalist policies.[21] In some cases, as in Romania's fascist era, state policies were a continuation of practices that had emerged in civil society.

In Latin America, budgets were smaller. Whereas in France the state budget spent in music was part of a larger institutional ecosystem made of large opera theaters, private conservatories, music pedagogy at the public school system, cinema and broadcasting networks, and prizes involving the role of schools with global prestige playing into the intra-European musical concurrence, in Latin America the very foundations of the field were still being created.

An American musicologist traveling the region in 1940 on behalf of the US cultural diplomacy considered that collective singing in Latin America was barely emerging.

---

[18] Esteban Buch, *La Neuvième de Beethoven: Une histoire politique* (Paris: Gallimard, 1999); George Mosse, *The Nationalization of the Masses. Political Symbolism and Mass Movements in Germany from the Napoleonic Wars Through the Third Reich* (New York: H. Fertig, 1975).

[19] Popular music societies turned public life in France inclusive and democratic. In 1913 the movement gained prestige when the city of Paris organized a national and international festival of popular music. Paul Gerbod, "L'institution orphéonique en France du XIXe au XXe Siècle," *Ethnologie Française* 10, no. 1 (January 1, 1980): 27–44. On the emergence of popular music, see Matthew Gelbart, *The Invention of "Folk Music" and "Art Music": Emerging Categories from Ossian to Wagner* (Cambridge: Cambridge University Press, 2007).

[20] Marie-Claude Genet-Delacroix, "'Musiciens officiels' des années trente?," in *Musiques et musiciens à Paris dans les années trente*, ed. Danièle Pistone (Paris: H. Champion, 2000), 11–19.

[21] Roland Clark, "Collective Singing in Romanian Fascism," *Cultural and Social History* 10, no. 2 (2013): 251–71; Szu-Wei Chen, "The Rise and Generic Features of Shanghai Popular Songs in the 1930s and 1940s," *Popular Music* 24, no. 1 (2005): 107–25; Andrew F Jones, *Yellow Music: Media Culture and Colonial Modernity in the Chinese Jazz Age* (Durham, NC: Duke University Press, 2001).

In the choral music field, South America is far behind the United States. The Protestant choral tradition common in North America is non-existent. [. . .] Latin Americans sing as individuals to the accompaniment of the guitar and bandurria. This is perhaps the chief reason for the lack of choral groups in South America. The activities of Sojo in Venezuela, Ernani Braga and Villa-Lobos in Brazil, Letelier and Santa Cruz in Chile and Rosier in Colombia, however, are changing the picture.[22]

The very fact that collective singing was being implemented by those cultural nationalist champions—like Sojo, Villa-Lobos, or Santa Cruz—clearly indicates the *political* nature of the choir in Latin America.[23] Singing, and more generally practicing music, as a *policy*—ideologically grounded, financed through public budget, intended as an inclusive mechanism, and inspired in transnational exchanges of musicological expertise across political and ideological boundaries.

To reconstruct the history of state musical policies in the entire hemisphere is of course beyond the scope of this book. Here I propose to see more closely how state musical policies in three major Latin American national projects enabled regional and transnational musical dialogues, using collective singing as a common thread.

Why these countries instead of others? Collective singing and other musical policies implemented by modernizing state bureaucracies in Argentina, Mexico, and Brazil between 1920 and 1950 targeted together more than 60% of Latin America's population, in the three countries with (in that order) the region's highest Gross Domestic Products.[24] Mexico City, Rio de Janeiro, and Buenos Aires, together with Havana, were also the artistic capitals of the radio, recording, and movie industries until the 1960s. As the Iberian Peninsula was hit by civil war, dictatorships, and economic decline, these four metropolises became the main hubs of Spanish- and Portuguese-language music and publishing. Mexico and Havana in particular enjoyed close connections with US capitals and artists. Buenos Aires, Rio de Janeiro, Mexico City, and São Paulo were the largest metropolitan areas in terms of cultural markets, school population, and transnational exchanges. Buenos Aires reached one million inhabitants around 1900 and in 1950 became the region's first metropolitan

[22] Carleton Sprague Smith, *Musical Tour through South America, June-October, 1940.* (New York: Conference on Inter-American Relations in the Field of Music, 1940), xx.

[23] An example of state music policies centered on collective singing is Colombia, where a program to teach music and organize popular *orfeones* began in 1936. Catalina Muñoz, "'A Mission of Enormous Transcendence': The Cultural Politics of Music During Colombia's Liberal Republic, 1930–1946," *Hispanic American Historical Review* 94, no. 1 (2014): 77–105.

[24] Migration, industrialization, and lower mortality rates accounted for this rapid growth. Argentina's population was in both years larger than nine countries combined (Ecuador, Uruguay, El Salvador, Dominican Republic, Paraguay, Honduras, Nicaragua, Costa Rica, and Panama). Mexico's was even larger than those nine countries plus Guatemala, Haiti, and Venezuela. Brazil, finally, had both in 1920 and in 1950 more inhabitants than the rest of Latin America combined minus Mexico, Argentina, and Colombia. Lynn Smith, *Latin American Population Studies* (Gainesville: University of Florida Press, 1961), 72, Table 10.

area with more than 5 million people. Its population until 1940 was equivalent to those of Rio de Janeiro and São Paulo combined. During the same period, Rio de Janeiro, Mexico City, and São Paulo all grew from about 1 to about 3 million people.

From 1910 to 1950, these three countries experienced a conflictive process of citizenship and socioeconomic inclusion, through both authoritarian and democratic politics that brought together urban and rural working-class organizations with sections of the ruling elites under a shared ideology of nationalism and popular legitimacy. This is what I call populism in this book. Beyond the multiple positions within the long, global debate on this concept since the nineteenth century, we can simply notice that Latin America's contribution to that debate originated precisely in these early- and mid-twentieth-century ambitious experiences of state-driven social inclusion, in the name of "the people," of millions of inhabitants previously marginalized or disconnected from the state.[25] Let us see the musical side of this populism, and its intertwining of national projects with transnational and regional aesthetics.

BRAZIL

The majority of Brazilians were excluded from the benefits of the "Order and Progress" proclaimed on the 1889 republican flag. Universal suffrage would become a reality only a century later with the 1988 Constitution, and comprehensive policies of socioeconomic inclusion, aimed at the totality of the population, would only happen even later, under the Workers Party administrations in the twenty-first century. The expansion of social and economic rights during the Populist Era (1930–1964) focused on unionized urban sectors—and as we know, as soon as it aimed at rural workers and the urban poor, a military dictatorship stopped it. Brazilians thus have experienced their relationship with the state, even until today, as a combination of coercion, indifference, and bureaucratic exclusion, in what has been described a "poverty of rights."[26]

The influence of state-sponsored music policies was hence very limited. Musical life in Brazil traditionally embodied experiences—from love to clandestine lottery to social critique—that in fact could *not* be channeled through official institutions.

[25] Pierre Ostiguy and María Esperanza Casullo, "Left versus Right Populism: Antagonism and the Social Other," *67th Political Studies Association (PSA) Annual International Conference* (Glasgow, 2017); Charles Postel, *The Populist Vision* (New York: Oxford University Press, 2007); Maria Moira Mackinnon and Mario Alberto Petrone, *Populismo y neopopulismo en América Latina: el problema de la Cenicienta* (Buenos Aires: Editorial Universitaria de Buenos Aires, 1998); Franco Venturi, *Il Populismo Russo*, Biblioteca Di Cultura Storica 46 (Torino: Einaudi, 1952).

[26] Brodwyn Fischer, *A Poverty of Rights: Citizenship and Inequality in Twentieth-Century Rio de Janeiro* (Stanford, CA: Stanford University Press, 2008). Even those who did enjoy legal protections were often in fact, "drowning in laws" that were not actually functional. John D. French and Paulo Roberto Ribeiro Fontes, *Afogados em leis: a CLT e a cultura política dos trabalhadores brasileiros* (São Paulo: Editora Fundação Perseu Abramo, 2001).

A variety of musical traditions reflects the immense size of the country and the diversity of its cultural regions. And yet music became in the 1930s a major avenue for cultural and national identification, with samba in particular as the most popular music genre in radio, Carnival, journalism, and record sales, turning the musical aesthetics of Brazilians of African origin into a racially hybrid national symbol. Samba also became global, through nationalist imagery in war-propaganda-oriented Hollywood movies and in Parisian and European dance halls and commercial records. State bureaucrats attempted to sanitize and nationalize Carnival parades and lyrics and infuse popular broadcasting with an official discourse of national identity. But the state's operations were rather "reactive" vis-à-vis a lively popular music world.[27]

Alien to popular music, "art" music organized around a combination of public concert halls and orchestras and private networks and associations. During his 1935 visit to Rio de Janeiro, a young German-Uruguayan musicologist, Francisco Curt Lange, wrote that unfortunately, in that city the "European spirit" was musically and culturally subordinated to the local one—that is, samba. But a few years later, Lange was a bit more optimistic. Traveling the country in 1941 and this time also visiting São Paulo, he summarized his impressions in an official letter to the director of Uruguay's national Broadcasting Official Service (SODRE), where he worked.[28] Art music was still a "European island" amid the surrounding folk and commercial music, but it was expanding across the country. Brazil's musical life had improved, thanks to better transportation and communication between Rio, São Paulo, and the southern states of Paraná, Santa Catarina, and Rio Grande do Sul, where an increasing number of private musical institutions could afford to bring artists from the central cities. An aesthetic difference remained between Rio de Janeiro and São Paulo—the "excessively Italian ambience of the Paulista professional field" did not want to integrate Rio de Janeiro's main modernist composer Heitor Villa-Lobos's work into the city's concert life.[29] But from the perspective of the small and highly centralized country of Uruguay the increasing musical integration of many Brazilian cities into a larger

[27] Ruben George Oliven, "A malandragem na música popular brasileira," *Latin American Music Review* 5, no. 1 (1984), 66–96 and "Singing Money," in *Economic Representations: Academic and Everyday*, ed. David Ruccio (New York: Routledge, 2008), 211–32; Marcos Napolitano, *Cultura brasileira: utopia e massificação (1950–1980)* (São Paulo: Contexto, 2001); Marcelo Ridenti, *Em busca do povo brasileiro: artistas da revolução, do CPC à era da tv* (Rio de Janeiro: Editora Record, 2000); Hermano Vianna, *The Mystery of Samba: Popular Music & National Identity in Brazil* (Chapel Hill: University of North Carolina Press, 1999); José Vinci de Moraes, "Los tránsitos de la música popular en la Misión de Investigación de Folclor (1938)," *Boletín Música* 31 (2012), 3–14; Carol A. Hess, "Walt Disney's *Saludos Amigos*: Hollywood and the Propaganda of Authenticity," in *The Tide Was Always High: The Music of Latin America in Los Angeles*, ed. Josh Kun (Berkeley: University of California Press, 2017), 105–23; Anaïs Fléchet, *Si tu vas à Rio: la musique populaire brésilienne en France au XXe siècle* (Paris: Armand Colin, 2013), esp. chapter 1, "Premiers échos du Brésil," 37–61; Marc A. Hertzman, *Making Samba: a New History of Race and Music in Brazil* (Durham, NC: Duke University Press, 2013), 195–98; McCann, *Hello Hello Brazil*; Pablo Palomino, "Tango, Samba y Amor," *Apuntes de Investigación Del CECYP*, no. 12 (2007): 71–101.
[28] Letter January 1, 1942, Subsérie 2.1, AFCL.
[29] Letter Luiz Heitor Correa de Azevedo to Francisco Curt Lange, December 4, 1934, Subsérie 2.2, AFCL.

national system of classical music, and even the emergence of city rivalries, was impressive.

Lange suggested that the Uruguayan state should replicate the civil-society based Brazilian model by increasing the number of mid-size chamber-concert halls, for two or three hundred people, which would give Uruguayan composers options other than SODRE. He even considered integrating the country's musical scene—already commercially connected to Buenos Aires—with that of neighboring Southern Brazilian cities such as Pelotas, Porto Alegre, Florianopolis, and Curitiba, as well as São Paulo and Rio de Janeiro. In the interest of creating a vibrant concert system, cross-national circuits run by both public and private institutions seemed necessary and viable.

The foes of this European island—or rather, archipelago—of classical music in Brazil were, according to Lange, the conflicts among artists around "musical nationalism" and a weak organizational structure:

> The organization of musical life in Rio is a fiction . . . exemplified by the absence of a permanent national symphonic orchestra. The orchestra of the Municipal Theater is dedicated to opera, the one formed by [Hungarian-German composer exiled since 1933, Eugen] Szenkar has neither stability nor official funding yet, and the one directed by [Brazilian composer] Mr. [Camargo] Guarneri is made of aficionados. I think musical nationalism has provoked many troubles in our countries . . . Today, being a nationalist musician does not mean a principle of professional ethics or artistic ideals, but a shield to hide the lowest human passions . . . People revere the political authorities, who generally do not understand music . . . Ineptly or gracefully, compositions are dressed with multicolor costumes and imposed upon a musically ill-prepared public, itself heterogeneous.[30]

This was a professional field under construction, judged by a musicologist trained in early twentieth-century Munich. Classical music's underdeveloped institutional structure lacked stable funding, was based on political favoritism, and failed to educate a still "heterogeneous" and "ill-prepared public." The national Institute of Music in Rio de Janeiro published a magazine for fewer than two hundred subscribers, and its librarian, the young Luiz Heitor Correa de Azevedo—who after the war would become a key figure at UNESCO's cultural exchange office—worked almost in total isolation.[31] In sum, a weak official structure from the times of the empire in Rio, an Italianized concert system built by immigrants in São Paulo, and a mushrooming of musical clubs—many of them ethnic, sponsored for example by Jewish

---

[30] Letter January 1, 1942, Subsérie 2.1, AFCL.
[31] Letter Luiz Heitor Correa de Azevedo to Francisco Curt Lange, December 4, 1934, Subsérie 2.2, AFCL.

associations[32]—were barely interconnected by a rhetoric of musical nationalism manipulated for personal careerism.

In such context, the state project of "choral masses" led by Heitor Villa-Lobos to reach hundreds of thousands of Brazilians via classical musical education was politically and musically notable. In the mind of its promoters, this project aimed at forming a new citizen, at once aesthetically sensitive and emotionally Brazilian, by ritually singing together at school and in massive gatherings of school communities. Whereas in countries such as Argentina and Spain musical policies were intended to "re-educate" audiences (in Spain by imposing them at the Francoist prisons), in Brazil they were aimed at creating a new musical public from scratch.[33] Collective singing was particularly well-suited to counter patrimonialism, clientelism, and *coronelismo* (the specific Brazilian form of patriarchal patronage), which had generated, in the realm of music as well, only processes of individual, not collective or corporative, incorporation.[34]

Villa-Lobos was recognized by his Latin American peers as an ambitious and modernist cultural broker.[35] He was the son of a Spanish immigrant, who had obtained a musical education and an employee position at the National Library thanks to the sponsorship of a political boss and then died young, and a mother who had sustained the family by washing the linens of the fancy Colombo Bakery in downtown Rio. In 1904 Villa-Lobos joined the Instituto Nacional de Música, where he was trained in both the Italian and the Wagnerian-Romantic traditions that divided the classical world in the 1890s. But his career revolved around the new modernist canon of Debussy, which he performed at an orchestra in the Amazonian boomtown of Manaus and with small orchestras in cinemas and cafes back in Rio, where he interacted with amateur musicians.

In 1921 Villa Lobos composed some "folkish" pieces, participated in the famous Modern Art Week of 1922 in São Paulo, and in 1923 he was sent to Paris, funded by both public and private money. He stayed there several years and realized that what Parisian vanguard artists such as Jean Cocteau expected from non-European composers like him was not imitations of Debussy, but local styles. (The Parisian legitimation of Brazilian music has a deep history. For example, French composer Darius

---

[32] For example, the network of Jewish associations that sustained Nina Sibirtzeva's hemispheric tours. See Pablo Palomino, "Nina Sibirtzeva, or the Hidden Half of Musical Globalization," *Journal of Social History* 52, no. 2 (2018): 260–82.

[33] Analía Cherñavsky, "O nacionalismo musical e a necessidade de formação do público" (presented at the XVIII Congress of ANPPOM, Salvador, Bahía, 2008); on Spain, see Belén Pérez Castillo, "Music for Redemption in Francoist Prisons" (Colloque Musique et sorties de guerres, Université de Montréal, 2018).

[34] José Murilo de Carvalho, "Mandonismo, coronelismo, clientelismo: uma discussão conceitual," *Dados* 40, no. 2 (January 1997): 229–50. http://www.scielo.br/scielo.php?script=sci_arttext&pid=S0011-52581997000200003.

[35] Alberto Ginastera, the leading Argentine nationalist composer, wrote to Villa-Lobos that Ginastera himself, like "all musicians have always thought of him as our Continent's top figure." Letter from Ginastera to Heitor Villa-Lobos, August 8, 1952, AHVL.

Milhaud, who lived in Brazil between 1917 and 1919 as part of the French delegation, premiered in 1920 in Paris *Le Boeuf sur le Toit*, after a 1910 composition by Donga, the popular composer and putative father of samba, greatly increasing the value of "Brazilian" music in France and more widely in Europe.) Back in Rio de Janeiro he became a champion of *Brazilian* music—paradoxically produced by "the imaginary Brazil of the Parisians."[36]

Meanwhile, choral singing had been part of the São Paulo public curriculum since the 1910s and a central concern at the federal level in the elementary school curricula since the 1920s. Its first promoters had the goal of civilizing the limited school population through the propagation of Western erudite music.[37] Singing exercises were imparted on a daily basis and ranged from simple popular songs to complex hymns. Lyrics were considered important for conveying moral and civic values. State activism in the 1930s made collective singing events more regular, and teachers, students, and their families gathered more often throughout the year. At the same time, official pedagogues increasingly censored popular poetry in lowbrow styles such as tangos, sambas, and maxixes (an Afro-Brazilian dance) and replaced it with solemn, proper, and patriotic lyrics.[38]

Upon returning from France, Villa-Lobos joined this movement by supervising elementary school students' demonstrations of "orpheonic singing" in Sao Paulo, where he directed up to "approximately 12,000 voices of teachers, students, academics, soldiers, workers and other sectors of society."[39] In 1932, supported by Rio de Janeiro's Municipal Department of Education, which was directed by Anísio Teixeira, he established teacher training in choral singing as director of the SEMA (*Superintendencia de Educação Musical e Artística*). Collective singing—*canto orfeónico*–was adopted as a required subject in all schools in Brazil beginning in 1934. Villa-Lobos organized singing events in São Paulo and Rio de Janeiro that involved no less than 40,000 students. In November 1942 Villa-Lobos became director of the National Conservatory of Choral Chant (*Conservatório Nacional de Canto Orfeónico*, CNCO), which had been created by national Secretary of Education Gustavo Capanema. Villa-Lobos directed CNCO until his death in 1959.

But this was just one aspect of Villa-Lobos's broader role as artistic figure and cultural mediator. In addition to choral masses, Villa-Lobos also entertained performances of works by German-British baroque composer Handel and Brazilian

---

[36] Paulo Renato Guérios, "Heitor Villa-Lobos and the Parisian Art Scene: How to Become a Brazilian Musician," *Mana* 1 (2006), 13; Anaïs Fléchet, *Villa-Lobos á Paris: un écho musical du Brésil* (Paris: L'Harmattan, 2004) and *Si tu vas a Rio* . . . .

[37] Renato de Sousa Porto Gilioli, "Civilizando pela música: a pedagogia do canto orfeônico na escola paulista da Primeira República (1910–1930)" (MA thesis, Universidade de São Paulo, 2003).

[38] Flavio Oliveira, "Orpheonic Chant and the Construction of Childhood in Brazilian Elementary Education," in *Brazilian Popular Music and Citizenship*, ed. Idelber Avelar and Christopher Dunn (Durham, NC: Duke University Press, 2011), 51–53.

[39] Ibid., 58.

romantic Carlos Gomes and maintained relations with Parisian companies.[40] During World War II and in the postwar years he visited and performed in the United States,[41] and in 1951 he even attempted to conquer America's big screen by offering his services to Hollywood.[42] The nationalism and populism of those times were aesthetically heterogeneous and transnational.

Civic formation and artistic elevation were for him two sides of the same coin.[43] Civilizing the population certainly involved, for many among the Brazilian cultural elites, a "whitening" of the national culture and identity.[44] But strictly musical and pedagogical criteria were paramount to musicians and pedagogues. Villa-Lobos's institutional policies were intended to increase the folkloric repertoire, train music teachers, organize choirs, and improve children's musical skills. From his point of view, this was an opportunity to fulfill a widespread ambition among avant-garde artists around the world: to directly intervene in the relationship between art and society toward the goal of building a unanimous "people." His books of "orpheonic songs" for the schools (*Marchas, canções e cantos marciais para a educação consciente da "Unidade Movimento,"* in 1940, and *Marchas, canções, cantos: cívicos, marciais, folclóricos e artísticos para a formação consciente da apreciação do bom gusto na música,* in 1951) brought together a wide collection of composers from all over the country, from popular and folk to military and erudite. These regional roots generated a broad definition of what constituted a national and elevated ("good taste") canon.[45] His rhetoric on national and civic identity was at the service of his aesthetic project. Aesthetic programs like Villa-Lobos's were not a mere ideological façade, and they need to be

---

[40] "Yesterday I organized a Civic Concentration in commemoration of Independence Day with a group of 20,000 school students and 1,000 band musicians, and now I have the pleasure of sending to you, attached, the newspaper clips. [. . .] In October I will execute a series of cultural concerts, including a premiere of Handel's Oratorio *Judas Maccabaeus*. At the Centennial commemoration of [nineteenth-century Brazil's national composer] Carlos Gomes, I will perform 'Columbus,' with staging, at the Municipal Theater and at a field with school students, professors, bands, orchestra, etc. Attached you will find also a description of the French artists that have danced the ballet 'Jurupary' in Paris at both the Opera and the Pleyel Hall." Letter from Heitor Villa-Lobos to Francisco Curt Lange, September 8, 1936, Subsérie 2.2, AFCL.

[41] Richard Cándida Smith, *Improvised Continent: Pan-Americanism and Cultural Exchange* (Philadelphia: University of Pennsylvania Press, 2017), 161–62 and 169.

[42] Unfortunately for him, "Mr. Walt Disney's studio production [was then] firmly blue-printed for the next five years, with feature length cartoon treatments of Peter Pan, Hiawatha and Sword in the Stone prominent on the drawing boards." Hence, "Mr. Disney [was] not at present seeking story material other than that which he already possesses. However, Mr. Disney thanks you sincerely for the kind thought that has prompted you to write to him." Letter from Walt Disney Mickey Mouse Ltd. to Villa-Lobos, August 1, 1951, AHVL.

[43] Ricardo Goldemberg, "Educação Musical: a Experiência Do Canto Orfeônico No Brasil," *Pro-Posições* 6, no. 3 (November 1995): 103–109.

[44] Jerry Dávila, *Diploma of Whiteness: Race and Social Policy in Brazil, 1917–1945* (Durham, NC: Duke University Press, 2003).

[45] Alessandra Coutinho Lisboa, "Villa-Lobos e o Canto Orfeônico: Música, Nacionalismo e Ideal Civilizador" (Dissertação de mestrado inédita. Universidade Estadual Paulista Júlio de Mesquita Filho, 2005), 90–101.

understood in their own terms. He was, above anything else, a musician. In Paris he realized that Parisian musical organizations—specially its *orpheons*—if applied to what he explicitly considered the ignored "racial music" of Brazil, could allow him to realize the vanguard dream of introducing "intellectuals and artists" to the "multitudes," who had until then been "uninterested in culture and divorced from the great and true musical art."[46] He intended to blend Brazil's "race" with the language of what was considered the greatest art music of the time. Of course, the institutional power of Villa-Lobos and the larger state apparatus under Getulio Vargas and his successors paled in comparison to other contemporary musical programs, such as in Soviet Russia.[47] In the end, his project to build a permanent structure of well-trained music teachers across the nation failed due to the structural limits of the Brazilian state.[48]

Another project aimed at creating a musical audience in Brazil was built around folkloric missions. Lange noted when visiting musical institutions in São Paulo that the city's Municipal Recording Collection, which had been organized according to his own advice, had now surpassed in size its model, Uruguay's SODRE. He was impressed and even wanted to receive a donation of some of their recordings. The *Discoteca Pública Municipal* of the State of São Paulo had been created in 1935 under the direction of the young musicologist and poet Oneyda Alvarenga—one of the very few women in an overwhelmingly masculine milieu—who had been assigned to the position by her colleague, Mário de Andrade, who was the head of the Department of Culture and also a musicologist. The *Discoteca* was intended to feed folkloric documentary materials to erudite composers so they could create a national style of musical composition.[49] In 1936 Andrade invited French anthropologist Dina Lévi-Strauss—then living and conducting fieldwork in Brazil with her husband, Claude Lévi-Strauss—to teach a course on folklore and ethnographic methods, out of which the Society of Ethnography and Folklore was created within São Paulo's Department of Culture. Alvarenga attended that course. And under Alvarenga's direction, in 1937 the *Discoteca* researchers, including classical pianist Camargo Guarneri, began registering, both as sound and text recordings, folkloric music from isolated places in the Northeast, in addition to recording some music at their own studio in São Paulo.[50]

Collecting and recording folkloric music, like collective singing, was a worldwide trend. Initiated in the 1890s in Europe, it had been promoted by official institutions in Berlin and Paris—German ethnomusicologists were the first recorders of folk music in the Americas. By the late 1920s and early 1930s, folk music recording in the

[46] Heitor Villa-Lobos, *A música nacionalista no govêrno Getulio Vargas* (Rio de Janeiro: Departamento de Imprensa e Propaganda, 1941), 17. Gerbod, "L'institution orphéonique."

[47] Pauline Fairclough, *Classics for the Masses: Shaping Soviet Musical Identity under Lenin and Stalin* (New Haven, CT: Yale University Press, 2016).

[48] Goldemberg, "Educação musical," 108–109.

[49] Alvaro Carlini, "Recuperação e preservação do acervo histórico-fonográfico da Discoteca Municipal de São Paulo," *Folha de São Paulo—Leitura*, December 12, 1993, 6.

[50] Roberto Barbato Júnior, *Missionários de uma utopia nacional-popular: os intelectuais e o Departamento de Cultura de São Paulo* (São Paulo: FAPESP/Annablume, 2004).

Americas, from Chile and Argentina to the United States, had grown in size and technical quality.[51] The notion of folklore as a *treasure* and as a *patrimony* was too irresistible not to become a common symbol and the goal of musical policies for all sorts of governments. In Brazil, as Lange noticed, both the Department of Publications and Propaganda (DIP) and the section of the Secretary of Education, from which Villa-Lobos had organized collective singing, had produced folk records.

These folk studies were, according to historian Roberto Barbato, an attempt at defining what Gramsci called the *"nacional-popular"* culture.[52] The same mix of populist and civilizing impulses can be found in Mário de Andrade's music listening guides (which included instructions as to when to applaud), designed to orient the people who attended the free *concertos populares* that featured Beethoven, Schumann, and national modernist composers such as Francisco Mignone. *Popular* here meant state pedagogy for the people; some performances had folk content, but they were accompanied by an erudite explanation of the procedures by which an author took a folk rhythm or melody and expanded it into a full composition. The preference for national authors (Mignone, but also Nepomuceno, Camargo Guarnieri, and Artur Pereira) was also an explicit attempt at nationalizing the musical scene of São Paulo, which was dominated, like the cities of the Rio de la Plata region, by Italian immigrants, companies, and repertories. Weekend and holiday concerts were aimed at granting access to art music to people who did not frequent it due to market and social barriers. This intellectual generation was explicitly committed to make popular taste meet high art, on the grounds that not only had highbrow artists always benefited from popular sources, but also that they had infused the popular repertoire, for example in the aristocratic and Portuguese *modinhas* that became popular in nineteenth-century Rio de Janeiro. A national-popular civilizing utopia, thus, by intellectuals within the state apparatus, mediated between the popular and the erudite, two separate but historically mutually dependent cultures. In April 1942 Radio Nacional started its popular programming oriented to civilizing and purifying popular culture. Besides broadcasting "true samba" (*samba de verdade*), it also broadcast a repertoire for children to cultivate their sensitivity "to music of civic character, and *orfeônico* and folkloric singing."[53]

A crucial conceptual shift happened in the transit from the 1940s to the 1950s, in Brazil as in many other countries in the region, regarding the value of popular music. Until the 1940s, *música popular* meant music that had not been written by an identifiable author, nor been recorded or commercialized; in other words, *rural*

[51] Corinne Pernet, "For the Genuine Culture of the Americas: Musical Folklore, Popular Arts, and the Cultural Politics of Pan Americanism, 1933–1950," in *Decentering America*, ed. Jessica Gienow-Hecht (New York: Berghahn Books, 2007), 132–68.

[52] Barbato, *Missionários*, 132–33.

[53] Mônica Pimenta Velloso, *Os intelectuais e a política cultural do Estado Novo* (Rio de Janeiro: Fundação Getulio Vargas, Centro de Pesquisa e Documentação de História Contemporânea do Brasil, 1987), 30. See also McCann, *Hello, Hello Brazil*.

music. Even Mário de Andrade, who unlike other early folklorists appreciated urban music and who in 1937 wrote an essay on the problems of recorded music ("Sung pronunciation and the problem of the Brazilian nasal through records"),[54] usually used the term *popular* music to refer to music of rural origins, and *popularesca* to refer—somewhat derogatorily—to urban music.[55] (Popularesca, it must be noted, means something closer to what "meso-música" or "middle-level music" mean in the contemporary work of Argentine musicology's founding father Carlos Vega.) In 1950, at a folklore conference, Oneyda Alvarenga explicitly argued that even if folkloric music was the source of national character, popular music influenced by commercialism and cosmopolitanism had at least a "thread of conformity with the people's deepest tendencies."[56] By the 1950s, the term *popular* had gained full legitimacy as including urban commercial music. Sandroni notes that in 1950 a Rio journal devoted to music and radio was called *Revista de Música Popular*, and by 1977 the *Enciclopédia da Música Brasileira*'s subtitle was *Erudita, Folclórica, Popular* ("Erudite, Folkloric, and Popular").

At the same time, Northeastern brokers proclaimed their *region* to be a popular alternative to the hegemony of Rio de Janeiro's samba as the one and only popular music of Brazil. But there was another regional musical project that further complicated the definition of national music. In addition to the Northeastern-Southeastern debate and the São Paulo-Rio de Janeiro rivalry, the state of Minas Gerais reemerged in the 1940s with its own brand of regional expression of nationalist modernism. In 1944 Curt Lange arrived in Belo Horizonte, the modern capital of Minas Gerais, with support from Governor Juscelino Kubitschek to develop a research project that took him for several months to the old cities of Diamantina, Sabará, Ouro Preto, Mariana, and São João D'El Rei with the goal of "rescuing" colonial music sheets that had been forgotten in the region's many churches. The results contributed to the development of a musicological argument about the "first" original music of the Americas: the Baroque music composed by African and mixed-race musicians.[57] Lange's research supported Minas Gerais's claim to being the cradle of Brazilian culture, a title that until then had been disputed by Rio de Janeiro and Northeastern intellectuals. Historical manuscripts from this research were exhibited at a Pan American Union event in 1948, and the explanatory text included Lange's main theses: that these eighteenth-century musicians from Minas Gerais were grouped in corporations, that performed the work of their European contemporaries—"Haydn, Mozart,

---

54 Mario de Andrade, "A pronúncia cantada e o problema do nasal através dos discos," *Projeto História : Revista do Programa de Estudos Pós-Graduados de História* 26 (June 2003) [1937]: 75–91.

55 Carlos Sandroni, "Farewell to MPB," in *Brazilian Popular Music and Citizenship*, ed. Idelbar Avelar and Christopher Dunn (Durham, NC: Duke University Press, 2011), 64–73.

56 Renato de Almeida, *Música Folclórica e Música Popular* (Porto Alegre: Comissão Gaúcha de Folclore and Comissão Nacional de Folclore, 1958), 9–10, quoted in Sandroni, "Farewell to MPB," 67.

57 Lange's disciple, Lauro Ayestarán, would later find and analyze in Peru even earlier musical works and colonial documents for the history of Latin America. See Coriún Aharonián's prologue in Lauro Ayestarán, *Textos breves*, ed. Coriún Aharonián, Biblioteca Artigas (Montevideo: Ministerio de Educación y Cultura, 2014), xi.

Beethoven, while they were still alive"—that there was a circulation of works among Lisbon, Rio de Janerio, and Minas Gerais, and that performers were "99% negros y mulatos" (and most composers too).[58]

Lange's project in Minas Gerais promoted an argument about Baroque music as the origin of Latin American musical culture itself that was consequential: researchers and performers recovered this transnational Catholic legacy many years later with material found in the Jesuit missions of Chiquitos, Bolivia.[59] In parallel to Lange, Catholic musicologist Miguel Bernal Jiménez published in 1939 in Mexico a research on the Baroque repertoire of religious choirs in the colonial churches of Morelia, Michoacán.[60]

The interest throughout the Americas in the transnational colonial roots of religious music was not contradictory with nationalist aesthetic programs that during the central decades of the twentieth century, in virtually every country, aimed at shaping popular musical practices.

MEXICO

In Mexico, a country large and diverse as Brazil, but with a comparatively stronger tradition of political centralization and a closer relationship with the United States, musical brokers actively promoted "national music" since the revolution further strengthened the power of the state agencies in the 1920s. At the First National Congress of Music in Mexico City in 1926 the debate focused on art music and musicians, but it also extended to popular musical traditions.[61] The recognition of a specific Mexican folk music tradition was fundamental for the National Conservatory curriculum in the following years and for the atmosphere in which commercial radio started to broadcast "typical Mexican music" alongside many other musical traditions. In the 1920s nationalist composers, teachers, scholars, collectors, and musicians intensely circulated across state and civil institutions, including the Casa del Pueblo, which later on would become a rural school, "the Cultural Missions, and the popular nocturnal music schools" aimed at "rescuing [the urban poor] from vice" (sacar del vicio).[62] What began to be called "Mexican music" in those institutions were

[58] "Unión Panamericana—Departamento de Asuntos Culturales—División de Música y Artes Visuales," October 13, 1948, Organization of American States.

[59] Bernardo Illari, Domenico Zipoli: para una genealogía de la música latinoamericana (La Habana: Premio de Musicología Casa de las Américas, 2011).

[60] Miguel Bernal Jiménez, El archivo musical del Colegio de Santa Rosa de Santa María de Vallodolid, siglo XVIII, Morelia colonial (Morelia: Universidad michoacana de San Nicolás, 1939). I thank Lorena Díaz Nuñez for her references on Bernal Jiménez and his relevance to the history of Baroque and Mexican music. See Lorena Díaz Núñez, Como un eco lejano . . . La vida de Miguel Bernal Jiménez (México, D.F.: Consejo Nacional para la Cultura y las Artes, 2003).

[61] Alejandro L. Madrid, "The Sounds of the Nation: Visions of Modernity and Tradition in Mexico's First National Congress of Music," Hispanic American Historical Review 86, no. 4 (2006): 701.

[62] Marina Alonso Bolaños, La "invención" de la música indígena de México: antropología e historia de las políticas culturales del siglo XX (Buenos Aires: SB Ediciones, 2008), 41.

repertoires that resulted in fact from migrations and concoctions produced by the (civil) war against the French invasion, elite sociability, and urban popular artists and audiences; from transnational avant-garde and commercial circuits, especially in connection with the United States, Cuba, and Europe; and from a musicological "invention of indigenous music," which provided a historical and mythical nationalist background for modern music.[63] Mexican ideas on music invoked hence many geographies. Composer and nationalist titan Carlos Chávez proclaimed in 1925 that not just Mexican but also *Latin American* music was in fact Indo-Spanish. In 1934 he became head of the Department of Fine Arts at the SEP. The Mexican state became a very active musical sponsor. Its cadres and programs came directly from the forces that participated in the revolution.

The history of the military choirs is a great example of how the revolution shaped musical education. In 1918 the folklorist Rubén M. Campos published a history of a military band, the *Orfeón Militar*, and its influence on choral music during the revolution.[64] Aware of the cultural and political importance of choral music in the Mexican Revolution, he saw it as a continuation of the mythical Orpheus, a sort of primordial choir director and inventor of collective singing. Popular chant became in the nineteenth century, he argued, something secular and inherent to all nations. The Mexican Revolution created an *Orfeón Militar* in 1915 to propagate Mexican popular songs throughout the country via the schools: "children marching and singing by the streets of the metropolis [. . .] in harmony with a people that celebrated the recovery of its freedom. No popular spectacle had acquired such proportions: the union of the people and the young army through music." Far from evoking fear, soldiers became "the people itself." The Orfeón Militar instituted choral singing in the schools to make of each student not a soldier, but a future music teacher.[65]

[63] Alonso Bolaños, *La "invención"*; Marco Velázquez and Mary K. Vaughan, "Mestizaje and Musical Nationalism in Mexico," in *The Eagle and the Virgin: Nation and Cultural Revolution in Mexico, 1920–1940*, ed. Mary K. Vaughan and Stephen E. Lewis (Durham, NC: Duke University Press, 2006), 95–118; Guy P. C. Thomson, "The Ceremonial and Political Role of Village Bands, 1846–1974," in *Rituals of Rule, Rituals of Resistance : Public Celebrations and Popular Culture in Mexico*, ed. William H. Beezley, Cheryl English Martin, and William E. French (Wilmington, DE: SR Books, 1994), 564–625; María Esther Aguirre Lora, "En pos de la construcción del sentido de lo nacional. Universos sonoros y dancísticos en la escuela mexicana (1920–1940)," *Historia de la Educación* 25 (2006): 205–24.

[64] Rubén M Campos, *Los orfeones populares en la cultura nacional* (Mexico, D.F.: Secretaría de Guerra y Marina–Departamento de Militarización–Sección Cuarta–Orfeones, Publicaciones del Departamento de Militarización para su propaganda en toda la República–Imprenta Victoria, 1918).

[65] Ibid., 18–20: "Los niños han desfilado cantando por las calles de la metrópoli, y el pueblo se ha unido a esa manifestación de cultura y de alegría estruendosa, jubilosa, rítmica, en armonía con el júbilo del pueblo que celebraba sus fastos gloriosos al mismo tiempo que celebraba su triunfo de volver a la libertad. Ningún espectáculo popular había adquirido tales proporciones, como el de la unión del pueblo al juvenil ejército por la música [sic]. Jamás se había obtenido una fusión de sentimientos tan estrecha, espresada en la más sonora de las manifestaciones. [. . .] El ejército juvenil es hijo del pueblo. Han desaparecido los antiguos resquemores y las antipatías que hacían que el pueblo viera al soldado como a un paria, como a una amenaza, casi como a un enemigo. Hoy no. El soldado es el pueblo, el pueblo mismo, que venció y barrió al antiguo ejército y que hoy [. . .] educa a sus hijos en el

The musical and military organizer of this ambitious military choir was Jesús Reynoso Aráoz,[66] founder in September 1915 of the *Orfeón de las escuelas de tropa* that taught choral lessons to the Constitutionalist Army in Mexico City. Aráoz convoked colleagues from an older Mexico City popular choir (*Orfeón popular*) that had been active from 1907 to 1914. On September 15, Independence Day, the first 2,000 soldiers from different brigades got together to sing the national anthem in conjunction with a military march, and two weeks later the Orfeón was incorporated to the Troops School. By the end of 1915 they were teaching 3,600 students in twenty-six barracks, and at the city's penitentiary the eight original teachers grew to sixteen.

According to Aráoz, in May 1916 the Orfeón (now under the Secretary of Public Instruction and Fine Arts) was devoted first to the task of "militarizing the children." The teaching extended from the barracks to regular schools and some professional schools, and the Orfeón also expanded its roster and upgraded salaries. On May 1, 1917, at the Condesa hippodrome, 2,000 children sang a repertoire combining varied musical categories: "classical Mexican songs," "patriotic chants," and "musical art works."[67] In September, at the same place, 20,000 children "organized in battalions" did gymnastic exercises while 2,000 young children, 2,000 nurses, and 1,000 other performers organized into four bands played patriotic hymns, sang peace and war chants and popular songs, and displayed art works in front of the president. These singers, trained by the Orfeón teachers, were musically illiterate, having learned exclusively through auditory methods. This scale of celebration was a novelty. In 1918 the Orfeón was dissolved, with the goals of de-militarizing choral singing and instead generalizing its principles throughout the educational system under the name of *Canto Coral y Orfeónico*.

Always under the direction of Reynoso Aráoz, the 1915–1918 military *orfeones* became the Orfeón Popular that functioned within the National University between 1920 and 1922, then the 1923 Nocturnal Department of the National Music Conservatory, and finally the 1924 EPNM,[68] the Popular Music Night School, which targeted Mexico City's working-class youth. This final reincarnation was approved by the National Congress after a proposal by avant-garde composer Julián Carrillo, who wanted the National Music School to be released of the less prepared students, for whom a different type of professional training could be provided based on the

---

amor a la patria [. . .] y les da un idioma universal, el idioma de la música, para que por medio de él se unan y simpaticen fraternalmente en la formación de la patria de mañana."

[66] Jesus Reynoso Aráoz, "Apuntes biográficos del orfeón de la Escuelas de Tropa y orfeón del Departamento de Enseñanza Militar, con una breve reseña de sus trabajos desarrollados durante los años de 1915, 1916 y 1917, por Jesús Reynoso Aráoz," Mexico, January 1918, 21–45, in Campos, *Los orfeones populares*.

[67] Ibid., 37.

[68] Caja 47, Expediente 3, Departamento de Bellas Artes, SEP.

military choirs—which hence did not just turned into children choirs, but became ultimately a tool of job training for the working-class youth of Mexico City.[69]

The EPNM met from 5:00 p.m. to 10:00 p.m. every night and had five basic goals:

- to "keep people from dissolution"
- to "elevate them aesthetically"
- to give them "economic opportunities as music performers"
- to help them "organize the popular neighborhoods"
- to count with an "organized mass of people at official and cultural events"

By 1932 more than 13,000 students had attended classes, and many of them became music teachers themselves, members of bands, orchestras, theaters, film studios, and radio stations. The best among them entered the Music Department at the University and the conservatories of music, dance, and dramatic arts.

The debates about the musical orientation of the EPNM expressed larger ones about the cultural hierarchies that the state should respect, promote, or shape when intervening in the aesthetic life of society. While top modernist composers such as Julián Carrillo praised the labor of the EPNM, others argued instead that it should remain, musically speaking, within an "indigenist" conception of authentic popular music as a continuation of the Aztec pentatonic musical structure and therefore ban European classic forms "and even Italian opera" from the school's repertoire. Other critics argued that it should develop the true music of its time: modernist music. The EPNM director defended the school's aesthetic orientation in terms of improving the cultural and material conditions of the Mexican working class "as it is," meaning neither an idealized indigenous society of the past nor a dreamed-of futurist one. He based his position on an argument about the nature of popular music that fell halfway between positivism and populism:

> The School's mission is to develop the aesthetic and moral sentiments of the working class . . . It therefore has to be based on popular songs . . . but at the same time has to educate the aesthetic sentiments of the students . . . according to Haeckel's philo-genetic law, across the stages through which humanity developed its musical feelings. In consequence . . . the School has to go from popular songs and then lead the students to . . . at least Italian opera and other classic musical forms. It could eventually lead them also to German opera, since it has a sufficiently skilled staff of professors and students to deal with that genre; but unfortunately it lacks enough financial resources.[70]

[69] "Objeto del establecimiento del Departamento Nocturno de la Escuela Nacional de Música, su organización, plan de estudios, resultados prácticos y galardones obtenidos," Caja 46, Expediente 2, Departamento de Bellas Artes, SEP, March 10, 1923.

[70] "La misión de la escuela consiste en desarrollar los sentimientos estéticos y morales de las clases trabajadoras, y para tal fin, debe basarse ciertamente en las canciones populares que jamás se han descuidado en la Escuela; pero debe también educar los sentimientos estéticos de los alumnos, y para

The internal struggles and the fate of the EPNM continued and increased over the 1930s. But its broader populist goal of musically educating the Mexican people was incorporated by even more ambitious policies. In June 1937, President Lázaro Cárdenas decreed obligatory and free musical education through choral singing in primary, middle, and normal schools in all the states and municipalities of the Mexican confederation. "The education of the popular sentiment must be reach all social classes, and essentially the children" in order to "unite them" in their "common and egalitarian needs and aspirations," through a "musical culture based on our popular chants, to give shape to the artistic intuitions of the masses."[71] Critic and folklorist Gerónimo Baqueiro Foster, under the pseudonym Demóstenes, welcomed the decree but warned about the amount of resources required to implement it. The only way to enforce this policy would be to create an autonomous Department of Music in charge of every aspect of musical education in the country, which would mean upgrading the status of the Music Section of the Fine Arts Department within the SEP to make it independent from the artistic establishment and increase its financial resources. In Mexico City alone, according to Baqueiro, less than a third of the 200,000 children attending primary school received real musical education, due to the lack of teachers.[72] That gap between the ambition of inclusion and the reality of exclusion is what populist policies were intended to close.

At the same time, military bands, crucial musical actors since the previous century, declined after the revolution.[73] The city's four military bands were those of the Joint Chiefs Staff, the Sappers, the Artillery, and the Police. By the mid-1930s they were playing classic marches, double-steps, fashionable popular songs, and sometimes well-known opera overtures and selections at sport events, bullfights, and horse races, less frequently at school events, and sometimes in the street to attract the public to entertainment halls. According to critic Gerónimo Baqueiro Foster, the bands' decadence and lack of creativity, and the dwindling tradition of the Sunday concerts, turned audiences to the "degenerate" influence of radio programming.

---

ese fin, se hace necesario llevarlos siguiendo la ley filogenética de Haeckel, al través de las diversas etapas por las cuales la humanidad ha desarrollado sus sentimientos musicales. De consiguiente, si se desea que la Escuela realmente eduque a nuestras clases trabajadoras, es indispensable partir de la canción popular y conducir enseguida a los alumnos por las diversas etapas del desarrollo musical humano, hasta llegar cuando menos a la ópera italiana y a las otras formas clásicas musicales. Podría llegarse también a la ópera alemana, pues la escuela cuenta con profesores y alumnos suficientemente competentes para abordar ese género; pero desgraciadamente la falta de elementos pecuniarios lo ha impedido."

[71] "Art. 3: Que la educación del sentimiento popular debe ponerse al alcance de todas las clases sociales, esencialmente en los niños, con el fin de unirlos estrechamente en sus necesidades y aspiraciones comunes e igualitarias, de acuerdo con los siglos de una cultura musical fundada en nuestros cantos populares." Manuel Barajas, *México y la cultura musical* (México, D.F.: Departamento Autónomo de Prensa y Publicidad, 1938), 9.

[72] "La música y los músicos entre bastidores. El canto coral como medio de educación nacional, por Demóstenes," July 29, 1937, AGBF.

[73] Demóstenes, "Las Bandas Militares de Música," June 11, 1936, Manuscripts, AGBF.

During the revolution, the bands had been devoted to celebrating the victorious military leaders, whose favorite director would occupy the office of the General Inspection of Bands. Now the position became bureaucratically established and the band directors better trained. But the artistic inspiration was lost, as directors and musicians just rehearsed the traditional repertoire.

Baqueiro Foster argued in favor of returning to the crowded Sunday concerts at the plazas, where the public could identify with their favorite bands, and of encouraging more and newer Mexican compositions to be performed by these bands in place of the old repertoire. During the revolution the army's music bands, including the police band, crisscrossed the country disseminating and mixing metropolitan and provincial music, musicians, and audiences, "from town to town, like bees flying from flower to flower," and this strengthened musical nationalism.[74] But now bureaucrats reduced these activities to a minimal level of activity, without sponsoring new programs, study, or tours, and paying low salaries to bored musicians. The official rhetoric praised the musician-workers, but the actual policies abandoned the police band musicians to improvisation, poverty, and decreased musical quality.

Baqueiro's critical assessment of the activities of military bands exemplifies a common pattern across Latin America in the age of musical populism: the feeling among intellectuals that the capacity of music to improve social life was underestimated and restrained by the inability of the political personnel.

Both state officers and their critics shared an awareness of the policies being developed in other countries. The Mexican state attempted many forms of intervention through the Music Section of the SEP, finding inspiration in foreign models. For instance, bureaucrats analyzed the broadcasting systems implemented in Europe and other parts of the Americas and attempted to build one in which the president could monitor the broadcasted contents of the several branches of the state, such as war, education, agriculture, health, statistics, foreign relations, governors, and the legislative and judiciary powers.

From the Italian case, based on a Fascist choral singing program, the educational bureaucrats learned that elementary notions of music could be taught by using traditional patriotic hymns, folk songs, and also new, modernist hymns that celebrated the current regime (*Inno popolare della scuola fascista*). The SEP participated in a 1931 poll that was conducted by the International Institute of Intellectual Cooperation and directed at researching different uses of broadcasting at the school. These bureaucrats were also aware of *Progressive Education*, a US publication dedicated to pedagogy and the "new tendencies in education." In fact, the director of the Music Section, Moisés Sáenz, published in the February 1932 issue a study on "New Trends in Indian Education" that showcased the advances of the revolutionary states in the incorporation of Indian population into modern housing, musical training, and agricultural techniques through educational policies. Among these, he emphasized music

---

[74] Demóstenes, "El derrumbamiento de la Banda de Policía," January 7, 1937, Manuscripts, AGBF.

as a tool for community organization, innovative teaching, national symbolism, and social harmony. He celebrated the creation of local orchestras as a result and means of progress.

In April 1935, with Cárdenas in office, a group of socialist educators further promoted the transnationalization of the repertoire by translating Soviet proletarian songs and incorporating them within the national curriculum via the SEP music scores distribution.[75] In 1938 the National Music Conservatory professor and music pedagogist Manuel Barajas proposed to follow the example of cellist Pablo Casals's pedagogical labor, as composer and conductor, with the working classes of Barcelona. From 1926 to 1939 (the end of the Civil War), Casals organized the *Associació Obrera de Conciertos*. By 1938, Barajas quotes Casals, it had "25,000 members," and "workers were the orchestra professors, the quartet players, the trios, the choirs. Simple people who feel the music . . . who work during the day and then at night and in the holidays transmit to their brothers the musical treasures from the past and of today." Barajas combined in fact this proletarian ethos with the old civilizing trope of music as "harmonizing" society. He praised choirs in particular for making men to "forgive and forget differences of class and of ideas and, united, pay tribute to art, which is always above and beyond everything else." Everyone knows, after all, that peoples with choral societies "have a more harmonic, less rough social life."[76]

The opening of musical education to a socialist agenda brought new problems to the musicologists and amateur musicians working within the music section of the Fine Arts department, which was one of the several units of the SEP. The alliance with working-class organizations was so tight that in September 1934 the Tramway Union AOECTM (*Alianza de Obreros y Empleados de la Compañía de Tranvías de México*) sent a note on behalf of one of its members, Antonio Méndez, asking that he be auditioned by the Music Section. A long quarrel followed the rejection of Méndez after an examination proved that "the composer has no musical formation, and some excerpts of his songs are in fact copied from the National Anthem and the popular song La Pajarera [a woman who sells birds]." The Union reacted in defense of its member, suggesting elitism on the part of the SEP, to which the SEP responded offering Méndez the opportunity to participate in a national contest of popular music that sought to incorporate popular compositions into the national curricula. The contest took place; Méndez did not win, and this outcome allowed the SEP to argue that other popular composers were actually able to compose (unlike Méndez) original and consistent musical pieces. Méndez responded by addressing President Cárdenas directly in a May 20, 1936, letter that expressed several key ideological tropes of populism. "I am not a professional, but a simple aficionado" from a poor family, with no studies but natural talent, he wrote. "My music is entirely lyrical because I know no musical

---

[75] April 11, 1935, Caja 47, Bellas Artes, SEP.

[76] "Olvidan y perdonan las diferencias de clase, de ideas y de condición para, unidos, rendir tributo al arte, que está siempre sobre todo y más allá de todo." Manuel Barajas, *México y la cultura musical* (México, D.F.: Departamento Autónomo de Prensa y Publicidad, 1938), 21–22 and 30–31.

note." His petition of support from the SEP was due to his need to feed a family of five with a salary that did not suffice to pay for music lessons, in spite of which "I can't abandon the idea of improving because I am a believer in progress." He felt entitled to pursue a musical career because in forty-three years he had "observed the favorite music of my social class in its joys and suffering" and wanted to advance a "revolution in music, since professionals have prevailed in it, but seldom the poor artist who fights desperately against misery and, even more, against the selfishness of the so-called 'educators.'"[77]

In effect, the SEP was sending musical-anthropological missions of educators to isolated corners of Mexico, collecting and distributing music sheets of folk songs, and echoing a hemispheric current of *indigenismo*. Let us consider the way musicologist Luis Sandi, research head of the Music Section in 1933–1934, described his work.

Sandi sent a report to his boss at the Fine Arts department of the SEP, Carlos Chávez, in which he described the planning and actions of the Music Section between May 1933 and May 1934. The report exemplifies the variety of musical and ideological sources of the SEP policies. It starts by pointing out the problems that needed to be addressed: music teachers expected students to read music and to learn school songs, but the basis for both were "nineteenth-century *zarzuelas* and *cuplés*," which presented the students only the "formal and external difficulties" of music and forced them to use not just compositions of low quality, but also old ones. As a result, primary school children were not able to read a popular song composition after years of training, detested classical music, and ended up getting used to "the music of the city outskirts" [*un tipo de música extraído de los arrabales de la ciudad*] cultivated by merchants. The youngest children were more affected by the despicable quality (*canallesca*) of the "dictators" of radio music; the older generations had at least the habit of attending classic concerts and even modern ones. A "radical change" was required, thus, and it consisted, among other things, of putting children and adolescents in contact with "representative works of the diverse cultures of the world, and of the times of Mexican, Inca, and Western cultures," in order to form an intelligent and active musical audience" (*formar un público musical interesado e inteligente*) that would form the basis for future music teachers.

Sandi invited a group of young composers that were teaching for the Music Section to create and propose musical works for the schools. They were Eduardo Hernández Moncada, José Ríos, Vicente T. Mendoza, Daniel Ayala, Salvador Contreras, Alfonso del Río, Julio Bacmeister, Manuel León Mariscal, and Angel Salas, some of whom

---

[77] Caja 47/ Folder 25, Bellas Artes, SEP. "Yo sé que puedo componer música antigua y moderna en todos sus estilos, especialmente la que más gusta al pueblo, porque durante cuarenta y tres años que tengo de vida, y desde que tengo uso de razón, he venido observando la música predilecta de mi clase sufrida en sus penas y en sus alegrías, y ojalá fuera yo el exponente de esas melodías, sería un caso verdaderamente extraordinario en la revolución de la Música, ya que en su mayoría ha prevalecido la Profesional, y rara vez la del artista pobre que lucha desesperadamente con la miseria, y por añadidura el egoísmo de los llamados 'educadores.'"

would become leading musicologists in Mexico. Sandi describes the scope of the group's production:

> The group has produced the following works: almost 200 original music works in pentatonic, Greek, major and minor modes, for kindergarten; 14 original works in those same modes for students in first cycle of primary school; Chuparrosa—Yaqui chant; Los Xtoles—Mayan chant; Ténabari—Yaqui chant; La Estrella Matutina—Pápago chant; El Pequeño Hermano—Pápago chant; I-coos—Serí chant; Canción del Coyote—Yaqui chant; and Bura Bampo—Yaqui chant, selected and arranged for the first level of the second cycle; 7 Mexican popular songs selected for the second level of the second cycle; Yo tengo un buen pastel –Rondel by Adam de la Hale and Se tu m'ami by Pergolesi for the first level of the third cycle; Paloma Blanca—Peruvian chant; Veyñi amán—Araucano chant; Kuriquinga—Ecuadorian chant; Muchacha Bonita—Peruvian chant and Encantadora Sirena—Peruvian chant, selected and arranged for the second and third trimesters of the first level of the third cycle; two African chants and an Arab one for the first trimester of the second level of the third cycle; Canto de la Tarde—Moussorgsky, selected for the second trimester of the second level of the third cycle; three original chants in modern style and the "Bestiario" or "Cortejo de Orfeo" by Francis Poulenc for the third semester.

To this wide span of musical sources were to be added three research centers (*academias*) producing monographs and bibliographies and preserving the Music Section's archive—one of European music; another of music from Ancient, Oriental, Africa and Oceania; and a third for American music—as well as a center for teachers' training. These would be consulting centers for the Music Section. The section also sent "music collectors" to Sonora, Lagos (Jalisco), and Chiapas. Future trips would require "recording machines that record the scientifically exact truth" (*aparatos grabadores que registren la verdad científicamente exacta*) instead of the deficient and approximated version that results from the aural transcription of the "ever changing music, always more interesting as more changing, of the indigenous." The section also organized two traveling concert groups to perform the section's repertoire throughout the schools of Mexico, one of them a duo of piano and singer, the other a "Mariachi Quartet" exclusively dedicated to "anonymous popular music." In 1933 an official event was held that included performances from selected choirs of schoolchildren, who sang some parts of the repertoire they had learned at their choral singing lessons; the reconstruction of some indigenous works from the section's archive; and the performance of an orchestra that included instruments from the different regions of the country (this synthesis of regional orchestras was called *Orquesta Mexicana*).[78]

---

[78] May 4, 1934, Bellas Artes, Caja 47, Folder 9, SEP.

Another factor influencing musical activity on the part of the state was the demands of US institutions, which required the SEP to instruct them in the authentic features of Mexican music to be performed by orchestras of unemployed musicians sponsored by the Work Progress Administration and by the organizers of musical and patriotic events at US prisons with Mexican inmates, not to mention the countless schools, conservatories and universities in the United States that wrote continuously, asking for scores, lyrics, and bibliography.

Within Mexico these policies had a multiplying effect on poor communities. In June 1934 the professor of a Federal Rural School in La Quemada, Salvatierra, Guanajuato wrote to the SEP's Department of Fine Arts that "given the enthusiasm for music awakened in this community by forming a band of 25 musicians, and given the peasants' lack of resources to afford music scores," he required some music pieces and patriotic hymns to be played by them.

The SEP also published and distributed a booklet "4 Canciones de Cuna" lyrics by the Chilean poet Gabriela Mistral, music by Rafael Galindo. In August 1936 it sent materials on Mexican music and dance to the musical supervisor of schools in Orange County, California. In February 1937 the supervisor asked for more materials to train the county's teachers, specifically the official school version of the national anthem. These are just a few examples of the degree of international reach of the Music Section.

A Catholic Musical Transnationalism in the Service of Nationalism

Conservative and anti-revolutionary intellectuals had similar transnational debts. As a response to secularist state musical practices, Catholic intellectuals decided to reinvigorate the religious framework of music that had been dominant in colonial times. This Catholic musical revisionism developed in the 1950s as a reaction to the activism of the SEP in the 1930s and 1940s, with which it shared a sense of musical nationalism.

Priest, organist, and composer Miguel Bernal Jiménez pointed out in 1948 that the religious music housed in the Santa Rosa College in Morelia, Michoacán, made it "the first conservatory of America" (1743) and as important in the history of sacred music as its contemporary Saint Thomas in Leipzig, directed by Johann Sebastian Bach.[79] His archival research on the Santa Rosa College happened a few years before Francisco Curt Lange conducted similar research to find the baroque musical treasures in the churches of Minas Gerais, Brazil, and he similarly claimed that he had discovered the first music of the Americas (Lange and Bernal had an intermittent intellectual dialogue over time). Choral music was a key component of Bernal's research, and he in fact developed a methodology for its teaching and practice.[80]

[79] Miguel Bernal Jiménez, "Música nuestra: breve ensayo sobre la música mejicana," *Estudios Americanos* 1, no. 1 (1948): 109–17.
[80] Miguel Bernal Jiménez, *La disciplina coral* (Morelia: Escuela Superior de Música Sagrada, 1947).

Bernal was a Hispanista nationalist who kept a keen eye on both Iberian roots and Mexican originality. Writing to a Spanish journal in 1947, he explained:

It seems to me that in the deepest and most archaic of our folklore we can recognize the Castilian and Andalusian *solera*: in some of the chants of our childhood, in the classic *corridos*, and in the use of the guitar. By contrast, our songs, from the past century to the present, sound to me more like mountain music. An economist would find perhaps an easy explanation, by arguing that in colonial times Seville was the door to overseas, whereas afterwards the door opened more readily to the U.S.

Today Mexican and Spanish folklore are distinct. You have noticed it in the songs that our cinema brought to Spain. The sympathy they inspire and that makes them popular in Spain is a signal of an affinity of feelings and kinship; but the fact that you recognize them as Mexicans [*Mejicanas*, with the Hispanist "j" instead of the Nahuátl "x"] proves that they acquired a distinct identity.[81]

Bernal went on to explain that erudite Mexican composers between the sixteenth and the nineteenth centuries needed to learn and incorporate the work of European composers—particularly Italians and French—by imitating it. In the nineteenth century some indigenous elements were incorporated as well. But it was not until the twentieth century that the time was ripe for a nationalist movement—which was not too late, he added, since musical nationalism had just begun in Europe as well. Manuel Ponce was the initiator of this movement: "He valorized the folkloric treasure, elevated it to the category of art and produced works that are European in their technical mastery and Mexican in their inspiration." Mexican composers gave their country a citizenship within the "Republic of the Universal Art" by emphasizing both the *indigenista* trend (Carlos Chávez) and the *mestiza* one (Silvestre Revueltas, Candelario Huízar, Blas Galindo, Daniel Ayala, Rafael Tello, José Vazquez, De Elías, Paredes, and others). Bernal himself participated in a series of musical "missions" organized by the SEP, by which teachers and experts from the Federal District reached distant schools in the country. Finally, another vital trend, he thought, was the "sacred musical movement: eight Schools of Sacred Music work regularly in different parts of the country under a unified plan of studies, inspired by the Roman Pontifical Institute."

---

[81] "Paréceme que en lo más hondo y arcaico de nuestro folklore puede reconocerse la solera castellana y andaluza: algunos de nuestros cantos infantiles, los clásicos 'corridos', el uso de la guitarra. Por el contrario, nuestras canciones, sel siglo pasado para acá, me saben más a música montañesa. Un economista hallaría tal vez una fácil explicación, diciendo que, durante el virreinato, Sevilla era la puerta hacia ultramar: mientras que después lo fueron los pueblos del norte. No obstante estos puntos de contacto, hoy día el folklore mexicano y el español son diferentes. Vosotros lo habréis advertido en las canciones que el cinematógrafo y el cine os han traído. La simpatía que os inspiran y las vuelven populares en tierras españolas, señal es de afinidad de sentires y similitud de progenie; pero el hecho de que las distingáis como mejicanas, prueba que poseen ya un elemento de identificación, un factor diferencial."

One of the schools, the one in Morelia, published the journal *Schola Cantorum*. A central committee headed by a bishop organized two regional congresses per year—the first national one was in 1937—and was then organizing in Guadalajara, Mexico, the First Inter-American Congress of Sacred Music, which took place in 1948. Several activities explicitly addressed the training of musicians (their "spiritual" and "artistic improvement") and popular participation in the religious choir ("the participation of the people in the diverse services through Gregorian chant").[82]

In 1950, a worldwide congress took place in Rome. In 1903 the Pope Pius X had established Gregorian chant, classic polyphony, Latin language, and organ as the only legitimate tools for performing sacred music. The fact that in 1928 and 1947 his two successors had to officially insist on this reveals both the frequent abandonment of those strict rules and the importance given to them by the church's authorities. But the Second Inter-American Congress never took off, and all the proposals of the first one vanished sooner or later. The main engine of this "restoration" of sacred music, Bernal Jimenez, died in 1956, and the reforms of the 1962 Second Vatican Council went in the opposite direction, toward more respect for the vernacular.[83] Bernal's 1948 plans of "establishing an Inter-American office of information, exchange and cooperation" did not prosper.[84]

The most salient feature of this Catholic musical nationalism was precisely its proclivity for producing inter-American exchanges and, ultimately, global ones. Its ideological base was an interpretation of the history of the Church in Mexico as part of a universal spiritual project that involved Latin America as a whole.

ARGENTINA

In Argentina collective singing provided a template for discipline and egalitarianism in the public educational system. But here the school choir was intended to organize and imprint the national identity on a population that enjoyed civil rights and economic opportunities—including in the music business—to a much higher degree than in the other countries. In fact, collective singing as a popular practice began in Argentina with immigrant associations (*orfeones*), especially from Catalonia, Galicia, and the Basque Country, in the late nineteenth century.[85]

Each and every nation in the Americas initially modeled its musical institutions after European traditions, but in Argentina the considerable size and prosperity of Italian immigration since the mid-nineteenth century—they were the largest

[82] "Primer Congreso Inter-Americano de Música Sacra," *Frumentum: Sugerencias Filosóficas y Religiosas* (Mexico, D.F.: Casa de Estudios M.Sp.S., 1949), 198.

[83] Eduardo Escoto Robledo, "El primer Congreso Interamericano de Música Sacra," *Boletín Eclesiástico del Arzobispado de Guadalajara* 6, no. 12 (2012). https://arquidiocesisgdl.org/boletin/2012-12-4.php.

[84] "Primer Congreso Inter-Americano de Música Sacra," 200.

[85] Alicia Chust, *Tangos, orfeones y rondallas: una historia con imágenes* (Barcelona: Carena, 2008), esp. chapter 3.

immigrant group—made their music particularly influential on the programs of musical pedagogy implemented by the cultural intelligentsia. Musical pedagogue Clemente Greppi, born in Italy and a naturalized Argentine, is a good example.[86] Besides exposing generation after generation of Argentine students up to the present to his adaptation of the patriotic hymn "March of San Lorenzo," Greppi published two books on musical education, in 1907 and 1922, aimed at shaping musical teaching and the national official curriculum.[87] An immigrant himself, he saw the pedagogy of the State as the right antidote to the dispersing effect of commercial music.

In his 1907 *Singing in Primary Schools* he proposed a variety of principles for a successful and patriotic musical education at the school.[88] The right school songs needed to have, according to him, an appropriate moral content ("fatherland, family, school, nature, sciences, virtues, affections") and a metric and tone adjusted to the children's ability to memorize, breathing, and pitch range; and last but not least, they needed to be *liked* by them. Whereas the solemn tone of "patriotic" songs—martial, imposing, and classic—risked boring the students, and the *arias* (pieces for solo voice) were only good for one performer, the "songs extracted from operas" were the most useful for the learning process. Once rid of their religious or political meanings and the morally correct ones selected, "the dramatic style," argued Greppi, "gives life to the music. Its rhythm, melodic force, and descriptive power capture the attention of the children, and they, fascinated, put all their will into overcoming the challenges of the learning process." "Experience," in sum, dictated that opera pieces were the best teaching tool for both boys and girls above the age of eleven.

Modern pedagogy like the one promoted by Greppi was used by the state as a tool for fabricating citizens, and therefore it was also a contested battlefield of professional, ethical, and ideological positions among educational actors.[89] In music, education was initially conceived as a set of techniques oriented to enhance individual creativity, expression, judgment, and intelligence. The "rhythm, melodic force, and descriptive power" of musical theater were for Greppi expressive values that were valid by themselves, beyond any nationalist concern. In fact, given that there were too few useful works in Spanish, music teachers should take advantage of operas in Italian and French. Their linguistic closeness with Spanish made them comprehensible to students, and professors could translate them almost literally. A French or Italian opera could even be an opportunity for foreign language training. Opera's theatricality had more advantages: the use of costumes in comic songs, musical

[86] I thank Aníbal Cetrangolo for this reference.

[87] Clemente Greppi, *El canto en las escuelas primarias. Consejos para la educación de la voz infantil y enseñanza de cantos escolares* (Buenos Aires: Librería del Colegio, 1907) and *La educación musical de los niños* (Buenos Aires: Librería del Colegio, 1922).

[88] Greppi, *El canto en las escuelas*, 31–37.

[89] Adriana Puiggrós, *Qué pasó en la educación argentina: breve historia desde la conquista hasta el presente* (Buenos Aires: Galerna, 2002); Lilia Ana Bertoni, *Patriotas, cosmopolitas y nacionalistas: la construcción de la nacionalidad argentina a fines del siglo XIX* (Buenos Aires: Fondo de Cultura Económica, 2001); Beatriz Sarlo, *La máquina cultural: maestras, traductores y vanguardistas* (Buenos Aires: Ariel, 1998).

pantomimes, "melodramas, operettas, zarzuelas, duets, romanzas, etc." could liberate children's spontaneity and talent from the constraints of their social conditions. Finally, any type of song had to be fundamentally "true" and "natural," and for this reason it could not be sung when marching or practicing any type of gymnastic movement. Music was not a way of animating a military parade, nor a physical or mental imposition, but an avenue for true expression.

Fifteen years later, in 1922, Greppi's musical principles had been challenged by the rapid expansion of the educational system, the ongoing influx of immigrants, and the emergence of new popular and avant-garde currents. He became pessimistic and conservative. Gone were the old good times when Italian teachers monopolized musical good taste. Greppi complained that the decline of opera turned the public to tangos and operettas, not to mention modernism and countless other "isms" full of dissonance, polyrhythm, and atonalism that scared good singers away.[90] His solution was conservative and nationalist: a return to opera by creating a national version of it. "It is time that Argentina takes its place in the musical world," he exhorted; "we crave the coming of the founder of *a national art* and of an *Argentine opera* composer able to honor his fatherland by making his name famous beyond the frontiers" (my emphasis). It is easy to understand the reasons for such a nationalistic claim: what had been lost in the expanded musical market was his generation's monopoly on the legitimate musical scene. Greppi saw profit and politicians replacing "true art" in the realm of education. In Buenos Aires alone, there were more than 100 private musical conservatories attended by 20,000 students, instead of just a public national conservatory.[91] Needless to say, whereas a single, big national conservatory could impose a model of music and pedagogy, in a diversified market many voices, even "illegitimate" ones, could make a profit and shape audiences' musical expectations.

Two years later the influential writer Ricardo Rojas, champion of Argentine cultural nationalism, also noticed the expansion of private musical activity but saw it in an optimistic vein, as a symptom of cultural vitality, and suggested that it could have nothing less than a civilizing role in universal culture. In his 1924 *Eurindia*, Rojas argued that Argentina was destined, in the same way that ancient Greece bridged Asia and Europe, to complete the bridging of Europe and America, a process started in the sixteenth century that was close to being achieved.[92] A modern equivalent of the classic Greek, Argentine culture was only comparable with that of the United States and was probably superior to it:

> Buenos Aires became one of the main musical centers of the cosmopolitan world, due to the importance of its lyrical theater, its numerous conservatories, specialized bookstores, its well-prepared critics, the open attitude of its

---

[90] Greppi, *La Educación Musical*, 195–99.
[91] Ibid., 203–205.
[92] Ricardo Rojas, *Eurindia. Ensayo de estética sobre las culturas americanas* (Buenos Aires: Losada, 1949). Originally published as a series of essays in 1924 in La Nación and a Spanish newspaper, 12.

maestros, and the support of the public. Not many cities can surpass us in this regard. From the greatest and most classics to the most extravagant and contemporary in music, everything is familiar to the *porteño* audiences. Besides Europe, only New York pays with generosity the European virtuosi, and these recognize that we are ahead of the *Yanqui* [Yankee] in musical sensibility.[93]

In effect, Argentine economic prosperity in the 1920s was reflected in increasing living standards and modern infrastructure as well as in artistic and musical spaces of all sorts, from the Teatro Colón to Jewish musical associations and from tango orchestras to musical venues at neighborhood and sport clubs. Rojas considered Buenos Aires' intense musical life in hierarchical and diffusionist terms:

It would be [...] interesting, although very hard, to track the evolution of [...] the repertoire of theaters, conservatories and concert halls of Buenos Aires during the last hundred years [...] among the urban lower classes and the peasantry, to find out how its themes could have been transformed or assimilated in our medium.[94]

For him, music traveled downward. Popular music consisted of adaptations from higher forms, in the same way for the older Greppi a truly musical education expanded from an aesthetic center (a National Conservatory, an Official Educational System, the Opera), in concentric waves, to the children and the uninitiated. For Rojas the "bridge between Europe and America" could not be the cultural mix of millions of poor European immigrants crossing the Atlantic and the Argentines of African, Criollo, or Indigenous descent, any more than for Greppi it was thinkable to believe that the *market* could be the engine of musical education. Nonetheless, music historian Sergio Pujol estimated that in the city of Buenos Aires alone, the 5,000 shows in 1905 (operas, operettas, and "ethnic" dramas and comedies, mainly Spanish, Italian, French, and Yiddish) increased to 25,000 in 1910, to 72,000 in 1914 and 108,000 in 1923. The yearly number of single attendances grew from 2.5 to 26 million in the same period. The greatest expansion happened between 1914 and 1930, when the largest number of theater halls were founded.[95]

Both Rojas and Greppi recognized the complexity of the Buenos Aires musical world and judged it from a particular ideological perspective. Greppi, a defender of creativity and expression, lamented the market because he considered that it somehow produced an uncontrolled variety of music of bad quality. Rojas, enthusiastic about this extraordinary musical expansion, could not see in it the participation of the popular classes, but saw the civilizing role of the upper classes upon the lower ones.

---

[93] Ibid., chapter LXVII, "Nuestra música cosmopolita," 189–90.
[94] Ibid.
[95] Sergio Alejandro Pujol, *Las canciones del inmigrante: Buenos Aires, espectáculo musical y proceso inmigratorio: de 1914 a nuestros días* (Buenos Aires: Editorial Almagesto, 1989), 34–36.

Folklore ideologues took a different approach to this changing musical world. Increasingly in charge of designing educational policies from the state, they did valorize popular musical traditions, but only those deemed "folkloric" and therefore truly national. In March 16, 1921, an official decree created the Argentine Folklore Survey, an unprecedented initiative aimed at literally mapping and collecting the country's folklore in order to use it as a nationalizing tool. A few months later the National Council of Education received 3,700 files produced by schoolteachers from all over the country; among the files, "the popular songs, inspired mainly in love and pain, permanent motifs of popular affection, constitute perhaps the biggest folkloric section collected by the teachers."[96]

Folklore was being promoted not just by the state. In 1921, the same year that the Folklore Survey was initiated, musician and music researcher Andrés Chazarreta's troupe of musicians from the northwestern provinces gave a folkloric show in Buenos Aires, and at around the same time Buenos Aires and Montevideo received an *Indigenista* musical troupe produced by the Cuzco avant-garde in Peru, after its performances in Peru's capital, Lima, and La Paz, Bolivia's biggest city.[97] In the late nineteenth century, before the spread of Indigenista themes and the northwestern mestizo musical tradition, several patterns began to shift the country's cultural foundations away from an exclusive link to France, England, and Italy: *gauchesca* literature and, later on, *criollismo*, as well as neocolonial style in architecture and the diffusion of the figure of the gaucho as national icon valorized the country's rural and colonial past. Alberto Williams and Julián Aguirre were the main gauchesco music composers and the first Argentine "national composers."[98] In 1928 German ethnologist Friedrich Lehman-Nitsche, who had founded key scientific institutions in Argentina, published an article in the journal of the Society of Americanists arguing that the word "gaucho," shared by Argentines and Southern Brazilians, had Bohemian and Andalusian origins, but this transnational conversation was obliterated by a scholarly tradition oriented to national identity.[99] The success of the myth of the gaucho can be explained—in terms of the philosophical anthropology of Mircea Eliade—as a "structural homology" between the educational system and the modern media, so strong in the urban areas, on the one hand, and mythical narratives on "the

[96] Manuel de Ugarriza Aráoz, "Antecedentes relativos al origen de esta Colección," in *Catálogo de La Colección de Folklore* (Buenos Aires: Facultad de Filosofía y Letras, Universidad de Buenos Aires, Instituto de Literatura Argentina, 1925), xix.

[97] Zoila S. Mendoza, "Crear y sentir lo nuestro: la Misión Peruana de Arte Incaico y el impulso de la produccion artístico-folklórica en Cusco," *Latin American Music Review* 25, no. 1 (2004): 57–77; Deborah Poole, "Figueroa Aznar and the Cusco Indigenistas: Photography and Modernism in Early Twentieth-Century Peru," *Representations* 38 (1992): 39–75.

[98] See Melanie Plesch, "Demonizing and Redeeming the Gaucho: Social Conflict, Xenophobia and the Invention of Argentine National Music," *Patterns of Prejudice* 47, no. 4–5 (September 1, 2013): 337–58 and Deborah Schwartz-Kates, "Alberto Ginastera, Argentine Cultural Construction, and the Gauchesco Tradition," *The Musical Quarterly* 86, no. 2 (2002): 248–81.

[99] Robert Lehmann-Nitsche, "Le mot 'gaucho', son origine gitane," *Journal de la Société des Américanistes* 20, no. 1 (1928): 103–105.

other"—the literary myth of the gaucho offered a model to a society in transforma-tion.[100] Folklore ended up entering the commercial metropolitan scene in the 1920s and then spread by the airwaves in the late 1930s and 1940s, in part as a soundtrack of the migration of poor rural workers to the growing industrial neighborhoods of Buenos Aires' metropolitan area. Via Andean indigenismo, the rescue of Hispanic roots, and European experts, folklore became part of the cosmopolitan musical scene of urban Argentina.

Reactionary Musical Nationalism and Public Institutions

By the 1930s folkloric nationalism, Hispanism, cultural Catholicism, and the Colonial-Criollo tradition was mature enough to take over Argentina's state agen-cies. For instance, the Didactic Commission of the National Educative Commission established on June 16, 1939, aimed at the "protection and diffusion of folklore" and "the people's spiritual culture." Following international standards—especially the resolutions of the First International Congress of the Popular Arts in Prague 1928, dedicated to preserving and collecting cultural heritage—the members of this com-mission explained the Argentine particularities and problems in quite extreme terms:

As a country of immigration, exposed to the influence of different, if not antagonistic races, ideologies, and cultures, it needs to neutralize its cosmo-politism by reaffirming its personality regarding what comes from the core of its history and soil [. . .] It has forgotten the high philosophy of the popular refrains, the science elaborated by the gaucho in the prairie and the mountain [. . .] Tradition is the strongest link that brings human groups together [. . .] Tradition distinguishes neighboring peoples, despite common origins and ide-als. It is also [. . .] more susceptible of reaching the child's soul than the cold reasoning of the historian.

Among the traditional "infantile rhymes and cradle songs" suggested as an anti-dote to cosmopolitanism, the commission included "Mambrú se fue a la guerra"—originally a French folk military song, "Marlbrough s'e va-t-en guerre," that entered the Spanish traditional songbook and through it, the Hispanic American one—and also Spanish religious songs to the Virgin. Their Hispanism made them write in italic all the words that came from the Argentine variant of Spanish, for example, "*salí si sabés* querer [. . .] *venite y vení*," and so on.[101] There were no signs of the repertoire from

---

[100] Raúl O. Fradkin, "Centaures de la pampa. Le gaucho, entre l'histoire et le mythe," *Annales. Histoire, Sciences Sociales* 58e année, no. 1 (2003): 109; Mircea Eliade, *Mitos, sueños y misterios* (Buenos Aires: Compañía General Fabril Editora, 1961), 28–30. See also Ezequiel Adamovsky, "La cuarta fun-ción del criollismo y las luchas por la definición del origen y el color del ethnos argentino (desde las primeras novelas gauchescas hasta c. 1940)," *Boletín del Instituto de Historia Argentina y Americana Dr. Emilio Ravignani* 41 (2014): 50–92.

[101] Consejo Nacional de Educación (Argentina), *Antología folklórica argentina para las escuelas primarias* (Buenos Aires: Kraft, 1940).

the urban outskirts that was also considered "folklore" by Lehmann-Nitsche several years before.[102] The members of the National Educative Commission, like Greppi and Rojas years before, resisted accepting actual urban popular music as national music.

In 1935 a proposal to the Ministry of Justice to call a Hispanic American conference on folklore argued that whereas teaching folklore was important for any country of elevated culture, in Argentina it was even more necessary "because immigration constitutes the base of our social formation," as demonstrated by the most recent census data, which showed that foreign male adults outnumbered native ones.[103] That folklore was considered the best mechanism for integrating the foreign population may seem strange, given folklorists' insistence on the Spanish origins of Argentine roots, even the supposedly indigenous ones: "Even the Quechua verses found here, despite their apparent link with the indigenous culture revealed by the archeology, are in fact translations, some of them literal, of Spanish verses" of the Spanish Golden Age (*Siglo de Oro*), preserved by oral tradition.[104] This traditional substratum was considered at risk of disappearing with the death of the oldest men and women of the rural areas in the northwestern provinces. But interestingly, it was considered less Argentine than *hispanoamericano* and therefore part of a shared background with the rest of Spanish America. Hence, the "traditional popular art" and the "American poetry" celebrated as the antidote to the European immigration was considered not native nor Argentine but Hispanic American. Since the Argentine is a "Hispanic American culture, its study requires the study of the folklore of all the Spanish-speaking countries, in order to establish the scope of the dispersion and the probable origins of the collected pieces." The United States provided a model: "This is how an Institute of folkloric research in the United States has sent a researcher to Spain to collect popular folklore, with the goal of establishing the Spanish origins of the folk tales collected in New Mexico."[105] A Hispanic American congress of folklore should articulate the efforts of different countries and bring the results together in common publications. The day proposed was, of course, October 12, the "Día de la Raza" that commemorated the Spanish "discovery" of the new world. If there was a Hispanic race, folklore was its cultural manifestation. To educate foreigners in Hispanic folklore was therefore to assimilate them, in a strange and spiritual manner, *racially*. The project never took off. But its arguments are the ones that the cultural establishment of the time judged convincing and adequate grounds for public policies.

---

[102] Roberto Lehmann-Nitsche, *Santos Vega* (Buenos Aires: Coni Hermanos, 1917), 159. Brian Bockelman, "Between the Gaucho and the Tango: Popular Songs and the Shifting Landscape of Modern Argentine Identity, 1895–1915," *American Historical Review* 116, no. 3 (June 2011): 577–601.

[103] "La inmigración constituye la base de nuestra formación social." Juan Mantovani, October 16, 1935, 3, in Manuel de Yriondo, *Congreso del folklore hispánico e hispano-americano: proyecto de la Inspección General de Enseñanza Secundaria y Decreto del Poder Ejecutivo* (Buenos Aires: Penitenciaría Nacional, 1936).

[104] Ibid., 4.

[105] Ibid., 4–5.

By the early 1940s a national mythology that centered on folk music was common currency, but it began to revert to a mythical understating of the Argentine *geography* as part of an effort to separate the specifically Argentine folkloric element from the common Spanish American background. In 1941 Oreste Schiuma published the article "Argentine Music" in the magazine *Mundo Musical*, which circulated among all sorts of musical organizations—such as the Yiddish musical association Joel Engel, where I found this particular issue. Schiuma argued that even if the Italian tradition was "the most accurate interpreter of human passions," what reigned in Argentina was "the sadness, the melancholy, the vastness of the landscape and the loneliness of the criollo," which required a specific musical expression.[106] It was in the infinite pampas of the past—not in contemporary dance halls—that people began to gather and dance.

Hence, the Argentine countryside turned into a space for the organic life of the collectivity [. . .] and the skies were filled with harmonies. From the highlands behind the Andes, and from the Europe of *minué* [*minuetto, menuet*], the wave of music—also an emigration of feelings in search of equilibrium—established itself in this virgin land. Adapted and newly elaborated, with its own modalities, and in agreement with the time and the place, a series of Argentine dances emerged with a great wealth of melodic nuances, to tell us through the *Malambo, Zapateado, Contradanza, Escondido, Firmeza, Cielito, Huella, Sombrerito, Media Caña, Gato, Chacarera, Zamba,* and *Pericón* a whole range of passions, hopes, and joys. Argentine music, transplanted from folklore by maestros of the highest hierarchy after slightly more than a quarter of century, has enough merits to be considered as alive and having a character on its own [*tiene el mérito suficiente para ser considerada con vida y carácter propios*].[107]

In other words, a mythical experience of desolation—the vastness of the pampas—expressed through the encounter of two ancestral cultures—Spanish and Inca—produced a folkloric music that, once it was transformed by "maestros of the highest hierarchy," became a national music.

This interpretation of folklore gave room to an elitist and racist rejection of actual popular and modern music practices, which were considered manifestations of something deeper and worse than folkloric or rural music: the "commodification" of music, seen as decadent and a consequence of democracy. Julio Viggiano Esain is perhaps the most expressive representative of the reaction against modern musical markets and popular musical consumption.[108] I will quote him extensively, because his diatribes are revealing.

---

[106] Oreste Schiuma, "Música argentina," *Mundo Musical* 34, no. 3 (July 1941).

[107] Box "Asociación Pro-Cultura Musical 1," IWO.

[108] Julio Veggiano Esaín, *Cultura musical. Notas relativas a este problema en nuestro país* (Córdoba, Argentina: Imprenta de la Penitenciaría, 1937).

Viggiano was founder of the Orchestra Professors School in Rosario—Argentina's second largest city—and professor of violin in two private conservatories between 1925 and 1936. In 1936 he moved to Córdoba and soon became member of the Institute of Archeology, Linguistics, and Folklore at the University of Córdoba, where he developed a career as a musicologist and folklorist, publishing many books on provincial folklore and regional songbooks. According to Viggiano in 1937, Latin America was rich in indigenous and colonial cultural treasuries, but it was also corrupted by modern radio, the recording industry, the tango, the lack of state intervention, the indifference of publishers and critics, and a generalized cultural decadence. In Argentina—unlike Italy, Germany, Denmark, Norway, or Russia—the state did not control broadcasting and had "completely surrendered to commercial exploitation." There was not even "national music": the national holidays of May 25 and July 9, respectively, were "celebrated with 'The Barber of Seville' [. . .] and 'Tosca'," while the Municipal Band of Buenos Aires played Wagner. Schoolteachers trained students' choruses with excerpts of opera—this confirms the success of Greppi's 1907 recommendations—and popular music in its vulgar expression, "which damages the development of the children's aesthetic feelings." Private lessons, for their part, "promote a generalized bad taste in all social strata." The lack of state regulation of music meant that a "true education" had been hijacked by monetary interests.[109]

Viggiano depicted the musical scene in racial terms, although he did not organize the racial hierarchy exactly as his contemporary European conservative counterparts did. For him, the best music students "come in general from European homes, and among them, the ones that profess the Jewish religion, because given their deep and exact sense of music's nature and complexity, they apply to the study a systematic discipline and method." Non-European students, by contrast, did not study techniques, were "intuitive" and "improvisational," and preferred to make money on the radio after a short period of study. In a country with no artistic tradition, he argued, the youth were dominated by "moral materialism, superficiality and laziness." In Europe and the United States, "philanthropy" created "great musical societies, instrumental associations, institutes, seminars, grants, and prizes," while in Argentina people just "vegetate," exactly like "our Andean people," surrounded by an unexplored wealth. Foreign musicians that came to Argentina—"Kreisler, Kleiber, Kempf, Casals, Elman, Iturbe, Cortot, Busch, Fuerman, Kraus, Cherniawsky, Rosenthal, Zigheti, Lamond, Milstein, Rubinstein and others"—only performed in Buenos Aires and a little bit in Rosario. But even Buenos Aires lacked a true musical tradition. Suffocated by Italian opera, it did not allow Mozart, Beethoven, Bach, and Handel to take root. German music was the true music, not Italian opera.[110]

Proof of the country's musical "mediocrity" (*nivel medio*) was the biggest tango star, Carlos Gardel. The massive funeral cortege that accompanied his repatriated corpse

---

[109] Ibid., 10–11, 14, and 20.
[110] Ibid., 12–16.

after having died in a plane crash when touring Medellín, Colombia, was a "smart display of a boisterous commercial fanfare," with "all social classes participating in a homage that not even the authentic and great workers of the spirit receive." The city's lawmakers even proposed naming a street after him. The musical atmosphere was "poisoned" by records and popular music everywhere, threatening education, morality, art, and even the sense "of nationhood . . . at the cinema, the café, the street, at school, at home, in many 'academic' institutions and above all [. . .] radio programming, [. . .] pervading every inch of every home, hitting night and day people's ears and forever destroying the seeds of aesthetic sentiments in the children with the sound and lyrics of so many scummy tango and so many cheap little song."[111]

Conservatories, state-sponsored bands, and fine arts commissions worked in vain: "One hour of good music can do nothing against the other 23 hours of bad music." Even intimate family parties, once musically delicate and refined, were "saturated by fox-trot, tango, and vulgar songs [. . .] We brought the outskirts to the aristocratic salon," he wrote, and failed to penetrate the "authentic sentiments of the people" with "grand art."[112]

Viggiano's crusade was civilizing and moral, a war of spirit against money, of an aristocracy of the spirit that sought to cultivate the people's souls against a people captured by musical merchants. His diagnosis could not have been more negative. Improvisation dominated legitimate art forms, such as "ballet, opera, operetta, zarzuela and sainete," which were "executed without major artistic scruples"; at the same time, "almost all the orchestras at cafés and radio stations play almost exclusively popular, inferior music." Interestingly, "sound cinema theaters sometimes offer good music when executing famous scores, adapted to the script. But even there bad music dominates, unarticulated; music of black rhythms, among which sometimes appear nice songs." Once again, as for Greppi, only the state could remediate the problem. In Germany, where this fight had given birth "to the greatest musical geniuses," musical instruction was mandatory and carefully implemented by the state, which "assigns to it a powerful moral influence, a force of social cohesion, a deep cultural sense, and a powerful force of authentic national sentiments."[113]

Only state intervention could properly filter "black rhythms" and stop "popular, inferior music" in favor of a good combination of erudite and folk music, as well stop "the propagation of small *conjuntos típicos* that invade all social sectors, from the aristocratic salon to the last hovel on the outskirts"—a denunciation that revealed a vital musical scene. Just a handful of Argentine composers, according to Viggiano, seriously attempted "a conciliation of European opera with the character, structure, and substance of native motifs," such as "Ollantay, Matrero, Tabaré, Huemac, La Sangre de las Guitarras." But nobody cared about them, and the Colón Theater, Argentina's main opera house, was until recently "a branch of Milan's Scala." The explanation of

[111] Ibid., 16–17.
[112] Ibid., 18.
[113] Ibid., 19.

this general state of things is, ultimately, political: "Our politicians [. . .] don't feel the need for music." Argentine men of state, unfortunately, were not like "Édouard Herriot, France's ex-Prime Minister, who stopped in Cairo during an official visit to give a conference . . . about universal suffrage? No, gentlemen: about Beethoven."[114]

As these examples prove, Argentine musical policymakers and influential critics of the first half of the twentieth century either ignored or condemned the most important musical currents, from opera to tango and jazz, that criollo and immigrant artists and audiences brought to life in Buenos Aires, the largest urban area. State policies, initially oriented toward promoting artistic expression within an Italian musical model, soon became instruments of nationalist folklore. The commercial success of folklore artists in the 1930s and 1940s among urban audiences was silenced by the invocation of metaphysical rural spaces and the nostalgy for the colonial past. The active and original musicological initiatives by conservative elites in the Northwest that historian Oscar Chamosa studied—initiatives that also influenced national policies and the very ideology of criollo identity—also emphasized a sort of abstract symbolism of the nation that rejected the economically and aesthetically rich musical developments of the urban centers.[115]

Conservative musical policies of the 1930s promoted folklore as well as classical "universal" music. They aimed, above all, at arousing an emotional loyalty toward the state among school children. In 1937, while Viggiano called the state to combat commercialism in the name of a true and elevated art music, an official regulation enforced collective singing as a tool for producing that emotional loyalty. The state imposed an official repertoire of the only songs that could be taught at the schools (article 22) and mandated that music teachers "accompany and direct the students in person, trying to infuse the utmost enthusiasm" (article 23). But it also allowed the Military and Adult Schools Inspection Department the centralized creation and direction, at each Buenos Aires night school, of a "choral mass" (*masa coral*) of students, "with the purpose of spreading within the people "the love and habit of singing patriotic and traditional Argentine songs, as well as a variety of "creations of the universal lyric."[116]

And yet these musical ideologies sometimes converged. In late 1933, the Argentine Circle of Music Authors and Composers organized a tango concert at the Teatro Colón to celebrate the promulgation of law 11.723 regulating intellectual copyright. According to tango composer Francisco Canaro, "seventy bandoneons, eighty violins, ten contrabasses, eight cellos, eight pianos, ten flutes, ten clarinets, and twenty singers" formed "the greatest *orquesta típica* registered in the history of tango," successively directed by several directors. While Canaro directed his own 1924 tango "Sentimiento Gaucho," composer, critic, and school inspector Miguel Mastrogianni,

---

[114] Ibid., 21, 22, and 25.

[115] Chamosa, *The Agentine Folklore Movement*.

[116] Consejo Nacional de Educación, *Digesto de Instrucción Primaria* (Buenos Aires, 1937), 351, "De la enseñanza."

who "did not like popular music," had to admit, with a mixture of rage and admiration, that "despite everything, it is good." According to Canaro, it was the eighty standing violinists playing the harmony in unison that made this old tango foe think that there was something deep at play. It was hence not enough for tango to propose a gaucho theme to be played at the Colón—that had been part of the tango world from the beginning. To convince a conservative critic, the tango had to be an avenue to massive unanimity.[117]

Music in Argentina grew immensely and circulated largely outside the small spheres of the state and of an old cultural elite that never fully established its rule. Buenos Aires, as well as smaller cities, with plentiful chorus groups, countless music bands, all types of orchestras, and the largest market for recorded and broadcasted music in Latin America, was perceived by the conservative establishment as needing an aesthetic and emotional unification that could only come from the state. Phonographs (fabricated and distributed by Victor and National Odeon firms) and microphones contributed to sonic, aesthetic, and commercial changes upon which no actor was able to exert full control, altering the musical status quo.[118] A growing circuit of dance halls, cinemas, sheet music, magazines, social clubs, and teaching institutes, both within Argentina and connecting this country with others in the region and abroad, increased the circulation of all sorts of music styles in ways unexpected by Rojas and uncontrolled by his cultural establishment. This whole process of change redefined what was considered Argentine music and altered the received basic notions of what an artist was. That was the musical scene in which nationalist policymakers intervened.

In a letter written on March 16, 1934, Francisco Curt Lange visited Argentina and wrote to the Council of Primary and Normal Education of Uruguay about the state of musical education in the neighboring country. After complaining about music inspector Mastrogianni—the one who had reluctantly recognized the value of tango at the Teatro Colón—having ignored his demands to visit music classes at public schools, and about his musical ignorance, Lange explained that there were two main currents among Argentine composers: one that followed contemporary European trends, and other that sought "a national expression, based on folklore so abundant in the provinces."

The last one, oriented toward folklore, was supported by the government and dominated the Conservatorio Nacional de Música y Declamación. This current was

---

[117] Francisco Canaro, *Mis bodas de oro con el tango y mis memorias, 1906–1956* (Buenos Aires: CESA, 1957), 322–23. Mastrogianni had been part of the founding staff in 1924 of the Conservatorio Nacional de Música y Declamación, created after the Teatro Colón Escuela de Arte Lírico y Escénico, directed by Carlos López Buchardo until his death in April 1948. In 1939 it became the National Conservatory of Music and Arte Escénico.

[118] Technicians and producers became more important than ever. Marina Cañardo, "Cantantes, orquestas y micrófonos: la interpretación del tango y la tecnología de grabación," *Afuera: Estudios de Crítica Cultural* 10 (May 2011); Matthew B. Karush, *Culture of Class: Radio and Cinema in the Making of a Divided Argentina, 1920–1946* (Durham, NC: Duke University Press, 2012).

behind "the intensification of choral singing at the schools": Lange praised the fact that "many composers turned to the creation of a surprisingly elevated number of chants and children's choirs, in a relatively short period of time." Besides the works that were "true musical jewels," such as those by Julián Aguirre, there were children's song contests organized by the Wagnerian Association. The Buenos Aires branch of Ricordi Publishers from Milano, Italy, published three volumes of "coros escolares argentinos," ready to be taught in schools.

Lange thought that these materials should be adopted in Uruguay as well. He was very clear about this cultural borrowing: "With the exception of some patriotic or festive marches dedicated to specific national institutions, and perhaps also of certain Northern songs whose characteristics are not familiar to early-years students, all those materials currently available can perfectly be used in our choral teaching." The main folkloric elements featured in Argentine songs "plainly respond to the River Plate sentiment [*sentir rioplatense*], and could strengthen the inclination for our characteristic and autochthonous aspects of our environment and history." These children's songs could be added to the few already written by Uruguayan composers and could even stimulate Uruguayan creators to compose songs for children.

The perspective of an informed outsider such as Lange reveals the importance of choral singing in music education in Argentina. He visited several schools and admired the results of the many female chant teachers working with very young children. "*Action* was the principal element in children's musical expression," and it was based on the dramatization of verses from national authors. At one school, the teacher surprised him by having the students sing both the Argentine and Uruguayan anthems, and at another school—a Normal School for girls in the Belgrano neighborhood of Buenos Aires, where he had given a conference on Wagner—the school choir performed the chorus of the spinners from Wagner's opera *The Flying Dutchman*. He also listened to "a choir, of many voices, 600 girls, which made a significant impression on me." Even if their teaching methods were outdated compared with in basic musical teaching in postwar Germany that Lange knew but that were unknown to Buenos Aires teachers, "outdated methods can lead to satisfactory and even impressive results when the teacher communicates consciously and enthusiastically with the students."

A week later, he sent invitations to dozens of contacts to collaborate on the first volume of the Boletín Latino-Americano de Música, which would appear in August 1935, and simultaneously proposed to the Instituto de Estudios Superiores a set of courses on Schubert's lyricism, Russian national music, and Wagner. In other words, he saw in the European traditions the basis for both Uruguay's musical culture and his own income, and in Latin American music his intellectual horizon. The combination of good music professors, state sponsorship, folklore inspiration, and national composers applied to collective singing truly impressed Lange.[119]

---

[119] Letter from Lange to SODRE, March 16, 1934, Subsérie 2.1, AFCL.

STATE POLICIES FROM A REGIONAL PERSPECTIVE

State musical policies in Brazil, Mexico, and Argentina shared a common interest in collective singing, the exploration of folk traditions, and a selective valorization of modern and urban popular styles. But the implementation varied widely due to structural factors. In Brazil, a weak state apparatus attempted to intervene through civilizing policies the musical life of a very heterogeneous and disenfranchised population; in Mexico, the revolutionary state reach out to peasant and urban musical cultures through the army and the school, whereas most musicians confronted a precarious marketplace; in Argentina, the school and the associational life of immigrants had already shaped the musical life, and populist policies became a battlefield between conservative officials and commercial entrepreneurs around state sponsorship and censorship.

The Argentine cultural policy in the 1930s was a conservative attempt at combating tango, the most popular musical style at home and the Argentine symbol abroad, and promoting folk-Spanish roots against Buenos Aires cosmopolitism, hence turning the universalism and democratizing aspects of earlier state policies into essentialist, Catholic, and Hispanist ones. Brazilian cultural policy in the 1930s was a modernizing attempt at bringing the population into some kind of relationship with the state, something that in Argentina the school had already done; turning a mosaic of regions into an integrated nation, rather than regionalizing an already metropolitan-centered culture like in Argentina; and elevating popular culture to official status as national culture, unlike the Argentine attempt at inventing a folk culture against the urban popular one. Whereas in Mexico the revolution provided an heterogeneous population with a shared experience and a common vocabulary, in Brazil there was an abyss separating promoters and receptors of the state policies. This was thus the first elite systematic attempt at valorizing popular culture.

But Mexico went much further in the populist aim of educating the people and giving them aesthetic and economic resources; in Argentina, literacy and an extended cultural market had provided those opportunities earlier, and populist policies would arrive only later, through Peronism in 1946, without really challenging the categories already in place in the musical realm—but subverting the rules of access to musical practice. In Brazil, subaltern, grassroots, and commercial musical practices were, compared to Argentina and Mexico, always ahead of the state, which, despite the sophistication of its modernist cadres, left the majority of the population out of its educational policies.

Of the three cases, Mexico had the most Latin Americanist rhetoric. But it took an intellectual and *programmatic* formulation of Latin American music to fully activate the possibilities of a regional aesthetic framework whose seeds were already planted.

4

THE TRANSNATIONAL FORMATION OF LATIN

AMERICAN MUSICOLOGY

A SCIENTIFIC AND systematic discourse on Latin America emerged in 1934–1935, and despite its marginal origins, it ended up constituting an influential field in the sociological sense: Latin American musicology.

Composers, performers, journalists, and audiences in the urban public spheres of Latin America had created at the turn of the twentieth century local fields of musical competition and hierarchies of prestige, where symbolic and economic capital circulated. Modernist magazines across the region shared a cosmopolitan culture that reflected the established taste and canons of a European bourgeoisie that served as model.[1] The *Revista de América* in Buenos Aires, for example, published texts about national music from different countries—from Russia to Mexico—by nationalist critics who framed their nationalist projects in larger ethno-regional perspectives: the critic Gastón Talamon celebrated in 1920 the renaissance of Spanish musical nationalism, with its attention to popular songs as expressions of "la raza," as a "sibling" (*arte hermano*) of the one developing in America.[2] Nationalism slowly materialized

---

[1] For instance, the Mexican weekly magazine *El Mundo Ilustrado*, published from 1894 to 1911, celebrated on one cover the elite of "The Mexican Musicians" (February 26, 1911) and portrayed with ethnographic style a group of peasant musicians as "Spontaneous National Artists" on another cover (January 17, 1904), but the only (few) cases of musical criticism were by or about European artists.

[2] Gastón Talamón, "Los compositores españoles y el folk-lore," *Música de América*, April 1920. See Vera Wolkowicz, "En busca de la identidad perdida: los escritos de Gastón Talamón sobre música académica de y en Argentina en la revista Nosotros (1915–1934)," in *Música y construcción de identidades : poéticas,*

The Invention of Latin American Music. Pablo Palomino, Oxford University Press (2020). © Oxford University Press.
DOI: 10.1093/oso/9780190687403.001.0001

in public policy, especially in the capital cities, in the 1920s and 1930s, as new technologies (film industry, recording, radio), civil associations (unions, choirs, clubs), and entertainment sites (cabarets, dance halls), especially in the main hubs of the region—Havana, Mexico City, Rio de Janeiro, and Buenos Aires—but also in smaller cities—like Medellín or Porto Alegre—adapted and produced repertoires that both nationalized and transnationalized musical forms and discourses.

Music actors were also organizing internationally: in 1921, classical composers organized the International Composers' Guild, which promoted modern music by sponsoring concerts that featured European and United States composers. Between 1928 and 1934 the Pan American Association of Composers brought together Cuban and Mexican composers with US ones and also organized concerts characterized by a pan-American musical sensibility.[3] And between the world wars, an array of international organizations—the International Musical Society, the International Society for Musicology, the International Society for Contemporary Music, the Permanent Council for the International Co-operation between Composers, and the League of Nations—fully incorporated "the politics of music" into the realm of international relations and institutions.[4] In 1936 the International Society for Music Education (ISME) organized its first world congress on music education in Prague—attended by 700 delegates from twenty-one countries—around a universalistic idea of music, even if—or rather, precisely because—the participants (with the exception of Heitor Villa-Lobos) were European or from the United States.[5] Those resources provided a basis during World War II for an unprecedented amount of music organizing that was taking place in many countries, for instance in the United States under the auspices government, army, and civil associations.[6] Music as a matter of private practice, local community reproduction, and loose patronage made room for larger, more ambitious, and more complex national and transnational organizations.

But in Latin America the labor of writing, analyzing, and critiquing musical practices in newspapers, folklore research, and literary writing was still confined to urban

---

diálogos y utopías en Latinoamérica y España, ed. Victoria Eli Rodríguez and Elena Torres Clemente (Madrid: Sociedad Española de Musicología, 2018), 33–44.

[3] Jennifer Campbell, "Shaping Solidarity: Music, Diplomacy, and Inter-American Relations, 1936–1946" (PhD diss., University of Connecticut, 2010). R. Allen Lott, "'New Music for New Ears': The International Composers' Guild," *Journal of the American Musicological Society* 36, no. 2 (July 1, 1983): 266–86. Deane Root, "The Pan American Association of Composers (1928–1934)," *Yearbook for Inter-american Musical Research* 7 (1972): 49–70. Stephanie Stallings, "Collective Difference: The Pan-American Association of Composers and Pan-American Ideology in Music, 1925–1945" (PhD diss., Florida State University, 2009).

[4] Christiane Sibille, "The Politics of Music in International Organizations in the First Half of the Twentieth Century," *New Global Studies* 10, no. 3 (2017): 253–81.

[5] Wilfried Gruhn, "Leo Kestenberg 1882–1962: Honorary President of ISME 1953–1962 Outstanding Musician, Visionary Educator, Pragmatic Reformer and Utopian Realist," *International Journal of Music Education* 22, no. 2 (2004): 103–29; Marie McCarthy, "The Birth of Internationalism in Music Education 1899–1938," *International Journal of Music Education* 21 (1993): 3–15

[6] Annegret Fauser, *Sounds of War: Music in the United States during World War II* (New York: Oxford University Press, 2013).

musical worlds that remained basically unknown to one another. It took a marginal Latin Americanist project to entice a new class of specialized writers, educators, researchers, and critics across the region to engage in a common transnational field, from which they could also foster the consolidation of their respective national fields. Latin American musicology emerged as a transnational field of nationalist experts. In 1934–1935 a musicological discourse systematically addressed from Montevideo, Uruguay, both *Latin American music*—the regional aesthetic category—and *music in Latin America*—the regional space—as legitimate endeavors.

EARLY NOTIONS OF LATIN AMERICAN MUSIC

Three types of rhetoric preceded the emergence of this field.

The first was a spiritual rhetoric, such as the one in Cortijo Alahija's 1919 *Musicología Latino-Americana*,[7] a country-by-country list of notorious figures, styles, and compositions, where Latin American music appears as a racial cliché of the "spirit" of the folklore and "primitive" music of each nation, explained through "personality traits" of the native, African, and European population. This rhetoric reappeared in 1930 in an essay by José Rolón, a composer from Jalisco trained in Paris and by then well established within the classical scene in Mexico City. Echoing at least twenty years of musical nationalism in Mexico, Rolón argued that the Latin American musicians' claim to universality can only be produced within every single national discourse, as a product of the rigorous and technical "development" of the aesthetic "embryos" provided by its "race." This race had "dual origins" (*vigénita*)—"aboriginal and criolla"—in almost all of Latin America and "triple origins" (*trigénita*) in Cuba and Brazil, where there was also an African origin. As a whole, then, Rolón defined Latin American music as a sui-generis music that expressed the "amalgam" of three "dissimilar races" and sensitivities: Moorish indolence, Indigenous ancestral sadness, and African exaltation" (Esa amalgama de razas, esa mezcla de sensibilidades tan divergentes y disímbolas [sic] ha creado, sin embargo, una música sui generis cuya fisonomía participa de la indolencia morisca, de la tristeza ancestral india y de la exultación negra).[8]

A second rhetoric was civilizational, one produced by diplomatic Pan American Union events in Washington, DC and other classical concerts in the United States. This *othering*, imperial notion of Latin America organized music by specific countries: it included no Latin American musicians, only national ones. For instance, in 1916 the twenty-year-old virtuoso *"senhorita* Guiomar Novaes" performed in New York after her European tour was cancelled due to the war. Novaes, whose examination committee in France included Gabriel Faure and Claude Debussy, appears in the pages of the

---

[7] Cortijo Alahija, *Musicología Latino-Americana: La música popular y los músicos célebres de la América Latina* (Maucci, Barcelona, 1919).

[8] José Rolón, "El porvenir de la música latino americana," *Música–Revista Mexicana* 2, no. 1 (1930): 31–34.

Pan American Union report as an example of "what *Brazilians* have accomplished in the world of music."[9] Here the claim of universality was based not on her race, but on her mastery of a European musical technique.

The third and final rhetoric of Latin American music was produced by musically minded Latin American intellectuals and disseminated by popular magazines. These publications began to vaguely define "our" music, still in national terms, in contrast to the US music of the time, jazz, with which it competed in Latin America and Europe. In 1929 the exiled Peruvian political leader Víctor Raúl Haya de la Torre described the popularity of Mexican music in Berlin as a triumph of the "música latinoamericana," and Cuban writer Alejo Carpentier described the success of Don Aspiazú's Cuban orchestra at the Empire Theater in Paris in 1932 as a "vanguardia de la música latinoamericana."[10] In December of 1934 the Buenos Aires magazine *Caras y Caretas* praised the Italian-Argentine classical director maestro Percuocco for his decision to broadcast through Radio Belgrano a bit of "*música latinoamericana*" to counterbalance the hegemony of jazz.[11] Latin American intellectuals were engaging with an increasingly dense international arena of diplomatic, cultural, and scientific exchanges, and at the same time, they were turning their gaze inward, organizing old and recent ethnic mixtures into coherent national narratives.[12] But they began also to produce a regionalist rhetoric around music.

It wasn't until 1934 that Latin American musicology as such was inaugurated with the publication of a manifesto with a still ambiguous name: "*Americanismo musical*." The author of the manifesto, Francisco Curt Lange, had been until then an almost complete outsider in the regional press and intellectual conversations.

MONTEVIDEAN ORIGINS OF LATIN AMERICANIST MUSICOLOGY

Franz Kurt Lange was born into a prosperous family in the small town of Eilenburg, Saxony, in 1903. In studying, according to his own account, architecture, musicology, and philosophy at the universities of Munich, Heidelberg, Berlin, Leipzig, and Bonn, Lange was partly following the footsteps of his parents—his father was an acoustic engineer, his mother a housewife and pianist. This was in the turbulent aftermath of the Great War, which brought misfortune to the family's property and his father's health. As a teenager, Franz participated in several battles against Communists and

---

[9] *Bulletin of the Pan American Union*, XLII, Jan–June 1916, p. 110–12.

[10] Víctor Raúl Haya de la Torre, "Latinoamericanización musical de Europa—Triunfo de la música típica de México," August 21, 1930, *La Industria*, Trujillo, Peru, in *Obras completas*, vol. 2 (Lima: J. Mejía Baca, 1977), 294–97; "Don Aspiazu in Paris," in *Crónicas*, Vol. 2, Instituto Cubano del Libro—Editorial Arte y Literatura, 1975, (orig. published in Revista Carteles, November 20, 1932), p. 109–14.

[11] *Caras y Caretas*, Buenos Aires, December 1, 1934 issue 1,887, p. 107.

[12] Patricia Funes, *Salvar la nación: intelectuales, cultura y política en los años veinte latinoamericanos* (Buenos Aires: Prometeo Libros, 2006); Michael Goebel, "Globalization and Nationalism in Latin America, c.1750–1950," *New Global Studies* 3, no. 3 (2010): 16–18.

Spartacists in the streets of Munich during 1918 and 1919. He financed his studies by playing piano in bars until the lack of better opportunities made him decide to emigrate in 1923.[13]

Among Lange's professors may have been Erich von Hornbostel and other creators and early disciples of comparative musicology, which aspired to classify all the musical manifestations of the world within a single universal system. Initiated in Wilhelminian Germany and continuing during the Weimar years, this perspective linked musicology with linguistics, ethnology, acoustics, psychology, and phonographic techniques, providing the foundations of current ethnomusicology.[14] This disciplinary development, combined with those in classical or Western musicology, the romantic cult of Beethoven, and the prestige of the Wagnerian tradition made Germany a serious competitor with France as the country after which the republics of the New World modeled their musical education systems and institutions.[15] The tension in the German intellectual milieu between a cosmopolitan and pluralistic tradition and a racist and nationalist one, which intensified after the defeat in the Great War, did not diminish the country's musicological influence.[16] Young researchers like Lange had at their disposal a variety of approaches to the Herderian perspective on the *Volk* in between those two ideological poles and used them to interrogate and locate musical expressions within a universal scheme.

Lange's youth and early writings were tinged by the philosophical trope of "cultural crisis" that penetrated in the interwar years every intellectual current, from reactionary writings such as Oswald Spengler's to radical critiques of modern culture such as the work of the Frankfurt School. Nazism and World War II scattered that German intellectual world into different fragments, sending some of its practitioners to exile; others to their death in concentration camps, at the front, or in the allied bombings; and still others into either silent or actively complicit survival in wartime Germany. Although he left Germany still a young man, several years before Hitler's designation as chancellor, Lange kept professional and personal contacts

---

[13] This biographical account is based on Lange's letters at the Acervo Curt Lange (Universidade Federal de Minas Gerais, Belo Horizonte, Brazil) and on the following works: Jorge Velazco, "La confluencia intelectual y académica en la formación escolástica y la obra de investigación de Francisco Curt Lange," *Revista Musical de Venezuela* X, no. 28 (1989): 207–23 (also in *Anales del Instituto de Investigaciones Estéticas*, vol. 16, 1992); Rui Mourão, *O alemão que descobriu a América* (Brasília; Belo Horizonte: Instituto Nacional do Livro; Editora Itatiaia, 1990); and Luis Merino Montero, "Francisco Curt Lange (1903–1997): Tributo a un americanista de excepción," *Revista Musical Chilena* 52, no. 189 (1998): 9–36.

[14] Alan Merriam, "Definitions of 'Comparative Musicology' and 'Ethnomusicology': An Historical-Theoretical Perspective," *Ethnomusicology* 21, no. 2 (May 1977): 189–204. Alexander Rehding, *Hugo Riemann and the Birth of Modern Musical Thought* (Cambridge: Cambridge University Press, 2003).

[15] In the United States, for instance, according to David Suisman, first and second generations of German and Jewish-German individuals were largely over-represented among orchestra directors, music educators, editors, critics, and piano makers. David Suisman, *Selling Sounds: The Commercial Revolution in American Music* (Cambridge, MA: Harvard University Press, 2009), 33–34.

[16] Glenn Penny and Matti Bunzl, eds., *Worldly Provincialism: German Anthropology in the Age of Empire* (Ann Arbor: University of Michigan Press, 2003).

with Germany throughout his life. After he moved to Uruguay, he adapted his intellectual formation to institutional and scientific practices organized around a particular idea of Latin America as a historical, racial, cultural, and especially musical entity.

In moving to Latin America, Franz was following the advice of his romance philology professor, Karl Vossler, who advised him that he would easily be able to get a job there as an architect or music teacher. His personal diary for January and February 1923, as he was preparing to migrate to Buenos Aires, shows him painfully navigating an economically desperate situation. He spent his final months in Munich fixing and tuning pianos to avoid his and his mother's judiciary eviction from his house, and paying for medical exams, travel, and police and visa paperwork during a time of hyperinflation—he notes the German mark's variations by the thousands from one day to the next. His prospects in Buenos Aires were modest: working as a piano fixer and tuner. His vision of those days was quite somber: on Sunday, February 4, among notes on his fevered correspondence (probably with Rio de la Plata contacts), he writes that the French army invaded Baden (in response to Germany's default in its war compensations); the next day, that he managed to sell pieces of iron and copper to buy razor blades that he could bring on his migration to Buenos Aires; on February 8, that he must keep his family from being evicted from the house they lived in; and on Tuesday, February 13, he remembers that Wagner died forty years ago that day in Venice. Feelings of chaos, desperation, and determination permeate this diary.

Later that year, Lange arrived in Buenos Aires, where he worked for a short time as a salesman in a German music firm, probably selling instruments or sheet music. In the city he also contacted a prestigious German émigré, professor Robert Lehman-Nitsche, pioneer of folklore research in Argentina and by then professor of folklore studies at the Natural Museum of La Plata University and the University of Buenos Aires. The two developed a close relationship. But instead of staying in Argentina to look for an academic position, he decided to move to Minas, Uruguay, a small city one hundred miles from the capital city of Montevideo. It's unclear why he made this move, though in some notes he mentions health problems, which may have inclined him to seek in the hills of Minas a less aggressive environment than Buenos Aires or even Montevideo. In Minas, he married the patrician María Luiza Vértiz and Hispanicised his name to Francisco Curt before moving to Montevideo.[17] According to his own account, he worked since 1925 in an imports business until the director of the SODRE, which was launched in 1930, asked him to organize the record collection. In a letter to the Uruguayan consul in Vienna, he asks for support to contact the Viennese pedagogue Anna Lechner, whose pedagogic method he wants to learn in order to educate the Uruguayan children musically, and to finish his own studies. Also, "as you know Mr. Consul, due to the racial and psychological links that tie Uruguay to France, we have grossly neglected the literature, philosophy, and other

[17] I thank Inés de Torres for sharing her views on Lange and an excerpt of his diary, and Katrin Zinsmeister and her aunt for translating it.

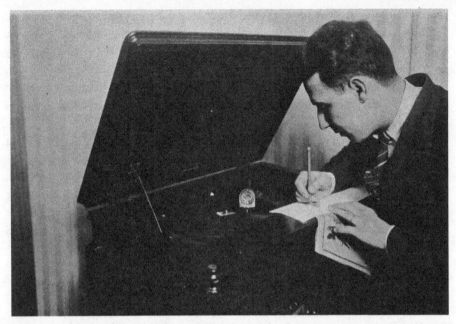

FIGURE 4.1 Francisco Curt Lange's collaborator Lauro Ayestarán, "measuring records," *Boletín Latino Americano de Música* 4, 1938.

arts from Germany and Austria," ignored by students and teachers. This is something to be corrected in the "enormous labor of musical education of the people."[18]

Between 1925 and 1934 Lange built a professional career thus around conferences on Austrian and German music but above all as Director of the National Record Disc Collection at the recently founded SODRE (Official Service of Electric Broadcasting) (see Figure 4.1).

This official station followed the model of the British BBC and of the Municipal Radio of Buenos Aires.[19] It was praised by a cultural diplomat from Fascist Italy in 1934 as a model of state intervention in musical life for its music programming; the frequent concerts of its multinational orchestra, composed of Europeans from many countries as well as natives; its rich and perfectly organized collection of records ranging from classic to popular music; and its catalogues. A cultural diplomat from the New Deal pointed out a few years later that Uruguayans were fed classical music by the state when in fact their musical preferences were probably more varied.[20] In any

---

[18] *"Grandísima obra de educación musical del pueblo."* AFCL Subsérie 2.1, November 24, 1931, letter to Eliseo Ricardo Gómez.

[19] María Inés de Torres, "El surgimiento de la radiodifusión pública en Hispanoamérica. Contexto, modelos y el estudio de un caso singular: el SODRE, la radio pública estatal de Uruguay (1929)," *Revista internacional de Historia de la Comunicación*, no. 5 (2015): 122–42.

[20] Adriano Lualdi, *Viaggio musicale nel Sud-America* (Milano: Istituto Editoriale Nazionale, 1934), 157–61, and Carleton Sprague Smith, *Musical Tour through South America, June-October, 1940* (New York: Washington Conference on Inter-American Relations in the Field of Music, 1940), XXXII.

case, SODRE was an example of the convergence of musicological activism and state building. Lange was also appointed professor of German at the National University, collaborated with the Riemann *Lexikon* directed in Berlin by Alfred Einstein—a very prestigious credential—then became an adviser of Uruguay's Education Council and, in 1934, created and directed the Section on Musical Research at Uruguay's Institute of Advanced Studies, where he launched his two most significant projects: his *Musical Americanism* textbook and the *Boletín Latino Americano de Música*.

At the end of 1934, Lange traveled for the first time outside the Rio de la Plata region. He started in Rio de Janeiro, where he gave conferences and met members of Brazil's musical establishment, and shortly afterward traveled to Chile, Bolivia, and Peru, where he drafted the content for two books published four years later: a philosophical-travel notebook of sorts, and a refutation of militaristic interpretations of Nietzsche's thought.[21] But that same year, before beginning his travels, Lange wrote a foundational text that served as his main intellectual credential: *Americanismo Musical*.

Americanismo Musical

The founding manifesto of Latin Americanist musicology begins by invoking Beethoven: "From one heart to many" (*¡De un corazón, que vaya hacia corazones!*).[22]

According to Lange, there is in the New World a "Latin soul" animating "a community of nations united by the same blood and driven by the same desires . . . bound together in the fight toward a common ideal." Among the arts, music is "predestined" to make this vital ideal the driving force of spiritual and cultural exchange among this community of nations. Music will interpret "the thousand hidden voices" of the Latin American peoples, who are ready to conquer their future by building on "the nebulous past of millenarian cultures, disappeared races, bloody conquests, and the awakening of the feelings of autonomy and freedom."

Through extreme figures and metaphors, like the trope of a vital force "defined by blood, conquering the future out of the ashes of its previous defeats," Lange presented music as an expression of cultures that he defined ethnically and geographically. The view of Latin America as a cultural region was being fostered by a wave of foundational institutions in Germany and the United States: an export-agriculture businessman financed the creation of the Middle America Research Institute at Tulane University in New Orleans in 1924, the Ibero-American Institute in Berlin was founded in 1930, the Institute of Latin American Culture at the University of Buenos

---

[21] Francisco Curt Lange, *Impresiones andinas. Argentina: antagonismo cultural. Bolivia: pueblo en desgracia* (Montevideo: Nueva América, 1938). Francisco Curt Lange, *La posición de Nietzsche frente a la guerra, el estado y la raza* (Santiago de Chile: Ercilla, 1938). The preface is signed in June 1936 in Montevideo, and the main text in February.

[22] Francisco Curt Lange, *Americanismo musical. La Sección de Investigaciones Musicales: su creación, propósitos y finalidades* (Montevideo: Instituto de Estudios Superiores—Sección de Investigaciones Musicales, 1934).

Aires and the Institute of Inter-American Affairs at the University of Florida in Gainsville were founded in 1931, and a few years later an Institute for Latin American Studies would be created at the University of Texas at Austin in 1940.[23]

Lange saw Latin American artists as living under the combined threat of modern mass media, commercial culture, and the hegemony of European art, which he considered in some way as foreign to the American reality. This is why artists must leave the capital cities, "with their fictitious exposition of values and mediocrities," and look both inside themselves and "at the central Pampa, the Sierras, at the magnificent heights of the Andes, at the tropical jungle, at the murmurous beaches of the Caribbean Sea, at the Atlantic and Pacific oceans, at the last vestiges of Incas and Aztecs, in direct contact with the races that still conserve some of their own life."[24] Musicians, historians, pedagogues, researchers, and above all composers must turn their backs on "the Atlantic"—a European space—and focus on the American "subconscious" where "musical destinies march along continental, national, and regional paths." He paraphrased James Monroe: *"American music for the Americans."* In his view, across the continent a "spiritual laboratory" of artists—still isolated from one another and from the state, the audiences, and the public—was waiting to be organized, to exchange ideas and artistic and scholarly works, to produce a reciprocal knowledge and stop admiring Europe and the United States. The main problems, in his diagnosis, were the almost complete ignorance of the musical production between neighboring countries and the lack of state intervention in their emerging broadcasting systems. States were too weak, commercial culture too widespread, and artists too isolated to change this reality. The solution to artistic isolation and commercial culture consisted, he thought, in creating *continental institutions.*

In 1934 Lange founded the Institute of Advanced Studies Section on Musical Research with the idea that it would become a hub for research and publication, including the creation of catalogues that would reach Latin America as a whole. His immediate goals were to create a Latin American music lexicon, a music library, a records collection, a score collection, a museum of native instruments, and a Latin American Music Congress, and to exchange materials with institutions from Europe "and other continents." He had virtually no budget for the section, which operated from a tiny office in Montevideo where his wife typed the letters—only later would he be assigned an assistant, Lauro Ayestarán, who went on to become a major Uruguayan musicologist. Despite these constraints, by 1935 he had managed to convince thirty-one of the most important composers, researchers, and institutional directors of the Southern Cone to support his initiative. These supporters came from Argentina, Brazil, Uruguay, and Chile and included Mário de Andrade,

---

[23] See Sonia Alvarez, Arturo Arias, and Charles R. Hale, "Re-visioning Latin American Studies," *Cultural Anthropology* 26, no. 2 (2011): 229.

[24] Beatriz Ocampo called these intellectual spaces an "inner nation." Ocampo, *La nación interior: Canal Feijóo, Di Lullo y los hermanos Wagner: el discurso culturalista de estos intelectuales en la provincia de Santiago del Estero* (Buenos Aires: Antropofagia, 2004).

Carlos Vega, Juan Carlos Paz, the Dean of Santiago de Chile's College of Fine Arts, the Director of Rio de Janeiro's Philharmonic Orchestra, and the Director of the Brazilian National Music Institute, among others. The *Boletín Latino Americano de Música* (BLAM) emerged out of this impulse. The United States was not represented in the name of the Boletín, but the very first issue includes an entire section dedicated to that country, which suggests that the United States was on the horizon from the beginning.

With Lange's tenacity as BLAM's main resource, the first issue planted in 1935 the seeds for developments that literally shaped the musicological discipline in Latin America. In 1938, after four years of intense lobbying, Lange prompted representatives at the Pan American Conference in Lima, Peru, to vote for the creation of an Inter-American Institute of Musicology based in Montevideo under his direction. He benefited from the prestige of BLAM's first four volumes.

The Boletín Latino Americano de Música as a Musical Map

Lange published the first volume (1935) in Montevideo, the second (1936) in Lima, the third (1937) again in Montevideo, and the fourth (1938) in Bogotá. After spending three years looking for resources, he published the fifth volume (1941) in Montevideo with private and public funding from the United States and Uruguay, and the sixth and last volume (1946) in Rio de Janeiro. Each volume is 600 to 900 pages long and is accompanied by a thick *Musical Supplement*, which made BLAM both impressive and expensive. For each volume Lange established partnerships with national institutions and intellectuals who saw in this initiative a possibility for international promotion and academic prestige.

The first volume, launched in April 1935, was distributed in Buenos Aires through Lange's personal contacts, in Brazil by the Music National Institute, in Chile by the College of Fine Arts at the University of Chile, and in Spain by the Iberian-American Publicity agency, based in Barcelona. Lange's editorial article had a crusade spirit. The BLAM, he argued, is a sign of the "artistic consciousness of our continent" and a tool for linking the isolated efforts of musicians, scholars, and musical institutions throughout Latin America. Neither his institute nor the contributors would receive any economic profit from the publication, which was intended as a tool for spiritual emancipation and as "propaganda" for Latin American musical art. Brazilian contributions would be published in Portuguese, and contributions in any other language would be translated into Spanish (this ended up being done by Lange himself). Notable painters would contribute, because this project was about not only music, but also art, which is "the supreme crystallization of any race's plans" and the way "it will acquire full consciousness of its mission in the universal concert." This first volume was organized in five sections: Latin American Studies, European Studies, United States Studies, Musical Pedagogy, and Aesthetic Education, plus a few editorial notes in which Lange asked for support and promoted his dream: the first congress of Latin American music.

The BLAM combined three distinct discourses: a civilizing idea of *education*, understood as means of elevating the national population; an idea of *race* as the synthesis of biology, history, and collective fate; and a conservative and elitist notion of *culture*, which made Lange consider "soccer, commercial broadcasting, and cinema" as "the collective diseases of the day in . . . Latin America, but especially in the region of the Rio de la Plata." Lange saw, on the one hand, institutionally rich, cosmopolitan cities hosting foreign collectivities isolated from each other and, on the other, "integrative" provincial cities that lacked institutions and cultural activity. What was needed, in his eyes, was an intensification of the art currents that connected these two poles. These cosmopolitan and provincial poles had to be connected continentally rather than just nationally. These currents needed to provide less "universal" and more "American" teachings, seeking an "absolute fusion with our soil of the children of foreigners who attend public schools, and the formation of an homogeneous and well-defined ethnic whole."[25] Racial thinking, public schools, and transnational Latin Americanism represented a truly original mix of themes articulated at the time by eugenicists, liberal nationalists, and revolutionary socialists.

What remained vague was the relationship between musical nationalism—a positive value that Lange assigned to ethnicity, authenticity, and indigenous roots—and a transnational Latin American identity, both of which he opposed to hollow cosmopolitanism and the imitation of Europe.

The articles in the three initial volumes, from 1935 to 1937, reveal the variety of issues the publication considered as part of a reflection on Latin American music. The first volume, for instance, presents an analysis of the legal and aesthetic dimensions of the an artwork as "property"; an interpretation of the avant-garde music of Juan Carlos Paz (the leader of the Argentine *Grupo Renovación*); a history of the musical instrument *Trutruka*; studies of Colombian folkloric poetry and Afro-Brazilian music; an ethno-historical study of Inca music; a collection of Argentine colonial songs; and a study of a classical composer from colonial Brazil.[26]

A representative combination of nationalism and Latin Americanism was by art professor and *indigenista* Guillermo Salinas Cossío, from Lima. Salinas praised the emergence of the Latin American artist as "a new man before a new world," the product of a "new race," and the creator of a "new sensibility" and "an original interpretation of reality."[27] On the one hand, he thought this new race would be expressed in

---

[25] Francisco Curt Lange, "Arte musical latino americano: raza y asimilación," *Boletín Latino Americano de Música* 1 (1935): 13–28.

[26] "Los derechos a la creación estética," by Eduardo J. Couture (Montevideo); "La obra musical de Juan Carlos Paz," by Héctor I. Gallac (Buenos Aires); "Un instrumento americano: la Trutruka," by C. Isamitt (Santiago de Chile); "Del folklore colombiano," by Emirto de Lima (Barranquilla); "Os Congos," by Mário de Andrade (São Paulo); "Ensayo sobre la música Inca," by André Sas (Lima); "Doce canciones coloniales del siglo XVII," notation and harmonization by Josué Teófilo Wilkes (Buenos Aires); "José Mauricio Nunes García (1767–1830). Ensaio histórico," by Luiz-Heitor Corrêa de Azevedo (Rio de Janeiro).

[27] Guillermo Salinas Cossío, "La música en la América Latina y su nacionalización," *BLAM* 2 (1936): 157–62.

"national schools," which, in the face of the rootless and "intoxicating" cosmopolitanism of the "so-called universal music," would filter and incorporate the "audacities" of modern and popular music the way the Russian, Spanish, and other European schools had done—like Weber, Chopin, or Smetana. On the other hand, he drew a diversified map of the region. Peru, Bolivia, and Ecuador, which he envisioned as ethnically homogeneous countries, would base their national schools of music and the arts in general on their indigenous past—a perspective that suited the *indigenismo* of Andean intellectuals of the day.[28] In Argentina and Uruguay, on the contrary, the base had to be *folk-criollo* music, with some African additions. In each country, according to the relative presence of Indian, African, and Spanish cultural heritage, the prevailing influence would be either "the melancholic and nostalgic influence of Indigenous music . . . the distant Oriental flavor of Spanish singing [or] the rhythmic orgy and frenetic, insatiable sensuality of black music, which although it has not created even a single melody, has introduced its unchaining of rhythms in the music of most Latin American countries." For Salinas, the distinct combination of essentialist racial contributions is what defined a nation. In this vision, Latin America was a mosaic of essences.

Salinas addressed the problem of musical hierarchy by valorizing *popular* music as a "spontaneous product of the people [and a] typical expression of its ethnic character," different from the *popularized* or *vulgar* music—*popularizada* or *populachera*—and differed from the "semipopular," produced by aficionados and commercial musicians. Phonographic recording paradoxically allowed not only commercialization but also "exact" reproduction, and therefore the analysis and authentication of different versions of a single tune by specialists. Salinas praised this technology for enabling a scientific classification of "the particular procedures and native forms of a race," which allowed trained composers to "nationalize" popular music by choosing and adapting harmonic, melodic, and rhythmic particularities into an "adequate realm" that "could fit all the innovations and conquests of modern polyphony."

We should retain at least three conclusions from Salinas's intervention. The first is modern technology as a legitimate tool for combating the commercialism and cosmopolitanism behind this very technology, because of its scientific and classificatory power to sustain a national canon.[29] The second is national canons, rooted in popular forms, required erudite techniques of composition to be adapted to a "universal" musical language. The third is that programmatic debates on how to build a national

---

[28] The modernist paternalism of Cuzco indigenistas vis-à-vis the popular classes was analyzed by Deborah Poole, "Figueroa Aznar and the Cusco Indigenistas: Photography and Modernism in Early Twentieth-Century Peru," *Representations* 38 (1992): 39–75. Rebecca Earle considers it part of an irresoluble tension between nation-building projects and the place of "our Indians" in Latin America. Rebecca Earle, *The Return of the Native: Indians and Myth-making in Spanish America, 1810–1930* (Durham, NC: Duke University Press, 2007).

[29] Appreciation of technology for the sake of authenticity was at the core of the reactionary modernism of Nazi and fascist movements in Europe. Jeffrey Herf, *Reactionary Modernism: Technology, Culture, and Politics in Weimar and the Third Reich* (New York: Cambridge University Press, 1984).

culture were inextricably linked to the definition of Latin America as a distinctive cultural area, a supra-identity of which national identities were particular variations. As we can see, a conservative and *indigenista* member of the Peruvian intellectual elite was able to invoke modern technology and erudite techniques under the assumption that Peruvian music was part of a pan-regional cultural area.

The promotion of erudite elaborations of folklore followed different national modulations. On Volume 3 (1937) of BLAM, for example, Argentine critic Mauricio Ferrari Nicolay expressed a conservative and elitist perspective: his piece attacks commercial broadcasting for its "concessions to ordinary people's degraded taste," for adopting low-quality melodies from the urban outskirts, for being "rhythmically poor," and for its "unspiritual lyrics, focused on the rude and unrefined aspects of life, that crowd a mixed and awkward radio broadcast devoted to a bastard internationalism." Official radio stations were guilty of advertising women's underwear and automobile lubricants between two movements of St. Matthews' Passion at the Colón Theater.[30] Mexican composer Juan León Mariscal, to the contrary, celebrated his fellows' work on "our folklore [. . .], the music of the Indian," whose intonations, calibrated through a "serious harmonization" with the "universal concept of auditory beauty," allow the "exotic timbres" of "our Indians" to convey feelings of placidity and joy that are "something fully ours." The image, once again, is of erudite composers elaborating refined music out of raw folkloric materials.[31] The modernist poet Julio Morales Lara from Venezuela also celebrated the folkloric inspiration of nationalist music, in his case by praising the ethnic and social concoctions of his country's *música criolla*, "until recently reduced to the cultivation of our popular style, the *joropo*" but now incorporating "our black and indigenous music" through the work of a new generation of musicians. The Orfeón Lamas (a chorus group), as well as "Vicente Emilio Sojo, Moisés Moleiro, Juan B. Plaza, José Antonio Calcagno C. y Miguel Angel Calcagno," are presenting "essentially national music, taken from humble popular themes and stylized in noble criteria of sensibility and art." These African and indigenous themes had been recovered from regional music from the Plain, Oriental, and Andean zones, where composers found "the melodic feelings of the defeated races" (*el sentir melódico de las razas vencidas*). With state support, Morales concludes, Venezuelan audiences will have, beside the traditional *joropo*, "a true national music."[32]

The *Boletín* presented Latin American music as a supra-national version of the nationalist discourses on music of the time, which subsumed within encompassing categories like "popular" and "artistic music" a vast array of ethnically and socially defined forms of music, from light theater to church music, from African-origin rhythms to European-inspired symphonies.[33]

---

[30] Mauricio Ferrari Nicolay, "Notas introductoras a la filiación musical de la cultura musical argentina," *BLAM* 3 (1937): 97–99.

[31] Juan León Mariscal, "La música moderna en México," *BLAM* 3 (1937): 109–12.

[32] Julio Morales Lara, "Panorama musical venezolano," *BLAM* 3 (1937): 81–82.

[33] Gerard Béhague, "Boundaries and Borders in the Study of Music in Latin America: A Conceptual Re-Mapping," *Revista de Musica Latino Americana (Austin)* 21, no. 1 (2000): 21.

The role of the United States was ambiguous. Lange was impressed by the modern musical organization of that country. For the *Boletín's* second volume (1936) he translated into Spanish an article about "The National Federation of Musical Clubs in the United States," in which one of the federation's authorities, Helen Harrison Mills, detailed the organizational aspects of 5,000 professional and amateur musical associations (comprising a total of 500,000 musicians) throughout the United States. A collaborator translated "Musical Education Through the Radio in the United States," by NBC officer Ernesto La Prade, which described the programs broadcast by CBS, NBC, and others that were dedicated to musical pedagogy, concerts, and promotion of some of the 50,000 school orchestras created in the country between 1920 and 1935. The impressive numbers associated with musical life in the United States—where civil organizations, commercial and public broadcasting, the school system, state policies, and private sponsorship seemed to flow and interact—confirmed to Lange the necessity of organizing institutionally Latin America's dispersed musical forces.

Sometime in 1936 Lange began to think that rather than replicating the US model, Latin America should improve its musical life by articulating its poorly funded institutions with US institutions through a hemispheric system. He probably realized that no single Latin American country could emulate the scale and synergy of the US musical system.

An article in the *Boletín's* third volume (1937) by Heitor Villa-Lobos explained the government's music education policies were based on his philosophy, which emphasized collective singing at patriotic events in which thousands of students and hundreds of schoolteachers followed his musical direction. This top-down state ritual was the largest musical organization in the country. There were also smaller and disconnected musical organizations. For example, urban groups of aficionados in Sao Paulo, Porto Alegre, and other cities were toured by a variety of local and foreign artists. Brazil also had an incipient broadcasting system, a small recording industry, a growing copyright-collection system still dominated by the representatives of foreign interests, popular neighborhood-based samba schools, and rural fairs and religious rituals that featured folk music. Musicologists and impresarios were impotent mediators compared with the musical market and associative movement in the United States. Meanwhile, Argentina's musical life was concentrated in the Buenos Aires metropolitan area and neglected the rest of the country. And in Mexico, though *bandas de pueblo*, musicians, and orchestras were everywhere, they were very far from being organized institutionally. The only cohesive (if incipient) elements of Mexican musical life were a few state-employed musicologists, the contested and weak orchestra musicians' unions described in chapter 3, and the first broadcasting impresarios analyzed in chapter 2. So from Lange's perspective, it made more sense to build a continental network than to try to replicate the US model nationally. He envisioned this hemispheric organization assigning its leading roles to musicologists, who were as a group, thanks to Lange and the BLAM, the most organized musical actors in Latin

America. The precise nature of the organization's relations with the United States remained vague in Lange's texts.

The Bulletin kept expanding institutionally and intellectually. The fourth volume (1938), published in Bogotá, Colombia, contained thirty-nine articles on a wide range of topics, perspectives, countries, and regions, and enlisted an impressive array of donors and sponsors. In Uruguay, these included government officials from the president of the republic to the mayor of Montevideo, the Jockey Club, private and public banks, military commanders, and university professors. In Chile and Ecuador, the heads of universities and education ministries joined in. And in Colombia, the heads of the most important cultural and musical institutions participated.

The fourth volume also featured the top tier of Latin American and US composers and musicologists, including Julián Carrillo and Vicente T. Mendoza from Mexico, Oneyda Alvarenga from Brazil, Carlos Isamitt from Chile, and the Russian-American critic Nicolás Slonimsky. This volume also included contributions from less-known musical spaces such as Paraguay, Honduras, and Costa Rica, as well as Brazilian cities other than Rio de Janeiro and São Paulo, such as Curitiba. The articles' subject matter also ranged widely: the volume included historical research on colonial and indigenous music and instruments, musical analysis of both folkloric and modernist compositions, studies of music pedagogy, and an article on classificatory systems for records collections. The thematic scope, the number of contributions, and the status and geographic diversity of its contributors made the BLAM an example of transnational intellectual cooperation. And its transnational nature made it a platform for showcasing the variety of personal, national, and disciplinary projects of the Latin American musical intelligentsia.

The letters Lange wrote while putting this volume together reveal no particular political or national allegiances; he seems to have been entirely focused on his own scientific and organizational goals. In a letter to the Brazilian musicologist Luiz Heitor Correa de Azevedo in January 1936, for example, Lange mentioned his goal of getting support from Pan American Union to increase musical exchange in the Americas. He commented on the "great Colonial musical treasure" he had just found in Caracas, Venezuela, and described his negotiations with the Uruguayan bureaucracy to extend his license to travel to Cuba and Mexico. A few days later, in a letter to Peruvian writer Luis Valcárcel, Lange asked for university support for research on indigenous and criollo folk music, "starting now, because nothing really serious has been done and research is urgent, before every living memory [of those musical traditions] disappears."[34]

Neither the origins of the collaborations nor the sources of funding really mattered to him, as long as he could bring together the best artists and scholars. There is an almost complete absence, in both his personal and official letters, of aesthetic

---

[34] January 18, 1938 and January 30, 1930, Subserie 2.1, AFCL.

judgments of the artists he recruited and the artists whose work was analyzed in the BLAM. Lange's spirit was that of a collector, organizer, and scholar, not an artist.

A quantitative analysis of the 12,767 letters he wrote between 1932 and 1947 gives us a sense of his international scope (see Figure 4.2). Buenos Aires and Montevideo were the letters' most frequent destinations but were hardly his only action zones.

If the sheer number of letters and the range of destinations are proof of Lange's ambition, the letters' content confirms the Boletín's transnational and organizational nature. For example, an early letter to A. Jurafsky, Secretary of the Wagnerian Association in Buenos Aires, mentioned Lange's collaboration on a South American Music Lexicon to be published in Germany, exemplifying his attempt to promote "an inter-American convergence and the promotion of South American authors and work in Europe."[35] And in August 1936, when the relationship between the intellectual establishments of Chile and Peru was quite complex, Lange suggested to the publishers of the Chilean journal The Voice of Indo-America that they consider the work of Peruvian writer and anthropologist José María Arguedas.[36] A month later, Lange wrote a long letter to Benedito Nicolau dos Santos in Curitiba, Brazil, praising Santos's recently published three-volume work Sound-metrics and Music, and describing Santos as "one of the many hidden heroes living in provincial cities" that strive for research and publishing opportunities despite the lack of funding. "This work is known in Paraná, São Paulo, and Rio de Janeiro; but its diffusion beyond Brazil can only be carried on by [Lange's] Musical Americanism."[37] Leo Rowe, director of the Pan American Union, wrote to Lange in January of 1936 congratulating him for the Bulletin and suggesting some contacts, like the secretary of Education of Venezuela, and also key figures such as "Sr. Fernando Ortiz . . . Señor don Ernesto Lecuona, Señor don Carlos Chávez."[38] In April 1939 Lange wrote to anthropologist Fernando Ortiz in Havana, to ask him to seek support from city authorities to fund a new BLAM issue. He wrote a similar letter to Harold Spivacke, chief of the Music Division at the Library of Congress, in which he offered to print the volume in Uruguay, where costs would be lower.[39] All these years, Lange's goal was to obtain funding. By 1938, his transnationalism had oriented him to the United States.

The Boletín's fourth volume was released right before the American International Conference held in Lima in December 1938. Its publication helped him convince the conference's delegates to recommend the creation of a hemispheric musicological center.

---

[35] October 24, 1932, Subsérie 2.1, AFCL.
[36] August 11, 1936 and August 13, 1936, Subsérie 2.1, AFCL.
[37] September 2, 1936, Subsérie 2.1, AFCL.
[38] January 12, 1936, Subsérie 2.2, AFCL.
[39] April 14, 1939 and April 19, 1939, Subsérie 2.1, AFCL.

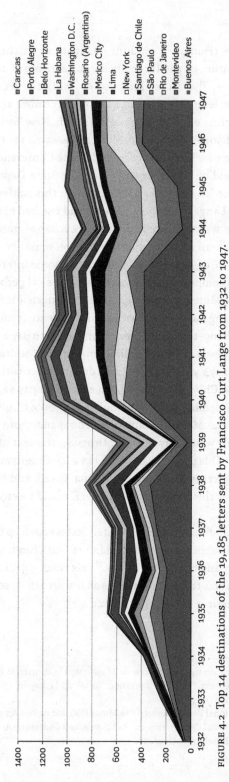

FIGURE 4.2 Top 14 destinations of the 19,185 letters sent by Francisco Curt Lange from 1932 to 1947.
Beginning in 1935, Lange wrote no less than 600 letters to the top 14 destinations, which represent just 66% of the total, and this number surpassed 1,200 in 1941. The ranking must be read from the bottom up: Buenos Aires, Montevideo, Rio de Janeiro, São Paulo, Santiago de Chile, New York, etc.

Source: Subsérie 2.1, AFCL.

Lange's cause seemed to have triumphed on June 26, 1940, when the president of Uruguay decreed the formation of the Inter American Institute of Musicology (IIAM), with Lange as director. The decree followed not only the recommendations of the Pan American Conference hosted in Lima on December 24, 1938, but also of the International Congress of Musicology celebrated in New York in 1939— which supported BLAM and Lange's Section on Musical Research for the sake of the "musical patrimony of the new hemisphere"—and of the Conference on Inter American Relations in the Field of Music, organized by the State Department in Washington the same year (200 US delegates participated in this conference, plus a few Latin Americans, led by Lange).[40] In theory, Lange had reached his goals: the new Inter-American Institute was dedicated to musical exchange, research, and congresses; hosted an inter-American music library, archive, museum, and publications; and began planning three new continental institutions: inter-American associations of contemporary composers, musicology, and musical pedagogy.

The IIAM operated under the Ministry of Foreign Relations, which was responsible for providing resources, but Lange wanted to involve governments from the entire hemisphere, so he proposed a budget in which every country had to pay according to its population. Countries with fewer than two million inhabitants (basically Central America and Paraguay) had to pay a yearly fee of $1,000 dollars; those with 2 to 5 million (Guatemala, Bolivia, Cuba, Chile, Ecuador, Venezuela) would pay $2,000; those with 5 to 12 million (Canada, Colombia and Peru) would pay $3,000; those with 12 to 50 million (Argentina, Brazil and Mexico) would pay $5,000; and those with more than 50 million (United States) would pay $12,000. Uruguay, the seat of the institute, would contribute $10,000. This proposal amounted to a US-Uruguayan financial partnership with substantial participation from Argentina, Brazil, and Mexico. The cultural and musical benefits of this partnership, however, would be enjoyed by all of them.

But securing this funding was difficult, and the United States ended up turning the fifth BLAM into a US-centered publication. Published in 1941 with funds from public and private sources in Uruguay and the United States,[41] this volume dedicated forty-five articles to US music and twelve to Latin America, and featured in its cover for the first time a full map of the Americas (see Figures 4.3 and 4.4).

---

[40] "Decreto de oficialización del Instituto Interamericano de Musicología" (Ministerio de Relaciones Exteriores y Ministerio de Instrucción Pública y Previsión Social de la República Oriental del Uruguay, June 26, 1940), *BLAM* 5 (1941): 15–16.

[41] Carnegie Endowment for International Peace, through the Music Division of Pan American Union, and National Committee on Intellectual Cooperation on the US side, and Consejo de Autor, Banco de la República, and Dr. Alejandro Gallinal, from Uruguay.

FIGURES 4.3 AND 4.4 A shift in the hemispheric representation from the 1938 to the 1941 covers of the *Boletín Latino Americano de Música.*

Lange's prologue was a complex reflection on inter-American musical relations.[42] He adopted a new rhetoric by locating "musical Americanism" in the "Western hemisphere" and expressed his preoccupation with the financial restrictions that the United States' entry into the war had created for the development of inter-American relations. Nonetheless, Lange wrote, the Great War had stimulated musical creation

---

[42] Francisco Curt Lange, "Suma de las relaciones interamericanas en el campo de la música," *BLAM* 5 (1941): 11–22.

FIGURES 4.3 AND 4.4 Continued

by increasing the autonomy of American institutions vis-à-vis Europe and spurring the migration of artists from the Old Continent, so World War II could also have positive effects. The main fight, as he saw it, was still against the Europeanist inclinations of too many New World musicians, composers, cultural authorities, and audiences. The hemispheric cultural autonomy that Lange envisioned was still to be achieved, both in the United States, with its countless musical organizations throughout its vast territory, and in Latin America, whose musical life was less developed and confined to a few capital cities. As Lange saw it, the situation in Latin America was worse than in the United States, because the roles played by universities, conservatories, and private institutions in the Unites States were in Latin America replaced by the state. "We are used to thinking with and through the state" (*nosotros estamos acostumbrados a pensar con el estado y a través del mismo*), he wrote—a state that he saw as supporting only erudite music, in total disconnection from the developments of popular music outside the formal institutions.

Thanks to this private institutional network, Lange argued, erudite music in the United States was beginning to show "signs of maturity." But Latin American composers could not benefit from the United States's vast system of chamber concerts due to the lack of institutional exchange and availability of music scores. In Latin America, the first Festival of Latin American Music held in Montevideo in 1935, which combined Latin American and European composers, barely drew an audience. Uruguay was a small country with a seaport historically oriented toward Europe; it was the cradle of musical Americanism, but it could not carry the whole mission on its back. Latin America and the United States should collaborate, Lange argued, by exchanging music scores, organizing tours, and working together to train young musicians. This shared mission would be the only way of defeating the shared threats of commercial radio and the European tradition.

By June 1942 many steps had been taken in the direction Lange desired. For the first time in hemispheric history, at least three institutional networks were operating in the field of music: the IIAM and the Inter-American Cooperative Publishing House of Composers, directed by Lange in Montevideo; the Music Division of the Pan American Union, directed by Charles Seeger in Washington, DC; and the Pan American Circle of Folklore in Natal (Brazil), directed by Luiz da Câmara Cascudo.[43] These links between the United States and Latin America were of utmost importance, in part because they coincided with the growing importance of the very idea of a *Latin American culture* and contributed to its consolidation.

During World War II, music was also part of a converging point for inter-American initiatives around folklore. In June 1941 a new magazine was founded, called—somewhat cumbersomely—"Folklore *of the-das-de las* Americas" (the title included the English, Portuguese, and Spanish ways of articulating the substantives "folklore" and "Americas" that are spelled the same way in the three languages). This publication came as an expansion of Ralph Steele Boggs's work as Hispanist at the university of North Carolina and at the *Handbook of Latin American Studies* (directed by the US Latin Americanist historian Lewis Hanke) and the Southern Folklore Quarterly between 1936 and 1938. Twice a year, this magazine published a series of short essays, directories, and bibliographies intended to bring together all the specialists from the hemisphere. In April 1940 membership cards for the *Folklore of the-das-de las Americas* association began to be distributed to the Americas' folklorists. At that point, interestingly, the leading US Latin Americanist musicologists were moving away from their traditional

---

[43] This unprecedented level of collaboration motivated the first two accounts of the history of musical exchanges within the hemisphere, by Eugenio Pereira Salas (University of Chile) and Eugenio Pereira Salas, *Notas para la historia del intercambio musical entre las Américas antes del año 1940.* (Washington, DC: Pan American Union, Music Division, 1941); and US Latin Americanist musicologist Gilbert Chase, "Materials for the Study of Latin American Music," *Notes: Journal of the Music Library Association* 13 (March 1942): 1–12.

hispanismo to embrace *Latin Americanism*: the first work by the towering scholar Gilbert Chase, published in 1941, was *The Music of Spain*, but then he immediately wrote in 1942 to the Library of Congress a bibliography of Latin American music; by 1962 he would found in Tulane University the Inter American Institute for Musical Research.

Who were these folklorists? The enumeration that follows is not intended as encyclopedic information, but as a collective portrait—its geographic scope, ethnic narratives, and institutional contexts—of the generation that established Latin American folklore as a legitimate regional field.

The June 1942 issue of the journal, now with a simpler name, *Folklore Americas*, provides short biographies of an important part of this intellectual establishment.[44] In the two years between its foundation in April 1940 and June 1942, the journal grew to include 26 members: 8 Argentines, 4 Americans, 3 Peruvians, 3 Brazilians, 2 Chileans, and 1 each from Bolivia, Dominican Republic, Ecuador, Mexico, Paraguay, and Uruguay. Each of them sent a self-presentation (most gave themselves the title of "professor") describing their arrival at folklore from music, law, business, and even politics. Being a folklorist meant dedicating time to learning and valorizing old cultural artifacts and artistic styles from their country, and at the same time establishing bonds with an international brotherhood of folklore amateurs and specialists. They were all male, and their origins diverged geographically, socially, and ethnically: the Americans presented themselves as "white," Peruvians as "mestizo," and many others as sons of German or Italian immigrants. The Brazilians grew professionally within state institutions, the Americans in universities, the rest held a variety of institutional positions. A remarkable fact about these biographies is the high degree of circulation between provinces and capital cities, between Latin America and European and US scientific centers, and in some cases across many countries. The Americas were for them a space of circulation wider than their distinct nations and represented at the same time a difference from Europe.

The eight Argentines had all been born in the provinces to Argentine, immigrant, or ethnically mixed parents and traveled more or less extensively within and outside Argentina. Bernardo Canal Feijóo, a forty-five-year-old who had been born "from Spanish father and Argentine mother" in Santiago del Estero, had traveled several times to Uruguay, Chile, and Brazil, but spent most of his life in Buenos Aires and in his field site of Santiago del Estero. Juan Alfonso Carrizo Reinoso, a forty-seven-year-old with Argentine parents, had been born in Catamarca and had also lived in Buenos Aires, Jujuy, Salta, Tucumán, and La Rioja before moving back to Buenos Aires—he became Argentina's most important folklorist. Augusto Raúl Cortázar, a thirty-two-year-old lawyer, had been born in Salta to Argentine parents, trained in Buenos Aires at Argentina's most prestigious educational institutions, and was an

---

[44] "Folklore Americas: Biographic Sketches of Members to 1942," *Folklore Americas* II, no. 1 (June 1942): 1–14.

authority on northern folklore. Juan Draghi Lucero, the forty-five-year-old son of
to an Italian father and an Argentine mother, had always lived in the South Andean
province of Mendoza and was a self-taught expert in the folklore of Cuyo. Dr. Santo
Faré, age forty-three, had been born in Paraná, Entre Ríos, and was a lawyer and
judge devoted to understanding folklore's "philosophy and psychology." Rafael Jijena
Sánchez, age thirty-eight, had been born in Tucumán to Argentine parents, had lived
in several provinces, and had become an important professor of folklore at many
public and Catholic institutions. Dr. Orestes Di Lullo, forty-four, had been born in
Santiago del Estero to Italian parents and had authored many books on Santiagueño
folklore. Finally, Carlos Vega, age forty-four, had been born to Andalusian parents in
Cañuelas, a province of Buenos Aires, and was a musicologist, folklorist, and leader
of Argentine folk music studies.

The four Americans, like the Argentines, came from and studied different regions.
Ralph Boggs, a forty-two-year-old scholar with "white American parents," was a well-
known promoter of folkloric and scholarly initiatives in the United States and Latin
America and was established in North Carolina. Arthur Leon Campa, age thirty-seven,
had been born to Mexican parents in Sonora, and was a university-trained folklorist
who had lived most of his life in Sonora, Baja California, and New Mexico and specialized in New Mexican Spanish folklore, folk drama, and song. Archer Taylor, age
fifty-two, had been born in Pennsylvania to white American parents, had lived in the
Northeast and Midwest, had trained at Harvard as a folklorist and Germanist, and
was a professor in Berkeley, California, specializing in riddles, proverbs, songs, and
tales. Finally, Stith Thompson, age fifty-seven, had been born in Kentucky to white
American parents, had lived all over the United States and traveled to Europe, had
been educated at Harvard, and was a promoter of international folklore associations
and a specialist in US Native American folktales. These were not members of a social
elite; they were classic specialized US scholars.

Peru offered quite representative members of its intellectual establishment: two
were from the *indigenista* heartland, and the third was a foreigner established in
the capital. José Farfán Ayerbe, age thirty-nine, had been born in Cuzco, Accha, to
"Peruvian parents of Spanish-Indian stock." He had trained in Cuzco and several
US Midwestern cities, had traveled to several parts of the Andes and the Americas,
and was an expert on Quechua language and folklore. Victor Navarro del Aguila,
age thirty-three, had been born to "Peruvian mestizo (Spanish-Indian) parents" in
Ayachucho and lived in that region before moving to Cuzco, and was a specialist in
pre-Columbian and colonial Peruvian archeology and Quechua language. Finally,
Federico Schwab, age forty, had been born to German parents in Bayern, had spent
his childhood and youth in several Middle Eastern and South American countries
before settling in Lima in 1930, had trained as librarian and bibliographer, and was
a historical folklorist.

Of the three Brazilian members, one was Lange's friend Luiz Heitor Correa de
Azevedo, a thirty-seven-year-old who had been born to "white Brazilian parents" in

the modest middle-class neighborhood of Cosme Velho in Rio de Janeiro, where he had taught history of music and been the librarian of the National Institute of Music for seven years. After World War II, he had become the head of UNESCO's musical directorate. Dr. Nicanor Miranda, age thirty-seven, had been born in São Paulo to "white Brazilian parents" and was head of several key educational institutions in São Paulo and an expert on Brazilian ethnography and folklore. Finally, Joaquim Bras Ribeiro, age thirty-five, had been born in Rio de Janeiro to "white Brazilian parents," one of whom had been a "prominent folklorist." Ribeiro had been an educational functionary in the 1930s and was now a professor specializing in the sociology of art and Brazilian folklore.

The two Chileans were Eugenio Pereira Salas and Yolando Pino Saavedra. Salas, age thirty-eight, had been born to Chilean parents in Santiago de Chile, had trained at the Universidad de Chile, Sorbonne, and Berkeley, conducted research in many European cities, and wrote about music and art in addition to folklore. Pino Saavedra, age forty-one, had been born to Chilean parents in Parral, Linares, in central Chile, had studied Spanish and German literature in Chile and Hamburg, and specialized in Chilean folklore.[45]

Each of the rest of these folklorists came from a different country. Bolivian Arthur Posnansky, age sixty-eight, had been born in Vienna from German parents and had lived in Germany, Sweden, England, and Brazil before establishing himself in La Paz. An entrepreneur and a scientist, he was one of Bolivia's first archeologists and had written a classic text on Tiwanaku as the cradle of South American civilization. Dominican Emilio Rodríguez Demorizi, age thirty-four, had been born in the small town of Sánchez, Samaná, to "white Dominican parents" and had become a diplomat, the director of the country's archive, a professor, and a cultural heritage promoter. Ecuadorian writer and folklorist Justino Cornejo Viscaíno, age thirty-eight, had been born to an old local family in the small agricultural city of Puebloviejo, Los Ríos, and had later moved to Quito and other parts of Ecuador. Paraguayan Guillermo Tell Bertoni, age fifty-three years, was the son of a distinguished Swiss botanist who, like many other Central European colonists, had migrated to Southeastern Paraguay in the 1880s. Bertoni was an agronomist and economist, had been Secretary of Agriculture and a professor at the University of Asunción, and was one of the founding fathers of Guaraní philology and folklore. Mexican Vicente Mendoza Gutiérrez, age forty-eight, had been born to Mexican parents in Cholula, Puebla, was a professor at the National Conservatory and president and founder of the Folklore Society of Mexico, and had authored foundational books on Mexican folklore, music, and Mexican-Spanish traditions. Uruguayan Ildefonso Pereda Valdés, age forty-three, had been born to a "Spanish father and Uruguayan mother" in Tacuarembó, Uruguay,

[45] Chilean folklorists were directly influenced by their Argentine colleagues. Ignacio Ramos-Rodillo, "Música típica, folklore de proyección y Nueva Canción chilena. Versiones de la identidad nacional bajo el desarrollismo en Chile, década de 1920 a 1973," Neuma 4, no. 2 (2011): 118–19.

had lived in Montevideo except for a few years in Buenos Aires, and was a lawyer and literary writer who was "interested chiefly in Negro and Uruguayan folklore."

Many of these biographies resemble Lange's and reflect his attempt to make the BLAM a common ground for a dispersed and heterogeneously trained Latin American intelligentsia. Scholars and musicians from different countries who wanted to promote their craft internationally developed transnational links around publications such as *Folklore Americas*. Folklore sparked one of the continental dialogues being created in those years: other cases were the Brazilian and Caribbean music critics who would discuss the concept of *mestizaje*; the writers, scholars, and diplomats who would establish Latin American cultural history as a new disciplinary field through the book series *Tierra Firme*, published by Fondo de Cultura Económica; the scholars of the African diaspora in the Americas; and the *indigenista* writers that also emerged in those years. Such links formed what Corinne Pernet called a "transnational cultural network(s) of professionals" that managed in some cases to incorporate its agenda into the realm of foreign relations, but more often simply infused with transnational views the culture and the politics of Latin America.[46]

Lange's *Musical Americanism* was aimed at discovering the "inner Other" that nationalist discourses promoted in each country, promoting international cultural exchange about Latin American identity, and converging with US institutions and disciplines. What distinguished it were its larger institutional goals in the realm of music. Moved by the BLAM's perpetual need for financial support, Lange perceived the State Department, the Pan American Union, the main private foundations in the United States, the Library of Congress, and some universities as institutional allies.

A HEMISPHERIC COUNTERPOINT: LANGE AND OTTO MAYER-SERRA

Lange's institutional goals contrasted and a times conflicted with the projects developed by his contemporary musicologists, as revealed by the epistolary relationship between Lange and another émigré, the German Jewish musicologist Otto Mayer-Serra, who also tried to promote, from Mexico City, musicological collaborations across the region.[47]

The dialogue between them began in German in 1935, when Mayer was exiled in Barcelona, writing on music for numerous Spanish and European journals, and Lange was in Montevideo kicking-off the first volume of the BLAM. Both were trying to

---

[46] Myers, "Gênese 'ateneísta' da história cultural Latino-Americana"; Corinne Pernet, "For the Genuine Culture of the Americas: Musical Folklore, Popular Arts, and the Cultural Politics of Pan Americanism, 1933–1950," in *Decentering America*, ed. Jessica Gienow-Hecht (New York: Berghahn Books, 2007), 132–68; Mareia Quintero-Rivera, *A cor e o som da nação: a idéia de "mestiçagem" na crítica musical do Caribe hispânico insular e do Brasil (1928–1948)* (São Paulo: FAPESP/Annablume, 2000).

[47] Subsérie 2.2, AFCL.

cement their reputation by promoting new forms of Spanish and Latin American musicology. On October 22, 1940, now established in Mexico City, Mayer explained to Lange, writing for the first time in Spanish, that he was finishing a Spanish version of the German *Atlantisbuch der Musik*, and thanked Lange for the names of several "folkloristas americanos": Paz, the Castro brothers, Wilkes, and Isamitt, to whom he solicited contribtuions. (Having lived in Germany and Spain during the previous three decades, he mentions with relief that the transition from the presidency of Lázaro Cárdenas to Ávila Camacho was happening in absolute calm.) On April 8, 1941, again in Spanish, Mayer depicts the difficulties of working as a Latin American musicologist in those days:

> You will easily understand that the only way out I have in this country is to work for our neighbor to the North. The new administration in the Department of Fine Arts began with big renovation projects, but politics drowned everything . . . and *"alles bleibt beim alten"* [everything remains the same]. Every month I receive a notice that a chair in musicology for me is "about" to be obtained. But I'm afraid I won't see this appointment made before I leave Mexico, which will surely happen in the next five or ten years . . . By the way, how is your next Bulletin going? Could you not get help from the new Pan American institutions in the U.S.A. that have real jets of dollars [*chorros de dólares*] at their disposal? Your work deserves it, if anything of all that has been done on this continent in musical matters deserves any support. But also in the U.S. . . . . politics takes precedence over our artistic things. . . . I plan to move, next winter, to Cuba to research Cuban music. I have realized that *only by means of comparative studies between the different Latin-American cultures* will it be possible one day to arrive at fruitful results. And this is precisely what I have set out for the future. *You can be very satisfied to know the whole continent and have a global vision of its problems and achievements* [my emphasis].

He shared a brief text, "Manuel M. Ponce. Cuatro Danzas Mexicanas para piano – Four Mexican Dances. Prefacio de Otto Mayer-Serra," in which he summarized the indigenous, Spanish, and Cuban traditions present in Mexican popular music, all of them reelaborated by Manuel Ponce. This was about the time he published *Panorama de la música mexicana*.[48] In 1943 Mayer also translated and adapted an *Enciclopedia de la Música* by M. Hürlimann y F. Hamel on Editorial Atlante, Mexico City (Atlante's director had worked in the publishing house Labor in Barcelona), in more than a thousand pages in three volumes that included his own addition, "Panorama de la Música Hispanoamericana (esbozo interpretativo)," later republished separately, where "Hispanoamérica" appears as a distinct "musical culture" in the "musical world," with Indigenous and colonial roots transformed by the Independence era

---

[48] Otto Mayer-Serra, *Panorama de la música mexicana: desde la independencia hasta la actualidad* (Mexico City: Colegio de México, 1941).

and the romantic nationalism, until reaching a present time marked by musical innovation.[49]

Prolific and ambitious, Mayer explained (March 22, 1943) the success of the *Enciclopedia*, particularly of his chapter on *Hispanoamérica* "in every country of the region," and shared with Lange a project that the latter would not tolerate. Mayer wanted to prepare for Atlante a new Encyclopedia,

> exclusively devoted to Hispanic-American music . . . a comprehensive panorama of the *cultura musical americana* in all its aspects: bibliographic, folkloric, historical, and organizative . . . As you can imagine, you are among the first people whose cooperation I wish to gain for this project to be accomplished as perfectly as possible. I will send you soon a questionnaire to be filled by the most outstanding musicians of your country. I would appreciate a list with names and address of all Latin American musicians that in your view should be incorporated to the dictionary, as well as ideas and suggestions . . . I am sure you have tons of unpublished material for which this project could be a good opportunity.

Lange did not respond to this nor to other letters insisting on the same. A letter Mayer wrote to Raul P. Silvera, secretary of the IIAM (September 27, 1943) apologized for his critical review at the Revista Musical Mexicana of the IIAM's publications. The apologies express the structural limitations of this field: he had always supported Lange and his work, and just wanted in his review to explain his disagreement, which was also shared by "the majority of young composers in Mexico who, up to now, have not wished to cooperate with the publishing house" of the IIAM, the Editorial Cooperativa.

> We continue to believe that the composer is no longer the romantic bohemian who lives on the margins of society and who has the right to share in its benefits [*el compositor ha dejado de ser el bohemio romántico que vive al margen de la sociedad y que tiene derecho a participar en los beneficios de ésta*]. It does not seem fair to us, therefore, that the composer should make a double contribution to the cooperative: that of his creative work and of his monetary contribution, without ever receiving more equivalent than that of the satisfaction that the publication of one of his works could produce.

Musicology's lack of funding made Lange charge composers to be published, instead of the other way around, which would have been the norm in a fully professional field.[50]

---

[49] Otto Mayer-Serra, *Panorama de la música hispanoamericana: esbozo interpretativo* (México: Editorial Atlante, 1943).

[50] The Editorial Cooperativa Interamericana de Compositores published more than 60 works by composers from all over Latin America. See *El Instituto Interamericano de Musicología—su labor de 1941 a 1947* (Montevideo: Ministerios de Relaciones Exteriores y de Instrucción Pública y Previsión Social del Uruguay, 1948).

Serra would finally publish his *Música y músicos de Latinoamérica* at Atlante in 1947, in two volumes. But there is just one reference to Lange, lost in the profuse bibliography. Serra founded in the 1950s a label, MUSART, which produced many records by Mexican musicians, with official support, combining popular and art music, and later on the discography magazine *Audiomúsica*, before his death in 1968. In 1951 Lange was working in Mendoza, at the Universidad de Cuyo, and where he received a letter (January 4, 1951) from Mayer with the letterhead of "El Músico" (The Musician), the monthly magazine from the Mexican Union of Music Workers, of which Mayer had been the Editor in Chief until recently, announcing his new gig at the XELA broadcasting, which "broadcasts good music" from discs and publishes *Carnet Musical*, a leading publication in Mexico City. On March 28, 1957, Mayer wishes good luck to Lange after the end of his appointment at Universidad de Cuyo and tells him about new work as Mexican representative for EMI to record Mexican artists performing Mexican repertoire for foreign markets—the United States, United Kingdom, France, and Germany—and also "some records of Latin American music" with pianist Miguel García Mora, "the best we have in Mexico." Mayer asked Lange to propose names, works, and also to write the records' notes. "If this works well, I'm convinced that the French branch of Columbia records and Capitol in the US would buy it, while we sell it as well in Mexico, Colombia, Peru, and some other country in the South." As we can see, Latin America in the 1950s was for Mayer, who began his career studying "Hispanic-American" music, a well established and globally marketable musical category.

Another interlocutor for Lange in those years was the Russian-American Nicolas Slonimsky, a prolific and influential music conductor who called Lange "the most idealistic publisher of Latin America"[51] and an "admirer of his relentless energy."[52] They entertained a correspondence from 1938 to 1960, during which Slonimsky published *The Music of Latin America* (1945), an encyclopedic-style panorama based on his experience with Latin American composers as conductor, organizer, and writer in New York, Havana and other places, and on a tour to "Central and South America" in 1941. This tour was related to Slonimsky's role as pan-American animator. On a letter written in French to Heitor Villa-Lobos during the tour, Slonimsky announces his arrival to Rio de Janeiro and "important news. Some "people interested in South American music" are offering handsome sums of money through a contest for Latin American composers of two Concertos for violin and orchestra ($750 and $250 dollars the first and second prize respectively), with two conditions: "that the Concertos are written in the style of indigenous musique, and that both compositions are between 20 and 30 minutes long." Even more, the winner Concerto would be played in 1942 on a South American

[51] Nicolas Slonimsky, *Music of Latin America* (New York: Thomas Y. Crowell Company, 1945), 12.
[52] "Admirador de su energía sin igual" (letter from 1952). Letters from Nicolas Slonimsky: August 23, 1938, 1942, 1952, and 1960. Subsérie 2.2, AFCL.

Tour by a US violinist.[53] Lange's Latin Americanism must be understood thus as counterbalancing these strong ideological and financial forces.

BLAM'S END

The sixth volume of the BLAM (Rio de Janeiro, 1946) signaled the end of the project and the beginning of a new era in Latin American musicology. This new era has been characterized by an array of disparate initiatives based in different universities and by UNESCO funding. This volume included 44 articles and 18 music scores, all of which were dedicated to Brazilian music or Brazil-related musical issues, which, according to Lange, made it almost a failure. In private letters, Lange bitterly expressed his discontent about Villa-Lobos taking over the volume, something Lange could not prevent due to the lack of other financial support. The volume revealed the vitality of Brazilian and Brazilianist musicology at the end of the first Vargas regime. It included collaborative work on sacred music, Portuguese influences, African styles, erudite and popular composers, musical pedagogy, and the sponsoring of music by the state. This wide-ranging subject matter represented a span of dimensions that no other national intelligentsia in the hemisphere had achieved. The volume included not only Brazilian authors, but also Lange himself and two American scholars. Lange's contribution was his first version of a work on Louis Moreau Gottschalk in Rio de Janeiro. American Melville Herskovits contributed a piece on *Afro-Bahiana* cult music, and Carleton Sprague Smith, chief of the Music Section of the Public Library of New York, wrote a history of the musical relations between Brazil and the United States.

Lange's personality may explain how he was able to publish no fewer than six original and extensive volumes, as well as his inability to institutionalize and consolidate this publishing project after 1946. His frank American contact, the musicologist and Latin American scholar William Berrien, wrote to Lange in 1941, "My dear Lange, you are losing your *sense of humor* [in English in the original] and your equilibrium with this *Americanismo Musical*. [. . .] You want everyone to share your enthusiasm for *your* musical Americanism and not *theirs*." In a blunt manner, Berrien echoed many comments that had circulated in the United States after Lange's visit and in the musicological world in general. "This is not possible, my dear Lange. [. . .] The rest of us cannot cope forever with this intensity of yours [. . .] Chileans, Brazilians, Mexicans, myself, each has a way and a rhythm to do things or not to do them, and I fear you will get sick of waiting for us all to follow Lange's

---

[53] "Un group des gens qui s'interesseent de la musique sudamericaine m'a demande d'inviter un nombre de compositeurs latino-américains . . . Les seules conditions son que le Concerto soit écrit dans le style de musique indigène, et que la composition soit de vingt jusqu'a trente minutes de duration [. . .] Le Concerto sera joué par un jeune violiniste américain pendant ces concerts dans l'Amerique du Sud en 1942." June 18, 1941, AHVL.

pace [. . .] My dear friend, stop condemning people to the gallows just because they don't do what you wish."[54]

Pan-regional perspectives in Latin Americanist musicology continued during the 1940s in the work of Spanish Republican exiles such as Vicente Salas Viu in Chile—who created in 1945 the profoundly Latin-Americanist *Revista Musical Chilena*—and Otto Mayer-Serra. But by the 1950s, UNESCO initiatives and Cold War cultural diplomacy created a more crowded and complex hemispheric picture. With the last volume of the BLAM, an era of individual pioneering and irregular connections came to an end. Rock and roll, the counterculture, youth culture, and radical politics shocked the hemisphere's musical currents and the meaning of Latin American music.

A new era began for Lange as well. His analytical skills and his historical perspectives fully emerged in the 1950s, once BLAM had ended and he had moved to a fully academic position at the University of Cuyo, Argentina. In this modernizing university in the province of Mendoza, Lange published many works on subjects ranging from the Argentine musical scene, colonial folklore, and ecclesiastic music, to Louis Moreau Gottschalk's journey to Rio de Janeiro and Baroque music from Minas Gerais, Brazil.[55]

Even though the BLAM had stopped production in the 1940s, it remained the basis of Lange's notoriously long and fruitful trajectory until the 1990s. He wrote and cowrote literally tens of thousands of pages, including books, journal articles, music scores, newspaper articles, unpublished volumes on colonial music in Argentina and Minas Gerais, translations of European and US literature on music, dictionaries, and encyclopedias. He lived in Uruguay until 1944, when he moved to Belo Horizonte, Brazil, to research and restore musical scores from the churches of Ouro Preto and several municipal, regional, and national archives. In 1948, after a brief return to Uruguay, he moved again, this time to Mendoza, in the Argentine Andes. There he started another music journal (*Revista de Estudios Musicales*, 1949–1956) and served as the director of the Musical Institute of the University of Cuyo until he was fired after the overthrow of Juan Perón. He returned to Brazil in 1958 as a UNESCO researcher and spent a few years in the early 1960s in the United States as visiting scholar and lecturer (at Vassar, Tulane, and Harvard, among other universities) and in Bonn as Cultural Attaché of the Uruguayan embassy. In 1986 he took on his last position as a Cultural Attaché in Caracas, again founding journals, archives, and

---

[54] Letter from William Berrien to Francisco Curt Lange, May 14, 1941. Subsérie 2.2, AFCL.

[55] Francisco Curt Lange, *Vida y muerte de Louis Moreau Gottschalk en Rio de Janeiro, 1869; el ambiente musical en la mitad del segundo imperio.* (Mendoza: Universidad Nacional de Cuyo, 1951); *Estudios brasileños (Mauricinas). Manuscritos musicales en la Biblioteca Nacional de Rio de Janeiro* (Mendoza: Dept. de Musicologia, Escuela Superior de Música, Universidad Nacional de Cuyo, 1951); *Archivo de música religiosa de la Capitanía Geral das Minas Gerais (Brasil, siglo XVIII)* (Mendoza: Departamento de Musicología, Escuela superior de música—Universidad nacional de Cuyo, 1951); *La música eclesiástica argentina en el período de la dominación hispánica, una investigación* (Mendoza: Universidad Nacional de Cuyo, 1954); *La música religiosa en el área de Rosario de Santa Fé y en el Convento San Carlos de San Lorenzo, durante el período aproximado de 1770 a 1820* (Rosario, Argentina: Tipogr. Llordén, 1956); *La música en Villa Rica (Minas Gerais, Siglo XVIII). El Senado de la Cámara y los servicios de música religiosa. Historia de un descubrimiento. Experiencias y conceptos* (Santiago de Chile: Universidad de Chile, 1967).

musical collections. Today the Curt Lange Archive at the Federal University of Minas Gerais in Brazil contains this vast correspondence, an extraordinary resource for understanding Latin American intellectual history.

BLAM was a transnational project populated by nationalist collaborations. It was the converging point of musical and intellectual trajectories emerging from multiple cultural establishments, each pursuing nationalist and modernist projects, in creative tension with European, avant-garde, folk, and popular aesthetics. Musicological specialists within state institutions were actively collecting, analyzing, selecting, valuing, and teaching music. The BLAM allowed both eminent and young professionals from all over the region to discuss methods and theories related to those activities and learn abpout the larger field beyond the individual relations that had predominated until then. Lange's project influenced the first congresses on Latin American music; many of the musicological journals of Brazil, Chile, Venezuela, and Argentina; and indirectly, the intellectual framing of programs such as UNESCO and the Music Division of the Pan American Union. In other words, BLAM created Latin American musicology as a transnational field out of previously scattered, isolated, and individual efforts.

Particularly important was Lange's influence in the musicological history of Ouro Preto and other cities in Minas Gerais, where his work between 1944 and 1946, supported by then governor Juscelino Kubitschek and by Villa-Lobos, had profound consequences in the scholarly discovery of Brazilian baroque music, and therefore in the development of a research tradition around eighteenth-century music not just in Brazil but in Bolivia and Argentina as well: this was the "rediscovery" of the first art music tradition of Latin America. In particular, his argument about *mulato* musicians as the key actors in the musical life of Minas Gerais confirmed his initial intuitions about Latin American music as expression of a distinct racial formation that was historically linked with Iberian (in this case, Portuguese) musical traditions and institutions. He also was decisive to the foundation of a municipal Record Disc Collection in Belo Horizonte, and entertained close relations with the group of young modernist composers around *Música Viva*. Lange developed in Minas a dialogue—at points a negotiation—with two local musical informants and custodians of music scores, Cândido Simplício Marçal e Justino da Conceição, who enabled him to connect with and understand the music societies and practices of colonial times. He was a foreigner through a quadruple mediation—coming to places like Diamantina, Sabará, Ouro Preto, or Mariana from the capital of the state, Belo Horizonte, after having been legitimized in the Brazilian capital, Rio de Janeiro, thanks to his official position in Montevideo, Uruguay, and speaking with his native German accent learned in Munich.[56]

---

[56] Francisco Curt Lange, "Um fabuloso redescobrimento (para justificação da existência de música erudita no período colonial brasileiro)," *Revista de História* 54, no. 107 (September 30, 1976): 45–67; Cláudio Roberto Dornelles Remião, "O caso Curt Lange: análise de uma polêmica (1958–1983)" (Pontifícia Universidade Católica do Rio Grande do Sul, 2018); Myrian Ribeiro Aubin, "Francisco Curt Lange e sua atuação nos meios musical e político em Belo Horizonte: constituição de uma rede de sociabilidades," *OPUS* 22, no. 1 (May 9, 2016): 299–338.

Like other proponents of a holistic idea of Latin American culture, such as Dominican essayist Pedro Henríquez Ureña (1884–1946), Lange operated as an intellectual by leaving his home—in his case, first Munich and then Montevideo. Ureña's social origins, intellectual formation, and academic experience in the United States allowed him to be well received in some of Latin America's most influential intellectual circles and scientific institutions, such as the Fondo de Cultura Económica publishing house in Mexico City and the University of Buenos Aires. Lange, a tenacious, self-made immigrant, made a rather peripheral journey—from Montevideo to the Argentine province of Mendoza, and briefly in Belo Horizonte, Caracas, and other sites in Europe and the United States. Ureña and Lange shared this nomadic condition with many revolutionary intellectuals, for instance the Peruvian revolutionary Apristas, so distant from them ideologically.[57]

The distinctive feature of Lange's transnationalism was its institutional scope. Whereas intellectuals like Ureña and revolutionaries like Haya de la Torre promoted intellectual and political visions of Latin America, Lange's project was closer to the modernizing and state-building projects that historians tend to consider at a national level. His was a conscious attempt to connect the musical life of the hemisphere, both institutionally and practically, through music collections and pedagogical exchanges. But it was very important ideologically as well: the BLAM created a network of composers and musicologists, critics and art professors, state authorities and intellectuals, who reconceptualized the popular, folkloric, and erudite music produced in their countries by invoking a vague, contradictory, but undoubtedly proud Latin American cultural identity. Attitudes toward popular music varied greatly within this heterogeneous network. In some cases, popular music simply provided raw input for erudite compositions, but in many other cases, music of popular, indigenous, African, Creole, and mixed cultural origins was for the first time incorporated into a positive definition of Latin American music as a distinct and promising aesthetic current. This flexibility allowed the BLAM to foster a transnational and conservatively populist understanding of folk and art music among the musical intelligentsia of the continent, including the United States. Lange's project articulated a hemispheric field of knowledge.

Latin American music began as a cause, *americanismo musical*, that Lange initiated in 1934 before any cohesive idea of Latin American culture existed in the public sphere. His *americanismo musical* stemmed from the perception, rooted in the German school of comparative musicology, of Latin America as a cultural area, a distinct zone whose unique characteristics deserved systematic analysis. Lange launched his manifesto just a few years after he arrived in the region, when his familiarity with Latin America was limited to a very peculiar corner: Buenos Aires, La Plata, Montevideo, and the small towns of the Uruguayan countryside, a region marked by European

---

[57] Martín Bergel, "Nomadismo proselitista y revolución. Notas para una caracterización del primer exilio aprista (1923–1931)," *EIAL: Estudios Interdisciplinarios de America Latina y El Caribe* 20, no. 1 (2009): 41–66, and "América Latina, pero desde abajo."

immigration, modern stockbreeding and intensive agriculture, expanding capitalist domestic markets, urbanization and secularizing, and ambitious state bureaucracies. But Lange's first definition of Latin America emerged *in contrast* to these spaces. He was obsessed with the "real" Latin America hidden below the despicable commercial modernity of the South Atlantic ports. But in these cities of the Rio de la Plata, modern social relations and musical organizations produced public and private broadcasting stations, conservatories, diverse musical audiences, a publishing industry, high literacy rates, and a densely organized civil society. It was this context what allowed Lange to imagine a modernizing intellectual project.

His goal was to attract all the threads of the "Americanist musical consciousness" dispersed throughout the American continent around regional infrastructure for music: musical publications, conferences, libraries, phonograph collections, academic centers, and public and private conservatories, to sustain the work of composers, musicians, folklorists, musicologists, educators, and public functionaries. But his Inter American Institute of Musicology (IAIM) never fully took off, and the disciplinary field of Latin American musicology was established around a constellation of other institutions that built on the dense personal networks that Lange and BLAM had created. Lange's organizational style, based on personal relationships, proved to be a good way to enable a continental conversation about music but an obstacle to institutionalizing it in the long run. Nonetheless, his career did continue after the end of the BLAM and the short-lived IAIM. He kept researching, publishing, and creating institutions until the 1990s. From the perspective of a transnational musical history of twentieth-century Latin America, his failed project in fact succeeded: it enabled a range of musical ideas and practices to circulate. This circulation taught the region's musical actors that they were facing the same challenges, and elevated national debates to a regional arena. It would take an imperial influence to consolidate this arena.

5

LATIN/PAN-AMERICAN MUSIC

WORLD WAR II turned Lange's emerging network of Latin Americanists into a quasi-imperial tool for US foreign policy. The Pan American Union's Music Division (MD) emerged as a wartime agency that formally represented all the American states but was mainly sponsored by the US State Department and managed by US musicologists.

The MD promoted the circulation and knowledge of Latin American music, as well as each national tradition in Latin America, in the context of a larger pan-American, hemispheric framework that served the US wartime interests. Once the war was over, the MD was closed.

But its impact was manifold. First, it produced catalogues of Latin American music aimed at music educators throughout the Americas who were willing to expand their musical collections beyond their national traditions. Second, it provided legitimacy for the emerging field of Latin American musicology. Finally, it offered a platform for postwar UNESCO's democratic, universalistic notion of culture and musical value as expressions of "the people"—a populist rhetoric that circulated both in erudite musicological and pedagogical programs as well as in the entertainment world. The overall result was an *imperial* musical project that valorized the *national folklore* of its subordinated allies by promoting a *regional* musical identity, based on a *populist* understanding of music (in the sense of music being the expression of a collective identity—"the people"—instead of individual genius or the aesthetic norms of the dominant social class). This odd combination helped consolidate the very legitimacy

The Invention of Latin American Music. Pablo Palomino, Oxford University Press (2020). © Oxford University Press.
DOI: 10.1093/oso/9780190687403.001.0001

of the category of Latin American music among musicologists and cultural officers, and ultimately, at school and in the marketplace, throughout the hemisphere.

US HEMISPHERIC MUSICAL PROGRAMS FROM THE NEW DEAL TO WORLD WAR II

How did music get involved in hemispheric relations? The first Pan American Conference in 1889 in Washington, DC, was intended to provide a framework for the expansion of US economic interests over Latin America and to displace European interests in the Western hemisphere.[1] Music was part of these interests only as it related to cinema, radio, and recording firms. But in the 1930s, a new, specifically *cultural* diplomacy emerged in Washington.

Three factors turned the State Department toward strengthening its position in the Western hemisphere through expanding its policies relating to cultural matters: (1) the economic crisis, which undermined private US educational and civil initiatives abroad; (2) the New Deal philosophy of state activism; and (3) the worsening European crisis. In 1936, US participation in the Inter-American Conference for the Consolidation of Peace in Buenos Aires initiated an array of cultural and scientific agreements with Latin America.[2] This was a strategic move: the State Department used the region as "the 'laboratory' for honing an approach that it eventually deploy worldwide."[3] At that conference, Francisco Curt Lange's *Boletín Latinoamericano de Música* was put forward as a solid foundation for future musical exchanges. Two years later, in 1938, pressure from Latin American delegates at the Pan American Conference in Lima created the short-lived Inter-American Institute of Musicology in Montevideo, under Lange's direction. But the State Department had created, in July of the same year, the first official agency for foreign cultural policy in the history of the United States: the Cultural Affairs Division, charged with planning cultural policies related to Latin America.[4]

---

[1] Lars Schoultz, *Beneath the United States: A History of U.S. Policy toward Latin America* (Cambridge, MA: Harvard University Press, 1998); Greg Grandin, "The Liberal Traditions in the Americas: Rights, Sovereignty, and the Origins of Liberal Multilateralism," *American Historical Review The American Historical Review* 117, no. 1 (2012): 68–91; Leandro Morgenfeld, *Vecinos en conflicto: Argentina y Estados Unidos en las conferencias panamericanas, 1880–1955* (Buenos Aires: Peña Lillo, 2011).

[2] Pan American Union Inter-American Conference for the Maintenance of Peace, ed., *Inter-American Conference for the Maintenance of Peace, Buenos Aires, December 1–23, 1936: Report on the Proceedings of the Conference* (Washington, DC: Pan American Union, 1937), 109. The only experience of Pan American musical exchanges so far had been a Pan American concert series for diplomatic audiences in Washington, DC since 1924. Another concert was organized in Mexico City in July 1937.

[3] Justin Hart, *Empire of Ideas: The Origins of Public Diplomacy and the Transformation of U.S. Foreign Policy* (Oxford: Oxford University Press, 2013), 3.

[4] Richard Arndt, *The First Resort of Kings: American Cultural Diplomacy in the Twentieth Century* (Washington, DC: Potomac Books Inc., 2005), 49–74. See also Frank Ninkovich, *The Diplomacy of Ideas: U.S. Foreign Policy and Cultural Relations, 1938–1950* (Cambridge: Cambridge University Press, 1981).

World War II broke out in September 1939 and the United States quickly attempted to displace German and Italian interests in the region, including musical interests, and strengthen both the image of the United States among Latin Americans and US domestic public opinion of Latin America. They targeted this "cultural front" with a set of propagandistic films, news, and broadcasting programs directed by the Office of the Coordinator of Inter-American Affairs (OCIAA), created by the White House in 1940.[5] From November 1940 to October 1941, the OCIAA had a short-lived but historically crucial Music Committee that promoted US musical tours in Latin America and, to a lesser extent, US performances of modern art music by Latin American composers. This was the starting point and model for US musical diplomacy in the long run in two respects: it generated collaboration between state and nonstate actors, and its results ironically "paled in comparison to the grandiose ideas for musical exchange [it] had envisioned."[6] The private, nonstate actors were active partners of the State Department: in 1940 the NBC and the CBS radio networks funded competing tours of Latin America by Arturo Toscanini and Leopold Stokowski, and in 1941 Walt Disney traveled to South America with official sponsorship, producing material for a few animated films. But these initiatives failed to enable actual exchanges in both directions.[7]

Less known is the parallel history that led to the MD's creation. In October 1939 the musicological establishment, a decentralized network of specialists at mostly public institutions across the country, converged at the Conference on Inter-American Relations in the Field of Music, organized in Washington, DC by the State Department's Cultural Affairs Division. As a result of the conference, musicologist Carleton Sprague Smith was commissioned to travel to South America from June to October 1940. Sprague, the Vienna-trained chief of the Music Division of the New York Public Library, was an important figure in the Music Library Association and the American Musicological Society, and also a veteran of the Federal Music

---

[5] Gisela Cramer and Ursula Prutsch, ¡Américas Unidas! : Nelson A. Rockefeller's Office of Inter-American Affairs (1940–46) (Madrid/Frankfurt: Iberoamericana Vervuert, 2012). Brazilian "audiences" were treated as such, in the sense of a universe of preferences measurable through scientific surveys and having an "average" that could be addressed by advertising techniques. During the war, polls conducted by Gallup, as part of the OCIIA policies, produced information that was also shared by US military and intelligence agencies. Antônio Pedro Tota, O imperialismo sedutor: a americanização do Brasil na época da Segunda Guerra (São Paulo: Companhia das Letras, 2000), 51.

[6] Jennifer L. Campbell, "Creating Something Out of Nothing: The Office of Inter-American Affairs Music Committee (1940–1941) and the Inception of a Policy for Musical Diplomacy," Diplomatic History 36, no. 1 (2012): 36.

[7] Similarly, the US publishing industry served diplomatic interests by translating Brazilian literature in order to promote the image of a war ally virtually unknown by US readers. Here too the results fell behind the expectations. Cf. Richard Cándida Smith, "Érico Veríssimo, a Brazilian Cultural Ambassador in the United States," Tempo 19, no. 34 (2013): 147–73. On the other end of the relationship, among the broader unintended consequences of the United States' cultural activism in Brazil during World War II, there was the shaping of a regional identity in the Northeast. See Courtney Campbell, "The Brazilian Northeast, Inside Out: Region, Nation, and Globalization (1926–1968)" (PhD diss, Vanderbilt University, 2014).

Project—the musical branch of Franklin D. Roosevelt's New Deal. He was now in charge of probing South America's musical establishment and bringing back contacts and insights for musical diplomacy. He was to provide these contacts and insights to the newly created MD, formed by an initiative of the Library of Congress' Music Section Board on July 29, 1940. The MD was an open dismissal of Lange's Inter-American Institute of Musicology. Lange's German origins may have influenced this decision, as well as his hardly diplomatic personal style, but the decision ultimately suggested that the State Department considered inter-American relations to be an instrument of US interests.

Let us consider Carleton Sprague Smith's tour between June and October of 1940 and the insights it provided to the MD.

A SOUTH AMERICAN MUSICAL TRIP

Sprague visited every South American country except Paraguay and the European territories of Guiana and Surinam.[8] Musical life in South America seemed to him very different from in the United States and, above all, very diverse from one country to another. Despite this heterogeneity, the contrast with the United States allowed him to see Latin America as a whole region. For instance, his assessment of the broadcasting infrastructure revealed that (according to his own numbers) Argentina had more than half (56%) the region's receiving sets and a quarter of its radio stations, while Peru, Bolivia, and Ecuador each had 2% of the sets and 5% of the stations. But he observed that despite this contrast, in general "the number of loudspeakers in the streets around which crowds gather impresses the visitor" and made the number of radio listeners higher than the number of radios. And yet for this and other reasons, he wrote, "it is difficult to work out a type of broadcasting which will appeal to every country since audiences have distinctive preferences in each city."[9] In other words: a region of differences.

In the realm of classical music, Sprague realized that the United States was far behind Europe in influencing South America: "North American composers and conductors play no role in the musical life of the Southern Hemisphere," he observed. Instead, South American music was dominated by local modernist and nationalist composers and directors, on the one hand, and a sort of star-system of Italians, European Jews, and other European artists, on the other. A global network run by

---

[8] Carleton Sprague Smith, *Musical Tour through South America, June–October, 1940* (New York: Conference on Inter-American Relations in the Field of Music, 1940).

[9] Ibid., III–IV. The surveys and polls that in those years were consolidating a national market in the United States were absent in Latin America, with the exceptions of very specific experiences. See, for the Argentine case, Fernando Rocchi, "La americanización del consumo: las batallas por el mercado argentino, 1920–1945," in *Americanización: Estados Unidos y América Latina en el siglo XX. Transferencias económicas, tecnológicas y culturales*, ed. María Inés Barbero and Andrés Martín Regalsky (Buenos Aires: Universidad Nacional de Tres de Febrero, 2014), 150–216.

European impresarios hired the most famous European figures to perform in South America. "The favorite performers," he wrote, "are much the same as those in the United States, an international managerial syndicate controlling the concerts just as in North America. Indeed, it is practically the same group." Local "managerial chains" extended the reach of these networks through representatives mainly in the coastal cities. But the influence of classical music varied from one country to another. Although "popular music is preferred in practically every country," in Uruguay Francisco Curt Lange's "SODRE [the state broadcasting station] exercises important influence," and as a result the "Uruguayan public . . . is fed 'classics' by order of the government." Opera "has meant a good deal in Brazil and Argentina," more than in the other countries, he said, because "Italian companies have toured for the last hundred years in practically every city of importance, and towns with any pretension whatsoever have an opera house"—a description that should have included Uruguay. On the other hand, in the region as a whole, "*zarzuelas* are really more popular than grand operas and Spanish, Portuguese, French and Italian operettas have been performed many times."

The best orchestras "are in Rio, São Paulo, Buenos Aires and Montevideo. Peru and Colombia boast ensembles, but they cannot compare with those on the East Coast. Santiago [Chile] has a particularly avid public and is more musical for its size than Buenos Aires." But the overall underdevelopment was comparable to the United States: there was a lack of "good native conductors in South America exactly as in the United States. Germans and Italians hold many of the most important orchestral posts."[10] There was, however, a lively scene around the practice of the *recital*, the small concert organized by local, private music associations, which Sprague described as "undoubtedly the most usual type of concert given in Latin American cities." The civil-society resources behind *recitales* were scarce compared to the massive public investments made in the United States under the New Deal: "The equipment is antiquated and the instruction less intense than in the United States. We have made very rapid strides in North America in Public School Music and in our conservatories during the past few years." He added that such striking difference in resources made it "one field where we may really be helpful to our Southern friends."[11] For Sprague, a man of the New Deal who had directed a library program at the New York Public Library under the Federal Arts Project, the idea of building up pan-American musical programs was a natural continuation of that same civilizational and public-centered ethos.[12]

Regarding the field of musicology, Sprague identified a number of pioneering studies that traced the history of classical music life and folklore in the region, especially by the Rio de la Plata musicologists Lange, Lauro Ayestarán, and Gastón Talamon. But

---

[10] Sprague Smith, *Musical Tour*, XXXII–XXXIII.

[11] Ibid., XX.

[12] John Shepard, "The Legacy of Carleton Sprague Smith: Pan-American Holdings in the Music Division of The New York Public Library for the Performing Arts," *Notes* 62, no. 3 (2006): 621–22.

he also noticed institutional weaknesses: "There is no outstanding Latin American music library [. . .] Some of the conservatories have material but it has not been assembled scientifically." The dominance of European music was the cause of this scarcity of resources regarding local traditions, he wrote: "Foreign music from Europe was assiduously aped and copied during most of the 19th century with the result that local music and archives were neglected."[13]

From the perspective of this US traveler, the dominance of bands over choirs was a striking feature of South American musical culture. The population was more used to participating in and listening to bands—both in small towns and at urban carnivals—than to singing in choirs, which could explain both their novelty and their limitations. But bands did not help music markets thrive: they acted locally, disconnected from one another, and lacked the managerial networks of classical music.

This heterogeneous musical space required, for this New Dealer, a unifying policy from above. Lange's *Boletín* was undoubtedly the single most important step in integrating the musical systems of the Americas, and his *americanismo musical* helped develop many musicological initiatives across the region. But the *Boletín* and the Montevideo Institute lacked financial and institutional resources. They were basically the results of Lange's personal work with aid from his wife and a young assistant, Lauro Ayestarán. Lange finally managed to obtain support and funding in the United States for the fifth volume of the *Boletín* (1941),[14] but only as part of a wider set of initiatives organized in Washington, DC. By contrast, less than six months after its creation in July 1940, the MD received $15,000 from the brand new OCIAA, a grant later renewed for a second and a third year with funds from the Carnegie Foundation. The MD was one of many public programs funded by private philanthropic foundations.[15] The direction of the MD was assigned to someone alien to the Latin American musical scene but close to the New Deal's musical activism: the American composer and musicologist Charles Seeger.

CHARLES SEEGER AND THE MUSIC DIVISION

Who was Charles Seeger? He was born in Mexico, where his father, a US businessman (and pianist) had moved to import US goods, and where he learned Spanish as a kid.[16] After his musical formation in the United States and Germany, he was involved

---

[13] Sprague Smith, *Musical Tour*, XXV.

[14] From William Berrien (American Council of Learned Societies), Irving Leonard (historian from Brown University), Concha Romero James (PAU Intellectual Cooperation), Harold Spivacke (Library of Congress Music Section), Charles Seeger (MD), and Carleton Sprague Smith (American Musicological Association and New York Public Library Music Section).

[15] The OCIAA's director, for instance, was John D. Rockefeller Jr., son of the creator of Standard Oil and a businessman himself. Corporate interests not only funded, but also *directed* public programs.

[16] Malena Kuss, "Leitmotive de Charles Seeger sobre Latinoamérica," *Revista Musical Chilena* 34, no. 151 (1980): 29–37.

in musical politics as a member of the Composers Collective, a New York offshoot of the official musical organization of the Communist Party, from its foundation in 1931 until 1935. The Composers Collective composed anti-capitalist songs for workers, some of which became part of the musical repertoire of the left, although as a historian put it, its aesthetics "hardly connected with America's masses."[17] This connection, however, made them an object of congressional "Anti-American" investigation from the late 1930s to the late 1940s. Seeger's political engagement with music was shared by a multifarious movement of folk musicians, composers and collectors, mainly on the Left, that produced a "folk revival," based on the appreciation of Southern rural traditions, on college campuses, in clubs, at festivals, and in radio programming during this decade.[18] Like many other progressive artists and intellectuals, Seeger joined public service under the New Deal and especially during World War II as a form of democratic and anti-fascist activism. His experience as a music specialist began in 1935 under the Resettlement Administration and continued under the Federal Music Project, the musical branch of Roosevelt's Federal Arts Project. The arts project included programs dedicated to theater, arts, and writing, but its musical branch was "the largest of the cultural programs [of the New Deal] in terms of both employment and attendance."[19] It designated public money for hiring unemployed musicians, promoting national composers, and subsidizing public consumption of classical music.[20] Seeger had been classically trained at Harvard and Cologne, but his work with unemployed musicians and promotion of national composers contributed to turning him into a passionate folklorist.[21] When this project, like most of the Works Progress Administration, was cancelled in 1940, Seeger was assigned to the MD.

Seeger faced three major challenges as head of the MD. The first was political: how to get individual and institutional actors throughout the Americas on board for an

[17] Ronald D. Cohen, *Rainbow Quest: The Folk Music Revival and American Society, 1940–1970* (Amherst: University of Massachusetts Press, 2002), 17. See also Jennifer Ashe, "Modernism and Social Consciousness: Seeger, Cowell, Crawford, and the Composers Collective, 1931–1936" (PhD diss., New England Conservatory of Music, 2006); Steven Garabedian, "Reds, Whites, and the Blues: Lawrence Gellert, 'Negro Songs of Protest,' and the Leftwing Folksong Revival of the 1930s and 1940s," *American Quarterly* 57, no. 1 (2005): 179–206; Sarah McCall, "The Musical Fallout of Political Activism : Government Investigations of Musicians in the United States, 1930–1960" (PhD diss., University of North Texas, 1993), 15; Ann Pescatello, *Charles Seeger: A Life in American Music* (Pittsburgh: University of Pittsburgh Press, 1992).

[18] Cohen, *Rainbow Quest*.

[19] Peter L. Gough, "'The Varied Carols I Hear': The Music of the New Deal in the West" (PhD diss., University of Nevada, Las Vegas, 2009), iii.

[20] Kenneth J. Bindas, *All of This Music Belongs to the Nation: The WPA's Federal Music Project and American Society* (Knoxville: University of Tennessee Press, 1995).

[21] Helen Rees, "'Temporary Bypaths'? Seeger and Folk Music Research," in *Understanding Charles Seeger, Pioneer in American Musicology*, ed. Bell Yung and Helen Rees (Urbana: University of Illinois Press, 1999), 92–93. Charles Seeger's son, Peter Seeger, would be a key figure, from the late 1940s through the 1960s, in the full blossoming of the folk revival closely linked to the radicalism of US youth during those years.

initiative mostly funded and commanded by the United States. The second was conceptual: how to promote a common musical identity for the Americas by valorizing folklore, a discipline oriented toward the particular. The "sister republics" were distinct nations characterized by specific combinations of history, territory, blood, and costumes; how would the MD match individual nationalisms with hemispheric rhetoric? The third challenge was geopolitical: the State Department promoted pan-American policies, but it aimed, especially by the end of the war, at creating global, not regional, institutions.[22]

Seeger did not lack support: he was not only Chief of the Music Division, but also simultaneously held many other appointments within the country's cultural bureaucracy.[23] This multiple positioning enabled the MD to collaborate with other organizations, including the Music Division of the Library of Congress, the Music Educators National Conference, the National Endowment for the Arts, the American Council of Learned Societies, and the Works Administration of the Federal Endowment of Defense. Vanett Lawler, the appointed MD's Music Education Consultant, was also the liaison to the Music Educators National Conference, which during its first year also worked with the OCIAA music committee. So unlike in Europe and Latin America, where centralized state policies were the usual practice, US musical diplomacy was born as a cluster of organizations and agencies.

US-sponsored cultural initiatives enabled the consolidation of an emerging transnational network of Latin American folklore scholars, who used them to autonomously develop an array of folklore-related projects in many Latin American countries.[24] (For others, like the Spanish composer Gustavo Durán, who had been militarily active Republican in the Civil War, the MD was a station in a longer career in diplomacy and espionage).[25] From Seeger's perspective, these initiatives were aimed at fostering folklore-related activities with the goal of integrating the musical and musicological life of the hemisphere under US leadership.

The MD began its work by publishing a collection called "Music Series," which initially consisted of a list of Latin American music obtainable in the United States, a historical index of US musicians, and a historical account of the musical exchanges between the Americas. Later on, the collection added a series of folk songbooks and popular music songbooks and a series of national collections: "Music in Chile,"

---

[22] The postwar mindset among policymakers was marked by global concerns: "At least in the United States no generation was so thoroughly indoctrinated in Universalist values as the one coming of age around mid-century." Robert H. Wiebe, *Who We Are: A History of Popular Nationalism* (Princeton, NJ: Princeton University Press, 2002), 1.

[23] He was member of the Consultant Commission of the State Department's Division of Cultural Affairs, and of the Music Commission of the Council of National Defense. He remained (founding) member of the American Musicological Society, of the American Folklore Society, and became chairman of the Inter-American Committees of the Music Library Association and the Music Teachers National Association.

[24] Pernet, "For the Genuine Culture of the Americas."

[25] Jorge de Persia, "Centro de Documentación—Gustavo Durán," *Revista Residencia* 1, June (1997) http://www.residencia.csic.es/bol/num1/duran.htm.

"Music in Peru," and so on. With funds from the OCIAA, the MD catalogued its own music collection for public access, created a bibliography of Latin American music, conducted a study of music teaching in South American schools, and published Latin American music scores to give to US orchestras, music centers, and schools.[26] Other funds were designated for sponsoring long stays in the United States for invited composers and musicologists, including many heads of public offices, such as Luiz Heitor Corrêa de Azevedo, the librarian of the National School of Music in Rio de Janeiro. The MD also conducted surveys on the availability of Latin American music scores at US schools and gathered choral materials in the United States that could be useful for international exchange.[27]

The musicians themselves did not travel as much as Seeger would have liked, but their music still reached the United States. By mid-1942 the MD had gathered 5,240 volumes and references to 6,400 works of Iberian American music and had begun to develop an ambitious cataloguing project with the American Council of Learned Societies.[28] It had also expanded these resources domestically. The OCIAA's project of building a "Directory of Ibero-American Musicians and Musical Societies" was transferred to the MD in January 1942. That year, sixty-one Latin American music scores were published by twenty-one of the most important US music publishers, many of which went on to take part in music contests and festivals organized in 1943. More than 50,000 US military bands, orchestras, and choirs across the country now had access to this repertoire.[29] The MD also collected and catalogued Spanish-language music that had been recorded in the United States, especially by Southwestern and Texan musicians. In part thanks to a Rockefeller Foundation grant, several important music educators toured the United States giving conferences and advising their colleagues, and several young Latin American musicians received grants to study music in the United States.[30] Finally, the MD expanded its web of collaborative work to include the Instituto Indigenista Pan Americano (in Mexico City), the Inter American Institute of Folkloric Research (in Panama), and the Archive of American Folk Song at the Library of Congress, among others.

---

[26] Here the MD continued a trend of library accumulation on Latin American collections, which stemmed from multiple private, philanthropic, and university initiatives, and had a hemispheric dimension, as suggested by the 1934 Inter-American Conference on Bibliography celebrated in Havana. Cf. Ricardo Salvatore, "Library Accumulation and the Emergence of Latin American Studies," *Comparative American Studies* 3, no. 4 (2005): 415–36.

[27] Leila Fern, "Origin and Functions of the Inter-American Music Center," *Notes* 1, no. 1 (1943): 14–22.

[28] Pan American Union, *Informe Anual del Director General de la Unión Panamericana* (Washington, DC, 1941–1942), 99.

[29] The number of bands is an estimate by the National Federation of Musical Clubs in the United States. See "The National Federation of Musical Clubs in the United States," *Boletín Latino Americano de Música*, Vol. 2 (Lima: 1936).

[30] Such as Filomena Salas (Fine Arts, University of Chile), Juan Bautista Plaza (music professor in Venezuela), Luis Sandi (Mexico, Secretaría de Educación Pública, Mexico), Domingo Santa Cruz (composer and Fine Arts Dean, University of Chile), Antonio Sa Pereira (director, National School of Music, Rio de Janeiro), and several others. These educators visited musical centers of Des Moines, Kansas City, Chicago, Joliet, Cleveland, Rochester, Boston, New Haven, and New York.

What was Latin America in these projects? Each of them had a particular underlying definition: Latin America was referred to as either a cultural area, a collection of republics, or a series of musical regions (e.g., the Andes, the Brazilian *sertão*). But none of these initiatives originated *in* Latin America. This imperial feature reflected in part the fact that in 1942–1943 the United States provided 54% of the PAU budget. By contrast, the four major Latin American contributors (contributions were calculated on the basis of population) were Brazil at 16%, Mexico at 7%, Argentina at 4.7%, and Colombia at 3%.

From Seeger's perspective, the two Americas were becoming musically independent from Europe, a process that was accelerated by the war and depended on its result. "Dependence upon Europe [. . .] is by no means ended. Belief, however, that the contribution of the New World to music may be substantial, is more and more commonly held. *That this contribution is related to the outcome of the war is obvious*" (my emphasis).[31] Still, there was an uneven contribution between the two Americas, given their economic differences. "The United States, while it comprises but about 50% of the population of the member republics of the Union, comprises upwards of 90% of its music resources."[32] Those music resources were highly organized professional resources—"composition, performance, education, scholarship, library"—and commercial ones—"publication, industry, merchandising, concert management, mass communication." During the war, he argued, the MD had to orient the 90% of US resources toward the entire hemisphere.

Reorienting these resources required stronger state intervention. Broadcasting, recording, music publishing, and even copyright legislation were domains in which inter-American relations were quite advanced, but Seeger noticed that the US government was absent from these relations. In this regard, the government had much to learn from Latin America, whereas

> most of the American Republics had long shown an interest in music as a concern of government, had established Ministries of Education and Fine Arts, and had subsidized opera and concert activity, the United States had always resisted proposals to establish a Department of Fine Arts, or to subsidize music composition, performance, or education. National music programs in emergency agencies of the New Deal were continually under fire and finally liquidated.[33]

World War II, which drastically transformed US economic and institutional structures, represented an opportunity for the state to orient the country's cultural forces—or at least promote certain strands of it that market dynamics would not.

---

[31] Charles Seeger, "Review of Inter-American Relations in the Field of Music, 1940–1943," s/f. [c. 1944], Archive OAS, 2.

[32] Charles Seeger, "Brief History of the Music Division of the Pan American Union," June 9, 1947, Archive OAS, 3.

[33] Ibid., 3–4.

And Latin America, with its centralized cultural authority, provided the model for Seeger and other former New Deal officers.

A powerful current of civil organizations had produced an array of musicological projects in the years immediately before the United States entered the war, and the war strengthened these efforts by generating national policies around which these organizations converged. Seeger wanted to consolidate this process so that it would continue after the war ended. In early 1941, the National Music Council (NMC) included twenty-eight member associations ranging from professional to corporate organizations, including the American Musicological Society, League of Composers, National Association of Broadcasters, National Federation of Music Clubs, and Music Teachers National Association. NMC leaders proudly announced that now, unlike during the Great War, "all of the most important musical interests of the country are represented." They were ready, they said, both to accept the "inevitable" wartime state regulations and to intervene whenever the state's lack of "wisdom and experience" might require those interests "speak with one voice."[34] NMC's strategy was to promote its members' interests by serving the state's needs. For instance, they pushed for a program called "Advancement of Music in Smaller Cities Through Opera in English," which they designed to employ foreign musicians received as war refugees, consolidate English-speaking opera productions, and partner with the state to create a nationwide market for American music in small cities.[35] At the same time, the NMC collaborated with the War Department by providing the names of army officers with musical skills, as well as civilian assistance in music-related activities on military bases.

The MD added a Latin American branch to this current by inserting the Latin American repertoire into a wide range of activities. Its 1943 report described the repertoire performed at the *Day of the Americas*: a choral concert interpreting "European music contemporary to the discovery of America, American music from the colonial period, and music by contemporary composers." An Inter-American Folk Music Festival included dances and songs from seventeen American countries, and in 1942, the annual PAU Summer Concerts featured US military bands performing with Latin American classic-trained singers.[36] At the same time, other organizations implemented several projects the MD had devised: the New School of Social Research distributed US music in Latin America, the ACLS provided technical equipment to the University of Chile, and the International Institute of Education awarded grants to young Latin American music students to attend classes in the United States. Independently from these efforts but in a similar direction, in August 1943 the Federation of Inter-American Societies of Authors and Composers (FISAC)

[34] National Music Council, *Bulletin* 1: 3, New York (March 1941), 6.
[35] Ibid., 7.
[36] Pan American Union, *Informe Anual del Director General de la Unión Panamericana* (Washington, DC, 1942–1943), 117–18.

was pushing hemispheric copyright legislation at the Inter-American Conference of Lawyers held in Mexico City.

Despite all these initiatives and musical organizations, US musicologists tended to agree, according to Seeger, "with the verdict of the nine Latin American musicians who visited the United States [in 1942] and saw high school bands, orchestras and choruses in action: 'What a marvelous mechanism for performing such terrible music!'"[37] To these musicologists, the United States had a great institutional system in place for music performance, but the system's repertoire and the performances themselves needed improvement. More ambitious policies for musical education were needed. And here, musicologists needed to elevate their standards. ("Compared to the predictable results offered by sanitary experts, engineers, and even economists," Seeger complained, "the promoters of music projects sooner or later have a hard time to keep from being regarded as bluffers."[38])

A KEY SITE ACROSS THE AMERICAS: THE SCHOOL

In documents produced in 1945 and 1946, it became clear that schools were the key instrument for inter-American relations and music development in general and that Latin America provided the model for the whole hemisphere. For Brunilda Cartés, a Chilean musicologist who had joined the MD, "the current organization of music education in Latin America is almost uniform," and therefore the plans for organizing it at a hemispheric level could be based on "common principles and ideals."[39] She was summarizing debates about the state of music education in Latin America that had taken place among seventeen Latin American musicians and educators at the Music Educators National Conference (MENC) convention in Cleveland in March 1946 (funding provided by a Rockefeller grant). Interestingly, the Committee seemed to have agreed that Latin America, a model for the state promotion of music, nonetheless needed to imitate the US emphasis on the formation of music teachers. They concluded that the key to any successful plan in music education was to involve children and adults in educational and community contexts. Cartés recommended that every school have a department of music education responsible for "reaching every child in school" through "choral singing with participation of the school as a whole, connecting music with other disciplines such as history, literature, geography, etc." This hemispheric plan for music education addressed national and subnational goals such as "providing every child the opportunity of listening good music, by orienting

---

[37] Charles Seeger, "Musicology and the Music Industry," paper prepared for the Annual Meeting of the National Music Council, May 10, 1945, in National Music Council, *Bulletin* 5:3 (May 1945).

[38] Seeger, "Brief History."

[39] Brunilda Cartés, "Informe de la Secretaria del Comité Consejero en Educación Musical para las Repúblicas Latinoamericanas (ALADEM) de la Confederación Nacional de Educadores en Música de los Estados Unidos," Oficina de Música, Pan American Union, 1946.

him towards the appreciation of music by the national composers" and "promoting the interest for folkloric music by initiating him in the folkloric music of his region." By folk music, they meant music with either Indigenous, African, or Spanish origins, and they suggested that educators themselves needed to be encouraged to appreciate the national composers, as well as folkloric and contemporary music.[40] The committee also recommended that official and private broadcasters agree on their programming content to counterbalance commercial music.

These musicologists arrived at the same conclusions as the Mexican revolutionary policymakers, old Argentine liberals and nationalists, and Brazilian modernists we saw in previous chapters. And French republicans, German nationalists, and many other regimes and political movements around the world had reached similar conclusions in the previous century: choirs and collective musical practice were powerful society-builders and stabilizers. At school, students, teachers, and parents can come together through collective singing. At industrial centers, folkloric clubs, and other civil associations, collective singing and music bands and orchestras were means to promote musical advancement, social improvement, and symbolic and emotional bonds. Folklore and nationalism were just means for accomplishing social and cultural goals. Cartés went further in this direction by stating:

> Educators must emphasize the idea that we live in one world, that we are citizens of the world, that we need to know other peoples in order to understand them. This is not against the idea of nationalism. . . . On the contrary, the richness of the world culture is based upon national diversities as long as they are harmonized in a greater whole. This is why educators should prepare the child, not only to become an efficient citizen of his country but an efficient citizen of the world. This means that education in international relations involves the whole range of human life and welfare.[41]

The goal of serving "the school, the community, the country, and the hemisphere" through music education was broad enough to represent a variety of ideological actors in the field of music.[42] The idea of the broader world beyond the hemisphere was already looming in this project, as it later appeared in the presence of Latin American music in world music collections in the 1980s.

FOLKLORE VERSUS MUSICAL MARKETS

Despite their multifaceted musical projects, musicologists, educators, and diplomats viewed their own impact as minor compared with the influence of market relations

---

[40] Ibid., 5–8.
[41] Brunilda Cartés, "Music Education in Latin America" (PhD diss., Northwestern University, 1946), preface.
[42] Cartés, "Informe," 13.

and the evolution of popular taste. Carleton Sprague Smith pointed out in 1940 that whatever the State Department did to strengthen links with Latin American music and dance would be based on exchanges that were already taking place. "North American Dance Music has certainly done a tremendous lot to win the youth of the southern hemisphere and young people in the United States are grateful for the Tango, Rumba and Conga." In fact, he added, "North and Southern Americans are really co-partners in the field of modern dancing."[43] Hollywood and Tin Pan Alley were responsible for an explosion of popularity of Latin American music styles and artists in the United States during the war that could hardly be matched by the efforts of cultural diplomats.[44] Through its adoption by many Hollywood musicals that circulated globally, Latin American music became popular for instance in India, inspiring the music of "jazzy cabarets" and early cinema productions in Mumbai.[45] As early as 1929, a popular Argentine newspaper interviewed jazz orchestra leader Paul Whiteman and titled the interview by quoting him: "With foxtrot and tango we have repaid Europe for discovering us."[46] Inter-American musical diplomacy was, however, influential in music ideologies and music education.

The ideology of musical inter-Americanism was ambiguous. Cultural officers from across the Americas gathered in 1943 to sign a common document related to folklore and education, in which a peculiar concept of cultural identity emerged. First, culture was considered, above all, as folklore, and folklore as a series of profound "spiritual manifestations of the people," present in "each local tradition," which institutions have the mission of supervising (*vigilar*) to keep them safe "from superficial, strange and destructive influences." Folklore is therefore a spiritual heritage, now threatened by commercial music. Second, although folklore is traditionally a local phenomenon, there is "a rich American folkloric tradition" that provides a common ground for "solidarity and friendship." Third, folklore "has to be cultivated at the school" with two goals in mind: fulfilling its "patriotic duties" while at the same time "contributing to the formation of a hemispheric consciousness."[47] The signatories' recommendations consisted of adding a hemispheric sensibility to the patriotism of each country's musical education and promoting more musical and pedagogical exchanges. The key roles were to be played by the school and the cultural experts—from musicologists to broadcasters—that fed schools with musical resources.

---

[43] Sprague Smith, *Musical Tour*, 283–84.

[44] John Storm Roberts, *The Latin Tinge: The Impact of Latin American Music on the United States*, 2nd ed. (New York: Oxford University Press, 1999), chapter 5.

[45] Bradley Shope, "Latin American Music in Moving Pictures and Jazzy Cabarets in Mumbai, 1930s–1950s," in *More than Bollywood: Studies in Indian Popular Music*, eds. Gregory D. Booth and Bradley Shope (New York: Oxford University Press, 2014), 201–15.

[46] "Con el Fox Trot y con el Tango hemos pagado a Europa el Descubrimiento de América, dice P. Whiteman, el Rey del Jazz," *Crítica*, July 6, 1929. I thank Martín Bergel for this reference.

[47] Pan American Union, "Resolución sobre el folklore, entre las aprobadas por la junta de ministros y directores de educación de las repúblicas americanas, reunida en Panamá, 27 de septiembre a 4 de octubre de 1943," in Ralph Steele Boggs, "El folklore en la escuela," in *Folklore Americas* 6: 1/2 (1946), 11–12.

Music was hence, simultaneously, a cultural tradition, a commercial trade, and a pedagogic matter in which experts could intervene. Hemispheric programs influenced the folklore initiatives of Latin American nationalists. In late 1943, for instance, a Center of Folkloric Research was created in Brazil's National School of Music and immediately launched a series of publications. The first, *A Escola Nacional de Música e as pesquisas de folclore musical no Brasil*, was defined by its author as a resource for the School of Music and a tool for cooperating with similar organizations dedicated to the study of popular arts "in Brazil, in the hemisphere, and tomorrow, once the furies of the war are gone, in the pacific and scholarly world as a whole."[48]

A folk canon of Latin American music began to be taught at US schools (see Figure 5.1). In part, this was a result of folk music's increasing legitimacy in the United States due to its proliferation in festivals, archival collections, and radio and the recording industry. It was also the continuation of a recently established pedagogical trend. According to music education historian Terese Volk, in the 1930s foreign songs began to be adapted, translated, or rearranged and then presented in Western notation, without much attention to the intricacies and particularities of different rhythms and ways of executing them.[49] This arguably ethnocentric appropriation was in fact a form of musical globalization. Music educators in the United States had begun this trend by incorporating music from Eastern Europe and the Balkans in the 1930s, but the war prompted the Music Education National Conference to adopt an inter-American policy and bring Latin American music and, to a lesser extent, African and Asian music into an increasingly global pedagogical repertoire.[50] Behind all these programs was MENC leader Vannette Lawler, who during the war created for US schools the "Music to Unify the Americas" program, which adapted Latin American musical material provided by Seeger's PAU. Lawler later became a founding figure at both UNESCO and ISME. Inter-Americanism during the war thus enabled a global ambition within the US musical establishment.

Music education and folk roots became important concerns among cultural officers. In the summer of 1941, these concerns motivated two researchers to travel to a variety of Latin American countries, funded by the PAU through the MENC program "Music for Uniting the Americas." They wrote a series of articles on music education in Latin America published by the *Music Educators Journal* in 1941–1942.[51]

---

[48] Luiz H. Corrêa de Azevedo, *A Escola Nacional de Música e as pesquisas de folclore musical no Brasil* (Rio de Janeiro: Centro de Pesquisas Folclóricas—Universidade Federal do Rio de Janeiro, 1944).

[49] "Music Speaks to the Hearts of All Men: The International Movement in American Music Education: 1930–1954," *Bulletin of the Council for Research in Music Education* 133 (Summer, 1997): 143–52.

[50] After the war, the internationalism of music educators gave impulse to the foundation in 1953 of the International Society for Music Education (ISME).

[51] MENC directive Leon Roddick argued that despite differences such as the fact that US music "is more highly developed, that there is more widespread use of music in the United States, that public school music as we know it is not prevalent in South America, that some efforts of Latin American composers seem very simple and direct," music is still "the expression of a people or the voice of art in neighboring republics, each another of the Americas," and therefore something to be valued and shared

FIGURE 5.1 Cover of *The Latin-American Song Book*. Ginn and Company, 1942.

The two MENC travelers, John Beattie and Louis Curtis, offered revealing depictions of the global nature of musical life in South America. In Ecuador, for instance, they contacted a local expert, Juan Gorrell, who was in fact a transplanted New Englander whose father, Henry Gorrell, had Anglicized his name from Enrico Gorrelli, after a career as opera singer in Italy that ended with him teaching voice lessons in Kansas City. His son Juan (John) moved to Ecuador to engage "in the recording of native Ecuadorian music." Juan Gorrell sponsored a local trio of guitars, *Los nativos andinos* (The Native Andeans) and the *Grupo Típico Castro*, also dedicated to folkloric songs, and recorded both for RCA-Victor. His other business was as an international

across the hemisphere. Leon Ruddick, "Music for Uniting the Americas," *Music Educators Journal* 28, no. 3 (January 1942): 10–11.

impresario who brought foreign stars to perform in Quito, Ecuador's capital.[52] This portrait of Juan Gorrell captures the difficulties of isolating an authentically Latin American folk tradition.

A response to Beattie and Curtis's views came from Chile's top musical figure, Domingo Santa Cruz—dean of fine arts, organizer of the national symphonic orchestra, creator of music programs for public and private schools, and supporter of many other key musical activities. Santa Cruz attended MENC's conference in Milwaukee in 1942 and wrote an article for the Music Educators Journal shortly afterward. As his comments suggest, the growing interest in folk music bumped up against the advanced commercialization of music making in Latin America. After thanking Beattie and Curtis for their visit and acknowledging the extraordinary importance of learning from US musical institutions, he pointed out a discrepancy in how musicologists in the United States and Latin America perceived Latin American folk music. "First of all," he wrote, "we . . . would like to see here [in the United States] a deeper and more careful understanding of our artistic and musical life. We would like to banish the 'picturesque' aspect and the preference for the obviously exotic, with which the selection of Latin American music is made." He asked them to collaborate more with Latin American experts so they would understand "the boundaries between the so-called folklore and the musical pastiches of our cafés," and avoid mistakes such as publishing two supposedly Chilean folk songs in a US songbook for schools that were "written and harmonized as four-voice part songs in the very serious form of a Protestant chorale."[53]

"Why should we Americans not be able to create music that, though typical and national, would have universal appeal?" The words of Heitor Villa-Lobos at the Milwaukee conference revealed a new problem. Not only was folk music hard to isolate from commercialization, but also the very champions of musical nationalism were simultaneously making claims of musical universalism while embracing a musical ideology that was both Latin and pan-Americanist.[54] This ideological shift from pan-Americanism to a global perspective on music was analogous to the geopolitical shift of the foreign cultural policies of the State Department.

---

[52] John Beattie and Louis Woodson Curtis, "South American Music Pilgrimage II: Ecuador and Peru," *Music Educators Journal* 28, no. 3 (1942): 12–18.

[53] Domingo Santa Cruz, "On Hemispherical Unity," *Music Educators Journal* 28, no. 6 (1942): 13.

[54] Heitor Villa-Lobos, "Hands Across the Air," *Music Educators Journal* 28, no. 6 (1942): 14. Leading Mexican musicologists Luis Sandi and Baqueiro Foster were also attentive to the connections between Mexican folklore, African music ("La Bamba" was for Sandi a "*Nigro tang*"), and ancient Greek music, an argument that gave Mexican folk a universal dimension. Theodore Cohen, "Among Races, Nations, and Diasporas: Genealogies of 'La Bamba' in Mexico and the United States," *Studies in Latin American Popular Music* 35 (2017): 51–78.

FROM PAN-AMERICANISM TO UNESCO

In 1944 the Coordinator of Inter-American Affairs cut the MD's funding and instead promoted a similar office within the State Department: the Division of Cultural Relations. Seeger believed that the new organization would be more powerful and that inter-American policies would be now part of larger, universal ones. Among the recommendations he gave to the successor organization were "the formation of an inter-American organization of authors and composers" and the "formation of an inter-American association of music educators."[55]

During the final year of war and in the immediate postwar, cooperation and concurrence among the victors led to a reorganization of global cultural cooperation along US and UK interests around UNESCO, against different proposals by French, Latin American, and other diplomatics actors.[56] Relieved of wartime pressures, Seeger suggested to UNESCO in 1947 some core principles that had guided his work and some lessons he had learned along the way. UNESCO's goal, he wrote, is world peace, but "to be avoided here is the belief that music is *in itself* [his emphasis] good for world peace. To the contrary, it is a highly competitive field and can be used as a medium for aggression as easily as any other." This principle operated both among large audiences and within the "small world" of professional music. There was no music that was *in itself* suitable for peace or war. Music, to the contrary, conveys a specific meaning

> in each particular instance. In a radio broadcast, for example, the music used should be what the people who are to receive it like best and want most. This may or may not be the music thought "best" for the program by specialists in Hollywood, New York or Paris. Music of all regions should be used without prejudice, as needed, using the idiom—primitive, folk, popular, fine art or any hybrid—most suitable for the audience addressed and the theme and occasion chosen. [...] The *frame* in which music is presented, often determines the *value*.

Another threat to be avoided was competition among national identities. "The music program of UNESCO should be intercultural rather than international [...] UNESCO must not become a list in which 'national' musics joust for advantages in competitive preliminaries traditionally leading to war." The focus of UNESCO had to be "the building of strong national music organizations, upon which strong international music organization can be based." To keep the stronger nations from subordinating the weaker ones, UNESCO had to seek a balanced development, among the different countries, of "unions or syndicates of performing musicians, associations of music educators, and of allied activities such as concert management, rights collection, and

---

[55] Seeger, "Brief History."

[56] Corinne A. Pernet, "Twists, Turns and Dead Alleys: The League of Nations and Intellectual Cooperation in Times of War," *Journal of Modern European History* 12, no. 3 (2014): 342–58.

music industry."[57] (In a similar letter from November 1946, Seeger suggested to the State Department that "the music of the various cultures and regions, but not of the nations, of the world" should be the players in the global cultural exchange, because nationalism is a "pernicious myth," and musicians, not governments, should run the exchanges.)[58] The musical content of such intercultural exchange would be determined not by governments or even traditional musical hierarchies, but by the intentions and expectations of music producers, consumers, and mediators.

Two years later, in 1949, Luiz Correa de Azevedo addressed the recently founded International Folk Music Council (IFMC). He described UNESCO's goal as creating, under conditions of peace, "a spiritual union of the men of all races, of all religions and political views, over a common ground in which their beliefs and expectations, far from being dissimilar, will tend to the same goal: the spiritual improvement through education, science and culture." Azevedo was proposing to create an International Institute of Music, a "worldwide super-organization for music." In his words, the first step toward such an overarching institution would be creating a kind of

council of the international musical organizations in charge of coordinating the activities of the different organizations, encouraging the creation of new international organizations in the areas where there is none yet, encouraging the creation of musical organizations in the countries that need it, counseling UNESCO in any music-related matter, preparing or promoting Festivals or International Congresses of Music, and finally organizing the creation of an International Institute . . . We hope to establish such Council by 1950.[59]

This Brazilian musicologist had begun his career studying his country's musical nationalism. His internationalist words illustrate the successive historical shifts in the MD's approach: from a New Deal–style of cultural nationalism to pan-Americanism and then to the promotion of global exchanges.

Seeger imagined music interests around the globe organized on two levels, a governmental one and a civil one. His vision in 1948 was "an inter-government agency," UNESCO, "surrounded by a planetary family of autonomous specialized organizations with which it can deal, but which are controlled and directed by private initiative." Individuals and organizations would be able to operate at both levels through their governments or by means of the international association of their particular field. In the first case—the governmental level—ingenuity was necessary to overcome the bureaucratic mediations that threatened to dilute any proposal from civil society as it made its way to UNESCO's top decision-makers. And among civil society

[57] Seeger, "Brief History," 7.

[58] Letter to William Benton, Assistant Secretary of State (for Public Affairs), November 18, 1946. University of Chicago Library—Special Collections. I thank Mauricio Tenorio for sharing this letter.

[59] Luiz H. Corrêa de Azevedo, "L'Unesco et la musique populaire," *Journal of the International Folk Music Council* 1 (1949): 19–21 (my translation).

organizations, rivalries among countries were to be avoided, because they could lead to another war. Seeger was blunt in this regard: "The worst wars in modern times [. . .] have been fought between nations that have been 'interchanging' and 'understanding' for centuries."

This was an important conceptual shift: from agreements among governments that represented nations to global cultural exchanges among civil associations. Even so, Seeger considered national agreements essential: "Each Member State is urged, but not required, to form a 'national cooperating body' or commission to secure mass participation of citizens within the Member State. Six, among them the United States, had done this by September 1, 1947." The United States had done so by gathering top officers from the Department of State, National Music Council, American Library Association, National Education Association, American Council on Education and American Council of Learned Societies.[60] In Seeger's view, international exchanges and cooperation did not undermine the integration of different institutions within each nation.

Pan-American music policies shifted from the hemisphere to the globe by bridging the folk revival and musical nationalism of the 1930s with the global ideologies of the 1950s represented by UNESCO. From this perspective, the valorization of the "music of the Americas" in both in its folk and classical (but not commercial) forms appears as a model for the "music of the world."

The OCIAA programs were in general inconsequential for Latin American audiences' sympathy for the United States: Latin Americans liked and rejected US culture for reasons other than cultural diplomacy.[61] More consequential were the MD-funded catalogues and publications that helped establish folklore and music education as a transnational conversation among Latin Americans.[62]

There were two important aspects to this hegemonic project. First, unlike the previous European musical hegemony and the postwar Americanization, World War II hemispheric musical diplomacy explicitly valorized Latin American musical practices, knowledge, and actors. The MD's goal was to articulate Latin Americans *institutionally* with more financially and politically powerful cultural organizations in the United States through hemispheric networks under US hegemony. Second, the MD rearticulated its institutional and ideological energies on a fully global scale after the war by incorporating American, European, and Latin American cultural diplomats into UNESCO, particularly the International Council of Music, founded in 1949. As historian Anaïs Fléchet has shown, the ICM brought first art music and later folk or

---

[60] Charles Seeger, "UNESCO, February 1948," *Notes* 5, no. 2 (1948): 165–68.

[61] Weimar Germany's cultural policy on Latin America suffered from a similar weakness: the assumption of the malleability of the region's cultural élites. Cf. Michael Goebel, "Decentering the German Spirit: The Weimar Republic's Cultural Relations with Latin America," *Journal of Contemporary History* 44, no. 2 (2009): 226.

[62] Pan American exchanges also shaped the careers of major Latin American composers like Villa-Lobos, Carlos Chavez and Alberto Ginastera, as analyzed in Carol Hess, *Representing the Good Neighbor: Music, Difference, and the Pan American Dream* (New York: Oxford University Press, 2013).

traditional music into a vast theater of exchanges and conflicts concerning the globalization of music.[63] Thanks in part to the MD catalogues, by the 1960s folk music and its populist ethos were already rooted in Latin America's musical education and national imagination and were feeding both its anti-imperialist left and its nationalist conservative right.

Considered from the perspective of the history of the globalization of culture, the MD represented the imperial acceptance, in the space of just a few years, of a series of discourses on folklore, art music compositions, and musical pedagogy. This acceptance legitimized Latin American expertise. But more importantly, it also nurtured both a US ideology of *Latin* music and culture that keeps developing today, as well as the idea of a global, non-European-centered musical heritage.

A new era of musical globalization took place after the war, by artists, companies, experts, and musical associations increasingly connected with one another around the world. In Latin America, these networks further expanded a musical life whose nature had always been, to a great extent, transnational, but now the regional category, *Latin American music*, would shape and infuse an unexpected array of projects.

---

[63] Anaïs Fléchet, "Le Conseil international de la Musique et la politique musicale de l'Unesco," *Relations internationales* 156 (2014): 53–71.

6

MUSIC AND REGIONALISM SINCE THE 1950S

THE INVENTION OF Latin American music in the 1930s was successful. Its general-ized adoption during World War II contributed to consolidate the view, in the postwar years, of Latin America and the Caribbean as a cultural area, both from within and from without. Latin American music became a regional aesthetic symbol, adopted by all kinds of projects: anti-imperialist ones since the 1960s, integrationist ones in the 1990s and 2000s, and by myriad organizations that naturalized it as much as musical audiences did. What follows is a panoramic view of the history of the intertwining of Latin America as a regional project and Latin American music as its symbol since the 1950s.

The architecture of the postwar international order allowed for the consolidation of Latin America as a region both organizationally and conceptually. From within, regional thought became a tool for economic reformism.[1] From the outside, it became a policy framework for United States economic and military power. In 1948, the Pan American Union became the Organization of American States, which institutional-ized an inter-American system contradictorily marked by US hemispheric hegemony and by multilateralism as the accepted legal norm of the Americas. On the one hand, in 1946 the United States created in the Panama Canal Zone a "Latin American Ground

---

[1] Jimena Caravaca and Ximena Espeche, "América Latina como problema y como solución: Robert Triffin, Daniel Cosío Villegas, Víctor Urquidi y Raúl Prebisch 'antes' del Manifiesto Latinoamericano (1944–1946)," *Desarrollo Económico* 55, no. 217 (2016): 411–35.

The Invention of Latin American Music. Pablo Palomino, Oxford University Press (2020). © Oxford University Press.
DOI: 10.1093/oso/9780190687403.001.0001

School," later on renamed as the infamous School of the Americas (and since 1984, Western Hemisphere Institute for Security Cooperation in Fort Benning, Georgia), tying together the armed force officials of the continent. But on the other hand, in 1949 Latin America was conceptualized as a separate economic area by the Economic Commission for Latin America (CEPAL, part of the Department of Economics Affairs at the United Nations), further entrenching the view of Latin America as a separate and unified region. Argentine economist Raúl Prebisch seemed to echo Lange's and Seeger's progressive, regionalist, scientific, and institutional aims in music when explained his organization's challenges: "As in many other domains, we are faced with a precarious knowledge of the economic structure of our countries," and therefore scientific research and professional formation are required to "capture the evolving manifestations of reality" and "collaborate to find solutions" for the "economic development of Latin America."[2] The 1964 foundation of the United Nations Conference on Trade and Development (UNCTAD), also directed by Prebisch, showed the natural correlation between Latin America's regionalism and its model for global, multilateral organizations.[3]

"Ibero-América" also fostered the re-creation of the region's identity. In 1950, a minor, Spanish-Argentine neofascist network proposed the idea of a "Hispanic Community of Nations." The project did not prosper, but its rhetoric reappeared much later, as "historical and cultural affinities" at the 1991 first Iberian-American Summit and a series of commemorations of the Fifth Centennial of the "encounter" between the two regions—"encounter" replacing the traditional language of an Iberian "discovery" of America. The *indigenista* tradition, on the other hand, had held in 1940 the First *Inter*-American Indigenista Congress in Páztcuaro, Mexico, which echoed previous international declarations by promoting the integration of the "descendants of the first inhabitants of the American land" into the national societies across the Americas. Fifty years later indigenous activists discussed instead five hundred years of *continental* "Indian resistance."[4]

---

[2] "En esto, como en muchos otros casos, nos encontramos con un conocimiento precario de la estructura económica de nuestros países . . . Si se logra realizar su investigación con imparcialidad científica y estimular la formación de economistas capaces de ir captando las nuevas manifestaciones de la realidad, previendo sus problemas y colaborando en la busca de soluciones, se habrá hecho un servicio de incalculable importancia para el desarrollo económico de la América Latina." Raúl Prebisch, "El desarrollo económico de la América Latina y algunos de sus principales problemas," *El Trimestre Económico* 16, no. 63 (1949): 431. See also United Nations CEPAL, "Economic Survey of Latin America, 1949," January 1, 1951,

[3] Juan Pablo Scarfi, *The Hidden History of International Law in the Americas: Empire and Legal Networks* (Oxford: Oxford University Press, 2017); Lesley Gill, *The School of the Americas: Military Training and Political Violence in the Americas* (Durham, NC: Duke University Press, 2004); Matias Margulis, ed., *The Global Political Economy of Raúl Prebisch* (Abingdon: Routledge, 2017).

[4] "Descendientes de los primeros pobladores de las tierras americanas." The board of the Instituto Indigenista created in 1940 was commanded for many years by F.D.Roosevelt's indigenous "expert," John Collier. See Laura Giraudo, "'No hay propiamente todavía Instituto': Los inicios del Instituto Indigenista Interamericano (Abril 1940–Marzo 1942)," *América Indígena* LXII, no. 2 (June 2006): 6–32, and Marc Becker, "Comunistas, indigenistas e indígenas en la formación de la Federación Ecuatoriana

The tension between the region's indigenous and Iberian identities continues to this day: the Museum of the Americas in Madrid, founded in 1940 under a Catholic, authoritarian, and Hispanicist rhetoric, recently became a multicultural yet ethnocentric celebration of the Hispanic civilizing mission, targeting primarily an audience of immigrant children from Latin America. The very Spanish identity is of course debated as well—vis-à-vis the European Union, its internal nationalisms and regionalisms, and its immigrants from all over the world, including Latin America—providing yet another context for the remaking of Latin American identities.[5] In Argentina, a monument to Columbus (a donation of the Italian community in 1921), located behind the Presidential Palace, was removed by the government in 2015 and replaced by a countermonument to Juana Azurduy, a female mestiza and anticolonial Independence warrior from Bolivia. The inauguration featured the Ballet Nacional Folclórico de Bolivia dancing to traditional and modern Bolivian music and was infused with Latin-Americanist discourses.[6] In Los Angeles, Latino political representatives in 2018 also removed a Columbus statue, (donated in 1973 by an Italian association as well), for being a "genocidal" symbol. At the same time, politicians of both the traditional and the extreme right in Spain praised Latin American immigrants, from any "brother Hispanic-American country, with the same culture, language, and worldview," because they are people who consider that "the best thing that can happen to them is that their daughter marries a Spaniard," unlike those undesirable migrants from "the Muslim countries." Migrations, markets, and identities follow complex routes as well among Brazil, Portugal, and Africa, a "Lusophone migratory system" of changing nuclei and peripheries and transnational cultural policies.[7] Hence, the cultural definition of Latin America vis-à-vis Iberia is still in flux.

de Indios y el Instituto Indigenista Ecuatoriano," *Íconos. Revista de Ciencias Sociales* 27 (January 2007): 135–44; Continental Conference on 500 Years of Indian Resistance et al., eds., *Indigenous Alliance of the Americas on 500 Years of Resistance: resolutions from the First Continental Conference on 500 Years of Indian Resistance, July 17–21, 1990* (Quito, Ecuador, and Berkeley, CA: Confederación de Nacionalidades Indígenas del Ecuador and South and Meso-American Indian Information Center, 1990); Daniel G. Kressel, "The Hispanic Community of Nations: The Spanish-Argentine Nexus and the Imagining of a Hispanic Cold War Bloc," *Cahiers Des Amériques Latines* 79 (2015): 115–33.

[5] Joshua Tucker, "Sounding the Latin Transatlantic: Music, Integration, and Ambivalent Ethnogenesis in Spain," *Comparative Studies in Society and History* 56, no. 4 (October 2014): 902–33; Jessaca Leinaweaver, "Transatlantic Unity On Display: The 'White Legend' and the 'Pact of Silence' in Madrid's Museum of the Americas," *History and Anthropology* 28, no. 1 (2017): 39–57.

[6] Pablo Ortemberg, "Monumentos, memorialización y espacio público: reflexiones a propósito de la escultura de Juana Azurduy," *Tarea* 3, no. 3 (2016): 96–125. The new government displaced the Azurduy monument in 2017 to a nearby plaza with no fanfare or music, leaving an empty space. A few months earlier the secretary of education had proposed "a new Conquest of the Desert [the military ethnic cleansing of Patagonia in the nineteenth century], now through education instead of the sword" ("la nueva Campaña del Desierto, pero no con la espada sino con la educación").

[7] Iñigo Aduriz, "El PP, un día después de la irrupción de Vox: 'Lo mejor que les puede pasar a los hispanoamericanos es que su hija se case con un español,'" eldiario.es, March 12, 2018 (https://www.eldiario.es/politica/PP-despues-irrupcion-Vox-hispanoamericanos_0_842365921.html); "Abascal (Vox): 'No es lo mismo un inmigrante hispanoamericano que la inmigración de los países islámicos,'" eldiario.es, April 17, 2018 (https://www.eldiario.es/canariasahora/sociedad/

Migration patterns to Latin America changed precisely around 1950, when the region shifted from primarily receiving European immigrants to producing domestic migrations, emigration to the United States, Spain, and other parts of Europe, and at a smaller but significant scale, between Latin American countries.[8] Carlos Monsiváis wrote that the twentieth century in Latin America is a century of continuous cultural migrations, a movement that "invents and legitimizes urban scenes, family hierarchies and habits, consumption styles, structures of feeling and sentimentalism,". including "the relations between the cultural industry and everyday life, between commercial culture and worldviews."[9]

The "cultural migrants" that transformed modern culture in Latin America in the twentieth century, and especially with the industrialization and economic expansion after the 1950s, ranged from rural migrants to urbanite avant-garde artists. They migrated not only within national boundaries but also transnationally. Like the multiple Afro-Caribbean diasporas that crisscrossed the circum-Caribbean ports in the 1920s and 1930s,[10] some of these migrants pursued both economic goals and politico-cultural projects. All of them learned from cinema melodramas how US, Mexican, and Argentine playwrights and actors narrated modern life.[11] In this context, Latin American music became a market niche—a standard, run-of-the-mill category. Popular music was an inseparable part of the experience of the postwar generation, many of them children of domestic and transnational migrants, that grew up in the region from the late 1950s to the early 1970s. These young people broke away from their parents' generation in several fundamental ways, but their music didn't break away entirely. Instead, they took old and new boleros, cumbias, tangos, sambas, rumbas, mambos, valses, and cuecas from all over the region and naturalized them as either commercial, folkloric, "tropical," or simply Latin American music, alongside European melodic pop and the twist and rock and roll of the United States.[12] CBS and

VIDEO-Abascal-Vox-hispanoamericano-inmigracion_0_761874455.html); Pablo Ximénez de Sandoval, "Los Ángeles retira una estatua de Colón: 'No hay que celebrar al responsable de un genocidio,'" *El País*, November 12, 2018; Pedro Góis and José Carlos Marques, "A emigração portuguesa e o sistema migratório lusófono: complexidade e dinâmicas de um país de migrações," *Informe OBIMID (Observatorio Iberoamericano sobre Movilidad Urbana, Migraciones y Desarrollo)*, March 19, 2016; Bart Paul Vanspauwen, "Lusofonia in *Musidanças*. Governance, Discourse and Performance" (PhD diss., Universidade Nova de Lisboa, 2017), chapter 1.

[8] Alejandro I. Canales, "Panorama actual de la migración internacional en América Latina," *Revista Latinoamericana de Población*, no. 4–5 (October 31, 2015): 65–91.

[9] Carlos Monsiváis, *Aires de familia: cultura y sociedad En América Latina* (Barcelona: Editorial Anagrama, 2000), 155.

[10] Lara Putnam, *Radical Moves: Caribbean Migrants and the Politics of Race in the Jazz Age* (Chapel Hill: University of North Carolina Press, 2013).

[11] Matthew B. Karush, *Culture of Class: Radio and Cinema in the Making of a Divided Argentina, 1920–1946* (Durham, NC: Duke University Press, 2012); Maricruz Castro and Robert McKee Irwin, *El cine mexicano "se impone": mercados internacionales y penetración cultural en la época dorada* (México: Universidad Nacional Autónoma de México, 2011).

[12] I thank Eduardo Morales and Héctor Palomino for this insight. See also Valeria Manzano, *The Age of Youth in Argentina: Culture, Politics, and Sexuality from Peron to Videla* (Chapel Hill: University of North Carolina Press, 2014), esp. chapter 3, "Surfing the New Wave." In 1940, a musical and cimenatographic

RCA Victor expanded into the regional market by promoting the "Nueva Ola," and this expansion planted the seeds of a musical youth culture that in the 1980s would massively adopt rock music sung in Spanish. At the same time, romantic ballads remained central, as in the 1969 and 1970 Mexican government-sponsored "Festival Mundial de la Canción Latina" in Mexico City, and in its continuation by the "Festival OTI de la Canción" (Organización de la Televisión Iberoamericana, an international alliance of Latin American and Iberian media corporations that created a spin-off of the Eurovision contest), held until 2000 in multiple cities from Madrid to Belo Horizonte and from Miami to Santiago de Chile. The original name of the great prize was "Gran Premio de la Canción Iberoamericana"—it assumed the existence of a unifying genre of Iberian American songs.

The Cuban revolution produced in the 1960s a cultural rhetoric and policies that were heavily Latin Americanist and Caribbeanist, as well as anti-colonial and Third-Worldist. Its global-reaching news press was called *Prensa Latina*. The cultural policies of this revolution were primarily invested in literature but also reached music, dance, and other arts. In 1962, the Institute of Folkloric Research became the Seminario de Música Popular, oriented to Cuban musical traditions. But in 1965, Havana's *Casa de las Américas*, which had been launched in 1959 immediately after the revolution, created a music department, which in 1970 began publishing a music bulletin, and since 1979 awards musicological works on Latin American and Caribbean music, with committees and awardees hailing from the entire region. Pan-American music festivals have been organized in Havana since 1965.[13]

During the Cold War, the idea of Latin America also regained attention within Area Studies sustained by U.S. federal funding, and as intrinsic to the notion of a "Western Hemisphere," in an influential rereading by Lewis Hanke of Herbert Bolton's 1932 idea of the *Greater America*.[14] This view, and hemispheric interests in the music field, produced many international initiatives. When the Pan American Union's music division stopped operating, Latin American art music continued to be performed in the United States at the Tanglewood music festivals in Massachusetts; the Festivales de Música in Caracas, Venezuela, from 1954 to 1966; the OAS-sponsored Consejo Inter-Americano de Música (CIDEM), created in 1956 under the direction of Guillermo

---

"Mexican invasion" allowed Chileans the "discovery of our own continent." See José Miguel Varas and Juan Pablo González, *En busca de la música chilena: crónica y antología de una historia sonora* (Santiago de Chile: Editorial Catalonia, 2005).

[13] Guillermo Rodriguez Rivera, *Decirlo todo: políticas culturales (en la Revolución cubana)* (La Habana: Editorial Ojalá, 2017), 40. Robin Moore, *Music and Revolution: Cultural Change in Socialist Cuba* (Berkeley: University of California Press, 2006), 154; *Casa de las Américas, 1959–2009* (La Habana: Casa de las Américas, 2014); Patrick Iber, *Neither Peace nor Freedom: The Cultural Cold War in Latin America* (Cambridge, MA: Harvard University Press, 2015); Elizabeth Schwall, "'Cultures in the Body': Dance and Anthropology in Revolutionary Cuba," *History of Anthropology Newsletter* (blog), December 14, 2017 (http://histanthro.org/notes/cultures-in-the-body/).

[14] Lewis Hanke, *Do the Americas Have a Common History?: A Critique of the Bolton Theory* (New York: Knopf, 1964).

Espinosa; and CIDEM's Inter-American Festivals in Washington, DC starting in 1958.[15] In 1961 the Chilean composer and musicologist Juan Orrego Salas, with funding from the Rockefeller Foundation, created the Latin American Music Center at the University of Indiana, Bloomington, which a few years later expanded its focus to include popular music as well as art music. The academic and art music scenes in the United States continued hence paying attention to Latin American composers and to Latin American-inspired compositions by US artists, as musicologist Carla Hess put it, in an ambiguous game of pan-American sameness and ethnocentric otherness.[16] And we should not forget that musical diplomacy toward Latin America was in fact just a section within a global effort of cultural hegemony.[17]

The terms in which a prominent Argentine musicologist, Pola Suárez Urtubey, celebrated Alberto Ginastera's 1960 "Cantata para América mágica" reveal the flexibility of the Latin American regional musical category among musicologists: Ginastera is described as a "universal" musician, among the top ones in the "Western world" and acclaimed in the "Northern hemisphere" because he is essentially an "Argentine" and "Americano" composer, capable of interpreting the "magical" poetry of the "primitive" America that survived thanks to the Christian colonizers that saved it.[18] National, universal, and Western frameworks sustain a musician's (Latin) Americanness.

Meanwhile, in Buenos Aires, composers from across the region had been forging bonds of friendship since 1961 under the direction of the same Ginastera at the Latin American Center for Music Experimentation (CLAEM), founded through the Rockefeller Foundation. When the center closed in 1971, these musicians continued to interact until 1989 through the *Cursos Latinoamericanos de Música Contemporánea*,

---

[15] Miguel Astor, "Los ojos de Sojo: el conflicto entre nacionalismo y modernidad en los Festivales de Música de Caracas (1954–1966)" (PhD diss., Universidad Central de Venezuela, 2008). I thank Hernán Vázquez for his guidance on the history of Latin American Art music festivals.

[16] Carol A. Hess, *Representing the Good Neighbor: Music, Difference, and the Pan American Dream* (New York: Oxford University Press, 2013).

[17] Danielle Fosler-Lussier, *Music in America's Cold War Diplomacy* (Berkeley: University of California Press, 2015).

[18] "Si Ginastera es hoy un músico universal . . . ; si figura entre los primeros compositores vivientes del *mundo occidental* y si su obra "existe" y tiene lugar en el *hemisferio norte* . . . es porque ha sabido caracterizar a su música dándole *una perspectiva de lugar y de historia*; porque transmite con ella el *genio de un pueblo* . . . sin ese desapego amargo que suele ser típico del *creador americano*. Ginastera viene a dar la razón a cuantos se han dedicado a especular sobre la *cultura argentina o americana en general*. La deficiencia, el atraso –se ha señalado– de *nuestras culturas* se debe a la imposesión de sí mismo del *creador americano*. Se vive y se crea enajenado y ausente de su propio ámbito y sólo se consigue con ello crear una obra despaisada, que nadie reconoce, ni sus compatriotas ni el resto del universo. Cuando Ginastera usa la palabra '*mágica*' en el título de su obra le da a aquella el sentido de '*primitiva.*' Parte de la base de que han coexistido dos corrientes en la formación cultural y espiritual del continente sudamericano: la etapa mágica o precolombina y la cristiana. Y sostiene Ginastera que la primera no ha muerto por completo . . . como si se tratara del latido de *una invencible vena poética y musical*. Los poemas que los primeros sacerdotes cristianos recogieron en las avanzadas culturas mayas, aztecas e incaicas, son las alas que han transportado las civilizaciones precolombinas a través del tiempo y del espacio." Pola Suarez Urtubey, "'La Cantata Para América Mágica', de Alberto Ginastera," *Revista Musical Chilena* 17, no. 84 (1963): 19–36.

in which many CLAEM alumni worked practically as honorary teachers.[19] In 1962, following a recommendation by the 1956 Inter-American Music Council, the OAS funded an Inter-American Institute of Musical Education at the Universidad de Chile.[20] In Salta, Argentina, the first Festival Latinoamericano de Folklore was organized in 1965.[21] In Caracas, the Inter-American Institute of Ethnomusicology and Folklore, founded in 1970, produced research across the region with support from the OAS, and provided the basis for the 1977 work by Isabel Aretz published by UNESCO, with a prologue from Alejo Carpentier that argued in favor of approaching Latin American music from all social determinations "as a block."[22] The other centers of Latin Americanist musicology were Tulane University, UCLA, and the University of Texas, Austin, where Gilbert Chase, Robert Stevenson, and Gerard Béhague, respectively, set up the foundations for today's Latin Americanist ethnomusicology.[23]

And yet the image of a Latin American regional identity—in politics, culture, and music—was far from universally accepted. Jorge Luis Borges was probably right in doubting that there were many "Argentines or Mexicans who are also Americans . . . beyond the effusiveness of a toast"; "the sentiment of Americanism or Iberian-Americanism," he argued, "is sporadic."[24] But at the same time, in other popular and modern realms, like soccer, nationalism and regional integration went hand in hand, as evidenced by the idea of a "South American football" since the 1930s and the organization of the *Copa Libertadores de América* since 1960.

---

[19] Hernán Gabriel Vazquez, *Conversaciones en torno al CLAEM: entrevistas a compositores becarios del Centro Latinoamericano de Altos Estudios Musicales del Instituto Torcuato Di Tella* (Buenos Aires: Instituto Nacional de Musicología "Carlos Vega," 2015); Eduardo Herrera, "The Rockefeller Foundation and Latin American Music in the 1960s: The Creation of Indiana University's LAMC and Di Tella Institute's CLAEM," *American Music* 35, no. 1 (2017): 51–74, and "Perspectiva internacional: lo 'latinoamericano' del Centro Latinoamericano de Altos Estudios Musicales," in *La música en el Di Tella. Resonancias de la modernidad*, ed. José Luis Castiñeira de Dios (Buenos Aires: Secretaría de Cultura de la Nación, 2011), 30–35.

[20] Comité Editorial, "El Instituto Interamericano de Educación Musical," *Revista Musical Chilena* 30, no. 134 (January 1, 1976): 111–14.

[21] Fernando Rios, "'They're Stealing Our Music': The Argentinísima Controversy, National Culture Boundaries, and the Rise of a Bolivian Nationalist Discourse," *Latin American Music Review* 35, no. 2 (2014): 197–227.

[22] Isabel Aretz, ed., *América Latina en su música* (Paris: UNESCO, 1977), 17; Ana Maria Locatelli de Pergamo, "Recordando a Isabel Aretz (13/04/1909-01/06/2005)," *Latin American Music Review* 26, no. 2 (2005): 158–63. The wider ideological aspects of the OAS music recordings were analyzed in Ramiro Mansilla Pons et al., "Las revoluciones y los surcos. Política cultural hemisférica y edición fonográfica," in *VIII Jornadas de Investigación en Disciplinas Artísticas y Proyectuales* (Universidad Nacional de La Plata, 2016).

[23] Juan Pablo González, *Pensar la música desde América Latina: problemas e interrogantes* (Buenos Aires: Gourmet Musical, 2013), 24.

[24] "No sé si hay muchos argentinos o mexicanos que sean americanos también, más allá de la firma de una declaración o de las efusiones de un brindis . . . el sentimiento de americanidad o de hispano-americanidad sigue siendo esporádico." Jorge Luis Borges, "Prólogo," *Obra crítica de Pedro Henríquez Ureña*, ed. Emma Susana Speratti Piñero (México, D.F.: Fondo de Cultura Económica, 1960).

Scholars in the United States began to acknowledge the deep roots of the "Latin" influence on US music in 1979.[25] The circulation of "Latin" *commercial* music, which had begun in the 1910s—Argentine tangos and Brazilian maxixes—and became mainstream in the 1930s and 1940s in Paris, New York, and Hollywood, converged with the emergence in the mid-1940s of a *Latin* jazz heavily inspired by Cuban styles that musicians such as the Spanish-Cuban Xavier Cugat had made fashionable. Meanwhile, by the late 1940s, the Chilean Parra sisters were performing "boleros, corridos, rancheras, tangos, tonadas, and cuecas" from multiple parts of the hemisphere in Santiago de Chile; they recorded some of them with RCA Victor.[26] They then turned to collecting and composing Chilean folklore, building a repertoire that would turn Violeta Parra—who had built her career in Santiago and Paris while also performing in Buenos Aires, London, Geneva, and Concepción—into a folk icon of Chile and of Latin America. This is how a new "Latin" *folk* music and "Latin" *jazz* coexisted during the 1950s and 1960s. Then a boom of *pop* and *melodic* music in Spanish joined the soundscape. By the 1980s, "Latin" *rock*, or *rock en español*, became a hemispheric reality as well. United States recording companies were key to all these developments. As Matthew Karush showed with the example of Argentine artists, several generations of artists and audiences throughout the region connected those multiple "Latin" musical streams with each other, as they circulated through national, hemispheric, and global markets.[27]

Reflection on how the musical history of Latin America is approached and written began in the 1960s. "Panorama de la musicología latinoamericana" was written in 1959 by the Argentine musicologist Daniel Devoto, and "The Present State and Potential of Musical Research in Latin America" was written in 1972 by L. H. Correa de Azevedo.[28] (A precedent was Gilbert Chase's *Guide to Latin American Music*, first published in 1945 and republished in 1962 with more texts.)

An important continuation of Francisco Curt Lange's *Bulletin of Latin American Music* in the consolidation of Latin America as a region from the musicological perspective was the creation in 1961 of an Inter-American Institute for Musical Research at Tulane University in New Orleans, followed by a 1963 big conference in Washington, DC, where many of the actors of this history reunited, including Lange. In the report, its director Gilbert Chase gave the tone to this very much US-centered

[25] "Until Roberts's *The Latin Tinge* (1979), the influence of Latin rhythms in American music went largely unacknowledged," Gustavo Pérez Firmat, "Latunes: An Introduction," *Latin American Research Review* 43, no. 2 (2008): 180–203, 183, footnote.

[26] Ericka Verba, "To Paris and Back: Violeta Parra's Transnational Performance of Authenticity," *The Americas* 70, no. 2 (October 2013): 274

[27] Matthew Karush, *Musicians in Transit: Argentina and the Globalization of Popular Music* (Durham, NC: Duke University Press, 2017), chapter 2; Gustavo Pérez Firmat, "Latunes: An Introduction."

[28] Juliana Pérez González, *Las historias de la música en hispanoamérica, 1876–2000* (Bogotá: Universidad Nacional de Colombia, Facultad de Ciencias Humanas, Departamento de Historia, 2010), 34.

initiative: Latin America as a "laboratory" where US musicologists could extend their curiosity:

> As Charles Seeger has said, Latin America offers a splendid laboratory for the musicologist, since it covers the whole spectrum of music-making, from the primitive tribal music to the most complex fine-art forms, and only in this continent can they be observed side-by-side in a tremendous process of acculturation that has gone on for more than four- and-a-half centuries.[29]

In 1965, the institute published its first *Yearbook*, which Chase introduced as an "anniversary and new start": a place for US and Latin American scholars to converge in truly inter-American musical research, exactly thirty years after Lange had "established not only the foundation but also the basic edifice of inter-American musicology."[30] Following Lange's "heroic, militant phase," when BLAM promoted hemispheric musicology, the yearbook and the institute would now offer permanent support. In 1970, the yearbook moved to the University of Texas in Austin, but in 1975 it ceased to be published. Lange had operated with a scanty support system that included only his individual official position at SODRE, his laborious wife María Luisa Vértiz and son Hermann Lange Vertiz, and an assistant, Lauro Ayestarán. But even with a more solid and better-funded structure in the United States, hemispheric musicology remained a difficult enterprise. In 1980, still at UT Austin, the *Latin American Music Review* resumed the task, now under the direction of Gerard Béhague. But its first issue was presented on a brief note, without fanfare, as a regular academic endeavor, without even mentioning Lange; the note only mentioned Chase and Charles Seeger, who had just passed away. The "heroic, militant phase" was thus forgotten. Musicology in the United States was now well established as a combination of musical analysis, historical musicology, folklore, and ethnomusicology, and Latin America became naturalized as a cultural unit that included, together with the music of Latin America and the Caribbean, the music of "Mexican Americans, Puerto Ricans, Cubans, Spaniards, and Portuguese in the United States and Canada."[31]

Latin Americanism kept mushrooming in unexpected places. During the 1970s and 1980s, military Cold War authoritarianism across the region also framed its nationalist and Christian-Western cultural views within a Latin Americanist rhetoric: the Christian Family Movement of Argentina, for example, promoted the idea of a Latin American type of family that demanded specific "cultural concepts" from a "Latin American family theology."[32] This was in part spurred by a debate around the notes

---

[29] "Summary Report of the First Inter-American Conference on Musicology, Washington, D.C., 1963," *Anuario / Yearbook / Anuário of the Inter-American Institute for Musical Research* 1 (1965): 139–50, 140.

[30] Gilbert Chase, "An Anniversary and a New Start," *Anuario / Yearbook / Anuário of the Inter-American Institute for Musical Research* 1 (1965): 1–10.

[31] Gerard Béhague, "Editorial Note," *Latin American Music Review / Revista de Música Latinoamericana* 1, no. 1 (1980): 1–1.

[32] Isabella Cosse, "¿Una teología de la familia para el público latinoamericano? La radicalización del Movimiento Familiar Cristiano en Argentina (1968–1974)," *Iberoamericana* XVIII, no. 18 (2018): 57–75.

and illustrations to the 1972 *Latin American Bible* (*La Biblia Latinoamericana*), which conservative Catholics viewed as too influenced by the Liberation Theology, an explicitly Latin Americanist movement as well.[33] Underground musical practices also produced Latin American discourses: at the convergence of the influences of Bob Dylan and *música cafona* (commercial pop) in the 1970s, and then of Latin American folk and pop in the 1990s, an explicitly Latin American musical identity emerged in Mato Grosso do Sul, in Southern Brazil. Its hub was the social and musical club Peña Eme-Ene, which provided, through arts, gastronomy, and above all music, a regional identity linked to the neighboring countries. A regionalist musical discourse coalesced as recently as the turn of the twenty-first century, through a Latin Americanist musical discourse undistinguishable from the local identity.[34] The category of Latin America seems to appear in the historical record in fulfillment of some kind of geocultural necessity by people engaged in some kind of transnational production.

The global musical market kept concocting sounds deemed Latin American, and so did between 1973 and 1985 the Cuban *Nueva Trova* and many "protest song" artists, who reached a peak in popularity through festivals and albums presented as Latin American.[35] A whole Latin Americanist movement, *New Song* (*Nueva Canción*), had emerged, generating specific meanings of Latin Americanism,[36] and in 1984 it was the subject of ethnomusicological analysis.[37] The international Human Rights movement converged with this rhetoric: campaigns by the exiled opposition to the Chilean dictatorship included music concerts organized by human rights and solidarity organizations whose names—"Community Action on Latin America" or "North American Congress on Latin America"—linked the regional category with artists who sung folk music that was in fact specifically Chilean (e.g., Inti-Illimani and Los Jaivas) or from the United States (e.g., Arlo Guthrie, Bob Dylan, Pete Seeger, and Joan Baez).[38]

---

[33] Pablo Gustavo Rodríguez, "Los mundos posibles de la pobreza en la Biblia" (III Reunión de Antropología del Mercosur, Posadas, Misiones (Argentina), 1999). https://www.aacademica.org/pablo.gustavo.rodriguez/74.pdf.

[34] Alvaro Neder, *"Enquanto este novo trem atravessa o Litoral Central." Música popular urbana, latino-americanismo e conflitos sobre modernização em Mato Grosso do Sul* (Rio de Janeiro: Mauad, 2014), esp. "Bienvenida entre nosotros: la Peña Eme-Ene e a construção coletiva de discursos de integração latino-americana," 240–69.

[35] Some of the titles of Gato Barbieri's Latin jazz albums are telling of this popular Latin branding: *The Third World* (1969), *Latin America* (1973), *Viva Emiliano Zapata!* (1974), *Caliente!* (1976), and *Trópico* (1978). See Karush, *Musicians in Transit*, chapter 2. Robin Moore, *Music and Revolution*, 155.

[36] Pablo Molina Palomino, "Los límites de lo latinoamericano. Distinción e identidad en la configuración de un circuito de Nueva Canción en Lima," in *Vientos del pueblo. Representaciones, recepciones e interpretaciones sobre la Nueva Canción Chilena*, eds. Simón Palominos Mandiola and Ignacio Ramos Rodillo (Santiago de Chile: LOM, 2018), 327–62.

[37] Jan Fairley, "La Nueva Canción Latinoamericana," *Bulletin of Latin American Research* 3, no. 2 (1984): 107–15.

[38] Patrick William Kelly, *Sovereign Emergencies: Latin America and the Making of Global Human Rights Politics* (Cambridge: Cambridge University Press, 2018). 110 and 199; Ashley Black, "Canto Libre. Folk Music and Solidarity in the Americas, 1967–1974," in *The Art of Solidarity: Visual and Performative Politics in Cold War Latin America*, ed. Jessica Stites Mor (Austin: University of Texas Press, 2018), 117–45.

A group of exiled Chilean and Uruguayan musicians in Mexico City founded in 1982 the Cuarteto Latinoamericano. Their trajectory is revealing of the broad regionalism of this category: the Cuarteto *Latinoamericano* won the Grammy *Latino* twice: in 2012 for an album of works by *Brazilian* composer Francisco Mignone, and in 2016 for an album of *Sephardic* music. The Quartet was based for a few years in Pittsburgh, and in Caracas it organized a Latin American Academy of String Quartets affiliated with the Venezuelan *Sistema* of orchestras. Almost half of their domestic concerts were devoted by 2003 to Latin American music repertoire, and the percentage rose to 70% when performing abroad. Their first concerts focused on the national composers of Argentina, Mexico, and Brazil (Ginastera, Revueltas, Villa-Lobos), seamlessly integrated into a Latin American repertoire to which they would keep adding throughout the years works from those and many other countries. This explicitly Latin Americanist project still involves the recovery and preservation of traditional and overlooked past music, and the performance of works composed for them by contemporary creators.[39]

Latin Americanism was present in Brazilian rock as well. In January of 1985, the largest international rock festival ever organized until then in Brazil, *Rock in Rio*, took place in Rio de Janeiro as the Electoral College was electing the first civilian president after twenty-one years of military dictatorship. The opening act was the Brazilian countercultural singer Ney Matogrosso (see Figure 6.1). Before hundreds of thousands of fans, wearing a feather headdress, "primitive" necklaces, and a leopard thong, and brandishing a donkey jawbone, like a shaman-cannibal, Matogrosso kicked off the festival with a song called "America do Sul" (1975): "*Deus salve a América do Sul* [. . .] *esses campos molhados de suor / Esse orgulho latino em cada olhar*" (God save South America . . . those fields wet by sweat, that Latino pride in everyone's sight).[40] The main acts of the festival were English-language super-stars like Queen, Iron Maiden, and George Benson, but the opening act was unequivocally Latin-Americanist.[41]

---

[39] I thank Claudio Lomnitz for this reference. See Consuelo Carredano, *Cuerdas revueltas: Cuarteto Latinoamericano, veinte años de música* (Ciudad de México: Fondo de Cultura Económica, 2003).

[40] "With his indigenous-art-déco visuals, a thong, an elaborated headdress and a jawbone on his hand, Ney was the Neanderthal Man for a new era, at ease on a stage so big that would have swallowed a less charismatic artist" ("con su visual indígene-art déco, de tanga, elaborado cocar y una quijada [de burro] en la mano, Ney era el hombre de Neanderthal para una nueva era, muy a gusto en un escenario tan grande que podía fácilmente tragarse a alguien con menos carisma"). Ana Maria Bahiana, "Rock in Rio: 11/1/1985 | Rock in Rio Brasil."

[41] Paulo Gustavo da Encarnação, "Rock in Rio—um festival (im)pertinente à música brasileira e à redemocratização nacional," *Patrimônio e Memória* 7, no. 1 (August 4, 2007): 348–68. The idea of South America was meaningful for many Brazilian popular artists in the 1970s. Matogrosso had composed in 1973, with his band Secos e Molhados, the song "Sangue latino" (Latin Blood): "*My life, my dead ones, my twisted roads / my Latin blood / my captive soul*" ("Minha vida, meus mortos, meus caminhos tortos / Meu sangue latino / Minh'alma cativa"). The same year Chico Buarque and Ruy Guerra wrote a song for the play *Calabar* called "Não existe pecado ao sul do Equador" (There is no sin below the equator), inspired in a seventeenth-century Latin expression (*ultra aequinoxialem non peccari*), which Buarque found quoted in his father Sérgio Buarque de Holanda's 1936 essay *Raízes do Brasil*. In 1976,

FIGURE 6.1 Ney Matogrosso in the opening act of Rock in Rio Festival, Rio de Janeiro, January 11, 1985. Photo: Sebastião Marinho / Agência O Globo–Negativo: 85-00702.

In 1996, after releasing successful collections of African, World, contemporary folk, Celtic, Caribbean, and Senegalese music (such are the categories that appear on the albums' packaging), the commercial New York label Putumayo Records released ¡Latino! ¡Latino!, followed by titles such as Afro-Latino, Nuevo Latino, Latin Groove, Radio Latino, Café Latino, and Vintage Latino, which together presented quite a wide notion of Latin American music. In 2002 the Smithsonian Institute released, as part of its prestigious collection Folkways, an album called, in Spanish, Raíces Latinas (Latin Roots).[42] Hence, as musicological categories keep changing (in 1981, for instance, UNESCO officially shifted from "folklore" to "traditional music" to designate music that was neither urban nor classical),[43] Latin American music remains relevant and widely used, even as an umbrella for vastly different and changing genres, styles, and origins. At the turn of the twenty-first century, Manu Chao,

the mythical Brazilian rocker Belchior released "Eu sou apenas um rapaz latino-americano" (I'm just a Latin-American boy), meaning a young with no money, no family connections, and coming from "the interior" (the poor provinces, in his case the Brazilian northeast). I thank Alexandra Lemos Zagonel for the latter reference.

[42] Joseph Maurer, "Latin, Latino, Latin American: music, people, and categorization in the United States," Colloquium: The Worlds of Latin American Music in the 20th Century, University of Chicago, April 18, 2017.

[43] In its Seoul 1981 meeting, the ICFM Consejo Internacional para la Música Foklórica changed its name to Consejo Internacional para las Músicas Tradicionales. See Coriún Aharonián, "Prólogo" to Lauro Ayestarán, Textos breves, ed. Coriún Aharonián, Biblioteca Artigas (Montevideo: Ministerio de Educación y Cultura, 2014), XVII.

producer Gustavo Santaolalla,[44] and others infused the Latin American rock culture with cumbia and other Latin styles—"*latino, sí, latino*" ends the 1998 cumbia-rock "Sr. Cobranza"—enriching a global, largely Miami-based corporate business around circum-Caribbean dance music today known as Latin music.[45]

Art music echoed these developments: being a Latin American composer became commonsense among composers, performers, and listeners. Contemporary composers such as Osvaldo Golijov in *Oceana* (1996) and Esteban Benzecry in *Colores de la Cruz del Sur* (2002) or *Rituales Amerindios* (2008) maintain the idea of a regional tradition from which to craft new music. Both José Abreu, founder and director of the Venezuelan *Sistema* of youth orchestras, and Gustavo Dudamel, its more famous and star conducer, present *Sistema* as both a Venezuelan project and a Latin American contribution to the world.[46]

In 1997, musicologists from the region who studied popular music created a Latin American and Caribbean branch within the International Association for the Study of Popular Music. As a regional project, in fact, Latin Americanist musicology was much older than other scientific associations, such as the North American Congress on Latin America (NACLA, 1966), the Latin American Council of Social Sciences (CLACSO, 1967), or the Latin American Studies Association (LASA, 1968). But despite having preceded this constellation of Latin American Studies of the 1960s, it renewed itself conceptually and methodologically later, thanks to the growth of ethnomusicology in the 1980s. (And to a lesser extent, to an Iberian American stream of research and publications emerged around 1992—the Fifth Centennial of the European arrival to America.) Today, Latin Americanist musicology is both an established and innovative field.[47]

One could ask whether in fact Latin American music exists as a musical tradition independently from the geopolitical frameworks that produced it—from Lange's Americanismo to today's Latin Americanist academic ethnomusicology. My research, and my reading of generations of musicological research, suggests that the music of this region only began to be perceived as Latin American when Latin America as an intellectual and geopolitical journey unfolded. It was never "out there," waiting to be uncovered. The ethno-musical threads we keep discovering in the past were not Latin American but were, say, Quechua, Basque, or Yiddish; it is our Latin Americanist framework what puts them in contact if they did not do so themselves.

---

[44] Karush, *Musicians in Transit*, chapter 6.

[45] "The Latin Recording Academy® Elects New Officers to Its Board of Trustees," Latin GRAMMYs, September 13, 2018.

[46] See Maria Majno, "From the Model of El Sistema in Venezuela to Current Applications: Learning and Integration through Collective Music Education," *Annals of the New York Academy of Sciences* 1252, no. 1 (April 1, 2012): 56–64; Freddy Sánchez, "El Sistema Nacional para las Orquestas Juveniles e Infantiles. La nueva educación musical de Venezuela," *Revista Da ABEM—Associação Brasileira de Educação Musical* 15, no. 18 (2007): 63–69.

[47] Juan Pablo González, "Musicología y América Latina: una relación posible," *Revista Argentina de Musicología*, no. 10 (2009): 43–72.

In the course of my life in the United States, I encountered a variety of cultural forms that have adopted a Latin American identity, most of which involve music. Every large US city has a Hispanic area. In Los Angeles, Miami, New York, and Chicago, this area covers immense portions of the metropolis; in smaller cities like San Francisco it is a neighborhood, where shops, street art, and associations signs make this population visible. In all of these cities, Latin American identity appears somehow related to music. In Berkeley, California, the restaurant/dance club/cultural center La Peña—*Peña* means a social gathering organized around music—recreates a regional identity strongly based on music and food, even though the people running it come from specific countries (in my time it was Chile and Peru). The Latin American Motorcycle Association (LAMA), present in several states since its foundation in 1977, uses salsa music in its promotional videos. Its bar in the Paseo Boricua of Chicago is decorated with symbols of Puerto Rican cultural and political identity, including advertisements for solidarity campaigns with jailed rebel nationalist heroes—and salsa music can be heard every few steps along the avenue. In Atlanta, the Latin American Association provides all kind of services—migratory, legal, educational, and economic—since its foundation in 1972, but its main collective event is the "Latin Fever Ball." The Mexican construction workers who moved to this city in the 1990s to build the infrastructure for the 1996 Centennial Olympics hang out today with their children, and with migrants form other countries, in a mall called Plaza Fiesta, which replicates a Mexican colonial town and is animated by diverse forms of Latin American music.

These are just a few examples from my own personal observations: the list would be endless if one considered all 58 million of people of Latin American descent in the United States, who make up 18% of its population.[48] Mexico, whose economy and population are the second largest in the region (after Brazil) and the most integrated with those of the United States, has adapted to this US version of Latin American identity. In 1998 Mexico City launched a music festival called *Vive Latino—Festival Ibero-Americano de Cultura Musical*, whose name articulates the US-based Latino identity with the old, Spanish-based Iberian one around the concept of musical culture. As two observers put it, the festival presents

> a musical frenzy, in which it will no be surprising to find a band of "Mayan rhythms" preceding a Spanish folk-rock singer, who in turn shares the stage with a US alternative rock band and a Colombian DJ . . . A demonstration of how Iberian-American rock, despite its foreign origins, has re-asserted and

---

[48] Antonio Flores, "How the U.S. Hispanic Population Is Changing," *Pew Research Center* (blog), September 18, 2017, http://www.pewresearch.org/fact-tank/2017/09/18/how-the-u-s-hispanic-population-is-changing/ (accessed October 2018). On the future of the political and statistical determinations of the future Latino identity, see Cristina Mora and Michael Rodríguez-Muñiz, "Latinos, Race, and the American Future: A Response to Richard Alba's 'The Likely Persistence of a White Majority,'" in *New Labor Forum* 26 (2017): 40–46.

re-defined the very idea of Latin America as a possibility of cultural unification that includes even Brazil, Spain, and the Spanish-speaking communities of the United States.[49]

Today, music festivals reinvent Latino identity across the United States, even in areas where Latin American immigration is less obvious or traditional, such as North Carolina.[50] Music was intrinsic to the Pan-Hispanic identity formed in the United States between the 1960s and the 1990s, and spread since then to Latin America through the Latino cultural symbols produced in the United States. (As a census category, "Hispanic/ Latino" has a cumbersome history: in 1930 the US Census included "Mexican" as an option, but this was too ambiguous for Mexican Americans, and totally off for Cubans, Puerto Ricans, and others. Still in 1969, "the U.S. Census Bureau classified Mexican Americans, Puerto Ricans, and Cuban Americans, the nation's three largest Latin American groups at the time, as white, effectively lumping their information in with data on Anglo Americans." By the mid-1980s, the Bureau instituted a new category, Hispanic.[51]) In a demographic sense, the transnational making of the region continues primarily among Latin American migrants in the United States, where individuals from different origins come to see themselves as *Latinos*—a term that is more friendly to Brazilians, who do not conceive of themselves as Hispanic. (A 2012 survey showed that half of the people of Latin American descent in the United States tend to use their family's country of origin rather than pan-ethnic terms; the other half identify as Latino/ Hispanic or American.) But a non-negligible 29% consider that US Latinos share a pan-ethnic culture.[52] This cultural regionalism has to do, among other factors, with the creation of an ethnic aesthetic identity through entertainment media that include music, as in the Billboard Latin Chart since the 1980s, the Latin Grammy awarded since 1999, and the MTV International and MTV Latino cable channels—in 2002 the first MTV Video Music

[49] "Un frenesí musical en el que no es sorprendente encontrar a una banda de "ritmos mayas" precediendo a un cantante de folk-rock español, quien a su vez comparte la cartelera con una banda de rock alterno de los Estados Unidos y un DJ de Colombia. . . . una demostración de cómo el rock iberoamericano, a pesar de sus orígenes extranjeros, ha reafirmado y redefinido la idea misma de América Latina como una posibilidad de unificación cultural que incluye incluso a Brasil, España y las comunidades de habla hispana en Estados Unidos," Mario Bahena Uriostegui and Ramón Garibaldo Valdéz, "El ruido y la nación: cómo el rock iberoamericano redefinió el sentido de comunidad en Latino América," *Diálogos: Revista electrónica de historia* 16, no. 1 (2015): 192.

[50] Samuel K Byrd, *The Sounds of Latinidad: Immigrants Making Music and Creating Culture in a Southern City* (New York: New York University Press, 2016).

[51] Cristina Mora, "Cross-Field Effects and Ethnic Classification: The Institutionalization of Hispanic Panethnicity, 1965 to 1990," *American Sociological Review* 79, no. 2 (April 1, 2014): 183–210, 183 and 190.

[52] Paul Taylor, Mark Hugo Lopez, Jessica Martínez and Gabriel Velasco, "When Labels Don't Fit: Hispanics and Their Views of Identity | Pew Research Center," April 4, 2012. A recent, gender-neutral term, *Latinx*, has been growing since 2014. Cristobal Salinas Jr. and Adele Lozano, "Mapping and Recontextualizing the Evolution of the Term Latinx: An Environmental Scanning in Higher Education," *Journal of Latinos and Education* (November 16, 2017): 1–14.

Awards–Latin America took place, and the overall winner was the Colombian singer Shakira.[53]

Music proves to be particularly capable of articulating a polysemic cultural sedimentation, from political projects, transnational experiences for Latino populations in the United States, commercial and community-oriented musical brokers, ethnomusicology, and of course, artists and audiences. The Latino festivals in both US and Mexican cities are adopting a category that results from a long prehistory of musical practices that, as I have shown in this book, invented Latin America as a cultural-aesthetic region in the 1930s.

---

[53] Cristina Mora, *Making Hispanics: How Activists, Bureaucrats, and Media Constructed a New American* (Chicago: University of Chicago Press, 2014). "Latino Solanas," a fictional character, first appeared on the Argentine public television in 2009, created by humorists Diego Capusotto and Pedro Saborido, made fun of the Latin American MTV US-based Latino rhetoric, and of the influence of Puerto Rican and Caribbean hip-hop music across the hemisphere. Latino Solanas's full stage name is (depending on the episode) "D+D Daddy Moncho Mamani/ Blackberry/ Dr. Dumbo Montoya Fidel Castro Hugo Chávez/ Dr. Bolas Ricardo Arjona Latino Solanas," but his real name is a European immigrant one: "Mariano Grunberg Hollester Jurguensen Smith/ Mastrodonato." See https://es-la.facebook.com/Latino-Solanas-125462528365/ (Season 5, 2009).

EPILOGUE

A Century of Latin American Music

IN THE FIRST decade of the 2000s Latin America was resurrected as a pragmatic regional project by a group of center-left and neodevelopmental governments. Economic growth, progressive policies (higher minimum wages, industrialization, and expansive labor and social rights), and agricultural exports to feed a booming East Asian demand enabled an integrationist revival, led by Brazil's promotion of regional and global alliances. Brazil's Latin Americanism was not a sudden innovation of the Workers Party and President Lula: it had been announced in the 1988 Constitution, whose Article 4 reads: "The Federative Republic of Brazil will seek the economic, political, social, and cultural integration of the peoples of Latin America, in order to create a Latin American community of nations."[1] When I began this research in 2007, Latin American and Caribbean governments moved toward the creation of new regional organizations, the most ambitious of which were the Union of South American Nations (UNASUR, 2008) and the Community of Latin American and Caribbean States (CELAC, 2011). It seemed as if a previous, long history of regional integration was being resumed with pragmatic impetus.

---

[1] "A República Federativa do Brasil buscará a integração econômica, política, social e cultural dos povos da América Latina, visando à formação de uma comunidade latino-americana de nações," http://www. planalto.gov.br/ccivil_03/Constituicao/Constituicao.htm.

The Invention of Latin American Music. Pablo Palomino, Oxford University Press (2020). © Oxford University Press.
DOI: 10.1093/oso/9780190687403.001.0001

Like in past attempts of integration, the geography and the end point of this new regionalism were uncertain.[2] At the time of the fight for decolonization, the Trinidadian C. L. R. James, a pre-eminent activist and historian of the Caribbean, pursued an independentist regionalism that saw the Caribbean future as intrinsically tied to Africa: when discussing in 1958 the future of the British Guyana—"a baby" lost in the "big, and very dark . . . Latin American woods"—he recommended its foreign relations to follow its "natural historical evolution," meaning its federation with the West Indian islands, with whom it shared the language and historical experience of British colonialism, but he also explicitly explored the possibility of a further widening of a federation to encompass Cuba and Haiti, countries of different colonial and linguistic roots.[3] The region's plurinational organizations evolved in fact like a puzzle: the Community of Andean Nations (CAN) created in 1969 and the Caribbean Community (CARICOM) from 1973 were joined by the Mercosur (1991), the Bolivarian Alliance (ALBA, 2004), and the Pacific Alliance (2011), each proposing a different geography and a different vision. The title of the first CARICOM book series in 2000 reflected the challenge of all these countries and organizations: *Unity in Adversity*.[4] UNASUR and CELAC were born precisely as comprehensive and ambitious organizations to encompass those multiple, overlapping regional projects, none of which was completely inclusive.[5] They would pave the road, in a still unforeseeable future, to common rules for regional autonomy, development, finance, defense, and last but not least, democracy. These organizations were purposely independent from the United States-dominated OAS (the former Pan American Union, the only fully hemispheric organization that includes also the United States and Canada). Brazil led the promotion of both UNASUR and CELAC as the region's largest economic and demographic actor and a long-term aspirant to a permanent seat at the UN Security Council. It also created two regionally oriented universities: one for Latin American Integration (UNILA in Foz do Iguazú, by the triple frontier with Paraguay and Argentina, in 2007) and another for the Afro-Brazilian Lusophony (UNILAB 2010, in the northeastern state of Ceará, aiming at Africa). Integration was thus a keyword around the first decade of the twenty-first century.

---

[2] This open and uncertain "constructedness" of the region is not exclusive to Latin America, but inherent to all supra- and transnational regions in global history. See Paul Kramer, "Region in Global History," in *A Companion to World History*, ed. Douglas Northtrop (Chichester, West Sussex: Blackwell, 2012), 201–12.

[3] C. L. R. James, "Lecture on Federation, (West Indies and British Guiana)," Marxists.org, 1958 (https://www.marxists.org/archive/james-clr/works/1958/06/federation.htm) and "The Artist In The Caribbean," *Caribbean Quarterly* 54, no. 1/2 (2008): 177–80. See also Minkah Makalani, "The Politically Unimaginable in Black Marxist Thought," *Small Axe: A Caribbean Journal of Criticism* 22, no. 2 (July 1, 2018): 18–34.

[4] Kenneth O. Hall, *CARICOM: Unity in Adversity* (Georgetown, Guyana: UWI-CARICOM Project, 2000). The publishing series is titled "The Integrationist Books."

[5] Nand C. Bardouille, "Caribbean Regionalisms in a Comparative-Historical Perspective: The Making of Four Regional Systems," *Canadian Journal of Latin American and Caribbean Studies / Revue Canadienne Des Études Latino-Américaines et Caraïbes* 43, no. 2 (May 4, 2018): 171–211. The institutional complexity

How did music play into these regional initiatives centered on economics, education, and politics? Just to take the example of Mercosur, in 1998 the Mercosur Youth Symphonic Orchestra debuted at the University of Morón in the Greater Buenos Aires area with a Europeanist program of vaguely Latin and broadly American connotations: Ravel's "Bolero," a Rachmaninov concerto, and Dvorjak's "New World" symphony. The musicians were members of regional orchestras that participated in UNESCO's system of youth orchestras, inspired by Venezuela's El Sistema. Whereas in 2003 music from the Mercosur countries was displayed in Buenos Aires' record stores under the label "World Music," in 2008, the Festival de la Música del Litoral, organized since 1963 in Posadas, Misiones, changed its name to the Festival de la Música del Litoral *y del Mercosur*, and began to include artists from nearby towns of Brazil and Paraguay. In 2009 the Parlasur, a congress of representatives from the Mercosur countries, launched a series called *Latin-American: Music for the Integration* (*Latinoamericana: Música para la Integración*) at the Teatro Solís in Uruguay, with artists from the Mercosur countries plus Chile. In November 2015 the first Festival Cultural del Mercosur took place in Asunción, Paraguay. Artists included Tonolec, a duo of electronic music from Chaco performing songs in Spanish and Toba.[6]

State and, as this book as shown, *regional* support for music is essential, in the form of funding but above all of the creation of economic and legal structures in which musicians could earn their lives. Music-related jobs keep growing in numbers in the twenty-first century, people increasingly professionalize their training, and the cultural industry and markets keep expanding. But labor markets, traditionally a model of flexibility, creates precarious jobs, combining both old and new forms of inequality.[7]

As I write these words in 2019, that integrationist movement has lost momentum and actually reversed. Right-wing governments across South America are simply

---

of the Caribbean organizations is shaped by the quite diverse sovereign statuses of the Caribbean countries, and to the weight of British Commonwealth, France, Netherlands, European Union, United States, and the global finance in them. The main projects are the Caribbean Community (CARICOM 1973, originally British former colonies, it expanded to non-Anglophone neighbors and since 2003 it has a common Caribbean Court of Justice); the Organization of Eastern Caribbean States (OECS, 1981, small Lesser Antilles, in 2010 advanced to economic union and already have single currency—the Western Caribbean Dollar, featuring Queen Elizabeth—and freedom of movement among them); the Caribbean Forum of the African, Caribbean, and Pacific Group of States (CARIFORUM, 1992, a wide but not really operative "forum"); and the Association of Caribbean States (ACS 1994, the largest but less formally institutionalized of them; it however takes the "Caribbean Sea" as a common environmental, cultural, and social space and the "Greater Caribbean" as a "political concept," 191).

[6] See Silvana Contreras, "Industria de la música, 'world music' y MERCOSUR," *Oficios Terrestres* 13 (2003): 132; https://www.lanacion.com.ar/86390-ya-suena-la-musica-del-mercosur; https://posadasantiguaymoderna.wordpress.com/festival-del-litoral-y-del-mercosur/; https://www.parlamentomercosur.org/innovaportal/v/1025/1/parlasur/latinoamericana-musica-para-la-integracion.html; and http://www.abc.com.py/espectaculos/musica/la-musica-del-cono-sur-reunida-1424498.html (accessed October 2018).

[7] Rocío Guadarrama Olivera, "Mercado de trabajo y geografía de la música de concierto en México," *Espacialidades. Revista de temas contemporáneos sobre lugares, política y cultura* 3, no. 2 (2013): 192–216.

abandoning UNASUR. The Parliament of the Mercosur is paralyzed. Some of the few remaining regional organizations, like the Pacific Alliance, focus less on integration than on "branding" their nations to attract foreign investments. CELAC became a marginal diplomatic forum. Governments throughout the region gave up supranational integration and the search of regional autonomy, to be brokers of trade agreements with the United States, China, the World Trade Organization, the European Union, and other bilateral agreements. The socially reformist aspects of integrationism are being buried by a neoliberal agenda that, as in the cycle of "structural reforms" of the 1980s and 1990s, subordinates the region's economy to global financial and trade interests.[8]

If the past is any guide, projects of regional integration have constantly re-emerged in the history of Latin America.[9] Despite the current decline of diplomatic integrationism, the region keeps feeding cross-pollinating movements of population, ideas, and politics, adding to the slow and persistent sedimentation of two centuries of projects. In a small but meaningful scale, the transnational academic field built around those sediments—Latin American studies—also transmits them, even in the work of scholars often unaware of the essentialist, racialist roots of the epistemological criteria that sustain the field, and of those who question, for good reasons, the very existence of the region. Latin America is not a historically rigorous delimitation, but neither it is just a romantic invocation or a melancholic lamentation of a racial and therefore radical sociocultural difference from the United States. Latin Americanist scholarship has expanded geographically toward the Atlantic, the Pacific, and the globe in the last decade—in some cases under the vague and ethnocentric category of the Global South, which confuses more than it clarifies.[10] Perhaps it is time to look at Latin America as *a history of cultural projects*. From this perspective, it definitely exists. The project of Latin American music, in particular, became a transnational academic and business field, and future political projects may make use of it.

Like Africa, the Muslim world, and other transnational categories, the Latin American and Caribbean region was object of *orientalizing*—in our case, as historian José Moya put it, *australizing*—imperial and intellectual interests. But as this book demonstrates, the region's history of musical practices also created its own discourses and identities. The ambiguities in its ethnic identity and its evidently politico-cultural nature made this invention successful. The region may have been

---

[8] Quinn Slobodian, *Globalists: The End of Empire and the Birth of Neoliberalism* (Cambridge, MA: Harvard University Press, 2018); Juan Carlos Torre, "El lanzamiento político de las reformas estructurales en América Latina," *Política y Gobierno (CIDE)* 4, no. 2 (1997): 471–96.

[9] Salvador Rivera, *Latin American Unification: A History of Political and Economic Integration Efforts* (Jefferson, NC: McFarland & Co., 2014).

[10] Allison Margaret Bigelow and Thomas Miller Klubock, "Introduction to Latin American Studies and the Humanities: Past, Present, Future," *Latin American Research Review* 53, no. 3 (September 28, 2018): 573–80.

invented, and it may even look like Frankenstein from some angles, but the invention is certainly alive.[11]

If anything, the formation of this musical region reveals that Latin America is neither a self-evident truth nor a colonial artifice, but rather a historical entity that *came to be* as a transnational project—one in which multiple ideological and episte-mological currents were able to pursue their goals and experience both success and failure. In 1919, Cortijo Alahija's published a strange and pioneering text on "Latin-American musicology." Today, music has an accepted place both in international aca-demia and as a symbol of a Latin American (and *Latino*) culture. Within one century, music played a central role in carving out a regional identity in a globalizing world. Latin America as a category may have had diplomatic and political origins, but music was the arena in which education, commerce, and popular culture disseminated it as a world-regional identity. National projects were essential to the development of this identity, through their participation in transnational exchanges. And the United States was always part of the picture—*the other* of Latin America, its unavoidable continuation, althoug partially being Latin American itself (somehow like the image historian Claudio Lomnitz proposed to capture the relationship between Mexico and the United States, likening them to the North and the South of Antonio Gramsci's Italy).

The role of musical practices in creating the very concept of Latin America has been surprisingly absent from scholarly reflection. Whereas the romantic view of the early scholars valorized authenticity over political inventions, modern ethnomusicolo-gists, whose field developed just as Latin America and the Caribbean were becom-ing legitimate areas of study, wanted to explore the research possibilities of Latin America and consolidate it as a field, rather than questioning the category of Latin America itself. And yet music was the arena in which erudite traditions, popular cul-ture, state populism, and commercial transnationalism converged most naturally, in the 1930s, to *create* shared images of the region. It was so successful at it, that no one questioned the reality of this musical region.

The category of Latin American music emerged at a different time of nationalism and globalization. It infused state public education and connected with listening and performing habits in turn shaped by tradition and commercial culture. Those realms—musicology, state cultural policy, and popular culture—were, as this book has shown, deeply transnational, even when they channeled nationalist aspirations. Because music spoke then to the very making of Latin America, it provides a tem-plate for understanding now the mechanisms that keep producing the place of Latin America in the conflictive global culture we inhabit.

---

[11] Edmundo O'Gorman, *La invención de América: el universalismo de la cultura de occidente* (México, D.F.: Fondo de Cultura Económica, 1985 [1958]); Cemil Aydin, *The Idea of the Muslim World: A Global Intellectual History* (Cambridge, MA: Harvard University Press, 2017); Frederick Cooper, *Africa in the World: Capitalism, Empire, Nation-State* (Cambridge, MA: Harvard University Press, 2014).

Bibliography

Abreu, Martha. "Histórias musicais da Primeira República." *Artcultura* 13, no. 22 (2011): 71–83.

Abreu, Martha, and Carolina Vianna Dantas. "Música popular, folclore e nação no Brasil, 1890–1920." In *Nação e cidadania no Império: novos horizontes*, edited by José Murilo de Carvalho, 123–51. Rio de Janeiro: Civilização Brasileira, 2007.

Acree, William. *Everyday Reading: Print Culture and Collective Identity in the Río de La Plata, 1780–1910.* Nashville: Vanderbilt University Press, 2011.

Acree, William. "Hemispheric Travelers on the Rioplatense Stage." *Latin American Theatre Review* 47, no. 2 (2014): 5–24.

Adamovsky, Ezequiel. *Historia de la clase media argentina: apogeo y decadencia de una ilusión, 1919–2003.* Buenos Aires: Planeta, 2015.

Adamovsky, Ezequiel. "La cuarta función del criollismo y las luchas por la definición del origen y el color del ethnos argentino (desde las primeras novelas gauchescas hasta c. 1940)." *Boletín del Instituto de Historia Argentina y Americana Dr. Emilio Ravignani* 41 (2014): 50–92.

Aduriz, Iñigo. "El PP, un día después de la irrupción de Vox: 'Lo mejor que les puede pasar a los hispanoamericanos es que su hija se case con un español.'" *eldiario.es*, March 12, 2018.

Aguirre Lora, María Esther. "En pos de la construcción del sentido de lo nacional. Universos sonoros y dancísticos en la escuela mexicana (1920–1940)." *Historia de la Educación* 25 (2006): 205–24.

Aharonián, Coriún. "Carlos Vega y la teoría de la música popular: un enfoque latinoamericano en un ensayo pionero." *Revista Musical Chilena* 51, no. 188 (1997): 61–74.

Allende, Pedro Humberto. *Método original de iniciación musical para liceos y escuelas primarias de la América latina.* Santiago de Chile: Imp. y Lit. Casa Amarilla, 1937.

Almeida, Marcelo Crisafuli Nascimento. "Música popular em Minas Gerais no século XIX: São João del Rei, um estudo de caso." *Temporalidades* 2, no. 2 (2010): 43–49.

Alonso Bolaños, Marina. La "invención" de la música indígena de México: antropología e historia de las políticas culturales del siglo XX. Buenos Aires: SB Ediciones, 2008.

Alonso, Cecilio. "Semblanza de Editorial Mundo Latino (1915–1931)." Biblioteca Virtual Miguel de Cervantes—Portal Editores y Editoriales Iberoamericanos (siglos XIX–XXI), 2017.

Alvares, Felipe Batistella. "Milonga, chamamé, chimarrita e vaneira: origens, inserção no Rio Grande do Sul e os princípios de execução ao contrabaixo." Tesis de Licenciatura en Música, Universidade Federal de Santa María, 2007.

Alvarez, Sonia E., Arturo Arias, and Charles R. Hale. "Re-Visioning Latin American Studies." Cultural Anthropology 26, no. 2 (2011): 225–46.

Andrade, Mario de. "A pronúncia cantada e o problema do nasal através dos discos." Projeto História : Revista do Programa de Estudos Pós-Graduados de História 26 [1937] (June 2003): 75–91.

Applegate, Celia. "Introduction: Music Among the Historians." German History 30, no. 3 (September 1, 2012): 329–49.

Archetti, Eduardo. "Hibridación, diversidad y generalización en el mundo ideológico del fútbol y el polo." Prismas. Revista de Historia Intelectual 1 (1997): 53–76.

Archetti, Eduardo. "In Search of National Identity: Argentinian Football and Europe." International Journal of the History of Sport 12, no. 2 (1995): 201–19.

Archetti, Eduardo. Masculinities: Football, Polo, and the Tango in Argentina. Oxford: Berg, 1999.

Archetti, Eduardo. "Nationalisme, football et polo: tradition et créolisation dans la construction de l'Argentine moderne." Terrain: carnets du patrimoine ethnologique 25 (1995): 73–90.

Ardao, Arturo. "Panamericanismo y latinoamericanismo." In América latina en sus ideas, edited by Leopoldo Zea, 157–71. Mexico, D.F.: Unesco-Siglo XXI, 1986.

Aretz, Isabel, ed. América latina en su música. Paris: UNESCO, 1977.

Arndt, Richard T. The First Resort of Kings: American Cultural Diplomacy in the Twentieth Century. Washington, D.C.: Potomac Books Inc., 2005.

Ashe, Jennifer. "Modernism and Social Consciousness: Seeger, Cowell, Crawford, and the Composers [Sic] Collective, 1931–1936." PhD diss., New England Conservatory of Music, 2006.

Asociación Argentina de Autores y Compositores de Música. "Memoria y balance presentado a la Asamblea General Ordinaria, 1 de Agosto de 1929." Asociación Argentina de Autores y Compositores de Música, 1929.

Astor, Miguel. "Los ojos de Sojo: el conflicto entre nacionalismo y modernidad en los Festivales de Música de Caracas (1954–1966)." PhD diss., Universidad Central de Venezuela, 2008.

Atkins, E. Taylor. Blue Nippon: Authenticating Jazz in Japan. Durham, NC: Duke University Press, 2001.

Aubin, Myrian Ribeiro. "Francisco Curt Lange e sua atuação nos meios musical e político em Belo Horizonte: constituição de uma rede de sociabilidades." OPUS 22, no. 1 (May 9, 2016): 299–338.

Augusto, Antonio. "A civilização como missão: o conservatório de música no Império do Brasil." Revista Brasileira de Música 23, no. 1 (2010): 67–91.

Avelar, Idelber, and Christopher Dunn. Brazilian Popular Music and Citizenship. Durham, NC: Duke University Press, 2011.

Avila, Jacqueline A. "Los Sonidos Del Cine: Cinematic Music in Mexican Film, 1930–1950." PhD diss., University of California, Riverside, 2011.

Aydin, Cemil. *The Idea of the Muslim World: A Global Intellectual History*. Cambridge, MA: Harvard University Press, 2017.

Ayestarán, Lauro. *Textos breves*. Edited by Coriún Aharonián. Biblioteca Artigas. Montevideo: Ministerio de Educación y Cultura, 2014.

Azevedo, Luiz H. Corrêa de. *A Escola Nacional de Música e as pesquisas de folclore musical no Brasil*. Rio de Janeiro: Centro de Pesquisas Folclóricas–Universidade Federal do Rio de Janeiro, 1944.

Azevedo, Luiz H. Corrêa de. "L'Unesco et La Musique Populaire." *Journal of the International Folk Music Council* 1 (1949): 19–21.

Baim, Jo. *Tango: Creation of a Cultural Icon*. Bloomington: Indiana University Press, 2007.

Baldasarre, María Isabel. "América latina y la idea de una 'modernidad global', 1895–1915." *DezenoveVinte. Arte no Brasil do século XIX e início do XX*, December 2015. http://www.deze-novevinte.net/.

Barajas, Manuel. *México y la cultura musical*. México, D.F.: Departamento Autónomo de Prensa y Publicidad, 1938.

Barbato Júnior, Roberto. *Missionários de uma utopia nacional-popular: os intelectuais e o Departamento de Cultura de São Paulo*. São Paulo: FAPESP/Annablume, 2004.

Barbero, María Inés, and Andrés Martín Regalsky. *Americanización: Estados Unidos y América latina en el siglo XX: transferencias económicas, tecnológicas y culturales*. Buenos Aires: Universidad Nacional de Tres de Febrero, 2014.

Barbour, Philip L. "Commercial and Cultural Broadcasting in Mexico." *Annals of the American Academy of Political and Social Science* 208 (March 1, 1940): 94–102.

Bardouille, Nand C. "Caribbean Regionalisms in a Comparative-Historical Perspective: The Making of Four Regional Systems." *Canadian Journal of Latin American and Caribbean Studies / Revue Canadienne Des Études Latino-Américaines et Caraïbes* 43, no. 2 (May 4, 2018): 171–211.

Barth, Gunther Paul. *City People: The Rise of Modern City Culture in Nineteenth-Century America*. New York: Oxford University Press, 1980.

Beach, Frederick Converse, and George Edwin Rines, eds. *The Encyclopedia Americana: A Universal Reference Library. Comprising the Arts and Sciences, Literature, History, Biography, Geography, Commerce, Etc., of the World*. New York: Scientific American Compyling Department, 1904.

Bean, Annemarie, James Vernon Hatch, and Brooks McNamara. *Inside the Minstrel Mask: Readings in Nineteenth-Centuryblackface Minstrelsy*. Hanover, NH: Wesleyan University Press, 1996.

Beattie, John, and Louis Woodson Curtis. "South American Music Pilgrimage. II. Ecuador and Peru." *Music Educators Journal* 28, no. 3 (1942): 12–18.

Becker, Howard, and Robert R. Faulkner. *"Do You Know . . . ?": The Jazz Repertoire in Action*. Chicago: University of Chicago Press, 2009.

Becker, Marc. "Comunistas, indigenistas e indígenas en la formación de la Federación Ecuatoriana de Indios y el Instituto Indigenista Ecuatoriano." *Íconos. Revista de Ciencias Sociales* 27 (January 2007): 135–44.

Béhague, Gerard. "Boundaries and Borders in the Study of Music in Latin America: A Conceptual Re-Mapping." *Latin American Music Review / Revista de Música Latinoamericana* 21, no. 1 (April 1, 2000): 16–30.

Béhague, Gerard. "Editorial Note." *Latin American Music Review / Revista de Música Latinoamericana* 1, no. 1 (1980): 1–1.

Beilinson, Federico, Pablo Gindre, and Joaquín Zaidman, eds., *El libro de la folcloreishon.* Buenos Aires: Ediciones Biblioteca Nacional, 2014.

Benzecry, Claudio. *The Opera Fanatic: Ethnography of an Obsession.* Chicago: University of Chicago Press, 2011.

Benzecry, Claudio. "An Opera House for the 'Paris of South America': Pathways to the Institutionalization of High Culture." *Theory and Society* 43, no. 2 (March 1, 2014): 169–96.

Bergel, Martín. "América latina, pero desde abajo: prácticas y representaciones intelectuales de un ciclo histórico latinoamericanista, 1898–1936." *Cuadernos de Historia (Santiago)* no. 36 (June 2012): 7–36.

Bergel, Martín. *El Oriente desplazado. Los intelectuales y los orígenes del tercermundismo en la Argentina* (Bernal, Argentina: Universidad Nacional de Quilmes, 2015).

Bergel, Martín. "Nomadismo proselitista y revolución. notas para una caracterización del primer exilio aprista (1923–1931)." *EIAL: Estudios Interdisciplinarios de América Latina y el Caribe* 20, no. 1 (2009): 41–66.

Bernal Jiménez, Miguel. *El archivo musical del Colegio de Santa Rosa de Santa María de Vallodolid, siglo XVIII, Morelia colonial. Sociedad Amigos de la Música.* Morelia, Mexico: Universidad Michoacana de San Nicolás, 1939.

Bernal Jiménez, Miguel. *La disciplina coral.* Morelia: Escuela Superior de Música Sagrada, 1947.

Bernal Jiménez, Miguel. "Música nuestra: breve ensayo sobre la música mejicana." *Estudios Americanos* 1, no. 1 (1948): 109–17.

Bernal, Rafael. *México en Filipinas: estudio de una transculturación.* México: Universidad Nacional Autónoma de México, 1965.

Bernand, Carmen. "'Musiques Métisses', musiques criollas. Sons, gestes et paroles en Amérique hispanique." *L'Homme. Revue Française d'anthropologie* no. 207–208 (2013): 193–214.

Bertoni, Lilia Ana. *Patriotas, cosmopolitas y nacionalistas: la construcción de la nacionalidad argentina a fines del siglo XIX.* Buenos Aires: Fondo de Cultura Económica, 2001.

Bigelow, Allison Margaret, and Thomas Miller Klubock. "Introduction to Latin American Studies and the Humanities: Past, Present, Future." *Latin American Research Review* 53, no. 3 (September 28, 2018): 573–80.

Bindas, Kenneth J. *All of This Music Belongs to the Nation: The WPA's Federal Music Project and American Society.* Knoxville: University of Tennessee Press, 1995.

Black, Ashley. "Canto Libre. Folk Music and Solidarity in the Americas, 1967–1974." In *The Art of Solidarity: Visual and Performative Politics in Cold War Latin America*, edited by Jessica Stites Mor, 117–45. Austin: University of Texas Press, 2018.

Bocco, Andrea Alejandra. "Tensiones entre proyectos intelectuales, políticas estatales y emergencia de las masas en los cancioneros populares." *Anclajes* 13, no. 1 (June 2009): 27–40.

Bockelman, Brian. "Between the Gaucho and the Tango: Popular Songs and the Shifting Landscape of Modern Argentine Identity, 1895–1915." *American Historical Review* 116, no. 3 (June 2011): 577–601.

Boletín de la Secretaría de Educación Pública, México, 1922.

Boletín del Instituto de Cultura Latino-Americana. Universidad de Buenos Aires, 1937.

Boletín Latino-Americano de Música. 6 vols., 1935–1946.

Bolton, Herbert E. "The Epic of Greater America." *American Historical Review* 38, no. 3 (April 1933): 448–74.

Borge, Jason. "The Portable Jazz Age: Josephine Baker's Tour of South American Cities (1929)." In *Urban Latin America: Images, Words, Flows and the Built Environment*, edited by Bianca Freire-Medeiros and Julia O'Donnell, 127–41. New York: Routledge, 2018).

Borges, Jorge Luis. "El atroz redentor Lazarus Morell." In *Historia universal de la infamia [1935]*. Buenos Aires: Emecé, 1953.

Borges, Jorge Luis. "Prólogo." In *Obra crítica de Pedro Henríquez Ureña. Edición, bibliografía e índice onomástico por Emma Susana Speratti Piñero*, VII–X. México, D.F.: Fondo de Cultura Económica, 1960.

Borras, Gérard. *Chansonniers de Lima: le vals et la chanson criolla, 1900–1936*. Rennes: Presses Universitaires de Rennes, 2009.

Borucki, Alex. "From Colonial Performers to Actors of 'American Liberty': Black Artists in Bourbon and Revolutionary Río de La Plata." *The Americas* 75, no. 2 (April 2018): 261–89.

Braga Martins, Luiza Mara. *Os Oito Batutas: história e música brasileira nos anos 1920*. Rio de Janeiro: Editora Universidade Federal do Rio de Janeiro, 2014.

Bronfman, Alejandra. *Isles of Noise: Sonic Media in the Caribbean*. Chapel Hill: University of North Carolina Press, 2016.

Bronfman, Alejandra, and Andrew Grant Wood. *Media, Sound, and Culture in Latin America and the Caribbean*. Pittsburgh: University of Pittsburgh Press, 2012.

Buarque de Hollanda, Chico. *Sinal Fechado*. LP. Vol. 6349 122. Brazil: Phillips, 1974.

Buch, Esteban. "La censura del tango por la iglesia francesa en vísperas de la Gran Guerra (con una postdata de Erik Satie)." *Revista Argentina de Musicología*, no. 15–16 (2015): 79–102.

Buch, Esteban. *La Neuvième de Beethoven: Une histoire politique*. Paris: Gallimard, 1999.

Buch, Esteban, ed. *Tangos cultos: Kagel, J. J. Castro, Mastropiero y otros cruces musicales*. Buenos Aires: Gourmet Musical, 2012.

Buchanan, Fannie. *Musical Moments from Latin America*. Ames: Iowa State College of Agricultural and Mechanic Arts, 1940.

Burke, Peter. *Cultural Hybridity*. Cambridge: Polity, 2014.

Butsch, Richard. *The Making of American Audiences: From Stage to Television, 1750–1990*. Cambridge: Cambridge University Press, 2000.

Byrd, Samuel K. *The Sounds of Latinidad: Immigrants Making Music and Creating Culture in a Southern City*. New York: New York University Press, 2016.

Cadícamo, Enrique. *La historia del tango en París*. Buenos Aires: Ediciones Corregidor, 1975.

Calvo, Carlos. *Anales históricos de la revolución de la América Latina, acompañados de los documentos en su apoyo: Desde el año 1808 hasta el reconocimiento de la independencia de ese extenso continente*. A. Durand, 1865.

Campbell, Courtney. "The Brazilian Northeast, Inside Out: Region, Nation, and Globalization (1926–1968)." PhD diss., Vanderbilt University, 2014.

Campbell, Jennifer L. "Creating Something Out of Nothing: The Office of Inter-American Affairs Music Committee (1940–1941) and the Inception of a Policy for Musical Diplomacy." *Diplomatic History* 36, no. 1 (2012): 29–39.

Campbell, Jennifer L. "Shaping Solidarity: Music, Diplomacy, and Inter-American Relations, 1936–1946." PhD diss., University of Connecticut, 2010.

Campos, Rubén M. *Los orfeones populares en la cultura nacional.* Mexico, D.F.: Secretaría de Guerra y Marina–Departamento de Militarización–Sección Cuarta–Orfeones, Publicaciones del Departamento de Militarización para su propaganda en toda la República–Imprenta Victoria, 1918.

Canales, Alejandro I. "Panorama actual de la migración internacional en América Latina." *Revista Latinoamericana de Población* 4–5 (October 31, 2015): 65–91.

Cañardo, Marina. "Cantantes, orquestas y micrófonos: la interpretación del tango y la tecnología de grabación." *Afuera: Estudios de Crítica Cultural* 10 (May 2011). http://www.revistaafuera.com/articulo.php?id=170&nro=10.

Cañardo, Marina. *Fábricas de músicas. Comienzos de la industria discográfica en la Argentina (1919–1930).* Buenos Aires: Gourmet Musical, 2017.

Canaro, Francisco. *Mis bodas de oro con el tango y mis memorias, 1906–1956.* Buenos Aires: CESA, 1957.

Cándida Smith, Richard. "Érico Veríssimo, a Brazilian Cultural Ambassador in the United States." *Tempo* 19, no. 34 (2013): 147–73.

Cándida Smith, Richard. *Improvised Continent: Pan-Americanism and Cultural Exchange.* Philadelphia: University of Pennsylvania Press, 2017.

Caravaca, Jimena and Ximena Espeche. "América Latina como problema y como solución: Robert Triffin, Daniel Cosío Villegas, Víctor Urquidi y Raúl Prebisch 'antes' del Manifiesto Latinoamericano (1944–1946)." *Desarrollo Económico* 55, no. 217 (2016): 411–35.

Carlini, Alvaro Luiz Ribeiro da Silva. "Recuperação e preservação do acervo histórico-fonográfico da Discoteca Municipal de São Paulo." *Folha de São Paulo—Leitura*, December 12, 1993.

Carpentier, Alejo. *Crónicas.* La Habana: Instituto Cubano del Libro–Arte y Literatura, 1975.

Carredano, Consuelo. *Cuerdas revueltas: Cuarteto Latinoamericano, veinte años de música.* 1st ed. Colección popular 447. Ciudad de México: Fondo de Cultura Económica, 2003.

Carvalho, José Murilo de. "Mandonismo, coronelismo, clientelismo: uma discussão conceitual." *Dados* 40, no. 2 (1997): 229–50.

Casa de las Américas, 1959–2009. La Habana: Casa de las Américas, 2014.

Cassani, Joseph. *Glorias del segundo siglo de la compañia de Jesus, dibuxadas en las vidas y elogios de algunos de sus varones ilustres en virtud, letras y zelo de los almas que han florecido desde el año de 1640, primero del segundo siglo desde la aprobacion de la Religion.* Madrid: Manuel Fernandez, Impresor, 1734.

Castañeda, Daniel. "La música y la revolución Mexicana." *Boletín Latino Americano de Música* 5 (1941): 437–48.

Castro, J. Justin. *Radio in Revolution: Wireless Technology and State Power in Mexico, 1897–1938.* Lincoln: University of Nebraska Press, 2016.

Castro, Maricruz, and Robert McKee Irwin. *El cine mexicano "se impone": mercados internacionales y penetración cultural en la época dorada.* México: Universidad Nacional Autónoma de México, 2011.

Catálogo de la colección de folklore. Buenos Aires: Facultad de Filosofía y Letras, Universidad de Buenos Aires, Instituto de Literatura Argentina, 1925.

Caudarella, María Florencia. *La necesidad del espectáculo: aspectos sociales del teatro porteño, 1918–1930.* Rosario, Argentina: Prohistoria, 2016.

Cetrangolo, Aníbal Enrique. "Del arpa de Viggiano al organito porteño, músicos ambulantes y ópera." *Etno-Folk: Revista Galega de Etnomusicoloxía*, no. 14 (2009): 596–621.

Cetrangolo, Aníbal Enrique. *Ópera, barcos y banderas: el melodrama y la migración en Argentina (1880–1920)*. Madrid: Biblioteca Nueva, 2015.

Chamosa, Oscar. *The Argentine Folklore Movement : Sugar Elites, Criollo Workers, and the Politics of Cultural Nationalism, 1900–1955*. Tucson: University of Arizona Press, 2010.

Chase, Gilbert. "An Anniversary and a New Start." *Anuario / Yearbook / Anuário of the Inter-American Institute for Musical Research* 1 (1965): 1–10.

Chávez, Carlos. "Festivales Sinfónicos de Música Panamericana—Convocatoria." *Música—Revista Mexicana* 1, no. 4 (July 15, 1930): 3–4.

Chávez, Carlos. "Nacionalismo musical—II—El arte popular y el no popular." *Música—Revista Mexicana* 1, no. 4 (July 15, 1930): 18–22.

Chen, Szu-Wei. "The Rise and Generic Features of Shanghai Popular Songs in the 1930s and 1940s." *Popular Music* 24, no. 01 (2005): 107–25.

Cherñavsky, Analía. "O nacionalismo musical e a necessidade de formação do público." Salvador, Bahía, 2008.

Chevalier, Michel. "Letters on North America." Translated by Steven Rowan. *University of Missouri-St. Louis Institutional Repository Library—Original Edition Paris: Gosselin, 1836*, n.d., 434.

Chica Geliz, Ricardo, and Miguel Camacho Manjarrez. *El cine mexicano y la cartelera cinematográfica de Cartagena, 1939–1945*. Cartagena: Editorial Universitaria de la Universidad de Cartagena, 2017.

Chindemi Vila, Julia, and Pablo Vila. "La música popular argentina entre el campo y la ciudad: música campera, criolla, nativa, folklórica, canción federal y tango." *ArtCultura (Universidade Federal de Uberlândia)* 19, no. 34 (2017): 9–26.

Chouitem, Dorothée. "Cádiz, cuna de la murga uruguaya: ¿mitificación de los orígenes?" *Memorias: revista digital de historia y arqueología desde El Caribe* 32 (2017): 39–61.

Chust, Alicia. *Tangos, orfeones y rondallas: una historia con imágenes*. Barcelona: Carena, 2008.

Clark, Roland. "Collective Singing in Romanian Fascism." *Cultural and Social History* 10, no. 2 (2013): 251–71.

Cohen, Ronald D. *Rainbow Quest: The Folk Music Revival and American Society, 1940–1970*. Amherst: University of Massachusetts Press, 2002.

Cohen, Theodore. "Among Races, Nations, and Diasporas: Genealogies of 'La Bamba' in Mexico and the United States." *Studies in Latin American Popular Music* 35 (2017): 51–78.

Collier, Simon. *The Life, Music & Times of Carlos Gardel*. Pittsburgh: University of Pittsburgh Press, 1986.

Comité Editorial. "El Instituto Interamericano de Educación Musical." *Revista Musical Chilena* 30, no. 134 (January 1, 1976): 111–14.

Compagnon, Olivier. *L'adieu à l'Europe: l'Amérique latine et la Grande Guerre (Argentine et Brésil, 1914–1939)*. Paris: Fayard, 2013.

Consejo Nacional de Educación. *Antología folklórica argentina para las escuelas primarias*. Buenos Aires: Kraft, 1940.

Consejo Nacional de Educación. *Digesto de Instrucción Primaria*. Buenos Aires: Consejo Nacional de Educación, 1937.

Continental Conference on 500 Years of Indian Resistance, Confederación de Nacionalidades Indígenas del Ecuador, South and Meso-American Indian Information Center, and Indigenous Alliance of the Americas on 500 Years of Resistance, eds. *Indigenous Alliance of the Americas on 500 Years of Resistance: resolutions from the First Continental*

Conference on 500 Years of Indian Resistance, July 17–21, 1990. Quito, Ecuador and Berkeley, CA: Confederación de Nacionalidades Indígenas del Ecuador and South and Meso-American Indian Information Center, 1990.

Contreras, Silvana. "Industria de la música, 'world music' y MERCOSUR." Oficios Terrestres 13 (2003): 125–38.

Cook, Nicholas. "Theorizing Musical Meaning." Music Theory Spectrum 23, no. 2 (October 1, 2001): 170–95.

Cooper, Frederick. Africa in the World: Capitalism, Empire, Nation-State. Cambridge, MA: Harvard University Press, 2014.

Corradi, Juan. "'How Many Did It Take to Tango?. Voyages of Urban Culture in the Early 1900s." In Outsider Art: Contesting Boundaries in Contemporary Culture, edited by Vera Zolberg and Joni Maya Cherbo, 194–214. Cambridge: Cambridge University Press, 1997.

Corrado, Omar. "Victoria Ocampo y la música: una experiencia social y estética de la modernidad." Revista Musical Chilena 61, no. 208 (December 2007): 37–65.

Cortijo Alahija, Lucas. Musicología latino-americana. La música popular y los músicos célebres de la América latina. Barcelona: Maucci, 1919.

Cortijo Vidal, Mariano. Cuyanas, aires criollos. Letra y musica de M. Cortijo Vidal. Buenos Aires: Breyer Hermanos, 1911.

Cosse, Isabella. "¿Una teología de la familia para el público latinoamericano? La radicalización del movimiento familiar cristiano en Argentina (1968–1974)." Iberoamericana XVIII, no. 18 (2018): 57–75.

Costa Garcia, Tânia da. "Mundo Radial e o cancioneiro folclórico nos tempos de Perón." Nuevo Mundo Mundos Nuevos, no. Musique et politique en Amérique Latine, XXe-XXIe siècles (June 11, 2015).

Cramer, Gisela, and Ursula Prutsch. ¡Américas Unidas! : Nelson A. Rockefeller's Office of Inter-American Affairs (1940–46). Frankfurt: Iberoamericana Vervuert, 2012.

Cusicanqui, Silvia Rivera. "Ch'ixinakax Utxiwa: A Reflection on the Practices and Discourses of Decolonization." South Atlantic Quarterly 111, no. 1 (Winter 2012): 95–109.

Cusick, Suzanne G. "'You Are in a Place That Is out of the World. . .': Music in the Detention Camps of the 'Global War on Terror.'" Journal of the Society for American Music 2, no. 1 (February 2008): 1–26.

Dávila, Jerry. Diploma of Whiteness: Race and Social Policy in Brazil, 1917–1945. Durham, NC: Duke University Press, 2003.

Degiovanni, Fernando. Vernacular Latin Americanisms: War, the Market, and the Making of a Discipline. Pittsburgh: University of Pittsburgh Press, 2018.

Deihl, E. Roderick. "South of the Border: The NBC and CBS Radio Networks and the Latin American Venture, 1930–1942." Communication Quarterly Communication Quarterly 25, no. 4 (1977): 2–12.

Deutsch, Sandra McGee. Crossing Borders, Claiming a Nation: A History of Argentine Jewish Women, 1880–1955. Durham, NC: Duke University Press, 2010.

Di Meglio, Gabriel. 1816: La trama de la independencia. Buenos Aires: Planeta, 2016.

Díaz Núñez, Lorena. Como un eco lejano . . . La vida de Miguel Bernal Jiménez. México, D.F.: Consejo Nacional para la Cultura y las Artes, 2003.

Dumont, Juliette. "Latin America at the Crossroads. The Inter-American Institute of Intellectual Cooperation, the League of Nations, and the Pan American Union." In Beyond Geopolitics: New Histories of Latin America at the League of Nations, edited by

Alan McPherson and Yannick Wehrli, 155–67. Albuquerque: University of New Mexico Press, 2015.

Durang, Charles. *The Fashionable Dancer's Casket, Or, The Ball-Room Instructor: A New and Splendid Work on Dancing, Etiquette, Deportment, and the Toilet*. Philadelphia: Fisher & Brother, 1856.

Earle, Rebecca. *The Return of the Native: Indians and Myth-Making in Spanish America, 1810–1930*. Durham, NC: Duke University Press, 2007.

Edwards Bello, Joaquín. *El nacionalismo continental. Crónicas chilenas*. Madrid: Impr. G. Hernández y Galo Sáez, 1925.

El Instituto Interamericano de Musicología—Su labor de 1941 a 1947. Montevideo: Ministerios de Relaciones Exteriores y de Instrucción Pública y Previsión Social del Uruguay, 1948.

Eliade, Mircea. *Mitos, sueños y misterios*. Buenos Aires: Compañía General Fabril Editora, 1961.

Encarnação, Paulo Gustavo da. "Rock in Rio—um festival (im)pertinente à música brasileira e à redemocratização nacional." *Patrimônio e Memória* 7, no. 1 (August 4, 2007): 348–68.

Erenberg, Lewis A. *Steppin' Out: New York Nightlife and the Transformation of American Culture, 1890–1930*. Westport, CT: Greenwood Press, 1981.

Erlmann, Veit. *Reason and Resonance: A History of Modern Aurality*. New York: Zone Books, 2014.

Escoto Robledo, Eduardo. "El primer Congreso Interamericano de Música Sacra." *Boletín Eclesiástico del Arzobispado de Guadalajara* 6, no. 12 (2012). https://arquidiocesisgdl.org/boletin/2012-12-4.php.

Fairclough, Pauline. *Classics for the Masses: Shaping Soviet Musical Identity under Lenin and Stalin*. New Haven, CT: Yale University Press, 2016.

Fairley, Jan. "La Nueva Canción Latinoamericana." *Bulletin of Latin American Research* 3, no. 2 (1984): 107–15.

Fauser, Annegret. *Sounds of War: Music in the United States during World War II*. New York: Oxford University Press, 2013.

Federación de Estudiantes Latino-Americanos. *El estudiante latino-americano* 1, no. 1 (1918).

Feld, Steven. "Acoustemology." In *Keywords in Sound*, edited by David Novak and Matt Sakakeeny, 12–21. Durham, NC: Duke University Press, 2015.

Fern, Leila. "Origin and Functions of the Inter-American Music Center." *Notes* 1, no. 1 (1943): 14–22.

Fernández, Noelia. "'Hablando con el pueblo'. La creación de LS 11 bajo la gestión de Manuel Fresco en la provincia de Buenos Aires, 1936 – 1940." *Question* 1, no. 38 (June 28, 2013): 67–80.

Fernández Christlieb, Fátima. *La radio mexicana: centro y regiones*. México: J. Pablos Editor, 1991.

Fernández L'Hoeste, Héctor. "All the Cumbias, the Cumbia," in *Imagining Our Americas: Toward a Transnational Frame*, ed. Sandhya Shukla and Heidi Tinsman. Durham, NC: Duke University Press, 2007, 338–64.

Firmat, Gustavo Pérez. "Latunes: An Introduction." *Latin American Research Review* 43, no. 2 (2008): 180–203.

Fischer, Brodwyn. *A Poverty of Rights: Citizenship and Inequality in Twentieth-Century Rio de Janeiro*. Stanford, CA: Stanford University Press, 2008.

Fléchet, Anaïs. "Le Conseil International de La Musique et La Politique Musicale de l'Unesco (1945–1975)." *Relations Internationales* 156 (2014): 53–71.

Fléchet, Anaïs. *Si tu vas à Rio: la musique populaire brésilienne en France au XXe siècle.* Paris: Armand Colin, 2013.

Fléchet, Anaïs. *Villa-Lobos á Paris: Un écho musical du Brésil.* Paris: L'Harmattan, 2004.

Flores, Antonio. "How the U.S. Hispanic Population Is Changing." *Pew Research Center* blog, September 18, 2017. https://www.pewresearch.org/fact-tank/2017/09/18/how-the-u-s-hispanic-population-is-changing/.

Flores y Escalante, Jesús. *Salón México: historia documental y gráfica del danzón en México.* México, D.F.: Asociación Mexicana de Estudios Fonográficos, 1993.

Floyd Jr., Samuel A. Floyd. "Black Music in the Circum-Caribbean." *American Music* 17, no. 1 (April 1, 1999): 1–38.

Folklore Americas, 1941–1942.

Fosler-Lussier, Danielle. *Music in America's Cold War Diplomacy.* Berkeley: University of California Press, 2015.

Fox, Elizabeth. *Latin American Broadcasting: From Tango to Telenovela.* Luton: University of Luton Press, 1997.

Fradkin, Raúl. "Centaures de la pampa. Le gaucho, entre l'histoire et le mythe." *Annales. Histoire, Sciences Sociales* 58e année, no. 1 (2003): 109–33.

Francfort, Didier. "Le tango, passion allemande et européenne, 1920–1960." In *Littératures et musiques dans la mondialisation: XXe–XXIe siècles*, edited by Anaïs Fléchet and Marie-Françoise, 95–114. Lévy. Paris: Publications de la Sorbonne, 2015.

French, John, and Paulo Roberto Ribeiro Fontes. *Afogados em leis: a CLT e a cultura política dos trabalhadores brasileiros.* São Paulo: Editora Fundação Perseu Abramo, 2001.

Funes, Patricia. *Salvar la nación: intelectuales, cultura y política en los años veinte latinoamericanos.* Buenos Aires: Prometeo Libros, 2006.

Garabedian, Steven. "Reds, Whites, and the Blues: Lawrence Gellert, 'Negro Songs of Protest,' and the Leftwing Folksong Revival of the 1930s and 1940s." *American Quarterly* 57, no. 1 (2005): 179–206.

García Canclini, Néstor. "Contradictory Modernities and Globalisation in Latin America." In *Through the Kaleidoscope: The Experience of Modernity in Latin America*, edited by Vivian Schelling, 37–52. London: Verso, 2000.

García Canclini, Néstor. *Culturas híbridas: estrategias para entrar y salir de la modernidad.* México, D.F.: Grijalbo : Consejo Nacional para la Cultura y las Artes, 1990.

García, David F. *Arsenio Rodríguez and the Transnational Flows of Latin Popular Music.* Philadelphia: Temple University Press, 2006.

García, Rolando V, Luciano C Croatto, and Alfredo A Martín. *Historia de la música latinoamericana.* Buenos Aires: Librería Perlado, 1938.

Garí Barceló, Bernat. "La ensayística musicológica de Alejo Carpentier: eufónica vía a una poética de la novela." PhD diss., Universidad de Barcelona, 2015.

Garramuño, Florencia. *Modernidades Primitivas: Tango, Samba y Nación.* Buenos Aires: Fondo de Cultura Económica, 2007.

Garrido, Juan. *Historia de la música popular en México, 1896–1973.* México: Editorial Extemporáneos, 1974.

Geijerstam, Claes af. *Popular Music in Mexico.* Albuquerque: University of New Mexico Press, 1976.

Gelbart, Matthew. *The Invention of "Folk Music" and "Art Music": Emerging Categories from Ossian to Wagner.* Cambridge: Cambridge University Press, 2007.

Gerbod, Paul. "L'institution orphéonique en France du XIXe au XXe siècle." *Ethnologie Française* 10, no. 1 (January 1, 1980): 27–44.

Gilioli, Renato de Sousa Porto. "Civilizando pela música: a pedagogia do canto orfeônico na escola paulista da Primeira República (1910–1930)." Dissertação de Mestrado, Universidade de São Paulo, 2003.

Gill, Lesley. *The School of the Americas: Military Training and Political Violence in the Americas.* Durham, NC: Duke University Press, 2004.

Ginzburg, Carlo. *The Cheese and the Worms: The Cosmos of a Sixteenth-Century Miller.* Baltimore: Johns Hopkins University Press, 1980.

Giraudo, Laura. "'No hay propiamente todavía Instituto': Los inicios del Instituto Indigenista Interamericano (Abril 1940–Marzo 1942)." *América Indígena* LXII, no. 2 (June 2006): 6–32.

Glocer, Silvia. "Músicos judíos exiliados en Argentina durante el Tercer Reich (1933–1945): Los primeros tiempos en los nuevos escenarios." *Revista Argentina de Musicología*, no. 11 (2010): 99–116.

Glozman, Mara. "Combatir y conservar: posiciones y saberes sobre el lenguaje popular en los Boletines de la Academia Argentina de Letras (1933–1943)." *Gragoatá* 17, no. 32 (June 30, 2012): 227–45.

Glozman, Mara. "Corporativismo, política cultural y regulación lingüística: la creación de la Academia Argentina de Letras." *Revista Lenguaje* 41, no. 2 (May 12, 2013): 455–78.

Glozman, Mara. "Lenguas, variedades y filología en los discursos estatales (1946–1947): entre la comunidad hispánica y la identidad nacional." *Actas de las Primeras jornadas interdisciplinarias: lenguas, identidad e ideologías, Facultad de Filosofia y Letras, Universidad de Tucumán* (2006): 52–61.

Glozman, Mara, and Daniela Lauría, eds. *Voces y ecos: una antología de los debates sobre la lengua nacional (Argentina, 1900–2000).* Buenos Aires: Cabiria, 2012.

Gobat, Michel. "The Invention of Latin America: A Transnational History of Anti-Imperialism, Democracy, and Race." *American Historical Review* 118, no. 5 (December 1, 2013): 1345–75.

Godio, Julio. *Historia del movimiento obrero argentino: 1870–2000.* Buenos Aires: Corregidor, 2000.

Godio, Julio. *Historia del movimiento obrero latinoamericano.* San José, Costa Rica: Editorial Nueva Sociedad, 1987.

Goebel, Michael. "Decentring the German Spirit: The Weimar Republic's Cultural Relations with Latin America." *Journal of Contemporary History* 44, no. 2 (April 1, 2009): 221–45.

Goebel, Michael. "Una sucursal francesa de la reforma universitaria: jóvenes latinoamericanos y antiimperialismo en la París de entreguerras." In *Los viajes latinoamericanos de la Reforma Universitaria*, edited by Martín Bergel, 177–99. Rosario, Argentina: HyA Universidad Nacional de Rosario, 2018.

Góis, Pedro, and José Carlos Marques. "A emigração portuguesa e o sistema migratório lusófono: complexidade e dinâmicas de um país de migrações." *Informe OBIMID (Observatorio Iberoamericano sobre Movilidad Urbana, Migraciones y Desarrollo)*, March 2016, 19.

Goldemberg, Ricardo. "Educação musical: a experiência do canto orfeônico no Brasil." *Pro-Posições* 6, no. 3 (November 1995): 103–109.

González, Juan Pablo. "El trópico baja al sur: llegada y asimilación de música cubana en Chile, 1930–1960." *Boletín de Música Casa de Las Américas*, no. 11–12 (2003): 3–18.

González, Juan Pablo. "Musicología y América latina: Una relación posible." *Revista Argentina de Musicología*, no. 10 (2009): 43–72.

González, Juan Pablo. *Pensar la música desde América latina: problemas e interrogantes*. Buenos Aires: Gourmet Musical, 2013.

González, Juan Pablo, and Claudio Rolle. *Historia social de la música popular en Chile, 1890–1950*. Santiago, Chile: Ediciones Universidad Católica de Chile, 2005.

Gottschalk, Louis Moreau. *Les voyages extraordinaires de L. Moreau Gottschalk, pianiste et aventurier*. Lausanne: P. M. Favre, 1985.

Gottschalk, Louis Moreau. *Notes of a Pianist, during His Professional Tours in the United States, Canada, the Antilles, and South America*. Philadelphia: J. B. Lippincott, 1881.

Gough, Peter L. "'The Varied Carols I Hear': The Music of the New Deal in the West." PhD diss., University of Nevada, Las Vegas, 2009.

Gramsci, Antonio. *Gli intellettuali e l'organizzazione della cultura*. Torino: Einaudi, 1950.

Granados, Pável, and Mónica Barrón Echauri. *XEW, 70 años en el aire*. Mexico City: Editorial Clío, 2000.

Grandin, Greg. "The Liberal Traditions in the Americas: Rights, Sovereignty, and the Origins of Liberal Multilateralism." *American Historical Review* 117, no. 1 (2012): 68–91.

Greet, Michele. "Occupying Paris: The First Survey Exhibition of Latin American Art." *Journal of Curatorial Studies* 3, no. 2–3 (2014): 213–36.

Greet, Michele. *Transatlantic Encounters: Latin American Artists in Paris between the Wars*. New Haven, CT: Yale University Press, 2018.

Greppi, Clemente. *El canto en las escuelas primarias. Consejos para la educación de la voz infantil y enseñanza de cantos escolares*. Buenos Aires: Librería del Colegio, 1907.

Greppi, Clemente. *La educación musical de los niños*. Buenos Aires: Librería del Colegio, 1922.

Gronow, Pekka. "The Record Industry Comes to the Orient." *Ethnomusicology* 25, no. 2 (1981): 251–84.

Gruhn, Wilfried. "Leo Kestenberg 1882–1962: Honorary President of ISME 1953–1962 Outstanding Musician, Visionary Educator, Pragmatic Reformer and Utopian Realist." *International Journal of Music Education* 22, no. 2 (2004): 103–29.

Guadarrama Olivera, Rocío. "Mercado de Trabajo y geografía de la música de concierto en México." *Espacialidades. Revista de temas contemporáneos sobre lugares, política y cultura* 3, no. 2 (2013): 192–216.

Guérios, Paulo Renato. "Heitor Villa-Lobos and the Parisian Art Scene: How to Become a Brazilian Musician." *Mana* 1 (2006). http://socialsciences.scielo.org/scielo.php?script=sci_arttext&pid=S0104-93132006000100002&lng=en&nrm=iso&tlng=en.

Guilbault, Jocelyne. *Governing Sound: The Cultural Politics of Trinidad's Carnival Musics*. Chicago: University of Chicago Press, 2007.

Guilbault, Jocelyne. "Interpreting World Music: A Challenge in Theory and Practice." *Popular Music* 16, no. 1 (1997): 31–44.

Guilbault, Jocelyne. "The Politics of Labeling Popular Music in English Caribbean." *Revista Transcultural de Música* 3 (1997).

Hall, Kenneth O. *CARICOM: Unity in Adversity*. Georgetown, Guyana: UWI-CARICOM Project, 2000.

Halperin Donghi, Tulio. "Dos siglos de reflexiones sudamericanas sobre la brecha entre América Latina y Estados Unidos." In *La brecha entre América latina y Estados Unidos*, compiled by Francis Fukuyama, 31–78. Buenos Aires: Fondo de Cultura Económica, 2006.

Halperin Donghi, Tulio. *Historia contemporánea de América latina*. Madrid: Alianza Editorial, 1969.

Hanke, Lewis. *Do the Americas Have a Common History? A Critique of the Bolton Theory*. New York: Knopf, 1964.

Hart, Justin. *Empire of Ideas: The Origins of Public Diplomacy and the Transformation of U.S. Foreign Policy*. Oxford: Oxford University Press, 2013.

Haya de la Torre, Víctor Raúl. *Obras completas*. Vol. 2. Lima: J. Mejía Baca, 1977.

Hayes, Joy. "National Imaginings On the Air: Radio in Mexico, 1920–1940." In *The Eagle and the Virgin: Nation and Cultural Revolution in Mexico, 1920–1940*, edited by Mary K. Vaughan and Stephen E. Lewis, 243–58. Durham, NC: Duke University Press, 2006.

Hayes, Joy. *Radio Nation: Communication, Popular Culture, and Nationalism in Mexico, 1920–1950*. Tucson: University of Arizona Press, 2000.

Helal, Ronaldo, Antônio Jorge G Soares, and Hugo Rodolfo Lovisolo. *A invenção do país do futebol: mídia, raça e idolatria*. Rio de Janeiro: Mauad, 2001.

Henríquez Ureña, Pedro. "Música popular de América." *Boletín de Antropología Americana, Pan American Institute of Geography and History* 9 (July 1984): 137–57.

Henríquez Ureña, Pedro. *Obra crítica*, ed. Emma Susana Speratti Piñero. México-Buenos Aires: Fondo de Cultura Económica, 1960.

Herder, Johann Gottfried. *Song Loves the Masses: Herder on Music and Nationalism*, ed. Philip Bohlman. Berkeley: University of California Press, 2017.

Herf, Jeffrey. *Reactionary Modernism: Technology, Culture, and Politics in Weimar and the Third Reich*. Cambridge: Cambridge University Press, 1984.

Herrera, Ataliva, and Consejo Nacional de Educación. *Folklore y nativismo en la enseñanza primaria: resolución del Consejo Nacional de Educación creando la Comisión de Folklore y Nativismo*. República Argentina: Consejo Nacional de Educación, 1945.

Herrera, Eduardo. "Perspectiva internacional: lo 'latinoamericano' del Centro Latinoamericano de Altos Estudios Musicales." In *La música en el Di Tella. Resonancias de la modernidad*, edited by José Luis Castiñeira de Dios, 30–35. Buenos Aires: Secretaría de Cultura de la Nación, 2011.

Herrera, Eduardo. "The Rockefeller Foundation and Latin American Music in the 1960s: The Creation of Indiana University's LAMC and Di Tella Institute's CLAEM." *American Music* 35, no. 1 (2017): 51–74.

Hersch, Charles. *Subversive Sounds: Race and the Birth of Jazz in New Orleans*. Chicago: University Of Chicago Press, 2007.

Hertzman, Marc. "A Brazilian Counterweight: Music, Intellectual Property and the African Diaspora in Rio de Janeiro (1910s–1930s)." *Journal of Latin American Studies* 41, no. 04 (2009): 695–722.

Hertzman, Marc. "Making Music and Masculinity in Vagrancy's Shadow: Race, Wealth, and Malandragem in Post-Abolition Rio de Janeiro." *Hispanic American Historical Review* 90, no. 4 (November 1, 2010): 591–625.

Hertzman, Marc. *Making Samba: A New History of Race and Music in Brazil*. Durham, NC: Duke University Press, 2013.

Hess, Carol A. *Representing the Good Neighbor: Music, Difference, and the Pan American Dream*. New York: Oxford University Press, 2013.

Hess, Carol A. "Walt Disney's *Saludos Amigos*: Hollywood and the Propaganda of Authenticity." In *The Tide Was Always High: The Music of Latin America in Los Angeles*, edited by Josh Kun, 105–23. Oakland: University of California Press, 2017.

Hila, Antonio C. *Music in History, History in Music*. Manila: University of Santo Tomás, 2004.

Huyssen, Andreas. *After the Great Divide: Modernism, Mass Culture, Postmodernism*. Bloomington: Indiana University Press, 1986.

Ibarlucía, Ricardo. "La perspectiva del zorzal: Paul Celan y el 'tango de la muerte.'" *Revista Latinoamericana de Filosofía* 30, no. 2 (2004): 287–312.

Iber, Patrick. *Neither Peace Nor Freedom: The Cultural Cold War in Latin America*. Cambridge, MA: Harvard University Press, 2015.

Illari, Bernardo. *Domenico Zipoli: para una genealogía de la música latinoamericana*. La Habana: Premio de Musicología Casa de las Américas, 2011.

Ingwersen, Lance. "Mexico City in the Age of Theater, 1830–1901." PhD diss., Vanderbilt University, 2017.

Instituto Nacional de Musicología. "Carlos Vega." In *Antología del tango rioplatense*. Buenos Aires: Instituto Nacional de Musicologia "Carlos Vega," 1980.

Inter-American Conference for the Maintenance of Peace, Pan American Union, ed. *Inter-American Conference for the Maintenance of Peace, Buenos Aires, December 1–23, 1936: Report on the Proceedings of the Conference*. Washington, DC: Pan American Union, 1937.

International Bureau of American Republics. *Bulletin of the International Bureau of the American Republics*. Washington, DC: US Government Printing Office, 1910.

Irving, D. R. M. *Colonial Counterpoint: Music in Early Modern Manila*. New York: Oxford University Press, 2010.

Izikowitz, Karl Gustav. *Musical and Other Sound Instruments of the South American Indians, a Comparative Ethnographical Study*. Göteborg: Elanders boktr, 1935.

Jackson, Jeffrey H. *Making Jazz French: Music and Modern Life in Interwar Paris*. Durham, NC: Duke University Press, 2003.

James, C. L. R. "The Artist in the Caribbean." *Caribbean Quarterly* 54, no. 1/2 (2008): 177–80.

James, C. L. R. "Lecture on Federation, (West Indies and British Guiana)." Marxists.org, 1958.

Johnson, James. *Listening in Paris: A Cultural History*. Berkeley: University of California Press, 1996.

Jones, Andrew. "Black Internationale: Notes on the Chinese Jazz Age." In *Jazz Planet*, edited by E. Taylor Atkins, 225–43. Jackson: University Press of Mississippi, 2003.

Jones, Andrew. *Yellow Music: Media Culture and Colonial Modernity in the Chinese Jazz Age*. Durham, NC: Duke University Press, 2001.

Jones, Gareth Stedman. "Working-Class Culture and Working-Class Politics in London, 1870–1900; Notes on the Remaking of a Working Class." *Journal of Social History* 7, no. 4 (1974): 460–508.

Judkovski, José. *El tango y los judíos de Europa oriental*. Buenos Aires: Academia Porteña de Lunfardo and Fundación IWO, 2010.

Judkovski, José. *El tango: una historia con judíos*. Buenos Aires: Fundación IWO, 1998.

Kaliman, Ricardo Jonatas. "Dos actitudes ilustradas hacia la música popular: para una historia social de la industria del folklore musical argentino." *Revista Argentina de Musicología* 17 (December 2016): 37–56.

Karush, Matthew. *Culture of Class: Radio and Cinema in the Making of a Divided Argentina, 1920–1946*. Durham, NC: Duke University Press, 2012.

Karush, Matthew. *Musicians in Transit: Argentina and the Globalization of Popular Music*. Durham, NC: Duke University Press, 2017.

Katz, Michael. "'Go Argue with Today's Children': The Jewish Family in Sholem Aleichem and Vladimir Jabotinsky." *European Judaism* 43, no. 1 (May 30, 2010): 63–77.

Kelly, Patrick William. *Sovereign Emergencies: Latin America and the Making of Global Human Rights Politics*. Cambridge: Cambridge University Press, 2018.

Keppy, Peter. "Southeast Asia in the Age of Jazz: Locating Popular Culture in the Colonial Philippines and Indonesia." *Journal of Southeast Asian Studies* 44, no. 3 (October 2013): 444–64.

Kohan, Pablo. *Estudios sobre los estilos compositivos del tango (1920–1935)*. Buenos Aires: Gourmet Musical, 2010.

Kohan, Pablo. "Europa y el tango argentino: intercambios culturales en el origen del tango." In *Los caminos de la música: Europa y Argentina*, edited by Pablo Bardin et al., 153–75. Jujuy: Universidad Nacional de Jujuy, 2008.

Koolhaas, Rem. *Delirious New York: A Retroactive Manifesto for Manhattan*. New York: Monacelli Press, 1994.

Kramer, Paul. "Region in Global History." In *A Companion to World History*, edited by Douglas Northtrop, 201–12. Chichester, West Sussex: Blackwell, 2012.

Kressel, Daniel G. "The Hispanic Community of Nations: The Spanish-Argentine Nexus and the Imagining of a Hispanic Cold War Bloc." *Cahiers Des Amériques Latines* 79 (2015): 115–33.

Kuss, Malena. "Leitmotive de Charles Seeger Sobre Latinoamérica." *Revista Musical Chilena* 34, no. 151 (1980): 29–37.

Lacombe, Hervé, and Christine Rodriguez. *La Habanera de Carmen: Naissance d'un tube*. Paris: Fayard, 2014.

Landa, Enrique Guillermo Cámara de. "Tango 'de ida y de vuelta.'" *Revista de Musicología* 16, no. 4 (January 1, 1993): 2147–69.

Lange, Francisco Curt. *Americanismo musical. La Sección de Investigaciones Musicales: su creación, propósitos y finalidades*. Montevideo: Instituto de Estudios Superiores–Sección de Investigaciones Musicales, 1934.

Lange, Francisco Curt. "Arte musical latino americano: raza y asimilación," *Boletín Latino Americano de Música* 1 (1935): 13–28

Lange, Francisco Curt. *Impresiones andinas. Argentina: antagonismo cultural. Bolivia: pueblo en Desgracia*. Montevideo: Nueva América, 1938.

Lange, Francisco Curt. *La posición de Nietzsche frente a la guerra, el estado y la raza*. Santiago de Chile: Ercilla, 1938.

Lange, Francisco Curt. "Suma de las relaciones interamericanas en el campo de la música," *Boletín Latino Americano de Música* 5 (1941): 11–22.

Lange, Francisco Curt. *Archivo de música religiosa de la Capitanía geral das Minas Gerais (Brasil, siglo XVIII)*. Mendoza: Departamento de Musicología, Escuela superior de música–Universidad nacional de Cuyo, 1951.

Lange, Francisco Curt. *Estudios brasileños (Mauricinas). Manuscritos musicales en la Biblioteca Nacional de Rio de Janeiro*. Mendoza: Dept. de Musicologia, Escuela Superior de Música, Universidad Nacional de Cuyo, 1951.

Lange, Francisco Curt. *Vida y muerte de Louis Moreau Gottschalk en Rio de Janeiro, 1869; el ambiente musical en la mitad del Segundo Imperio*. Mendoza: Universidad Nacional de Cuyo, 1951.

Lange, Francisco Curt. *La música eclesiástica argentina en el período de la dominación hispánica, una investigación*. Mendoza: Universidad Nacional de Cuyo, 1954.

Lange, Francisco Curt. *La música religiosa en el área de Rosario de Santa Fé y en el Convento San Carlos de San Lorenzo, durante el período aproximado de 1770 a 1820*. Rosario, Argentina: Tipogr. Llordén, 1956.

Lange, Francisco Curt. *La música en Villa Rica (Minas Gerais, Siglo XVIII). El Senado de la Cámara y los servicios de música religiosa. Historia de un descubrimiento. Experiencias y conceptos*. Santiago de Chile: Universidad de Chile, 1967.

Lange, Francisco Curt. "Um fabuloso redescobrimento (para justificação da existência de música erudita no período colonial brasileiro)." *Revista de História* 54, no. 107 (September 30, 1976): 45–67.

Lastarria, José Victorino, Álvaro Covarrubias, Domingo Santa María González, and Benjamín Vicuña Mackenna, comps. *La patria común: pensamiento americanista en el siglo XIX*. Santiago de Chile: LOM, 2013.

Lazarsfeld, Paul, and Frank Stanton. *Radio Research, 1941*. New York: Duell, Sloan and Pearce, 1941.

Lehmann-Nitsche, Roberto. *Santos Vega*. Buenos Aires: Coni Hermanos, 1917.

Lehmann-Nitsche, Roberto. "Le mot 'gaucho,' son origine gitane." *Journal de la Société des Américanistes* 20, no. 1 (1928): 103–105.

Leinaweaver, Jessaca. "Transatlantic Unity on Display: The 'White Legend' and the 'Pact of Silence' in Madrid's Museum of the Americas." *History and Anthropology* 28, no. 1 (2017): 39–57.

Lena, Jennifer C. *Banding Together: How Communities Create Genres in Popular Music*. Princeton, NJ: Princeton University Press, 2012.

Levi-Strauss, Claude. "The Structural Study of Myth." *Journal of American Folklore* 68, no. 270 (1955): 428–44.

Levy, Aiala. "Stages of a State: From São Paulo's Teatro São José to the Teatro Municipal, 1854–1911." *Planning Perspectives* 28, no. 3 (July 1, 2013): 461–75.

Lewin, Linda. "A Tale of Two Texts: Orality, Oral History, and Poetic Insult in the Desafio of Romano and Inacio in Patos (1874)." *Studies in Latin American Popular Culture* 26 (2007): 1–25.

Link, Kacey, and Kristin Wendland. *Tracing Tangueros: Argentine Tango Instrumental Music*. New York: Oxford University Press, 2016.

Lisboa, Alessandra Coutinho. "Villa-Lobos e o Canto orfeônico: música, nacionalismo e ideal civilizador." M.A. thesis, Universidade Estadual Paulista Júlio de Mesquita Filho, 2005.

Lott, Allen. "'New Music for New Ears': The International Composers' Guild." *Journal of the American Musicological Society* 36, no. 2 (July 1, 1983): 266–86.

Lott, Eric. *Love and Theft: Blackface Minstrelsy and the American Working Class*. New York: Oxford University Press, 1993.

Lualdi, Adriano. *Viaggio musicale nel Sud-America*. Milano: Istituto Editoriale Nazionale, 1934.

Luker, Morgan James. *The Tango Machine: Musical Culture in the Age of Expediency*. Chicago: University of Chicago Press, 2016.

Machado Neto, Diósnio. "Administrando a festa: música e iluminismo no Brasil colonial." PhD Diss., Escola de Comunicação e Artes–USP, São Paulo, 2008.

Mackinnon, Maria Moira, and Mario Alberto Petrone. *Populismo y neopopulismo en América Latina: el problema de la Cenicienta*. Buenos Aires: Editorial Universitaria de Buenos Aires, 1998.

Madrid, Alejandro. *In Search of Julián Carrillo and Sonido 13*. New York: Oxford University Press, 2015.

Madrid, Alejandro. *Nor-Tec Rifa!: Electronic Dance Music from Tijuana to the World*. Oxford: Oxford University Press, 2008.

Madrid, Alejandro. "Renovation, Rupture, and Restoration. The Modernist Musical Experience in Latin America." In *The Modernist World*, edited by Allana Lindgren and Stephen Ross. London; New York: Routledge, 2015.

Madrid, Alejandro. *Sounds of the Modern Nation: Music, Culture, and Ideas in Post-Revolutionary Mexico*. Philadelphia: Temple University Press, 2008.

Madrid, Alejandro. "The Sounds of the Nation: Visions of Modernity and Tradition in Mexico's First National Congress of Music." *Hispanic American Historical Review* 86, no. 4 (2006): 681.

Madrid, Alejandro, and Robin D. Moore. *Danzón: Circum-Caribbean Dialogues in Music and Dance*. New York: Oxford University Press, 2013.

Magaldi, Cristina. "Cosmopolitanism and World Music in Rio de Janeiro at the Turn of the Twentieth Century." *The Musical Quarterly* 92, no. 3–4 (September 21, 2009): 329–64.

Majno, Maria. "From the Model of El Sistema in Venezuela to Current Applications: Learning and Integration through Collective Music Education." *Annals of the New York Academy of Sciences* 1252, no. 1 (April 1, 2012): 56–64.

Makalani, Minkah. "The Politically Unimaginable in Black Marxist Thought." *Small Axe: A Caribbean Journal of Criticism* 22, no. 2 (July 1, 2018): 18–34.

Malinowski, Bronislaw. *A Diary in the Strict Sense of the Term*. Stanford, CA: Stanford University Press, 1989.

Mansilla Pons, Ramiro, María Paula Cannova, Julián Chambó, and Alejandro Zagrakalis. "Las revoluciones y los surcos. política cultural hemisférica y edición fonográfica." In *VIII Jornadas de investigación en disciplinas artísticas y proyectuales*. La Plata: Universidad Nacional de La Plata, 2016.

Manuel, Peter, ed. *Creolizing Contradance in the Caribbean*. Philadelphia: Temple University Press, 2009.

Manzano, Valeria. *The Age of Youth in Argentina: Culture, Politics, and Sexuality from Peron to Videla*. Chapel Hill: University of North Carolina Press, 2014.

Margulis, Matias, ed. *The Global Political Economy of Raúl Prebisch*. Abingdon; Routledge, 2017.

Marichal, Carlos, and Alexandra Pita. "Algunas reflexiones sobre la historia de los intelectuales/diplomáticos latinoamericanos en los siglos XIX y XX." *Revista de Historia de América* 156 (June 2019): 97–123.

Marin Lopez, Javier. "A Conflicting Relationship: Music, Power and the Inquisition in Vice-Regal Mexico City." In *Music and Colonial Society in Colonial Latin America*, edited by Geoffrey Baker and Tess Knighton, 43–63. Cambridge: Cambridge University Press, 2011.

Marsilli-Vargas, Xochitl. "Listening Genres: The Emergence of Relevance Structures through the Reception of Sound." *Journal of Pragmatics* 69 (2014): 42–51.

Martel, Frédéric. *Mainstream: enquête sur cette culture qui plaît à tout le monde*. Paris: Flammarion, 2010.

Martí, José, and Pedro Henríquez Ureña. *Nuestra América*. Santo Domingo: Cielonaranja, 2016.

Martínez Moirón, Jesús. *El mundo de los autores. Incluye la historia de S.A.D.A.I.C.* Buenos Aires: Sampedro Ediciones, 1971.

Marx Delson, Roberta. "Some Brief Reflections on the Centennial of the Second Pan American Scientific Congress of 1915–1916." *Revista de Historia Iberoamericana* 9, no. 1 (2016): 90–102.

Mason, Kaley. "Musicians and the Politics of Dignity in South India." In *The Cambridge History of World Music*, edited by Philip Bohlman, 441–72. Cambridge: Cambridge University Press, 2013.

Matallana, Andrea. *Locos por la radio: una historia social de la radiofonía en la Argentina, 1923–1947*. Buenos Aires: Prometeo Libros, 2006.

Maurer, Joseph. "Latin, Latino, Latin American: Music, People, and Categorization in the United States." Colloquium The Worlds of Latin American Music, University of Chicago, 2017.

Mayer-Serra, Otto. *Panorama de la música hispanoamericana: esbozo interpretativo*. México: Editorial Atlante, 1943.

Mayer-Serra, Otto. *Panorama de la música mexicana. Desde la independencia hasta la actualidad*. Mexico City: Colegio de México, 1941.

McCall, Sarah. "The Musical Fallout of Political Activism : Government Investigations of Musicians in the United States, 1930–1960." PhD diss., University of North Texas, 1993.

McCann, Bryan. *Hello, Hello Brazil: Popular Music in the Making of Modern Brazil*. Durham, NC: Duke University Press, 2004.

McCarthy, Marie. "The Birth of Internationalism in Music Education 1899–1938." *International Journal of Music Education* 21 (1993): 3–15.

McCleary, Kristen. "Ethnic Identity and Elite Idyll: A Comparison of Carnival in Buenos Aires, Argentina and Montevideo, Uruguay, 1900–1920." *Social Identities* 16, no. 4 (2010): 497–517.

McCleary, Kristen. "Popular, Elite and Mass Culture? The Spanish Zarzuela in Buenos Aires, 1890–1900." *Studies in Latin American Popular Culture* 21 (2002): 1–27.

Mejía Barquera, Fernando. *La industria de la radio y la televisión y la política del estado mexicano*. México, D.F.: Fundación Manuel Buendía, 1989.

Mendívil, Julio. *En contra de la música: herramientas para pensar, comprender y vivir las músicas*. Buenos Aires: Gourmet Musical, 2016.

Mendoza, Zoila. "Crear y sentir lo nuestro: la misión peruana de arte incaico y el impulso de la produccion artístico-folklórica en Cusco." *Latin American Music Review* 25, no. 1 (2004): 57–77.

Merino Montero, Luis. "Francisco Curt Lange (1903–1997): tributo a un americanista de excepción." *Revista Musical Chilena* 52, no. 189 (1998): 9–36.

Merriam, Alan. "Definitions of 'Comparative Musicology' and 'Ethnomusicology': An Historical-Theoretical Perspective." *Ethnomusicology* 21, no. 2 (May 1977): 189–204.

Michaud, Éric. *Les invasions barbares: une généalogie de l'histoire de l'art*. Paris: Gallimard, 2015.

Miller, Karl Hagstrom. *Segregating Sound: Inventing Folk and Pop Music in the Age of Jim Crow*. Durham, NC: Duke University Press, 2010.

Miquel, Angel. *Disolvencias: literatura, cine y radio en México (1900–1950)*. México, D.F.: Fondo de Cultura Económica, 2005.

Miranda Pereira, Leonardo Affonso de. "Os anjos da meia-noite: trabalhadores, lazer e direitos no Rio de Janeiro da Primeira República." *Tempo* 19, no. 35 (2013): 97–116.

Molina Palomino, Pablo. "Los límites de lo latinoamericano. distinción e identidad en la configuración de un circuito de nueva canción en Lima." In *Vientos Del Pueblo. Representaciones,*

Recepciones e Interpretaciones Sobre La Nueva Canción Chilena, edited by Simón Palominos Mandiola and Ignacio Ramos Rodillo, 327–62. Santiago de Chile: LOM, 2018.

Mondragón, Rafael. "Anticolonialismo y socialismo de las periferias: Francisco Bilbao y la fundación de La Tribune Des Peuples." *Latinoamérica: Revista de Estudios Latinoamericanos* 56 (June 2013): 105–39.

Monsiváis, Carlos. *Aires de familia: cultura y sociedad en América Latina*. Barcelona: Anagrama, 2000.

Monsiváis, Carlos. *Escenas de pudor y liviandad*. México D.F.: Grijalbo, 1988.

Montgomery, Harper. *The Mobility of Modernism: Art and Criticism in 1920s Latin America*. Austin: University of Texas Press, 2017.

Moore, Rachel. *Performing Propaganda: Musical Life and Culture in Paris in the First World War*. Woodbridge, UK: Boydell Press, 2018.

Moore, Robin. *Music and Revolution: Cultural Change in Socialist Cuba*. Berkeley: University of California Press, 2006.

Moore, Robin. *Nationalizing Blackness: Afrocubanismo and Artistic Revolution in Havana, 1920–1940*. Pittsburgh, Pa: University of Pittsburgh Press, 1997.

Mor, Jessica Stites, and Daniel Alex Richter. "Immigrant Cosmopolitanism: The Political Culture of Argentine Early Sound Cinema of the 1930s." *Latin American and Caribbean Ethnic Studies* 9, no. 1 (January 2, 2014): 65–88.

Mora, Cristina. "Cross-Field Effects and Ethnic Classification The Institutionalization of Hispanic Panethnicity, 1965 to 1990." *American Sociological Review* 79, no. 2 (April 1, 2014): 183–210.

Mora, Cristina. *Making Hispanics: How Activists, Bureaucrats, and Media Constructed a New American*. University of Chicago Press, 2014.

Mora, G. Cristina, and Michael Rodríguez-Muñiz. "Latinos, Race, and the American Future: A Response to Richard Alba's 'The Likely Persistence of a White Majority.'" In *New Labor Forum* 26 (2017): 40–46.

Mora, María Elvira, and Clara Inés Ramírez. *La música en la revolución*. Mexico City: Comisión Nacional para las Celebraciones del 175 Aniversario de la Independencia Nacional y 75 Aniversario de la Revolución Mexicana, 1985.

Moraga Valle, Fabio. "¿Una nación íbero, latino o indoamericana? Joaquín Edwards Bello y el nacionalismo continental." In *Pensar el antiimperialismo: ensayos de historia intelectual latinoamericana, 1900–1930*, edited by Alejandra Pita González and Carlos Marichal Salinas, 247–79. Mexico D.F. y Colima: El Colegio de México y Universidad de Colima, 2012.

Moreno, Julio. *Yankee Don't Go Home!: Mexican Nationalism, American Business Culture, and the Shaping of Modern Mexico, 1920 - 1950*. Chapel Hill: University of North Carolina Press, 2003.

Moreno Rivas, Yolanda. *Historia de la música popular mexicana*. México, D.F.: Alianza Editorial Mexicana: Consejo Nacional para la Cultura y las Artes, 1989.

Morgenfeld, Leandro. *Vecinos en conflicto: Argentina y Estados Unidos en las conferencias panamericanas, 1880–1955*. Buenos Aires: Peña Lillo, 2011.

Mosse, George. *The Nationalization of the Masses: Political Symbolism and Mass Movements in Germany from the Napoleonic Wars through the Third Reich*. New York: Howard Fertig, 1975.

Mourão, Rui. *O alemão que descobriu a América*. Brasília and Belo Horizonte: Instituto Nacional do Livro and Editora Itatiaia, 1990.

Muniz de Albuquerque Jr., Durval. *A invenção do Nordeste e outras artes*. São Paulo: Editora Massangana, 1999.

Muñoz, Catalina. "'A Mission of Enormous Transcendence': The Cultural Politics of Music During Colombia's Liberal Republic, 1930–1946." *Hispanic American Historical Review* 94, no. 1 (2014): 77–105.

Myers, Jorge. "An 'Atlantic History' Avant La Lettre: Atlantic and Caribbean Transculturations in Fernando Ortiz." *Sociologia & Antropologia* 5, no. 3 (December 2015): 745–70.

Myers, Jorge. "Gênese 'Ateneísta' da história cultural Latino-Americana." *Tempo Social, Revista de Sociología da USP* 17, no. 1 (2004): 9–54.

Napolitano, Marcos. *Cultura brasileira: utopia e massificação (1950–1980)*. São Paulo: Contexto, 2001.

National Music Council. *Bulletin*. New York: National Music Council, n.d.

Neder, Álvaro. *"Enquanto este novo trem atravessa o Litoral Central": música popular urbana, latino-americanismo e conflitos sobre modernização em Mato Grosso do Sul*. Rio de Janeiro: Mauad, 2014.

Needell, Jeffrey. *A Tropical Belle Epoque: Elite Culture and Society in Turn-of-the-Century Rio de Janeiro*. New York: Cambridge University Press, 1987.

Ng, Stephanie. "Filipino Bands Performing in Hotels, Clubs and Restaurants in Asia: Purveyors of Transnational Culture in a Global Arena." PhD diss., University of Michigan, 2006.

Ninkovich, Frank. *The Diplomacy of Ideas: U.S. Foreign Policy and Cultural Relations, 1938–1950*. Cambridge: Cambridge University Press, 1981.

Nudler, Julio. *Tango judío: del ghetto a la milonga*. Buenos Aires: Editorial Sudamericana, 1998.

Ocampo, Beatriz. *La nación interior: Canal Feijóo, Di Lullo y los hermanos Wagner: el discurso culturalista de estos intelectuales en la provincia de Santiago del Estero*. Buenos Aires: Antropofagia, 2004.

Ochoa Gautier, Ana María. *Aurality: listening and knowledge in nineteenth-century Colombia*. Durham, NC: Duke University Press, 2014.

O'Connor, Francis V., and Federal Art Project. *Art for the Millions; Essays from the 1930s by Artists and Administrators of the WPA Federal Art Project*. Greenwich, CT: New York Graphic Society, 1973.

O'Gorman, Edmundo. *La invención de América: el universalismo de la cultura de occidente*. México, D.F.: Fondo de Cultura Económica, 1985.

Oliveira, Flavio. "Orpheonic Chant and the Construction of Childhood in Brazilian Elementary Education." In *Brazilian Popular Music and Citizenship*, edited by Idelber Avelar and Christopher Dunn, 44–63. Durham, NC: Duke University Press, 2011.

Oliven, Ruben George. "A malandragem na música popular brasileira." *Latin American Music Review* 5, no. 1 (1984): 66–96.

Oliven, Ruben George. "Singing Money," in *Economic Representations: Academic and Everyday*, edited by David Ruccio, 211–32. New York: Routledge, 2008.

Oliven, Ruben George. "'The Largest Popular Culture Movement in the Western World': Intellectuals and Gaúcho Traditionalism in Brazil." *American Ethnologist* 27, no. 1 (2000): 128–46.

Orrego, Antenor. *El pueblo continente: ensayos para una interpretación de la América latina*. Santiago de Chile: Ercilla, 1939.

Ortemberg, Pablo. "Geopolítica de los monumentos: los próceres en los centenarios de Argentina, Chile y Perú (1910–1924)." *Anuario de Estudios Americanos* 72, no. 1 (June 30, 2015): 321–50.

Ortemberg, Pablo. "Monumentos, memorialización y espacio público: reflexiones a propósito de la escultura de Juana Azurduy." *Tarea* 3, no. 3 (2016): 96–125.

Ortemberg, Pablo. "Ruy Barbosa en el Centenario de 1916: apogeo de la confraternidad entre Brasil y Argentina." *Revista de Historia de América* Enero-Junio, no. 154 (2018): 105–34.

Ortiz, Renato. *Otro territorio: ensayos sobre el mundo contemporáneo.* Buenos Aires: Universidad Nacional de Quilmes, 2005.

Osterhammel, Jürgen. *The Transformation of the World: A Global History of the Nineteenth Century.* Princeton, NJ: Princeton University Press, 2014.

Ostiguy, Pierre, and María Esperanza Casullo. "Left versus Right Populism: Antagonism and the Social Other." Conference paper, 67th Political Studies Association (PSA) Annual International Conference. Glasgow, 2017.

Pacini Hernandez, Deborah, Héctor Fernández l'Hoeste, and Eric Zolov, eds., *Rockin' Las Américas: The Global Politics of Rock in Latin/o America.* Pittsburgh: University of Pittsburgh Press, 2004.

Palomino, Pablo. "The Musical Worlds of Jewish Buenos Aires, 1910–1940." In *Mazel Tov, Amigos! Jews and Popular Music in the Americas,* edited by Amalia Ran and Moshe Morad, 25–53. Leiden: Brill, 2015.

Palomino, Pablo. "Nationalist, Hemispheric, and Global: 'Latin American Music' and the Music Division of the Pan American Union, 1939–1947." *Nuevo Mundo Mundos Nuevos* 4, no. 1 (June 11, 2015).

Palomino, Pablo. "Nina Sibirtzeva, or the Hidden Half of Musical Globalization." *Journal of Social History* 52, no. 2 (Winter 2018): 260–82.

Palomino, Pablo. "Tango, Samba y Amor." *Apuntes de Investigación Del CECYP* 12 (2007): 71–101.

Park, Paula Chungsun. "Transcolonial Listening: Dissonances in Cuban and Philippine Literature." PhD diss., University of Texas–Austin, 2014.

Pedelty, Mark. "The Bolero: The Birth, Life, and Decline of Mexican Modernity." *Revista de Música Latino Americana* 20, no. 1 (1999): 30–58.

Pelinski, Ramón. *El tango nómade: ensayos sobre la diáspora del tango.* Buenos Aires: Corregidor, 2000.

Pelinski, Ramón. "Tango nómade: una metáfora de la globalización." *Escritos sobre tango: en el Río de La Plata y en la diáspora,* edited by Teresita Lencina, Omar García Brunelli and Ricardo Salton, 65–128. Buenos Aires: Centro 'feca, 2008.

Penny, H. Glenn, and Matti Bunzl, eds. *Worldly Provincialism: German Anthropology in the Age of Empire.* Ann Arbor: University of Michigan Press, 2003.

Pereira, Leonardo Affonso de Miranda. "Do Congo ao tango: associativismo, lazer e identidades entre os afro-portenhos na segunda metade do século XIX." *Mundos do Trabalho* 3, no. 6 (2011): 30–51.

Pereira Salas, Eugenio. *Notas para la historia del intercambio musical entre las Américas antes del año 1940.* Washington, DC: Pan American Union, Music Division, 1941.

Pérez, Abel J. *República Oriental del Uruguay—Anales de Instrucción Primaria.* Montevideo: Imprenta El Siglo Ilustrado, 1908.

Pérez Castillo, Belén. "Music for Redemption in Francoist Prisons." Presentation at Conference Music and the Nation III: Music and Postwar Transitions (19th–21st Centuries), Université de Montréal, October 2018.

Pérez González, Juliana. *Las historias de la música en hispanoamérica, 1876–2000.* Bogotá: Universidad Nacional de Colombia, Facultad de Ciencias Humanas, Departamento de Historia, 2010.

Pérez, Louis A. *On Becoming Cuban: Identity, Nationality, and Culture.* Chapel Hill: University of North Carolina Press, 1999.

Pérez Montfort, Ricardo. "Circo, teatro y variedades: diversiones en la ciudad de México a fines del porfiriato." *Alteridades* 13, no. 26 (2003): 57–66.

Pérez Montfort, Ricardo. *Expresiones populares y estereotipos culturales en México, siglos XIX y XX : Diez ensayos.* México, D.F.: Centro de Investigaciones y Estudios Superiores en Antropología Social, 2007.

Pergamo, Ana Maria Locatelli de. "Recordando a Isabel Aretz (13/04/1909-01/06/2005)." *Latin American Music Review* 26, no. 2 (2005): 158–63.

Pernet, Corinne. "For the Genuine Culture of the Americas: Musical Folklore, Popular Arts, and the Cultural Politics of Pan Americanism, 1933–1950." In *Decentering America*, edited by Jessica Gienow-Hecht, 132–68. New York: Berghahn Books, 2007.

Pernet, Corinne. "Twists, Turns and Dead Alleys: The League of Nations and Intellectual Cooperation in Times of War." *Journal of Modern European History* 12, no. 3 (2014): 342–58.

Perrenoud, Marc. *Les musicos: enquête sur des musiciens ordinaires.* Paris: La Découverte, 2007.

Persia, Jorge de. "Centro de Documentación—Gustavo Durán." *Revista Residencia* 1 (June 1997). http://www.residencia.csic.es/bol/num1/duran.htm.

Pescatello, Ann. *Charles Seeger: A Life in American Music.* Pittsburgh: University of Pittsburgh Press, 1992.

Peterson, Richard A., and Roger M. Kern. "Changing Highbrow Taste: From Snob to Omnivore." *American Sociological Review* 61, no. 5 (October 1996): 900–907.

Piccato, Pablo. *City of Suspects: Crime in Mexico City, 1900–1931.* Durham, NC: Duke University Press, 2001.

Pistone, Danièle. *Musiques et musiciens à Paris dans les années trente.* Paris: H. Champion, 2000.

Pita González, Alexandra. *La Unión Latino Americana y el Boletín Renovación: redes intelectuales y revistas culturales en la década de 1920.* México, D.F. and Colima: Colegio de México and Universidad de Colima, 2009.

Plesch, Melanie. "Demonizing and Redeeming the Gaucho: Social Conflict, Xenophobia and the Invention of Argentine National Music." *Patterns of Prejudice* 47, no. 4–5 (September 1, 2013): 337–58.

Poole, Deborah. "Figueroa Aznar and the Cusco Indigenistas: Photography and Modernism in Early Twentieth-Century Peru." *Representations* 38 (1992): 39–75.

Postel, Charles. *The Populist Vision.* New York: Oxford University Press, 2007.

Prado, Gustavo H. *Rafael Altamira en América, 1909–1910: historia e historiografía del proyecto americanista de la Universidad de Oviedo.* Madrid: Consejo Superior de Investigaciones Científicas, 2008.

Prebisch, Raúl. "El desarrollo económico de la América latina y algunos de sus principales problemas." *El Trimestre Económico* 16, no. 63 (1949): 347–431.

Preuss, Ori. *Transnational South America: Experiences, Ideas, and Identities, 1860s-1900s.* New York, NY and Abingdon, UK: Routledge, 2016.

"Primer Congreso Inter-Americano de Música Sacra." *Frumentum: Sugerencias filosóficas y religiosas* (1949): 193–200.

Puiggrós, Adriana. *Qué pasó en la educación argentina: breve historia desde la conquista hasta el presente*. Buenos Aires: Galerna, 2002.

Pujol, Sergio Alejandro. *Las canciones del inmigrante: Buenos Aires, espectáculo musical y proceso inmigratorio, de 1914 a nuestros días*. Buenos Aires: Editorial Almagesto, 1989.

Putnam, Lara. *Radical Moves: Caribbean Migrants and the Politics of Race in the Jazz Age*. Chapel Hill: University of North Carolina Press, 2013.

Quesada, Ernesto. *El problema del idioma nacional*. Buenos Aires: Revista Nacional Casa Editora, 1900.

Quijada, Mónica. "Sobre el origen y difusión del nombre 'América latina' (o una variación heterodoxa en torno al tema de la construcción social de la verdad)." *Revista de Indias* 58, no. 214 (1998): 595–616.

Quijano Axle, Mario Roger. "Zarzuela y ópera en Yucatán (1863–1930). Actividad del teatro lírico y creación local." PhD diss., Universidad Complutense de Madrid, 2016.

Quintero-Rivera, Mareia. *A còr e o som da nação: a idéia de "mestiçagem" na crítica musical do Caribe hispânico insular e do Brasil (1928–1948)*. São Paulo: FAPESP/Annablume, 2000.

Racy, Ali Jihad. "Historical Worldviews of Early Ethnomusicologists: An East-West Encounter in Cairo, 1932." In *Ethnomusicology and Modern Music History*, edited by Stephen Blum, Philip V. Bohlman, and Daniel M. Neuman, 68–95. Urbana: University of Illinois Press, 1991.

Ramos-Rodillo, Ignacio. "Música típica, folklore de proyección y nueva canción chilena. Versiones de la identidad nacional bajo el desarrollismo en Chile, década de 1920 a 1973." *Neuma* 4, no. 2 (2011): 108–33.

Rehding, Alexander. *Hugo Riemann and the Birth of Modern Musical Thought*. Cambridge: Cambridge University Press, 2003.

Remião, Cláudio Roberto Dornelles. "O caso Curt Lange: análise de uma polêmica (1958–1983)." PhD diss., Pontifícia Universidade Católica do Rio Grande do Sul, 2018.

Restelli, Ernesto, ed. *Actas y tratados del Congreso sud-americano de derecho internacional privado (Montevideo 1888–1889)*. Buenos Aires: Imprenta y encuadernación de la Cámara de Diputados, 1928.

Revista latino-americana. 2 vols. Paris: Librería Española de E. Denné Schmitz, 1874.

Reyes, Alfonso. *Discurso por Virgilio*. Buenos Aires: Coni, 1937.

Richter, Daniel. "Mirrored Imaginaries: Urban Chroniclers in Buenos Aires and Montevideo, 1910–1936." *Journal of Urban History* (December 29, 2018): 1–20.

Ridenti, Marcelo. *Em busca do povo brasileiro: artistas da revolução, do CPC à era da tv*. Rio de Janeiro: Editora Record, 2000.

Rios, Fernando. "'They're Stealing Our Music': The Argentinísima Controversy, National Culture Boundaries, and the Rise of a Bolivian Nationalist Discourse." *Latin American Music Review* 35, no. 2 (2014): 197–227.

Rivera, Guillermo Rodriguez. *Decirlo todo: politicas culturales (en la Revolución cubana)*. La Habana: Editorial Ojalá, 2017.

Rivera, Salvador. *Latin American Unification: A History of Political and Economic Integration Efforts*. Jefferson, NC: McFarland & Co., 2014.

Rocchi, Fernando. "La americanización del consumo: las batallas por el mercado argentino, 1920–1945." In *Americanización: Estados Unidos y América Latina en el siglo XX: transferencias económicas, tecnológicas y culturales*, edited by María Inés Barbero and Andrés Martín Regalsky, 150–216. Buenos Aires: Universidad Nacional de Tres de Febrero, 2014.

Roberts, John Storm. *The Latin Tinge: The Impact of Latin American Music on the United States.* 2nd ed. New York: Oxford University Press, 1999.

Rodgers, Daniel T., Bhavani Raman, and Helmut Reimitz. *Cultures in Motion.* Princeton, NJ: Princeton University Press, 2014.

Rodriguez, Martha. "De historiadores y de los posibles usos de su saber: la contribución de los Congresos Internacionales de Historia de América en la conformación de una identidad americana (décadas de 1930 a 1960)." *História da Historiografia: International Journal of Theory and History of Historiography* 27 (2018): 91–117.

Rodríguez, Pablo Gustavo. "Los mundos posibles de la pobreza en la Biblia." Conference Paper at the III Reunión de Antropología del Mercosur, Posadas, Misiones (Posadas, Argentina), 1999.

Roghi, Vanessa. "Il dibattito sul diritto d'autore e la proprietà intellettuale nell'Italia fascista." *Studi Storici* 48, no. 1 (January 1, 2007): 203–40.

Rojas, Ricardo. "El arte americano." *Revista de América* 1, no. 1 (March 1920): 1–2.

Rojas, Ricardo. *Eurindia.* Buenos Aires: Librería "La Facultad" Juan Roldán, 1924.

Rolón, José. "El porvenir de la música latino americana." *Música—Revista Mexicana* 2, no. 1 (May 1930): 31–34.

Root, Deane L. "The Pan American Association of Composers (1928–1934)." *Anuario Interamericano de Investigacion Musical* 8 (1972): 49–70.

Rosselli, John. "Latin America and Italian Opera: A Process of Interaction, 1810–1930." *Revista de Musicología* 16, no. 1 (1993): 139–45.

Rosselli, John. "The Opera Business and the Italian Immigrant Community in Latin America 1820–1930: The Example of Buenos Aires." *Past & Present*, no. 127 (May 1990): 155–82.

Rouquié, Alain. *Amérique latine: introduction à l'extrême-occident.* Paris: Seuil, 1987.

Roy, William G., and Timothy Dowd. "'Race Records' and 'Hillbilly Music': Institutional Origins of Racial Categories in the American Commercial Recording Industry." *Poetics, Music in Society: The Sociological Agenda* 32, no. 3 (June 1, 2004): 265–79.

Ruddick, J. Leon. "Music for Uniting the Americas." *Music Educators Journal* 28, no. 3 (1942): 10–11.

Sacchi de Ceriotto, María Antonieta. *La profesión musical en el baúl: músicos españoles inmigrantes radicados en Mendoza a comienzos del siglo XX.* Mendoza, Argentina: Editorial de la Universidad Nacional de Cuyo, 2007.

Salas, Horacio. *El tango.* Buenos Aires: Planeta, 1986.

Salas, Samuel J. A., Pedro I. Pauletto, and Pedro J. S. Salas. *Historia de la música (América latina) adaptada a los nuevos programas de tercer año de la enseñanza secundaria.* Buenos Aires: Editorial Araujo, 1938.

Salinas Cossío, Guillermo. "La música en la América Latina y su nacionalización," *Boletín Latino Americano de Música* 2 (1936): 157–62.

Salinas Jr., Cristobal, and Adele Lozano. "Mapping and Recontextualizing the Evolution of the Term Latinx: An Environmental Scanning in Higher Education." *Journal of Latinos and Education* (November 16, 2017): 1–14.

Salvatore, Ricardo. *Disciplinary Conquest: U.S. Scholars in South America, 1900–1945.* Durham, NC: Duke University Press, 2016.

Salvatore, Ricardo. "Library Accumulation and the Emergence of Latin American Studies." *Comparative American Studies* 3, no. 4 (2005): 415–36.

Sánchez, Freddy. "El sistema nacional para las orquestas juveniles e infantiles. La nueva educación musical de Venezuela." *Revista da ABEM—Associação Brasileira de Educação Musical* 15, no. 18 (2007): 63–69.

Sandi, Luis. "Agustín Lara y la canción mexicana." *Música—Revista Mexicana* 1, no. 9–10 (Diciembre 1930): 46–49.

Sandoval, Pablo Ximénez de. "Los Ángeles retira una estatua de Colón: 'No hay que celebrar al responsable de un genocidio.'" *El País.* November 12, 2018.

Sandroni, Carlos. *Feitiço decente: transformações do samba no Rio de Janeiro, 1917–1933.* Rio de Janeiro, RJ: Jorge Zahar Editor : Editora Universidade Federal do Rio de Janeiro, 2001.

Santa Cruz, Domingo. "On Hemispherical Unity." *Music Educators Journal* 28, no. 6 (1942): 13–14.

Santamaría Delgado, Carolina. *Vitrolas, rocolas y radioteatros: hábitos de escucha de la música popular en Medellín, 1930–1950.* Bogotá, D.C.: Editorial Pontificia Universidad Javeriana, 2014.

Santana, Adalberto. "Bicentenario de la independencia, centenario de la Revolución Mexicana y de la UNAM." *Archipiélago. Revista cultural de nuestra América* 18, no. 68 (2010): 15–16.

Santos, Ramon Pagayon. *Musika: An Essay on the American Colonial and Contemporary Traditions in Philippine Music.* Manila: Cultural Center of the Philippines, 1994.

Saragoza, Alex. *The Monterrey Elite and the Mexican State, 1880–1940.* Austin: University of Texas Press, 1988.

Sarlo, Beatriz. *El imperio de los sentimientos: narraciones de circulación periódica en la Argentina, 1917–1927.* Buenos Aires: Catálogos Editora, 1985.

Sarlo, Beatriz. *La máquina cultural: maestras, traductores y vanguardistas.* Buenos Aires: Ariel, 1998.

Sarlo, Beatriz. *Una modernidad periférica: Buenos Aires, 1920 y 1930.* Buenos Aires: Ediciones Nueva Visión, 1988.

Savigliano, Marta. *Tango and the Political Economy of Passion.* Boulder, CO: Westview Press, 1995.

Savigliano, Marta. "Tango in Japan and the World Economy of Passion." In *Re-Made in Japan: Everyday Life and Consumer Taste in a Changing Society*, edited by Joseph Jay Tobin, 235–51. New Haven, CT: Yale University Press, 1992.

Sazbón, Daniel. "Sexto Continente: una apuesta por una tercera posición latinoamericanista en la cultura peronista." In *Polémicas intelectuales, debates politicos: Las revistas culturales en el siglo XX*, directed by Leticia Prislei, 149–91. Buenos Aires: Facultad de Filosofía y Letras, Colección Cátedra, 2015.

Schafer, R. Murray. *The Soundscape: Our Sonic Environment and the Tuning of the World.* Rochester, VT: Destiny, 1977.

Scarfi, Juan Pablo. "La emergencia de un imaginario latinoamericanista y antiestadounidense del orden hemisférico: de la Unión Panamericana a la Unión Latinoamericana (1880–1913)." *Revista Complutense de Historia de América* 39 (July 5, 2013): 81–104.

Scarfi, Juan Pablo. *The Hidden History of International Law in the Americas: Empire and Legal Networks.* Oxford: Oxford University Press, 2017.

Scharfeld, Arthur. "The Mexican Broadcasting Situation." *Journal of Radio Law* 1, no. 2 (July 1931): 193.

Schillinger, Ted. *Isa Kremer: The People's Diva*. New York: Women Make Movies, 2000.

Schiuma, Oreste. "Música argentina." *Mundo Musical* 34, no. 3 (July 1941).

Schoultz, Lars. *Beneath the United States: A History of U.S. Policy toward Latin America*. Cambridge, MA.: Harvard University Press, 1998.

Schwall, Elizabeth. "'Cultures in the Body': Dance and Anthropology in Revolutionary Cuba." *History of Anthropology Newsletter*. http://histanthro.org/notes/cultures-in-the-body/, December 14, 2017.

Schwartz-Kates, Deborah. "Alberto Ginastera, Argentine Cultural Construction, and the Gauchesco Tradition." *The Musical Quarterly* 86, no. 2 (2002): 248–81.

Schwoch, James. *The American Radio Industry and Its Latin American Activities, 1900–1939*. Urbana: University of Illinois Press, 1990.

Scott, Michelle. *Blues Empress in Black Chattanooga: Bessie Smith and the Emerging Urban South*. Urbana: University of Illinois Press, 2008.

Secretaría de Educación Pública de México. *El maestro rural. Órgano de la Secretaria de Educación Pública*. México D.F.: Secretaría de Educación Pública, 1934.

Seeger, Charles. "UNESCO, February 1948." *Notes* 5, no. 2 (1948): 165–68.

Semán, Ernesto. *Ambassadors of the Working Class: Argentina's International Labor Activists and Cold War Democracy in the Americas*. Durham, NC: Duke University Press, 2017.

Shepard, John. "The Legacy of Carleton Sprague Smith: Pan-American Holdings in the Music Division of The New York Public Library for the Performing Arts." *Notes* 62, no. 3 (2006): 621–62.

Shope, Bradley. "Latin American Music in Moving Pictures and Jazzy Cabarets in Mumbai, 1930s-1950s." In *More than Bollywood: Studies in Indian Popular Music*, edited by Gregory D. Booth and Bradley Shope, 201–15. New York: Oxford University Press, 2014.

Sibille, Christiane. "La musique à la Société des Nations." *Relations internationales* n° 155, no. 3 (Février 2014): 89–102.

Sibille, Christiane. "The Politics of Music in International Organizations in the First Half of the Twentieth Century." *New Global Studies* 10, no. 3 (2017): 253–81.

Sierra, Luis Adolfo. *Historia de la orquesta típica: evolución instrumental del tango*. Buenos Aires: A. Peña Lillo, 1976.

Siles González, Ignacio, Andrés Segura Castillo, Mónica Sancho, and Ricardo Solís Quesada. "Genres as Social Affect: Cultivating Moods and Emotions through Playlists on Spotify." *Social Media + Society* 5, no. 2 (May 25, 2019): 1–11.

Silva, Erminia. *Circo-teatro: Benjamim de Oliveira e a teatralidade circense no Brasil*. São Paulo: Editora Altana, 2007.

Silva, Joao Luis Meireles Santos Leitao. "Music, Theatre and the Nation: The Entertainment Market in Lisbon (1865–1908)." PhD diss., Newcastle University, 2012.

Simões, Julia da Rosa. "Na pauta da lei: trabalho, organização sindical e luta por direitos entre músicos porto-alegrenses (1934–1963)." PhD diss., Universidade Federal do Rio Grande do Sul, 2016.

Slobodian, Quinn. *Globalists: The End of Empire and the Birth of Neoliberalism*. Cambridge, MA: Harvard University Press, 2018.

Slonimsky, Nicolas. *Music of Latin America*. New York: Thomas Y. Crowell Company, 1945.

Smith, Carleton Sprague. *Musical Tour through South America, June–October, 1940.* New York: Conference on Inter-American Relations in the Field of Music, 1940.

Smith, T. Lynn. *Latin American Population Studies.* Gainesville: University of Florida Press, 1961.

Spencer Espinosa, Christian. "Imaginario nacional y cambio cultural: circulación, recepción y pervivencia de la zamacueca en Chile durante el siglo XIX." *Cuadernos de Música Hispanoamericana* 14 (2007): 143–76.

Stallings, Stephanie. "Collective Difference: The Pan-American Association of Composers and Pan-American Ideology in Music, 1925–1945." PhD diss., Florida State University, 2009.

Starr, Frederick. *Bamboula!: The Life and Times of Louis Moreau Gottschalk.* New York: Oxford University Press, 1995.

Sterne, Jonathan. *The Audible Past: Cultural Origins of Sound Reproduction.* Durham, NC: Duke University Press, 2003.

Stevenson, Robert. "Visión musical norteamericana de las otras Américas hacia 1900." *Revista Musical Chilena* 31, no. 137 (1977): 5–35.

Sturman, Janet. *Zarzuela : Spanish Operetta, American Stage.* Urbana: University of Illinois Press, 2000.

Suisman, David. *Selling Sounds: The Commercial Revolution in American Music.* Cambridge, MA: Harvard University Press, 2009.

"Summary Report of the First Inter-American Conference on Musicology, Washington, D. C., 1963." *Anuario / Yearbook / Anuário of the Inter-American Institute for Musical Research* 1 (1965): 139–50.

Szendy, Peter. *Écoute, une histoire de nos oreilles.* Paris: Minuit, 2001.

Szwed, John. *Alan Lomax: The Man Who Recorded the World.* New York: Viking Penguin, 2010.

Tagg, Philip. "Analysing Popular Music: Theory, Method and Practice." *Popular Music* 2 (1982): 37–67.

Tallon, José Sebastián. *El tango en sus etapas de música prohibida.* Buenos Aires: Instituto Amigos del Libro Argentino, 1959.

Tato, María Inés. "Propaganda de guerra para el Nuevo Mundo. El caso de la revista América-latina (1915–1918)1/War Propaganda for the New World. The Case of the Magazine América-Latina (1915–1918)." *Historia y Comunicación Social (Madrid)* 18 (2013): 63–74.

Taylor, Paul, Mark Hugo Lopez, Jessica Martínez and Gabriel Velasco, "When Labels Don't Fit: Hispanics and Their Views of Identity | Pew Research Center." April 4, 2012. https://www.pewresearch.org/hispanic/2012/04/04/when-labels-dont-fit-hispanics-and-their-views-of-identity/.

Taylor, William Robert, ed. *Inventing Times Square: Commerce and Culture at the Crossroads of the World.* New York: Russell Sage Foundation, 1991.

Tenorio Trillo, Mauricio. *Argucias de la historia: siglo XIX, cultura y "América Latina."* México: Paidós, 1999.

Tenorio Trillo, Mauricio. *Latin America: The Allure and Power of an Idea.* Chicago: University of Chicago Press, 2017.

Terán, Oscar. "El primer antiimperialismo latinoamericano." In *En busca de la ideología argentina,* 85–97. Buenos Aires: Catálogos Editora, 1986.

The Encyclopedia Americana: A Library of Universal Knowledge : In Thirty Volumes. Vol. 17. New York: The Encyclopedia Americana Corporation, 1919.

Thomson, Guy. "The Ceremonial and Political Role of Village Bands, 1846–1974." In *Rituals of Rule, Rituals of Resistance : Public Celebrations and Popular Culture in Mexico*, edited by William Beezley, Cheryl Martin, and William French, 564–625. Wilmington, DE: SR Books, 1994.

Tinhorão, José Ramos. *História social da música popular brasileira*. Lisboa: Editorial Caminho, 1990.

Toll, Robert C. *Blacking Up: The Minstrel Show in Nineteenth Century America*. New York: Oxford University Press, 1974.

Torre, Juan Carlos. *El proceso político de las reformas económicas en América latina*. Buenos Aires: Paidós, 1998.

Torres, María Inés de. "El surgimiento de la radiodifusión pública en Hispanoamérica. Contexto, modelos y el estudio de un caso singular: el SODRE, la radio pública estatal de Uruguay (1929)." *Revista internacional de Historia de la Comunicación*, no. 5 (2015): 122–42.

Tota, Antônio Pedro. *O imperialismo sedutor: a americanização do Brasil na época da Segunda Guerra*. São Paulo: Companhia das Letras, 2000.

Tucker, Joshua. "Sounding the Latin Transatlantic: Music, Integration, and Ambivalent Ethnogenesis in Spain." *Comparative Studies in Society and History* 56, no. 4 (October 2014): 902–33.

Turino, Thomas. "Are We Global Yet? Globalist Discourse, Cultural Formations and the Study of Zimbabwean Popular Music." *British Journal of Ethnomusicology* 12, no. 2 (2003): 51–79.

United Nations Economic Commission for Latin America and the Caribbean. *Economic Survey of Latin America, 1949*. Santiago de Chile: January 1, 1951.

Uriostegui, Mario Bahena, and Ramón Garibaldo Valdéz. "El ruido y la nación: cómo el rock iberoamericano redefinió el sentido de comunidad en Latino América." *Diálogos: Revista electrónica de historia* 16, no. 1 (2015): 6.

Urtubey, Pola Suarez. "'La Cantata para América mágica', de Alberto Ginastera." *Revista Musical Chilena* 17, no. 84 (1963): 19–36.

Valero Silva, José. *Polvos de olvido: cultura y revolución*. Mexico City: Universidad Autónoma Metropolitana, Unidad Azcapotzalco, División de Ciencias Sociales y Humanidades: Instituto Nacional de las Bellas Artes, 1993.

Vanspauwen, Bart Paul. "Lusofonia in Musidanças. Governance, Discourse and Performance." PhD diss., Universidade Nova de Lisboa, 2017.

Varas, José Miguel, and Juan Pablo González. *En busca de la música chilena: Crónica y antología de una historia sonora*. Santiago de Chile: Editorial Catalonia, 2005.

Vasconcelos, José. *Misión de la raza iberoamericana: notas de viajes a la América del Sud*. Madrid: Agencia Mundial de Librería, 1925.

Vaughan, Mary K. *Cultural Politics in Revolution: Teachers, Peasants, and Schools in Mexico, 1930–1940*. Tucson: University of Arizona Press, 1997.

Vaughan, Mary K., and Stephen E. Lewis. *The Eagle and the Virgin: Nation and Cultural Revolution in Mexico, 1920–1940*. Durham, NC: Duke University Press, 2006.

Vaz de Melo, Gabriel, Ana Flávia Machado, and Lucas de Carvalho. "Música digital no Brasil: uma análise do consumo e reproduções no spotify." Textos para Discussão no 592. Centro de Desenvolvimento e Planejamento Regional, Universidade Federal de Minas Gerais, November 2018.

Vazquez, Hernán Gabriel. *Conversaciones en torno al CLAEM: entrevistas a compositores becarios del Centro Latinoamericano de Altos Estudios Musicales del Instituto Torcuato Di Tella.* Buenos Aires: Instituto Nacional de Musicología "Carlos Vega," 2015.

Vega, Carlos. *Danzas y canciones argentinas: teorías e investigaciones.* Buenos Aires: G. Ricordi y C., 1936.

Vega, Carlos. *Estudios para los orígenes del tango argentino.* Buenos Aires: Editorial de la Universidad Católica Argentina, 2007.

Vega, Carlos. "Mesomúsica: un ensayo sobre la música de todos." *Revista Musical Chilena* 51, no. 188 (1997): 75–96.

Veggiano Esaín, Julio. *Cultura musical. Notas relativas a este problema en nuestro país.* Córdoba, Argentina: Imprenta de la Penitenciaría, 1937.

Velazco, Jorge. "La confluencia intelectual y académica en la formación escolástica y la obra de investigación de Francisco Curt Lange." *Revista Musical de Venezuela* X, no. 28 (1989): 207–23.

Velázquez, Marco, and Mary K Vaughan. "Mestizaje and Musical Nationalism in Mexico." In *The Eagle and the Virgin: Nation and Cultural Revolution in Mexico, 1920–1940*, edited by Mary Kay Vaughan and Stephen E. Lewis, 95–118. Durham, NC: Duke University Press, 2006.

Velloso, Mônica Pimenta. *Os intelectuais e a política cultural do Estado Novo.* Rio de Janeiro: Fundação Getulio Vargas, Centro de Pesquisa e Documentação de História Contemporânea do Brasil, 1987.

Veloso, Caetano. *Verdade tropical.* São Paulo: Companhia das Letras, 1997.

Venturi, Franco. *Il populismo russo.* Torino: Einaudi, 1952.

Verba, Ericka. "To Paris and Back: Violeta Parra's Transnational Performance of Authenticity." *The Americas* 70, no. 2 (October 2013): 269–302.

Verene, Donald Phillip. "Vico's Frontispiece and the Tablet of Cebes." In *Man, God, and Nature in the Enlightenment*, edited by Donald Mell, Theodore Braun and Lucia Palmer, 3–11. East Lansing: Michigan State University Press, 1988.

Vianna, Hermano. *O mistério do samba.* Rio de Janeiro: Jorge Zahar & Editora da Universidade Federal do Rio de Janeiro, 1995.

Vianna, Hermano. "Technobrega, Forró, Lambadão: The Parallel Music of Brazil." In *Brazilian Popular Music and Citizenship*, edited by Idelber Avelar and Christopher Dunn, 240–49. Durham, NC: Duke University Press, 2011.

Villa-Lobos, Heitor. *A música nacionalista no govêrno Getulio Vargas.* Rio de Janeiro: Departamento de Imprensa e Propaganda, 1941.

Villa-Lobos, Heitor. "Hands Across the Air." *Music Educators Journal* 28, no. 6 (1942): 14.

Vinci de Moraes, José Geraldo. "Los tránsitos de la música popular en la Misión de Investigación de Folclor (1938)." *Boletín Música* 31 (2012): 3–14.

Volk, T. M. "'Music Speaks to the Hearts of All Men:' The International Movement in American Music Education: 1930–1954." *Bulletin of the Council for Research in Music Education* 133 (Summer 1997): 143–52.

Wade, Peter. *Music, Race, & Nation: Música Tropical in Colombia.* Chicago: University of Chicago Press, 2000.

Warner, Charles Dudley, ed. *Library of the World's Best Literature: Ancient and Modern.* Vol. XXII. 46 vols. New York: R. S. Peale and J. A. Hill, 1896.

White, Bob W. *Music and Globalization: Critical Encounters.* Bloomington: Indiana University Press, 2014.

Wiebe, Robert H. *Who We Are: A History of Popular Nationalism*. Princeton, NJ: Princeton University Press, 2002.

Wolkowicz, Vera. "En busca de la identidad perdida: los escritos de Gastón Talamón sobre música académica de y en Argentina en la revista Nosotros (1915–1934)." In *Música y construcción de identidades : poéticas, diálogos y utopías en Latinoamérica y España*, edited by Victoria Eli Rodríguez and Elena Torres Clemente, 33–44. Madrid: Sociedad Española de Musicología, 2018.

Wolkowicz, Vera. "Incan or Not? Building Ecuador's Musical Past in the Quest for a Nationalist Art Music, 1900–1950." *Journal of Musicology* 36, no. 2 (April 1, 2019): 228–60.

Wong, Ketty. *Whose National Music? Identity, Mestizaje, and Migration in Ecuador*. Philadelphia: Temple University Press, 2012.

Wood, Andrew Grant. *Agustín Lara: A Cultural Biography*. New York: Oxford University Press, 2014.

Yampolsky, Philip Bradford. "Music and Media in the Dutch East Indies: Gramophone Records and Radio in the Late Colonial Era, 1903–1942." MA thesis, University of Washington, 2013.

Yriondo, Manuel de. *Congreso del folklore hispánico e hispano-americano: proyecto de la Inspección General de Enseñanza Secundaria y decreto del Poder Ejecutivo*. Buenos Aires: Penitenciaría Nacional, 1936.

Yung, Bell. *Understanding Charles Seeger, Pioneer in American Musicology*. Urbana: University of Illinois Press, 1999.

Index

Tables and figures are indicated by *t* and *f* following the page number

For the benefit of digital users, indexed terms that span two pages (e.g., 52–53) may, on occasion, appear on only one of those pages.